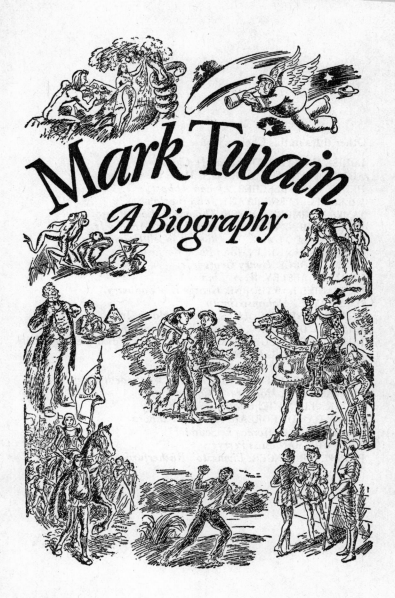

Mark Twain
A Biography

Other titles in this Chelsea House series:

MARK TWAIN
ALBERT BIGELOW PAINE

VOLUME III

INTRODUCTION BY
JAMES COX

American Men and Women of Letters Series

GENERAL EDITOR
PROFESSOR DANIEL AARON
HARVARD UNIVERSITY

CHELSEA HOUSE
NEW YORK, LONDON

1980

Copyright © 1980 by Chelsea House Publishers, a division of
Chelsea House Educational Communications, Inc.
Printed and bound in the United States of America

Library of Congress Cataloging in Publication Data

Paine, Albert Bigelow, 1861-1937.
    Mark Twain.

    (American men and women of letters)
    Reprint of the 1912 ed. published by Harper & Bros.,
New York.
    1. Clemens, Samuel Langhorne, 1835-1910--Biography.
2. Authors, American--19th century--Biography.   I. Se-
ries.
PS1331.P3 1980   818'.409 [B]   80-18842
ISBN 0-87754-170-1

Chelsea House Publishers
Harold Steinberg, Chairman & Publisher
Andrew E. Norman, President
A Division of Chelsea House Educational Communications, Inc.
70 West 40 Street, New York 10018

CONTENTS
VOLUME III

CONTENTS

CONTENTS

CONTENTS

CCXIV

MARK TWAIN AND THE MISSIONARIES

MARK TWAIN had really begun his crusade for reform soon after his arrival in America in a practical hand-to-hand manner. His housekeeper, Katie Leary, one night employed a cabman to drive her from the Grand Central Station to the house at 14 West Tenth Street. No contract had been made as to price, and when she arrived there the cabman's extortionate charge was refused. He persisted in it, and she sent into the house for her employer. Of all men, Mark Twain was the last one to countenance an extortion. He reasoned with the man kindly enough at first; when the driver at last became abusive Clemens demanded his number, which was at first refused. In the end he paid the legal fare, and in the morning entered a formal complaint, something altogether unexpected, for the American public is accustomed to suffering almost any sort of imposition to avoid trouble and publicity.

In some notes which Clemens had made in London four years earlier he wrote:

If you call a policeman to settle the dispute you can depend on one thing—he will decide it against you every time. And so will the New York policeman. In London if you carry your case into court the man that is entitled to win it will win it. In New York—but no one carries a cab case into court there. It is my impression that it is now more than thirty years since any one has carried a cab case into court there.

Nevertheless, he was promptly on hand when the case
was called to sustain the charge and to read the cab-
drivers' union and the public in general a lesson in good-
citizenship. At the end of the hearing, to a representative
of the union he said:

"This is not a matter of sentiment, my dear sir. It is
simply practical business. You cannot imagine that I
am making money wasting an hour or two of my time
prosecuting a case in which I can have no personal
interest whatever. I am doing this just as any citizen
should do. He has no choice. He has a distinct duty.
He is a non-classified policeman. Every citizen is a policeman, and it is his duty to assist the police and the
magistracy in every way he can, and give his time, if
necessary, to do so. Here is a man who is a perfectly
natural product of an infamous system in this city—a
charge upon the lax patriotism in this city of New York
where this thing can exist. You have encouraged him in
every way you know how to overcharge. He is not the
criminal here at all. The criminal is the citizen of New
York and the absence of patriotism. I am not here to
avenge myself on him. I have no quarrel with him. My
quarrel is with the citizens of New York, who have encouraged him, and who created him by encouraging him
to overcharge in this way."

The driver's license was suspended. The case made a
stir in the newspapers, and it is not likely that any one
incident ever contributed more to cab-driving morals in
New York City.

But Clemens had larger matters than this in prospect.
His many speeches on municipal and national abuses he
felt were more or less ephemeral. He proposed now to
write himself down more substantially and for a wider
hearing. The human race was behaving very badly: unspeakable corruption was rampant in the city; the Boers
were being oppressed in South Africa; the natives were

being murdered in the Philippines; Leopold of Belgium was massacring and mutilating the blacks in the Congo, and the allied powers, in the cause of Christ, were slaughtering the Chinese. In his letters he had more than once boiled over touching these matters, and for New-Year's Eve, 1900, had written:

A GREETING FROM THE NINETEENTH TO THE TWENTIETH CENTURY

I bring you the stately nation named Christendom, returning, bedraggled, besmirched, and dishonored, from pirate raids in Kiao-Chou, Manchuria, South Africa, and the Philippines, with her soul full of meanness, her pocket full of boodle, and her mouth full of pious hypocrisies. Give her soap and towel, but hide the looking-glass.[1]

This was a sort of preliminary. Then, restraining himself no longer, he embodied his sentiments in an article for the *North American Review* entitled, "To the Person Sitting in Darkness." There was crying need for some one to speak the right word. He was about the only one who could do it and be certain of a universal audience. He took as his text some Christmas Eve clippings from the New York *Tribune* and *Sun* which he had been saving for this purpose. The *Tribune* clipping said:

Christmas will dawn in the United States over a people full of hope and aspiration and good cheer. Such a condition means contentment and happiness. The carping grumbler who may here and there go forth will find few to listen to him. The majority will wonder what is the matter with him, and pass on.

A *Sun* clipping depicted the "terrible offenses against humanity committed in the name of politics in some of

[1] Prepared for Red Cross Society watch-meeting, which was postponed until March. Clemens recalled his "Greeting" for that reason and for one other, which he expressed thus:

"The list of greeters thus far issued by you contains only vague generalities and one definite name—mine: 'Some kings and queens and Mark Twain.' Now I am not enjoying this sparkling solitude and distinction. It makes me feel like a circus-poster in a graveyard."

the most notorious East Side districts"—the unmission-aried, unpoliced darker New York. The *Sun* declared that they could not be pictured even verbally. But it suggested enough to make the reader shudder at the hideous depths of vice in the sections named. Another clipping from the same paper reported the "Rev. Mr. Ament, of the American Board of Foreign Missions," as having collected indemnities for Boxer damages in China at the rate of three hundred taels for each murder, "full payment for all destroyed property belonging to Christians, and national fines amounting to thirteen times the indem-nity." It quoted Mr. Ament as saying that the money so obtained was used for the propagation of the Gospel, and that the amount so collected was moderate when compared with the amount secured by the Catholics, who had demanded, in addition to money, life for life, that is to say, "head for head"—in one district six hundred and eighty heads having been so collected.

The despatch made Mr. Ament say a great deal more than this, but the gist here is enough. Mark Twain, of course, was fiercely stirred. The missionary idea had seldom appealed to him, and coupled with this business of bloodshed, it was less attractive than usual. He printed the clippings in full, one following the other; then he said:

By happy luck we get all these glad tidings on Christmas Eve —just the time to enable us to celebrate the day with proper gaiety and enthusiasm. Our spirits soar and we find we can even make jokes; taels I win, heads you lose.

He went on to score Ament, to compare the missionary policy in China to that of the Pawnee Indians, and to propose for him a monument—subscriptions to be sent to the American Board. He denounced the national policies in Africa, China, and the Philippines, and showed by the reports and by the private letters of soldiers home, how

cruel and barbarous and fiendish had been the warfare
made by those whose avowed purpose was to carry the
blessed light of civilization and Gospel "to the benighted
native"—how in very truth these priceless blessings had
been handed on the point of a bayonet to the "Person
Sitting in Darkness."

Mark Twain never wrote anything more scorching,
more penetrating in its sarcasm, more fearful in its revelation of injustice and hypocrisy, than his article "To the
Person Sitting in Darkness." He put *aquafortis* on all
the raw places, and when it was finished he himself doubted
the wisdom of printing it. Howells, however, agreed that
it should be published, and "it ought to be illustrated by
Dan Beard," he added, "with such pictures as he made for
the *Yankee in King Arthur's Court*, but you'd better hang
yourself afterward."

Meeting Beard a few days later, Clemens mentioned the
matter and said:

"So if you make the pictures, you hang with me."

But pictures were not required. It was published in
the *North American Review* for February, 1901, as the
opening article; after which the cyclone. Two storms
moving in opposite directions produce a cyclone, and the
storms immediately developed; one all for Mark Twain and
his principles, the other all against him. Every paper in
England and America commented on it editorially, with
bitter denunciations or with eager praise, according to
their lights and convictions.

At 14 West Tenth Street letters, newspaper clippings,
documents poured in by the bushel—laudations, vitupera-
tions, denunciations, vindications; no such tumult ever
occurred in a peaceful literary home. It was really as if
he had thrown a great missile into the human hive, one-
half of which regarded it as a ball of honey and the
remainder as a cobblestone. Whatever other effect it may
have had, it left no thinking person unawakened.

Clemens reveled in it. W. A. Rogers, in *Harper's Weekly*, caricatured him as Tom Sawyer in a snow fort, assailed by the shower of snowballs, "having the time of his life." Another artist, Fred Lewis, pictured him as Huck Finn with a gun.

The American Board was naturally disturbed. The Ament clipping which Clemens had used had been public property for more than a month—its authenticity never denied; but it was immediately denied now, and the cable kept hot with inquiries.

The Rev. Judson Smith, one of the board, took up the defense of Dr. Ament, declaring him to be one who had suffered for the cause, and asked Mark Twain, whose "brilliant article," he said, "would produce an effect quite beyond the reach of plain argument," not to do an innocent man an injustice. Clemens in the same paper replied that such was not his intent, that Mr. Ament in his report had simply arraigned himself.

Then it suddenly developed that the cable report had "grossly exaggerated" the amount of Mr. Ament's collections. Instead of thirteen times the indemnity it should have read "one and a third times" the indemnity; whereupon, in another open letter, the board demanded retraction and apology. Clemens would not fail to make the apology—at least he would explain. It was precisely the kind of thing that would appeal to him — the delicate moral difference between a demand thirteen times as great as it should be and a demand that was only one and a third times the correct amount. "To My Missionary Critics," in the *North American Review* for April (1901), was his formal and somewhat lengthy reply.

"I have no prejudice against apologies," he wrote. "I trust I shall never withhold one when it is due."

He then proceeded to make out his case categorically. Touching the exaggerated indemnity, he said:

MARK TWAIN AND THE MISSIONARIES

To Dr. Smith the "thirteen-fold-extra" clearly stood for "theft and extortion," and he was right, distinctly right, indisputably right. He manifestly thinks that when it got scaled away down to a mere "one-third" a little thing like that was something other than "theft and extortion." Why, only the board knows!

I will try to explain this difficult problem so that the board can get an idea of it. If a pauper owes me a dollar and I catch him unprotected and make him pay me fourteen dollars thirteen of it is "theft and extortion." If I make him pay only one dollar thirty-three and a third cents the thirty-three and a third cents are "theft and extortion," just the same.

I will put it in another way still simpler. If a man owes me one dog—any kind of a dog, the breed is of no consequence—and I—but let it go; the board would never understand it. It can't understand these involved and difficult things.

He offered some further illustrations, including the "Tale of a King and His Treasure" and another tale entitled "The Watermelons."

I have it now. Many years ago, when I was studying for the gallows, I had a dear comrade, a youth who was not in my line, but still a scrupulously good fellow though devious. He was preparing to qualify for a place on the board, for there was going to be a vacancy by superannuation in about five years. This was down South, in the slavery days. It was the nature of the negro then, as now, to steal watermelons. They stole three of the melons of an adoptive brother of mine, the only good ones he had. I suspected three of a neighbor's negroes, but there was no proof, and, besides, the watermelons in those negroes' private patches were all green and small and not up to indemnity standard. But in the private patches of three other negroes there was a number of competent melons. I consulted with my comrade, the understudy of the board. He said that if I would approve his arrangements he would arrange. I said, "Consider me the board; I approve; arrange." So he took a gun and went and collected three large melons for my brother-on-the-half-shell, and one o..r. I was greatly pleased and asked:

"Who gets the extra one?"

"Widows and orphans."

"A good idea, too. Why didn't you take thirteen?"

"It would have been wrong; a crime, in fact—theft and extortion."

"What is the one-third extra—the odd melon—the same?"

It caused him to reflect. But there was no result.

The justice of the peace was a stern man. On the trial he found fault with the scheme and required us to explain upon what we based our strange conduct—as he called it. The understudy said:

"On the custom of the niggers. They all do it." [1]

The justice forgot his dignity and descended to sarcasm.

"Custom of the niggers! Are our morals so inadequate that we have to borrow of niggers?"

Then he said to the jury: "Three melons were owing; they were collected from persons not proven to owe them: this is theft; they were collected by compulsion: this is extortion. A melon was added for the widows and orphans. It was owed by no one. It is another theft, another extortion. Return it whence it came, with the others. It is not permissible here to apply to any purpose goods dishonestly obtained; not even to the feeding of widows and orphans, for this would be to put a shame upon charity and dishonor it."

He said it in open court, before everybody, and to me it did not seem very kind.

It was in the midst of the tumult that Clemens, perhaps feeling the need of sacred melody, wrote to Andrew Carnegie:

DEAR SIR & FRIEND,—You seem to be in prosperity. Could you lend an admirer $1.50 to buy a hymn-book with? God will bless you. I feel it; I know it.

N. B.—If there should be other applications, this one not to count. Yours, MARK.

P. S.—Don't send the hymn-book; send the money; I want to make the selection myself.

[1] The point had been made by the board that it was the Chinese custom to make the inhabitants of a village responsible for individual crimes; and custom, likewise, to collect a third in excess of the damage, such surplus having been applied to the support of widows and orphans of the slain converts.

MARK TWAIN AND THE MISSIONARIES

Carnegie answered:

Nothing less than a two-dollar & a half hymn-book *gilt* will do for you. Your place in the choir (celestial) demands that & you shall have it.

There's a new Gospel of Saint Mark in the *North American* which I like better than anything I've read for many a day.

I am willing to borrow a thousand dollars to distribute that sacred message in proper form, & if the author don't object may I send that sum, when I can raise it, to the Anti-Imperialist League, Boston, to which I am a contributor, the only missionary work I am responsible for.

Just tell me you are willing & many thousands of the holy little missals will go forth. This inimitable satire is to become a classic. I count among my privileges in life that I know you, the author.

Perhaps a few more of the letters invited by Mark Twain's criticism of missionary work in China may still be of interest to the reader: Frederick T. Cook, of the Hospital Saturday and Sunday Association, wrote: "I hail you as the Voltaire of America. It is a noble distinction. God bless you and see that you weary not in well-doing in this noblest, sublimest of crusades."

Ministers were by no means all against him. The associate pastor of the Every-day Church, in Boston, sent this line: "I want to thank you for your matchless article in the current *North American*. It must make converts of well-nigh all who read it."

But a Boston school-teacher was angry. "I have been reading the *North American*," she wrote, "and I am filled with shame and remorse that I have dreamed of asking you to come to Boston to talk to the teachers."

On the outside of the envelope Clemens made this pencil note:

"Now, I suppose I offended that young lady by having an opinion of my own, instead of waiting and copying hers. I never thought. I suppose she must be as much as twenty-five, and probably the only patriot in the country."

A critic with a sense of humor asked: "Please excuse seeming impertinence, but were you ever adjudged insane? Be honest. How much money does the devil give you for arraigning Christianity and missionary causes?"

But there were more of the better sort. Edward S. Martin, in a grateful letter, said: "How gratifying it is to feel that we have a man among us who understands the rarity of the plain truth, and who delights to utter it, and has the gift of doing so without cant and with not too much seriousness."

Sir Hiram Maxim wrote: "I give you my candid opinion that what you have done is of very great value to the civilization of the world. There is no man living whose words carry greater weight than your own, as no one's writings are so eagerly sought after by all classes."

Clemens himself in his note-book set down this aphorism: "Do right and you will be conspicuous."

CCXV

SUMMER AT "THE LAIR"

IN June Clemens took the family to Saranac Lake, to Ampersand. They occupied a log cabin which he called "The Lair," on the south shore, near the water's edge, a remote and beautiful place where, as had happened before, they were so comfortable and satisfied that they hoped to return another summer. There were swimming and boating and long walks in the woods; the worry and noise of the world were far away. They gave little enough attention to the mails. They took only a weekly paper, and were likely to allow it to lie in the post-office uncalled for. Clemens, especially, loved the place, and wrote to Twichell:

I am on the front porch (lower one—main deck) of our little bijou of a dwelling-house. The lake edge (Lower Saranac) is so nearly under me that I can't see the shore, but only the water, smallpoxed with rain splashes—for there is a heavy downpour. It is charmingly like sitting snuggled up on a ship's deck with the stretching sea all around but very much more satisfactory, for at sea a rainstorm is depressing, while here of course the effect engendered is just a deep sense of comfort & contentment. The heavy forest shuts us solidly in on three sides—there are no neighbors. There are beautiful little tan-colored impudent squirrels about. They take tea 5 P.M. (not invited) at the table in the woods where Jean does my typewriting, & one of them has been brave enough to sit upon Jean's knee with his tail curved over his back & munch his food. They come to dinner 7 P.M. on the front porch (not invited), but Clara drives them away. It is an occupation which requires some industry

& attention to business.   They all have the one name—Blenner-hasset, from Burr's friend—& none of them answers to it except when hungry.

Clemens could work at "The Lair," often writing in shady seclusions along the shore, and he finished there the two-part serial,[1] "A Double-Barrelled Detective Story," intended originally as a burlesque on Sherlock Holmes.   It did not altogether fulfil its purpose, and is hardly to be ranked as one of Mark Twain's successes. It contains, however, one paragraph at least by which it is likely to be remembered, a hoax—his last one—on the reader.   It runs as follows:

It was a crisp and spicy morning in early October. The lilacs and laburnums, lit with the glory-fires of autumn, hung burning and flashing in the upper air, a fairy bridge provided by kind nature for the wingless wild things that have their home in the tree-tops and would visit together; the larch and the pomegranate flung their purple and yellow flames in brilliant broad splashes along the slanting sweep of woodland, the sensu-ous fragrance of innumerable deciduous flowers rose upon the swooning atmosphere, far in the empty sky a solitary œsopha-gus slept upon motionless wing; everywhere brooded stillness, serenity, and the peace of God.

The warm light and luxury of this paragraph are facti-tious.   The careful reader will note that its various acces-sories are ridiculously associated, and only the most care-less reader will accept the œsophagus as a bird.   But it disturbed a great many admirers, and numerous letters of inquiry came wanting to know what it was all about. Some suspected the joke and taunted him with it; one such correspondent wrote:

MY DEAR MARK TWAIN,—Reading your "Double-Barrelled Detective Story" in the January *Harper's* late one night I came

<hr>

[1] Published in *Harper's Magazine* for January and February, 1902.

to the paragraph where you so *beautifully* describe "a crisp and spicy morning in early October." I read along down the paragraph, conscious only of its *woozy* sound, until I brought up with a start against your œsophagus in the empty sky. Then I read the paragraph again. Oh, Mark Twain! Mark Twain! How could you do it? Put a trap like that into the midst of a tragical story? Do serenity and peace brood over you after you have done such a thing?

Who lit the lilacs, and which end up do they hang? When did larches begin to flame, and who set out the pomegranates in that canyon? What are deciduous flowers, and do they always "bloom in the *fall*, tra la"?

I have been making myself obnoxious to various people by demanding their opinion of that paragraph without telling them the name of the author. They say, "Very well done." "The alliteration is so pretty." "What's an œsophagus, a bird?" "What's it all mean, anyway?" I tell them it means Mark Twain, and that an œsophagus is a kind of *swallow*. Am I right? Or is it a gull? Or a gullet?

Hereafter if you must write such things won't you please be so kind as to label them?

Very sincerely yours,
ALLETTA F. DEAN.

Mark Twain to Miss Dean:

Don't you give that œsophagus away again or I'll never trust you with another privacy!

So many wrote, that Clemens finally felt called upon to make public confession, and as one searching letter had been mailed from Springfield, Massachusetts, he made his reply through the *Republican* of that city. After some opening comment he said:

I published a short story lately & it was in that that I put the œsophagus. I will say privately that I expected it to bother some people—in fact, that was the intention—but the harvest has been larger than I was calculating upon. The œsophagus has gathered in the guilty and the innocent alike, whereas I was only fishing for the innocent—the innocent and confiding.

1137

MARK TWAIN

He quoted a letter from a schoolmaster in the Philippines who thought the passage beautiful with the exception of the curious creature which "slept upon motionless wings." Said Clemens:

Do you notice? Nothing in the paragraph disturbed him but that one word. It shows that that paragraph was most ably constructed for the deception it was intended to put upon the reader. It was my intention that it should read plausibly, and it is now plain that it does; it was my intention that it should be emotional and touching, and you see yourself that it fetched this public instructor. Alas! if I had but left that one treacherous word out I should have scored, scored everywhere, and the paragraph would have slidden through every reader's sensibilities like oil and left not a suspicion behind.

The other sample inquiry is from a professor in a New England university. It contains one naughty word (which I cannot bear to suppress), but he is not in the theological department, so it is no harm:

"DEAR MR. CLEMENS,—'Far in the empty sky a solitary œsophagus slept upon motionless wing.'

"It is not often I get a chance to read much periodical literature, but I have just gone through at this belated period, with much gratification and edification, your 'Double-Barrelled Detective Story.'

"But what in hell is an œsophagus? I keep one myself, but it never sleeps in the air or anywhere else. My profession is to deal with words, and œsophagus interested me the moment I lighted upon it. But, as a companion of my youth used to say, 'I'll be eternally, co-eternally cussed' if I can make it out. Is it a joke or am I an ignoramus?"

Between you and me, I was almost ashamed of having fooled that man, but for pride's sake I was not going to say so. I wrote and told him it was a joke—and that is what I am now saying to my Springfield inquirer. And I told him to carefully read the whole paragraph and he would find not a vestige of sense in any detail of it. This also I recommend to my Springfield inquirer.

I have confessed. I am sorry—partially. I will not do so

any more—for the present. Don't ask me any more questions; let the œsophagus have a rest—on his same old motionless wing.

He wrote Twichell that the story had been a six-day *tour de force*, twenty-five thousand words, and he adds:

How long it takes a literary seed to sprout sometimes! This seed was planted in your house many years ago when you sent me to bed with a book not heard of by me until then—*Sherlock Holmes*. . . .

I've done a grist of writing here this summer, but not for publication soon, if ever. I did write two satisfactory articles for early print, but I've burned one of them & have buried the other in my large box of posthumous stuff. I've got stacks of literary remains piled up there.

Early in August Clemens went with H. H. Rogers in his yacht *Kanawha* on a cruise to New Brunswick and Nova Scotia. Rogers had made up a party, including ex-Speaker Reed, Dr. Rice, and Col. A. G. Paine. Young Harry Rogers also made one of the party. Clemens kept a log of the cruise, certain entries of which convey something of its spirit. On the 11th, at Yarmouth, he wrote:

Fog-bound. The garrison went ashore. Officers visited the yacht in the evening & said an anvil had been missed. Mr. Rogers paid for the anvil.

August 13th. There is a fine picture-gallery here; the sheriff photographed the garrison, with the exception of Harry (Rogers) and Mr. Clemens.

August 14th. Upon complaint of Mr. Reed another dog was procured. He said he had been a sailor all his life, and considered it dangerous to trust a ship to a dog-watch with only one dog in it.

Poker, for a change.

August 15th. To Rockland, Maine, in the afternoon, arriving about 6 P.M. In the night Dr. Rice baited the anchor with his winnings & caught a whale 90 feet long. He said so himself. It is thought that if there had been another witness like Dr. Rice the whale would have been longer.

August 16th. We could have had a happy time in Bath but for the interruptions caused by people who wanted Mr. Reed to explain votes of the olden time or give back the money. Mr. Rogers recouped them.

Another anvil missed. The descendant of Captain Kidd is the only person who does not blush for these incidents. Harry and Mr. Clemens blush continually. It is believed that if the rest of the garrison were like these two the yacht would be welcome everywhere instead of being quarantined by the police in all the ports. Mr. Clemens & Harry have attracted a great deal of attention, & men have expressed a resolve to turn over a new leaf & copy after them from this out.

Evening. Judge Cohen came over from another yacht to pay his respects to Harry and Mr. Clemens, he having heard of their reputation from the clergy of these coasts. He was invited by the gang to play poker apparently as a courtesy & in a spirit of seeming hospitality, he not knowing them & taking it all at par. Mr. Rogers lent him clothes to go home in.

August 17th. The Reformed Statesman growling and complaining again—not in a frank, straightforward way, but talking at the Commodore, while letting on to be talking to himself. This time he was dissatisfied about the anchor watch; said it was out of date, untrustworthy, & for real efficiency didn't begin with the Waterbury, & was going on to reiterate, as usual, that he had been a pilot all his life & blamed if he ever saw, etc., etc., etc.

But he was not allowed to finish. We put him ashore at Portland.

That is to say, Reed landed at Portland, the rest of the party returning with the yacht.

"We had a noble good time in the yacht," Clemens wrote Twichell on their return. "We caught a Chinee missionary and drowned him.

Twichell had been invited to make one of the party, and this letter was to make him feel sorry he had not accepted.

RIVERDALE. A YALE DEGREE

THE Clemens household did not return to 14 West Tenth Street. They spent a week in Elmira at the end of September, and after a brief stop in New York took up their residence on the northern metropolitan boundary, at Riverdale-on-the-Hudson, in the old Appleton home. They had permanently concluded not to return to Hartford. They had put the property there into an agent's hands for sale. Mrs. Clemens never felt that she had the strength to enter the house again.

The Riverdale place had been selected with due consideration. They decided that they must have easy access to the New York center, but they wished also to have the advantage of space and spreading lawn and trees, large rooms, and light. The Appleton homestead provided these things. It was a house built in the first third of the last century by one of the Morris family, so long prominent in New York history. On passing into the Appleton ownership it had been enlarged and beautified and named "Holbrook Hall." It overlooked the Hudson and the Palisades. It had associations: the Roosevelt family had once lived there, Huxley, Darwin, Tyndall, and others of their intellectual rank had been entertained there during its occupation by the first Appleton, the founder of the publishing firm. The great hall of the added wing was its chief feature. Clemens once remembered:

"We drifted from room to room on our tour of inspection, always with a growing doubt as to whether we wanted that house or not; but at last, when we arrived in a dining-room that was 60 feet long, 30 feet wide, and had two great fireplaces in it, that settled it."

There were pleasant neighbors at Riverdale, and had it not been for the illnesses that seemed always ready to seize upon that household the home there might have been ideal. They loved the place presently, so much so that they contemplated buying it, but decided that it was too costly. They began to prospect for other places along the Hudson shore. They were anxious to have a home again—one that they could call their own.

Among the many pleasant neighbors at Riverdale were the Dodges, the Quincy Adamses, and the Rev. Mr. Carstensen, a liberal-minded minister with whom Clemens easily affiliated. Clemens and Carstensen visited back and forth and exchanged views. Once Mr. Carstensen told him that he was going to town to dine with a party which included the Reverend Gottheil, a Catholic bishop, an Indian Buddhist, and a Chinese scholar of the Confucian faith, after which they were all going to a Yiddish theater. Clemens said:

"Well, there's only one more thing you need to make the party complete—that is, either Satan or me."

Howells often came to Riverdale. He was living in a New York apartment, and it was handy and made an easy and pleasant outing for him. He says:

"I began to see them again on something like the sweet old terms. They lived far more unpretentiously than they used, and I think with a notion of economy, which they had never very successfully practised. I recall that at the end of a certain year in Hartford, when they had been saving and paying cash for everything, Clemens wrote, reminding me of their avowed experiment, and asking me to guess how many bills they had at New-Year's; he hastened to say that a horse-car would not have held them. At Riverdale they kept no car-

riage, and there was a snowy night when I drove up to
their handsome old mansion in the station carryall, which
was crusted with mud, as from the going down of the
Deluge after transporting Noah and his family from the
Ark to whatever point they decided to settle provision-
ally. But the good talk, the rich talk, the talk that
could never suffer poverty of mind or soul was there,
and we jubilantly found ourselves again in our middle
youth."

Both Howells and Clemens were made doctors of letters
by Yale that year and went over in October to receive
their degrees. It was Mark Twain's second Yale degree,
and it was the highest rank that an American institution
of learning could confer.

Twichell wrote:

I want you to understand, old fellow, that it will be in its
intention the highest public compliment, and emphatically so
in your case, for it will be tendered you by a corporation of
gentlemen, the majority of whom do not at all agree with the
views on important questions which you have lately promul-
gated in speech and in writing, and with which you are identified
to the public mind. They grant, of course, your right to hold
and express those views, though for themselves they don't like
'em; but in awarding you the proposed laurel they will make no
count of that whatever. Their action will appropriately signify
simply and solely their estimate of your merit and rank as a
man of letters, and so, as I say, the compliment of it will be of the
pure, unadulterated quality.

Howells was not especially eager to go, and tried to con-
spire with Clemens to arrange some excuse which would
keep them at home.

I remember with satisfaction [he wrote] our joint success in
keeping away from the Concord Centennial in 1875, and I have
been thinking we might help each other in this matter of the
Yale Anniversary. What are your plans for getting left, or
shall you trust to inspiration?

Their plans did not avail. Both Howells and Clemens went to New Haven to receive their honors.

When they had returned, Howells wrote formally, as became the new rank:

DEAR SIR,—I have long been an admirer of your complete works, several of which I have read, and I am with you shoulder to shoulder in the cause of foreign missions. I would respectfully request a personal interview, and if you will appoint some day and hour most inconvenient to you I will call at your baronial hall. I cannot doubt, from the account of your courtesy given me by the Twelve Apostles, who once visited you in your Hartford home and were mistaken for a syndicate of lightning-rod men, that our meeting will be mutually agreeable.

Yours truly,

W. D. HOWELLS.

DR. CLEMENS.

CCXVII

MARK TWAIN IN POLITICS

THERE was a campaign for the mayoralty of New York City that fall, with Seth Low on the Fusion ticket against Edward M. Shepard as the Tammany candidate. Mark Twain entered the arena to try to defeat Tammany Hall. He wrote and he spoke in favor of clean city government and police reform. He was savagely in earnest and openly denounced the clan of Croker, individually and collectively. He joined a society called The Acorns; and on the 17th of October, at a dinner given by the order at the Waldorf-Astoria, delivered a fierce arraignment, in which he characterized Croker as the Warren Hastings of New York. His speech was really a set of extracts from Edmund Burke's great impeachment of Hastings, substituting always the name of Croker, and paralleling his career with that of the ancient boss of the East India Company.

It was not a humorous speech. It was too denunciatory for that. It probably contained less comic phrasing than any former effort. There is hardly even a suggestion of humor from beginning to end. It concluded with this paraphrase of Burke's impeachment:

I impeach Richard Croker of high crimes and misdemeanors.

I impeach him in the name of the people, whose trust he has betrayed.

I impeach him in the name of all the people of America, whose national character he has dishonored.

I impeach him in the name and by virtue of those eternal laws of justice which he has violated.

I impeach him in the name of human nature itself, which he has cruelly outraged, injured, and oppressed, in both sexes, in every age, rank, situation, and condition of life.

The Acorn speech was greatly relied upon for damage to the Tammany ranks, and hundreds of thousands of copies of it were printed and circulated.[1]

Clemens was really heart and soul in the campaign. He even joined a procession that marched up Broadway, and he made a speech to a great assemblage at Broadway and Leonard Street, when, as he said, he had been sick abed two days and, according to the doctor, should be in bed then.

But I would not stay at home for a nursery disease, and that's what I've got. Now, don't let this leak out all over town, but I've been doing some indiscreet eating—that's all. It wasn't drinking. If it had been I shouldn't have said anything about it.

I ate a banana. I bought it just to clinch the Italian vote for fusion, but I got hold of a Tammany banana by mistake. Just one little nub of it on the end was nice and white. That was the Shepard end. The other nine-tenths were rotten. Now that little white end won't make the rest of the banana good. The nine-tenths will make that little nub rotten, too.

We must get rid of the whole banana, and our Acorn Society is going to do its share, for it is pledged to nothing but the support of good government all over the United States. We will elect the President next time.

It won't be I, for I have ruined my chances by joining the Acorns, and there can be no office-holders among us.

There was a movement which Clemens early nipped in the bud—to name a political party after him.

"I should be far from willing to have a political party named after me," he wrote, "and I would not be willing

---

[1] The "Edmund Burke on Croker and Tammany" speech had originally been written as an article for the *North American Review*.

to belong to a party which allowed its members to have political aspirations or push friends forward for political preferment."

In other words, he was a knight-errant; his sole purpose for being in politics at all—something he always detested—was to do what he could for the betterment of his people.

He had his reward, for when Election Day came, and the returns were in, the Fusion ticket had triumphed and Tammany had fallen. Clemens received his share of the credit. One paper celebrated him in verse:

> Who killed Croker?
> I, said Mark Twain,
> I killed Croker,
> I, the Jolly Joker!

Among Samuel Clemens's literary remains there is an outline plan for a "Casting-Vote party," whose main object was "to compel the two great parties to nominate their *best man always*." It was to be an organization of an infinite number of clubs throughout the nation, no member of which should seek or accept a nomination for office or any political appointment, but in each case should cast its vote as a unit for the candidate of one of the two great political parties, requiring that the man be of clean record and honest purpose.

From constable up to President [runs his final clause] there is no office for which the two great parties cannot furnish able, clean, and acceptable men. Whenever the balance of power shall be lodged in a permanent third party, with no candidate of its own and no function but to cast its *whole vote* for the best man put forward by the Republicans and Democrats, these two parties *will select the best man they have in their ranks.* Good and clean government will follow, let its party complexion be what it may, and the country will be quite content.

It was a Utopian idea, very likely, as human nature is made; full of that native optimism which was always overflowing and drowning his gloomier logic. Clearly he forgot his despair of humanity when he formulated that document, and there is a world of unselfish hope in these closing lines:

If in the hands of men who regard their citizenship as a high trust this scheme shall fail upon trial a better must be sought, a better must be invented; for it cannot be well or safe to let the present political conditions continue indefinitely. They can be improved and American citizenship should arouse up from its disheartenment and see that it is done.

Had this document been put into type and circulated it might have founded a true Mark Twain party.

Clemens made not many more speeches that autumn, closing the year at last with the "Founder's Night" speech at The Players, the short address which, ending on the stroke of midnight, dedicates each passing year to the memory of Edwin Booth, and pledges each new year in a loving-cup passed in his honor.

CCXVIII

NEW INTERESTS AND INVESTMENTS

THE spirit which a year earlier had prompted Mark Twain to prepare his "Salutation from the Nineteenth to the Twentieth Century" inspired him now to conceive the "Stupendous International Procession," a gruesome pageant described in a document (unpublished) of twenty-two typewritten pages which begin:

THE STUPENDOUS PROCESSION

At the appointed hour it moved across the world in the following order:

The Twentieth Century

A fair young creature, drunk and disorderly, borne in the arms of Satan. Banner with motto, "Get What You Can, Keep What You Get."

Guard of Honor—Monarchs, Presidents, Tammany Bosses, Burglars, Land Thieves, Convicts, etc., appropriately clothed and bearing the symbols of their several trades.

Christendom

A majestic matron in flowing robes drenched with blood. On her head a golden crown of thorns; impaled on its spines the bleeding heads of patriots who died for their countries— Boers, Boxers, Filipinos; in one hand a slung-shot, in the other a Bible, open at the text "Do unto others," etc. Protruding from pocket bottle labeled "We bring you the blessings of civilization." Necklace—handcuffs and a burglar's jimmy.

Supporters—At one elbow Slaughter, at the other Hypocrisy.

Banner with motto—"Love Your Neighbor's Goods as Yourself."

Ensign—The Black Flag.

Guard of Honor—Missionaries and German, French, Russian, and British soldiers laden with loot.

And so on, with a section for each nation of the earth, headed each by the black flag, each bearing horrid emblems, instruments of torture, mutilated prisoners, broken hearts, floats piled with bloody corpses. At the end of all, banners inscribed:

"All White Men are Born Free and Equal."

"Christ died to make men holy,
Christ died to make men free."

with the American flag furled and draped in crêpe, and the shade of Lincoln towering vast and dim toward the sky, brooding with sorrowful aspect over the far-reaching pageant. With much more of the same sort. It is a fearful document, too fearful, we may believe, for Mrs. Clemens ever to consent to its publication.

Advancing years did little toward destroying Mark Twain's interest in human affairs. At no time in his life was he more variously concerned and employed than in his sixty-seventh year. He was always alive, young, actively cultivating or devising interests—valuable and otherwise, though never less than important to him.

He had plenty of money again, for one thing, and he liked to find dazzlingly new ways for investing it. As in the old days, he was always putting "twenty-five or forty thousand dollars " as he said, into something that promised multiplied returns. Howells tells how he found him looking wonderfully well, and when he asked the name of his elixir he learned that it was plasmon.

I did not immediately understand that plasmon was one of the investments which he had made from "the substance of things hoped for," and in the destiny of a disastrous disappointment. But after paying off the creditors of his late publishing firm he had to do something with his money, and it was not his fault if he did not make a fortune out of plasmon.

It was just at this period (the beginning of 1902) that he was promoting with his capital and enthusiasm the plasmon interests in America, investing in it one of the "usual amounts," promising to make Howells over again body and soul with the life-giving albuminate. Once he wrote him explicit instructions:

Yes—take it as a medicine—there is nothing better, nothing surer of desired results. If you wish to be elaborate—which isn't necessary—put a couple of heaping teaspoonfuls of the powder in an inch of milk & stir until it is a paste; put in some more milk and stir the paste to a thin gruel; then fill up the glass and drink.

Or, stir it into your soup.

Or, into your oatmeal.

Or, use any method you like, so's you *get it down*—that is the only essential.

He put another "usual sum" about this time in a patent cash register which was acknowledged to be "a promise rather than a performance," and remains so until this day.

He capitalized a patent spiral hat-pin, warranted to hold the hat on in any weather, and he had a number of the pins handsomely made to present to visitors of the sex naturally requiring that sort of adornment and protection. It was a pretty and ingenious device and apparently effective enough, though it failed to secure his invested thousands.

He invested a lesser sum in shares of the Booklover's Library, which was going to revolutionize the reading world, and which at least paid a few dividends. Even the old Tennessee land will-o'-the-wisp—long since repudiated and forgotten—when it appeared again in the form of a possible equity in some overlooked fragment, kindled a gentle interest, and was added to his list of ventures.

He made one substantial investment at this period. They became more and more in love with the Hudson environment, its beauty and its easy access to New York. Their house was what they liked it to be—a gathering-place for friends and the world's notables, who could reach it easily and quickly from New York. They had a steady procession of company when Mrs. Clemens's health would permit, and during a single week in the early part of this year entertained guests at no less than seventeen out of their twenty-one meals, and for three out of the seven nights—not an unusual week. Their plan for buying a home on the Hudson ended with the purchase of what was known as Hillcrest, or the Casey place, at Tarrytown, overlooking that beautiful stretch of river, the Tappan Zee, close to the Washington Irving home. The beauty of its outlook and surroundings appealed to them all. The house was handsome and finely placed, and they planned to make certain changes that would adapt it to their needs. The price, which was less than fifty thousand dollars, made it an attractive purchase; and without doubt it would have made them a suitable and happy home had it been written in the future that they should so inherit it.

Clemens was writing pretty steadily these days. The human race was furnishing him with ever so many inspiring subjects, and he found time to touch more or less on most of them. He wreaked his indignation upon the things which exasperated him often—even usually—without the expectation of print; and he delivered himself even more inclusively at such times as he walked the floor between the luncheon or dinner courses, amplifying on the poverty of an invention that had produced mankind as a supreme handiwork. In a letter to Howells he wrote:

NEW INTERESTS AND INVESTMENTS

Your comments on that idiot's "Ideals" letter reminds me that I preached a good sermon to my family yesterday on his particular layer of the human race, that grotesquest of all the inventions of the Creator. It was a good sermon, but coldly received, & it seemed best not to try to take up a collection.

He once told Howells, with the wild joy of his boyish heart, how Mrs. Clemens found some compensation, when kept to her room by illness, in the reflection that now she would not hear so much about the "damned human race."

Yet he was always the first man to champion that race, and the more unpromising the specimen the surer it was of his protection, and he never invited, never expected gratitude.

One wonders how he found time to do all the things that he did. Besides his legitimate literary labors and his preachments, he was always writing letters to this one and that, long letters on a variety of subjects, carefully and picturesquely phrased, and to people of every sort. He even formed a curious society, whose members were young girls—one in each country of the earth. They were supposed to write to him at intervals on some subject likely to be of mutual interest, to which letters he agreed to reply. He furnished each member with a typewritten copy of the constitution and by-laws of the Juggernaut Club, as he called it, and he apprised each of her election, usually after this fashion:

I have a club—a private club, which is all my own. I appoint the members myself, & they can't help themselves, because I don't allow them to vote on their own appointment & I don't allow them to resign! They are all friends whom I have never seen (save one), but who have written friendly letters to me. By the laws of my club there can be only one member in each country, & there can be no male member but myself. Some day I may admit males, but I don't know—they are capricious & inharmonious, & their ways provoke me a good deal. It is a matter which the club shall decide. I have made four appointments in the past three or four months: You as a member for Scotland—oh, this good while!; a young citizeness of Joan of Arc's home region as a member for France; a Mohammedan girl as member for Bengal; & a dear & bright young niece of mine as member for the United States—for I do not represent a country myself, but am merely member-at-large for the human race. You must not try to resign, for the laws of the club do not allow that. You must console yourself by remembering that you are in the best company; that nobody knows of your membership except yourself; that no member knows another's name, but only her country; that no taxes are levied and no meetings held (but how dearly I should like to attend one!). One of my members is a princess of a royal house, another is the daughter of a village bookseller on the continent of Europe, for the only qualification for membership is intellect & the spirit of good-will; other distinctions, hereditary or acquired, do not count. May I send you the constitution & laws of the club? I shall be so glad if I may.

It was just one of his many fancies, and most of the active memberships would not long be maintained; though some continued faithful in their reports, as he did in his replies, to the end.

One of the more fantastic of his conceptions was a plan to advertise for ante-mortem obituaries of himself—in order, as he said, that he might look them over and enjoy them and make certain corrections in the matter of detail. Some of them he thought might be appropriate to read from the platform.

I will correct them—not the facts, but the verdicts—striking out such clauses as could have a deleterious influence on the other side, and replacing them with clauses of a more judicious character.

He was much taken with the new idea, and his request for such obituaries, with an offer of a prize for the best —a portrait of himself drawn by his own hand—really appeared in *Harper's Weekly* later in the year. Naturally he got a shower of responses—serious, playful, burlesque. Some of them were quite worth while.

The obvious "Death loves a shining Mark" was of course numerously duplicated, and some varied it "Death loves an Easy Mark," and there was "Mark, the perfect man."

The two that follow gave him especial pleasure.

OBITUARY FOR "MARK TWAIN"

Worthy of his portrait, a place on his monument, as well as a place among his "perennial-consolation heirlooms":

"Got up; washed; went to bed."

The subject's own words (see *Innocents Abroad*). Can't go back on your own words, Mark Twain. There's nothing *"to strike out"*; nothing *"to replace."* What *more* could be said of any one?

"Got up!"—Think of the *fullness* of *meaning!* The *possibilities* of life, its achievements—physical, intellectual, spiritual. Got up to the top!—the climax of human aspiration on earth!

"Washed"—Every whit clean; purified—body, soul, thoughts, purposes.

"Went to bed"—Work all done—to rest, to sleep. The culmination of the day well spent!

God looks after the awakening.

Mrs. S. A. OREN-HAYNES.

Mark Twain was the only man who ever lived, so far as we know, whose lies were so innocent, and withal so helpful, as to make them worth more than a whole lot of fossilized priests' eternal truths.

D. H. KENNER.

CCXIX

YACHTING AND THEOLOGY

CLEMENS made fewer speeches during the Riverdale period. He was as frequently demanded, but he had a better excuse for refusing, especially the evening functions. He attended a good many luncheons with friendly spirits like Howells, Matthews, James L. Ford, and Hamlin Garland. At the end of February he came down to the Mayor's dinner given to Prince Henry of Prussia, but he did not speak. Clemens used to say afterward that he had not been asked to speak, and that it was probably because of his supposed breach of etiquette at the Kaiser's dinner in Berlin; but the fact that Prince Henry sought him out, and was most cordially and humanly attentive during a considerable portion of the evening, is against the supposition.

Clemens attended a Yale alumni dinner that winter and incidentally visited Twichell in Hartford. The old question of moral responsibility came up and Twichell lent his visitor a copy of Jonathan Edwards's *Freedom of the Will* for train perusal. Clemens found it absorbing. Later he wrote Twichell his views.

DEAR JOE,—(After compliments.)[1] From Bridgeport to New York, thence to home, & continuously until near midnight

---

[1] Meaning "What a good time you gave me; what a happiness it was to be under your roof again," etc. See opening sentence of all translations of letters passing between Lord Roberts and Indian princes and rulers.

YACHTING AND THEOLOGY

I wallowed & reeked with Jonathan in his insane debauch; rose immensely refreshed & fine at ten this morning, but with a strange & haunting sense of having been on a three days' tear with a drunken lunatic. It is years since I have known these sensations. All through the book is the glare of a resplendent intellect gone mad—a marvelous spectacle. No, not *all* through the book—the drunk does not come on till the last third, where what I take to be Calvinism & its God begins to show up & shine red & hideous in the glow from the fires of hell, their only right and proper adornment.

Jonathan seems to hold (as against the Armenian position) that the man (or his soul or his will) never *creates* an impulse itself, but is moved to action by an impulse back of it. That's sound!

Also, that of two or more things offered it, it infallibly chooses the one which for the moment is most *pleasing* to ITSELF. *Perfectly* correct! An immense admission for a man not otherwise sane.

Up to that point he could have written Chapters III & IV of my suppressed *Gospel*. But there we seem to separate. He seems to concede the indisputable & unshaken dominion of Motive & Necessity (call them what he may, these are exterior forces & not under the man's authority, guidance, or even suggestion); then he suddenly flies the logical track & (to all seeming) makes the man & not those exterior forces responsible to God for the man's thoughts, words, & acts. It is frank insanity.

I think that when he concedes the autocratic dominion of Motive and Necessity he grants a *third* position of mine—that a man's mind is a mere machine—an *automatic* machine—which is handled entirely from the *outside*, the man himself furnishing it absolutely nothing; not an ounce of its fuel, & not so much as a bare *suggestion* to that exterior engineer as to what the machine shall do nor *how* it shall do it nor *when*.

After that concession it was time for him to get alarmed & *shirk*—for he was pointed straight for the only rational & possible next station on *that* piece of road—the irresponsibility of man to God.

And so he shirked. Shirked, and arrived at this handsome result:

1157

Man is commanded to do so & so.

It has been ordained from the beginning of time that some men *sha'n't* & others *can't*.

These are to blame: let them be damned.

I enjoy the Colonel very much, & shall enjoy the rest of him with an obscene delight.

Joe, the whole tribe shout love to you & yours! MARK.

Clemens was moved to set down some theology of his own, and did so in a manuscript which he entitled, "If I Could Be There." It is in the dialogue form he often adopted for polemic writing. It is a colloquy between the Master of the Universe and a Stranger. It begins:

I

If I could be there, hidden under the steps of the throne, I should hear conversations like this:

A STRANGER. Lord, there is one who needs to be punished, and has been overlooked. It is in the record. I have found it.

LORD. By searching?

S. Yes, Lord.

L. Who is it? What is it?

S. A man.

L. Proceed.

S. He died in sin. Sin committed by his great-grandfather.

L. When was this?

S. Eleven million years ago.

L. Do you know what a microbe is?

S. Yes, Lord. It is a creature too small to be detected by my eye.

L. He commits depredations upon your blood?

S. Yes, Lord.

L. I give you leave to subject him to a billion years of misery for this offense. Go! Work your will upon him.

S. But, Lord, I have nothing against him; I am indifferent to him.

L. Why?

S. He is so infinitely small and contemptible. I am to him as is a mountain-range to a grain of sand.

YACHTING AND THEOLOGY

L. What am I to man?

S. (Silent.)

L. Am I not, to a man, as is a billion solar systems to a grain of sand?

S. It is true, Lord.

L. Some microbes are larger than others. Does man regard the difference?

S. No, Lord. To him there is no difference of consequence. To him they are all microbes, all infinitely little and equally inconsequential.

L. To me there is no difference of consequence between a man & a microbe. Man looks down upon the speck at his feet called a microbe from an altitude of a thousand miles, so to speak, and regards him with indifference; I look down upon the specks called a man and a microbe from an altitude of a billion leagues, so to speak, and to me they are of a size. To me both are inconsequential. Man kills the microbes when he can?

S. Yes, Lord.

L. Then what? Does he keep him in mind years and years and go on contriving miseries for him?

S. No, Lord.

L. Does he forget him?

S. Yes, Lord.

L. Why?

S. He cares nothing more about him.

L. Employs himself with more important matters?

S. Yes, Lord.

L. Apparently man is quite a rational and dignified person, and can divorce his mind from uninteresting trivialities. Why does he affront me with the fancy that I interest Myself in trivialities—like men and microbes?

II

L. Is it true the human race thinks the universe was created for its convenience?

S. Yes, Lord.

L. The human race is modest. Speaking as a member of it, what do you think the other animals are for?

S. To furnish food and labor for man.

L. What is the sea for?

S. To furnish food for man. Fishes.

L. And the air?

S. To furnish sustenance for man. Birds and breath.

L. How many men are there?

S. Fifteen hundred millions.

L. (Referring to notes.) Take your pencil and set down some statistics. In a healthy man's lower intestine 28,000,000 microbes are born daily and die daily. In the rest of a man's body 122,000,000 microbes are born daily and die daily. The two sums aggregate—what?

S. About 150,000,000.

L. In ten days the aggregate reaches what?

S. Fifteen hundred millions.

L. It is for one person. What would it be for the whole human population?

S. Alas, Lord, it is beyond the power of figures to set down that multitude. It is billions of billions multiplied by billions of billions, and these multiplied again and again by billions of billions. The figures would stretch across the universe and hang over into space on both sides.

L. To what intent are these uncountable microbes introduced into the human race?

S. That they may eat.

L. Now then, according to man's own reasoning, what is man for?

S. Alas—alas—

L. What is he *for?*

S. To—to—furnish food for microbes.

L. Manifestly. A child could see it. Now then, with this common-sense light to aid your perceptions, what are the air, the land, and the ocean for?

S. To furnish food for man so that he may nourish, support, and multiply and replenish the microbes.

L. Manifestly. Does one build a boarding-house for the sake of the boarding-house itself or for the sake of the boarders?

S. Certainly for the sake of the boarders.

L. Man's a boarding-house.

S. I perceive it, Lord.

L. He is a boarding-house. He was never intended for anything else. If he had had less vanity and a clearer insight into the great truths that lie embedded in statistics he would have found it out early. As concerns the man who has gone unpunished eleven million years, is it your belief that in life he did his duty by his microbes?

S. Undoubtedly, Lord. He could not help it.

L. Then why punish him? He had no other duty to perform.

Whatever else may be said of this kind of doctrine, it is at least original and has a conclusive sound. Mark Twain had very little use for orthodoxy and conservatism. When it was announced that Dr. Jacques Loeb, of the University of California, had demonstrated the creation of life by chemical agencies he was deeply interested. When a newspaper writer commented that a "consensus of opinion among biologists" would probably rate Dr. Loeb as a man of lively imagination rather than an inerrant investigator of natural phenomena, he felt called to chaff the consensus idea.

I wish I could be as young as that again. Although I seem so old now I was once as young as that. I remember, as if it were but thirty or forty years ago, how a paralyzing consensus of opinion accumulated from experts a-setting around about brother experts who had patiently and laboriously cold-chiseled their way into one or another of nature's safe-deposit vaults and were reporting that they had found something valuable was plenty for me. It settled it.

But it isn't so now—no. Because in the drift of the years I by and by found out that a Consensus examines a new thing with its feelings rather oftener than with its mind.

There was that primitive steam-engine—ages back, in Greek times: a Consensus made fun of it. There was the Marquis of Worcester's steam-engine 250 years ago: a Consensus made fun of it. There was Fulton's steamboat of a century ago: a French Consensus, including the great Napoleon, made fun of it. There was Priestley, with his oxygen: a Consensus scoffed at him, mobbed him, burned him out, banished him. While a Consensus was proving, by statistics and things, that a steamship could not cross the Atlantic, a steamship did it.

And so on through a dozen pages or more of lively satire, ending with an extract from *Adam's Diary*.

Then there was a Consensus about it. It was the very first one. It sat six days and nights. It was then delivered of the verdict that a world could not be made out of nothing; that such small things as sun and moon and stars might, maybe, but it would take years and years if there was considerable many of them. Then the Consensus got up and looked out of the window, and there was the whole outfit, spinning and sparkling in space! You never saw such a disappointed lot.

ADAM.

He was writing much at this time, mainly for his own amusement, though now and then he offered one of his reflections for print. That beautiful fairy tale, "The Five Boons of Life," of which the most precious is "Death," was written at this period. Maeterlinck's lovely story of the bee interested him; he wrote about that. Somebody proposed a Martyrs' Day; he wrote a paper ridiculing the suggestion. In his note-book, too, there is a memorandum for a love-story of the Quarternary Epoch which would begin, "On a soft October afternoon 2,000,000 years ago." John Fiske's *Discovery of America*, Volume I, he said, was to furnish the animals and scenery, civilization and conversation to be the same as to-day; but apparently this idea was carried no further. He ranged through every subject from protoplasm to infinity, exalting, condemning, ridiculing, explaining; his brain was always busy —a dynamo that rested neither night nor day.

In April Clemens received notice of another yachting trip on the *Kanawha*, which this time would sail for the Bahama and West India islands. The guests were to be about the same.[1]

[1] The invited ones of the party were Hon. T. B. Reed, A. G. Paine, Laurence Hutton, Dr. C. C. Rice, W. T. Foote, and S. L. Clemens. "Owners of the yacht," Mr. Rogers called them, signing himself as "Their Guest."

YACHTING AND THEOLOGY

He sent this telegram:

H. H. ROGERS,
    Fairhaven, Mass.
Can't get away this week. I have company here from to-night till middle of next week. Will *Kanawha* be sailing after that & can I go as Sunday-school superintendent at half rate? Answer and prepay.   DR. CLEMENS.

The sailing date was conveniently arranged and there followed a happy cruise among those balmy islands. Mark Twain was particularly fond of "Tom" Reed, who had been known as "Czar" Reed in Congress, but was delightfully human in his personal life. They argued politics a good deal, and Reed, with all his training and intimate practical knowledge of the subject, confessed that he "couldn't argue with a man like that."

"Do you believe the things you say?" he asked once, in his thin, falsetto voice.

"Yes," said Clemens. "Some of them."

"Well, you want to look out. If you go on this way, by and by you'll get to believing nearly *every*thing you say."

Draw poker appears to have been their favorite diversion. Clemens in his notes reports that off the coast of Florida Reed won twenty-three pots in succession. It was said afterward that they made no stops at any harbor; that when the chief officer approached the poker-table and told them they were about to enter some important port he received peremptory orders to "sail on and not interrupt the game." This, however, may be regarded as more or less founded on fiction.

CCXX

MARK TWAIN AND THE PHILIPPINES

AMONG the completed manuscripts of the early part of
1902 was a *North American Review* article (published
in April)—"Does the Race of Man Love a Lord?"—a
most interesting treatise on snobbery as a universal
weakness. There were also some papers on the Philippine
situation. In one of these Clemens wrote:

We have bought some islands from a party who did not own
them; with real smartness and a good counterfeit of disinterested
friendliness we coaxed a confiding weak nation into a trap and
closed it upon them; we went back on an honored guest of the
Stars and Stripes when we had no further use for him and chased
him to the mountains; we are as indisputably in possession of
a wide-spreading archipelago as if it were our property; we have
pacified some thousands of the islanders and buried them;
destroyed their fields; burned their villages, and turned their
widows and orphans out-of-doors; furnished heartbreak by
exile to some dozens of disagreeable patriots; subjugated the
remaining ten millions by Benevolent Assimilation, which is the
pious new name of the musket; we have acquired property in the
three hundred concubines and other slaves of our business
partner, the Sultan of Sulu, and hoisted our protecting flag over
that swag.

And so, by these Providences of God—the phrase is the
government's, not mine—we are a World Power; and are glad
and proud, and have a back seat in the family. With tacks in
it. At least we are letting on to be glad and proud; it is the best
way. Indeed, it is the only way. We must maintain our
dignity, for people are looking. We are a World Power; we
cannot get out of it now, and we must make the best of it.

1164

And again he wrote:

I am not finding fault with this use of our flag, for in order not to seem eccentric I have swung around now and joined the nation in the conviction that nothing can sully a flag. I was not properly reared, and had the illusion that a flag was a thing which must be sacredly guarded against shameful uses and unclean contacts lest it suffer pollution; and so when it was sent out to the Philippines to float over a wanton war and a robbing expedition I supposed it was polluted, and in an ignorant moment I said so. But I stand corrected. I concede and acknowledge that it was only the government that sent it on such an errand that was polluted. Let us compromise on that. I am glad to have it that way. For our flag could not well stand pollution, never having been used to it, but it is different with the administration.

A much more conspicuous comment on the Philippine policy was the so-called "Defense of General Funston" for what Funston himself referred to as a "dirty Irish trick"; that is to say, deception in the capture of Aguinaldo. Clemens, who found it hard enough to reconcile himself to any form of warfare, was especially bitter concerning this particular campaign. The article appeared in the *North American Review* for May, 1902, and stirred up a good deal of a storm. He wrote much more on the subject—very much more—but it is still unpublished.

CCXXI

THE RETURN OF THE NATIVE

ONE day in April, 1902, Samuel Clemens received the following letter from the president of the University of Missouri:

My dear Mr. Clemens,—Although you received the degree of doctor of literature last fall from Yale, and have had other honors conferred upon you by other great universities, we want to adopt you here as a son of the University of Missouri. In asking your permission to confer upon you the degree of LL.D. the University of Missouri does not aim to confer an honor upon you so much as to show her appreciation of you. The rules of the University forbid us to confer the degree upon any one *in absentia*. I hope very much that you can so arrange your plans as to be with us on the fourth day of next June, when we shall hold our Annual Commencement.

Very truly yours,
R. H. Jesse.

Clemens had not expected to make another trip to the West, but a proffered honor such as this from one's native State was not a thing to be declined.

It was at the end of May when he arrived in St. Louis, and he was met at the train there by his old river instructor and friend, Horace Bixby—as fresh, wiry, and capable as he had been forty-five years before.

"I have become an old man. You are still thirty-five," Clemens said.

They went to the Planters Hotel, and the news presently got around that Mark Twain was there. There followed a sort of reception in the hotel lobby, after which Bixby took him across to the rooms of the Pilots Association, where the rivermen gathered in force to celebrate his return. A few of his old comrades were still alive, among them Beck Jolly. The same afternoon he took the train for Hannibal.

It was a busy five days that he had in Hannibal. High-school commencement day came first. He attended, and willingly, or at least patiently, sat through the various recitals and orations and orchestrations, dreaming and remembering, no doubt, other high-school commencements of more than half a century before, seeing in some of those young people the boys and girls he had known in that vanished time. A few friends of his youth were still there, but they were among the audience now, and no longer fresh and looking into the future. Their heads were white, and, like him, they were looking down the recorded years. Laura Hawkins was there and Helen Kercheval (Mrs. Frazer and Mrs. Garth now), and there were others, but they were few and scattering.

He was added to the program, and he made himself as one of the graduates, and told them some things of the young people of that earlier time that brought their laughter and their tears.

He was asked to distribute the diplomas, and he undertook the work in his own way. He took an armful of them and said to the graduates:

"Take one. Pick out a good one. Don't take two, but be sure you get a good one."

So each took one "unsight and unseen" and made the more exact distributions among themselves later.

Next morning—it was Saturday—he visited the old home on Hill Street, and stood in the doorway all dressed in white while a battalion of photographers made pictures of "this return of the native" to the threshold of his youth.

"It all seems so small to me," he said, as he looked through the house; "a boy's home is a big place to him. I suppose if I should come back again ten years from now it would be the size of a bird-house."

He went through the rooms and up-stairs where he had slept and looked out the window down in the back yard where, nearly sixty years before, Tom Sawyer, Huck Finn, Joe Harper, and the rest—that is to say, Tom Blankenship, John Briggs, Will Pitts, and the Bowen boys —set out on their nightly escapades. Of that lightsome band Will Pitts and John Briggs still remained, with half a dozen others—schoolmates of the less adventurous sort. Buck Brown, who had been his rival in the spelling contests, was still there, and John RoBards, who had worn golden curls and the medal for good conduct, and Ed Pierce. And while these were assembled in a little group on the pavement outside the home a small old man came up and put out his hand, and it was Jimmy MacDaniel, to whom so long before, sitting on the river-bank and eating gingerbread, he had first told the story of Jim Wolfe and the cats.

They put him into a carriage, drove him far and wide, and showed the hills and resorts and rendezvous of Tom Sawyer and his marauding band.

He was entertained that evening by the Labinnah Club (whose name was achieved by a backward spelling of Hannibal), where he found most of the survivors of his youth. The news report of that occasion states that he was introduced by Father McLoughlin, and that he "responded in a very humorous and touchingly pathetic way, breaking down in tears at the conclusion. Commenting on his boyhood days and referring to his mother was too much for the great humorist. Before him as he spoke were sitting seven of his boyhood friends."

On Sunday morning Col. John RoBards escorted him to the various churches and Sunday-schools. They were all new churches to Samuel Clemens, but he pretended not to recognize this fact. In each one he was asked to speak a few words, and he began by saying how good it was to be back in the old home Sunday-school again, which as a boy he had always so loved, and he would go on and point out the very place he had sat, and his escort hardly knew whether or not to enjoy the proceedings. At one place he told a moral story. He said:

Little boys and girls, I want to tell you a story which illustrates the value of perseverance—of sticking to your work, as it were. It is a story very proper for a Sunday-school. When I was a little boy in Hannibal I used to play a good deal up here on Holliday's Hill, which of course you all know. John Briggs and I played up there. I don't suppose there are any little boys as good as we were then, but of course that is not to be expected. Little boys in those days were 'most always good little boys, because those were the good old times when everything was better than it is now, but never mind that. Well, once upon a time, on Holliday's Hill, they were blasting out rock, and a man was drilling for a blast. He sat there and drilled and drilled and drilled perseveringly until he had a hole down deep enough for the blast. Then he put in the powder and tamped and tamped it down, but maybe he tamped it a little too hard, for the blast went off and he went up into the air, and we watched him. He went up higher and higher and got smaller and smaller. First he looked as big as a child, then as big as a dog, then as big as a kitten, then as big as a bird, and finally he went out of sight. John Briggs was with me, and we watched the place where he went out of sight, and by and by we saw him coming down— first as big as a bird, then as big as a kitten, then as big as a dog, then as big as a child, and then he was a man again, and landed right in his seat and went to drilling—just persevering, you see, and sticking to his work. Little boys and girls, that's the secret of success, just like that poor but honest workman on Holliday's Hill. Of course you won't always be appreciated. He wasn't. His employer was a hard man, and on Saturday night when he paid him he docked him fifteen minutes for the time he was up in the air—but never mind, he had his reward.

He told all this in his solemn, grave way, though the Sunday-school was in a storm of enjoyment when he finished. There still remains a doubt in Hannibal as to its perfect suitability, but there is no doubt as to its acceptability.

That Sunday afternoon, with John Briggs, he walked over Holliday's Hill—the "Cardiff Hill" of *Tom Sawyer*. It was just such a Sunday as that one when they had so nearly demolished the negro driver and had damaged a cooper-shop. They calculated that nearly three thousand Sundays had passed since then, and now here they were once more, two old men, with the hills still fresh and green, the river still sweeping by and rippling in the sun. Standing there together and looking across to the low-lying Illinois shore, and to the green islands where they had played, and to Lover's Leap on the south, the man who had been Sam Clemens said:

"John, that is one of the loveliest sights I ever saw. Down there by the island is the place we used to swim, and yonder is where a man was drowned, and there's where the steamboat sank. Down there on Lover's Leap is where the Millerites put on their robes one night to go to heaven. None of them went that night, but I suppose most of them have gone now."

John Briggs said:

"Sam, do you remember the day we stole the peaches from old man Price and one of his bow-legged niggers came after us with the dogs, and how we made up our minds that we'd catch that nigger and drown him?"

They came to the place where they had pried out the great rock that had so nearly brought them to grief. Sam Clemens said:

"John, if we had killed that man we'd have had a dead nigger on our hands without a cent to pay for him."

And so they talked on of this thing and that, and by and by they drove along the river, and Sam Clemens pointed out the place where he swam it and was taken with a cramp on the return swim, and believed for a while that his career was about to close.

"Once, near the shore, I thought I would let down," he said, "but was afraid to, knowing that if the water was deep I was a goner, but finally my knees struck the sand and I crawled out. That was the closest call I ever had."

They drove by the place where the haunted house had stood. They drank from a well they had always known, and from the bucket as they had always drunk, talking and always talking, fondling lovingly and lingeringly that most beautiful of all our possessions, the past.

"Sam," said John, when they parted, "this is probably the last time we shall meet on this earth. God bless you. Perhaps somewhere we shall renew our friendship."

"John," was the answer, "this day has been worth thousands of dollars to me. We were like brothers once, and I feel that we are the same now. Good-by, John. I'll try to meet you—somewhere."

CCXXII

A PROPHET HONORED IN HIS COUNTRY

CLEMENS left next day for Columbia. Committees met him at Rensselaer, Monroe City, Clapper, Stoutsville, Paris, Madison, Moberly—at every station along the line of his travel. At each place crowds were gathered when the train pulled in, to cheer and wave and to present him with flowers. Sometimes he spoke a few words; but oftener his eyes were full of tears—his voice would not come.

There is something essentially dramatic in official recognition by one's native State—the return of the lad who has set out unknown to battle with life, and who, having conquered, is invited back to be crowned. No other honor, however great and spectacular, is quite like that, for there is in it a pathos and a completeness that are elemental and stir emotions as old as life itself.

It was on the 4th of June, 1902, that Mark Twain received his doctor of laws degree from the State University at Columbia, Missouri. James Wilson, Secretary of Agriculture, and Ethan Allen Hitchcock, Secretary of the Interior, were among those similarly honored. Mark Twain was naturally the chief attraction. Dressed in his Yale scholastic gown he led the procession of graduating students, and, as in Hannibal, awarded them their diplomas. The regular exercises were made purposely brief in order that some time might be allowed for the conferring of the degrees. This ceremony was a peculiarly impressive one. Gardner Lathrop read a brief statement introducing "America's foremost author and best-loved citizen, Samuel Langhorne Clemens—Mark Twain."

Clemens rose, stepped out to the center of the stage, and paused. He seemed to be in doubt as to whether he should make a speech or simply express his thanks and retire. Suddenly, and without a signal, the great audience rose as one man and stood in silence at his feet. He bowed, but he could not speak. Then that vast assembly began a peculiar chant, spelling out slowly the word Missouri, with a pause between each letter. It was dramatic; it was tremendous in its impressiveness. He had recovered himself when they finished. He said he didn't know whether he was expected to make a speech or not. They did not leave him in doubt. They cheered and demanded a speech, *a speech*, and he made them one—one of the speeches he could make best, full of quaint phrasing, happy humor, gentle and dramatic pathos. He closed by telling the watermelon story for its "moral effect."

He was the guest of E. W. Stevens in Columbia, and a dinner was given in his honor. They would have liked to keep him longer, but he was due in St. Louis again to join in the dedication of the grounds, where was to be held a World's Fair, to celebrate the Louisiana Purchase. Another ceremony he attended was the christening of the St. Louis harbor-boat, or rather the rechristening, for it had been decided to change its name from the *St. Louis* [1] to the *Mark Twain*. A short trip was made on it for the ceremony. Governor Francis and Mayor Wells were of the party, and Count and Countess Rochambeau and Marquis de Lafayette, with the rest of the French group that had come over for the dedication of the World's Fair grounds.

Mark Twain himself was invited to pilot the harbor-

[1] Originally the *Elon G. Smith*, built in 1873.

boat, and so returned for the last time to his old place at the wheel. They all collected in the pilot-house behind him, feeling that it was a memorable occasion. They were going along well enough when he saw a little ripple running out from the shore across the bow. In the old days he could have told whether it indicated a bar there or was only caused by the wind, but he could not be sure any more. Turning to the pilot languidly, he said:

"I feel a little tired. I guess you had better take the wheel."

Luncheon was served aboard, and Mayor Wells made the christening speech; then the Countess Rochambeau took a bottle of champagne from the hand of Governor Francis and smashed it on the deck, saying, "I christen thee, good boat, *Mark Twain*." So it was, the Mississippi joined in according him honors. In his speech of reply he paid tribute to those illustrious visitors from France and recounted something of the story of French exploration along that great river.

"The name of La Salle will last as long as the river itself," he said; "will last until commerce is dead. We have allowed the commerce of the river to die, but it was to accommodate the railroads, and we must be grateful."

Carriages were waiting for them when the boat landed in the afternoon, and the party got in and were driven to a house which had been identified as Eugene Field's birthplace. A bronze tablet recording this fact had been installed, and this was to be the unveiling. The place was not in an inviting quarter of the town. It stood in what is known as Walsh's Row—fashionable enough once, perhaps, but long since fallen into disrepute. Ragged children played in the doorways, and thirsty lodgers were making trips with tin pails to convenient bar-rooms. A curious nondescript audience assembled around the little group of dedicators, wondering what it was all about. The tablet was concealed by the American flag, which could be easily pulled away by an attached cord.

Governor Francis spoke a few words, to the effect that they had gathered here to unveil a tablet to an American poet, and that it was fitting that Mark Twain should do this. They removed their hats, and Clemens, his white hair blowing in the wind, said:

"My friends, we are here with reverence and respect to commemorate and enshrine in memory the house where was born a man who, by his life, made bright the lives of all who knew him, and by his literary efforts cheered the thoughts of thousands who never knew him. I take pleasure in unveiling the tablet of Eugene Field."

The flag fell and the bronze inscription was revealed. By this time the crowd, generally, had recognized who it was that was speaking. A working-man proposed three cheers for Mark Twain, and they were heartily given. Then the little party drove away, while the neighborhood collected to regard the old house with a new interest.

It was reported to Clemens later that there was some dispute as to the identity of the Field birthplace. He said:

"Never mind. It is of no real consequence whether it is his birthplace or not. A rose in any other garden will bloom as sweet."

CCXXIII

AT YORK HARBOR

THEY decided to spend the summer at York Harbor, Maine. They engaged a cottage there, and about the end of June Mr. Rogers brought his yacht *Kanawha* to their water-front at Riverdale, and in perfect weather took them to Maine by sea. They landed at York Harbor and took possession of their cottage, The Pines, one of their many attractive summer lodges. Howells, at Kittery Point, was not far away, and everything promised a happy summer.

Mrs. Clemens wrote to Mrs. Crane:

We are in the midst of pines. They come up right about us, and the house is so high and the roots of the trees are so far below the veranda that we are right in the branches. We drove over to call on Mr. and Mrs. Howells. The drive was most beautiful, and never in my life have I seen such a variety of wild flowers in so short a space.

Howells tells us of the wide, low cottage in a pine grove overlooking York River, and how he used to sit with Clemens that summer at a corner of the veranda farthest away from Mrs. Clemens's window, where they could read their manuscripts to each other, and tell their stories and laugh their hearts out without disturbing her.

Clemens, as was his habit, had taken a work-room in a separate cottage " in the house of a friend and neighbor, a fisherman and a boatman ":

AT YORK HARBOR

There was a table where he could write, and a bed where he could lie down and read; and there, unless my memory has played me one of those constructive tricks that people's memories indulge in, he read me the first chapters of an admirable story. The scene was laid in a Missouri town, and the characters such as he had known in boyhood; but often as I tried to make him own it, he denied having written any such story; it is possible that I dreamed it, but I hope the MS. will yet be found.

Howells did not dream it; but in one way his memory misled him. The story was one which Clemens had heard in Hannibal, and he doubtless related it in his vivid way. Howells, writing at a later time, quite naturally included it among the several manuscripts which Clemens read aloud to him. Clemens may have intended to write the tale, may even have begun it, though this is unlikely. The incidents were too well known and too notorious in his old home for fiction.

Among the stories that Clemens did show, or read, to Howells that summer was "The Belated Passport," a strong, intensely interesting story with what Howells in a letter calls a "goat's tail ending," perhaps meaning that it stopped with a brief and sudden shake—with a joke, in fact, altogether unimportant, and on the whole disappointing to the reader. A far more notable literary work of that summer grew out of a true incident which Howells related to Clemens as they sat chatting together on the veranda overlooking the river one summer afternoon. It was a pathetic episode in the life of some former occupants of The Pines—the tale of a double illness in the household, where a righteous deception was carried on during several weeks for the benefit of a life that was about to slip away. Out of this grew the story, "Was it Heaven? or Hell?" a heartbreaking history which probes the very depths of the human soul. Next to "Hadleyburg," it is Mark Twain's greatest fictional sermon.

Clemens that summer wrote, or rather finished, his most

pretentious poem. One day at Riverdale, when Mrs. Clemens had been with him on the lawn, they had remembered together the time when their family of little folks had filled their lives so full, conjuring up dream-like glimpses of them in the years of play and short frocks and hair-plaits down their backs. It was pathetic, heart-wringing fancying; and later in the day Clemens conceived and began the poem which now he brought to conclusion. It was built on the idea of a mother who imagines her dead child still living, and describes to any listener the pictures of her fancy. It is an impressive piece of work; but the author, for some reason, did not offer it for publication.[1]

Mrs. Clemens, whose health earlier in the year had been delicate, became very seriously ill at York Harbor. Howells writes:

At first she had been about the house, and there was one gentle afternoon when she made tea for us in the parlor, but that was the last time I spoke with her. After that it was really a question of how soonest and easiest she could be got back to Riverdale.

She had seemed to be in fairly good health and spirits for several weeks after the arrival at York. Then, early in August, there came a great celebration of some municipal anniversary, and for two or three days there were processions, mass-meeting and so on, by day, with fireworks at night. Mrs. Clemens, always young in spirit, was greatly interested. She went about more than her strength warranted, seeing and hearing and enjoying all that was going on. She was finally persuaded to forego the remaining ceremonies and rest quietly on the pleasant veranda at home; but she had overtaxed herself and

---

[1] This poem was completed on the anniversary of Susy's death and is of considerable length. Some selections from it will be found under Appendix U, at the end of this work.

a collapse was inevitable. Howells and two friends called one afternoon, and a friend of the Queen of Rumania, a Madame Hartwig, who had brought from that gracious sovereign a letter which closed in this simple and modest fashion:

I beg your pardon for being a bore to one I so deeply love and admire, to whom I owe days and days of forgetfulness of self and troubles, and the intensest of all joys—hero-worship! People don't always realize what a happiness that is! God bless you for every beautiful thought you poured into my tired heart, and for every smile on a weary way.   CARMEN SYLVA.

This was the occasion mentioned by Howells when Mrs. Clemens made tea for them in the parlor for the last time. Her social life may be said to have ended that afternoon. Next morning the break came. Clemens, in his note-book for that day, writes:

Tuesday, August 12, 1902. At 7 A.M. Livy taken violently ill. Telephoned and Dr. Lambert was here in ½ hour. She could not breathe—was likely to stifle. Also she had severe palpitation. She believed she was dying. I also believed it.

Nurses were summoned, and Mrs. Crane and others came from Elmira. Clara Clemens took charge of the household and matters generally, and the patient was secluded and guarded from every disturbing influence. Clemens slipped about with warnings of silence. A visitor found notices in Mark Twain's writing pinned to the trees near Mrs. Clemens's window warning the birds not to sing too loudly.

The patient rallied, but she remained very much debilitated. On September 3d the note-book says:

Always Mr. Rogers keeps his yacht *Kanawha* in commission & ready to fly here and take us to Riverdale on telegraphic notice.

But Mrs. Clemens was unable to return by sea. When it was decided at last, in October, that she could be removed to Riverdale, Clemens and Howells went to Boston and engaged an invalid car to make the journey from York Harbor to Riverdale without change. Howells tells us that Clemens gave his strictest personal attention to the arrangement of these details, and that they absorbed him.

There was no particular of the business which he did not scrutinize and master. . . . With the inertness that grows upon an aging man he had been used to delegate more and more things, but of that thing I perceived that he would not delegate the least detail.

They made the journey on the 16th, in nine and a half hours. With the exception of the natural weariness due to such a trip, the invalid was apparently no worse on their arrival. The stout English butler carried her to her room. It would be many months before she would leave it again. In one of his memoranda Clemens wrote:

Our dear prisoner is where she is through overwork—day & night devotion to the children & me. We did not know how to value it. We know now.

And in a notation, on a letter praising him for what he had done for the world's enjoyment, and for his splendid triumph over debt, he said:

Livy never gets her share of these applauses, but it is because the people do not know. Yet she is entitled to the lion's share.

He wrote Twichell at the end of October:

Livy drags along drearily. It must be hard times for that turbulent spirit. It will be a long time before she is on her feet again. It is a most pathetic case. I wish I could transfer

it to myself. Between ripping & raging & smoking & reading
I could get a good deal of holiday out of it. Clara runs the house
smoothly & capitally.

Heavy as was the cloud of illness, he could not help
pestering Twichell a little about a recent mishap—a
sprained shoulder:

I should like to know how & where it happened. In the pulpit,
as like as not, otherwise you would not be taking so much pains
to conceal it. This is not a malicious suggestion, & not a
personally invented one: you told me yourself once that you
threw artificial power & impressiveness in your sermons where
needed by "banging the Bible"—(your own words). You have
reached a time of life when it is not wise to take these risks.
You would better jump around. We all have to change our
methods as the infirmities of age creep upon us. Jumping around
will be impressive now, whereas before you were gray it would
have excited remark.

Mrs. Clemens seemed to improve as the weeks passed,
and they had great hopes of her complete recovery.
Clemens took up some work—a new Huck Finn story,
inspired by his trip to Hannibal. It was to have two
parts—Huck and Tom in youth, and then their return
in old age. He did some chapters quite in the old vein,
and wrote to Howells of his plan. Howells answered:

It is a great lay-out: what I shall enjoy most will be the return of the old fellows to the scene and their tall lying. There
is a matchless chance there. I suppose you will put in plenty
of pegs in this prefatory part.

But the new story did not reach completion. Huck
and Tom would not come back, even to go over the old
scenes.

CCXXIV

THE SIXTY-SEVENTH BIRTHDAY DINNER

IT was on the evening of the 27th of November, 1902, at the Metropolitan Club, New York City, that Col. George Harvey, president of the Harper Company, gave Mark Twain a dinner in celebration of his sixty-seventh birthday. The actual date fell three days later; but that would bring it on Sunday, and to give it on Saturday night would be more than likely to carry it into Sabbath morning, and so the 27th was chosen. Colonel Harvey himself presided, and Howells led the speakers with a poem, "A Double-Barreled Sonnet to Mark Twain," which closed:

> Still, to have everything beyond cavil right,
> We will dine with you here till Sunday night.

Thomas Brackett Reed followed with what proved to be the last speech he would ever make, as it was also one of his best. All the speakers did well that night, and they included some of the country's foremost in oratory: Chauncey Depew, St. Clair McKelway, Hamilton Mabie, and Wayne MacVeagh. Dr. Henry van Dyke and John Kendrick Bangs read poems. The chairman constantly kept the occasion from becoming too serious by maintaining an attitude of "thinking ambassador" for the guest of the evening, gently pushing Clemens back in his seat when he attempted to rise and expressing for him an opinion of each of the various tributes.

"The limit has been reached," he announced at the

close of Dr. van Dyke's poem. "More that is better could not be said. Gentlemen, Mr. Clemens."

It is seldom that Mark Twain has made a better after-dinner speech than he delivered then. He was surrounded by some of the best minds of the nation, men assembled to do him honor. They expected much of him—to Mark Twain always an inspiring circumstance. He was greeted with cheers and hand-clapping that came volley after volley, and seemed never ready to end. When it had died away at last he stood waiting a little in the stillness for his voice; then he said, "I think I ought to be allowed to talk as long as I want to," and again the storm broke.

It is a speech not easy to abridge—a finished and perfect piece of after-dinner eloquence,[1] full of humorous stories and moving references to old friends—to Hay, and Reed, and Twichell, and Howells, and Rogers, the friends he had known so long and loved so well. He told of his recent trip to his boyhood home, and how he had stood with John Briggs on Holliday's Hill and they had pointed out the haunts of their youth. Then at the end he paid a tribute to the companion of his home, who could not be there to share his evening's triumph. This peroration —a beautiful heart-offering to her and to those that had shared in long friendship—demands admission:

Now, there is one invisible guest here. A part of me is not present; the larger part, the better part, is yonder at her home; that is my wife, and she has a good many personal friends here, and I think it won't distress any one of them to know that, although she is going to be confined to her bed for many months to come from that nervous prostration, there is not any danger and she is coming along very well—and I think it quite appropriate that I should speak of her. I knew her for the first time just in the same year that I first knew John Hay and

---

[1] The "Sixty-seventh Birthday Speech" entire is included in the volume *Mark Twain's Speeches*.

Tom Reed and Mr. Twichell—thirty-six years ago—and she has been the best friend I have ever had, and that is saying a good deal—she has reared me—she and Twichell together—and what I am I owe to them. Twichell—why, it is such a pleasure to look upon Twichell's face! For five and twenty years I was under the Rev. Mr. Twichell's tuition, I was in his pastorate occupying a pew in his church and held him in due reverence. That man is full of all the graces that go to make a person companionable and beloved; and wherever Twichell goes to start a church the people flock there to buy the land; they find real estate goes up all around the spot, and the envious and the thoughtful always try to get Twichell to move to their neighborhood and start a church; and wherever you see him go you can go and buy land there with confidence, feeling sure that there will be a double price for you before very long.

I have tried to do good in this world, and it is marvelous in how many different ways I have done good, and it is comfortable to reflect—now, there's Mr. Rogers—just out of the affection I bear that man many a time I have given him points in finance that he had never thought of—and if he could lay aside envy, prejudice, and superstition, and utilize those ideas in his business, it would make a difference in his bank-account.

Well, I liked the poetry. I liked all the speeches and the poetry, too. I liked Dr. van Dyke's poem. I wish I could return thanks in proper measure to you, gentlemen, who have spoken and violated your feelings to pay me compliments; some were merited and some you overlooked, it is true; and Colonel Harvey did slander every one of you, and put things into my mouth that I never said, never thought of at all.

And now my wife and I, out of our single heart, return you our deepest and most grateful thanks, and—yesterday was her birthday.

The sixty-seventh birthday dinner was widely celebrated by the press, and newspaper men generally took occasion to pay brilliant compliments to Mark Twain. Arthur Brisbane wrote editorially:

For more than a generation he has been the Messiah of a genuine gladness and joy to the millions of three continents.

It was little more than a week later that one of the old friends he had mentioned, Thomas Brackett Reed, apparently well and strong that birthday evening, passed from the things of this world. Clemens felt his death keenly, and in a "good-by" which he wrote for *Harper's Weekly* he said:

His was a nature which invited affection—compelled it, in fact—and met it half-way. Hence, he was "Tom" to the most of his friends and to half of the nation. . . .

I cannot remember back to a time when he was not "Tom" Reed to me, nor to a time when he could have been offended at being so addressed by me. I cannot remember back to a time when I could let him alone in an after-dinner speech if he was present, nor to a time when he did not take my extravagance concerning him and misstatements about him in good part, nor yet to a time when he did not pay them back with usury when his turn came. The last speech he made was at my birthday dinner at the end of November, when naturally I was his text; my last word to him was in a letter the next day; a day later I was illustrating a fantastic article on art with his portrait among others—a portrait now to be laid reverently away among the jests that begin in humor and end in pathos. These things happened only eight days ago, and now he is gone from us, and the nation is speaking of him as one who was. It seems incredible, impossible. Such a man, such a friend, seems to us a permanent possession; his vanishing from our midst is unthinkable, as was the vanishing of the Campanile, that had stood for a thousand years and was turned to dust in a moment.

The appreciation closes:

I have only wished to say how fine and beautiful was his life and character, and to take him by the hand and say good-by, as to a fortunate friend who has done well his work and goes a pleasant journey.

CCXXV

CHRISTIAN SCIENCE CONTROVERSIES

THE *North American Review* for December (1902) contained an instalment of the Christian Science series which Mark Twain had written in Vienna several years before. He had renewed his interest in the doctrine, and his admiration for Mrs. Eddy's peculiar abilities and his antagonism toward her had augmented in the mean time. Howells refers to the "mighty moment when Clemens was building his engines of war for the destruction of Christian Science, which superstition nobody, and he least of all, expected to destroy":

He believed that as a religious machine the Christian Science Church was as perfect as the Roman Church, and destined to be more formidable in its control of the minds of men. . . .

An interesting phase of his psychology in this business was not only his admiration for the masterly policy of the Christian Science hierarchy, but his willingness to allow the miracles of its healers to be tried on his friends and family if they wished it. He had a tender heart for the whole generation of empirics, as well as the newer sorts of scienticians, but he seemed to base his faith in them largely upon the failure of the regulars, rather than upon their own successes, which also he believed in. He was recurrently, but not insistently, desirous that you should try their strange magics when you were going to try the familiar medicines.

Clemens never had any quarrel with the theory of Christian Science or mental healing, or with any of the empiric practices. He acknowledged good in all of them, and he welcomed most of them in preference to *materia medica*. It is true that his animosity for the founder of the Christian Science cult sometimes seems to lap over and fringe the religion itself; but this is apparent rather than real. Furthermore, he frequently expressed a deep obligation which humanity owed to the founder of the faith, in that she had organized a healing element ignorantly and indifferently employed hitherto. His quarrel with Mrs. Eddy lay in the belief that she herself, as he expressed it, was "a very unsound Christian Scientist."

I believe she has a serious malady—self-edification—and that it will be well to have one of the experts demonstrate over her. [But he added]: Closely examined, painstakingly studied, she is easily the most interesting person on the planet, and in several ways as easily the most extraordinary woman that was ever born upon it.

Necessarily, the forces of Christian Science were aroused by these articles, and there were various replies, among them, one by the founder herself, a moderate rejoinder in her usual literary form.

"Mrs. Eddy in Error," in the *North American Review* for April, 1903, completed what Clemens had to say on the matter for this time.

He was putting together a book on the subject, comprised of his various published papers and some added chapters. It would not be a large volume, and he offered to let his Christian Science opponents share it with him, stating their side of the case. Mr. William D. McCrackan, one of the church's chief advocates, was among those invited to participate. McCrackan and Clemens, from having begun as enemies, had become quite friendly, and had discussed their differences face to face at considerable length. Early in the controversy Clemens one night wrote McCrackan a pretty savage letter. He threw it on the hall table for mailing, but later got out of bed and slipped down-stairs to get it. It was too late—the letters had been gathered up and mailed. Next evening a truly Christian note came from McCrackar, returning the hasty letter, which he said he was sure the writer would wish to recall. Their friendship began there. For some reason, however, the collaborated volume did not materialize. In the end, publication was delayed a number of years, by which time Clemens's active interest was a good deal modified, though the practice itself never failed to invite his attention.

Howells refers to his anti-Christian Science rages, which began with the postponement of the book, and these Clemens vented at the time in another manuscript entitled, "Eddypus," an imaginary history of a thousand years hence, when Eddyism should rule the world. By that day its founder would have become a deity, and the calendar would be changed to accord with her birth. It was not publishable matter, and really never intended as such. It was just one of the things which Mark Twain wrote to relieve mental pressure.

CCXXVI

"WAS IT HEAVEN? OR HELL?"

THE Christmas number of *Harper's Magazine* for 1902 contained the story, "Was it Heaven? or Hell?" and it immediately brought a flood of letters to its author from grateful readers on both sides of the ocean. An Englishman wrote: "I want to thank you for writing so pathetic and so profoundly true a story"; and an American declared· it to be the best short story ever written. Another letter said:

> I have learned to love those maiden liars—love and weep over them—then put them beside Dante's Beatrice in Paradise.

There were plenty of such letters; but there was one of a different sort. It was a letter from a man who had but recently gone through almost precisely the experience narrated in the tale. His dead daughter had even borne the same name—Helen. She had died of typhus while her mother was prostrated with the same malady, and the deception had been maintained in precisely the same way, even to the fictitiously written letters. Clemens replied to this letter, acknowledging the striking nature of the coincidence it related, and added that, had he invented the story, he would have believed it a case of mental telegraphy.

> I was merely telling a true story just as it had been told to me by one who well knew the mother and the daughter & all the beautiful & pathetic details. I was living in the house where it

1189

had happened, three years before, & I put it on paper at once while it was fresh in my mind, & its pathos still straining at my heartstrings.

Clemens did not guess that the coincidences were not yet complete, that within a month the drama of the tale would be enacted in his own home. In his note-book, under the date of December 24 (1902), he wrote:

Jean was hit with a chill: Clara was completing her watch in her mother's room and there was no one able to force Jean to go to bed. As a result she is pretty ill to-day—fever & high temperature.

Three days later he added:

It was pneumonia. For 5 days Jean's temperature ranged between $103\frac{1}{3}$ & $104\frac{2}{5}$, till this morning, when it got down to 101. She looks like an escaped survivor of a forest fire. For 6 days now my story in the Christmas *Harper's*—"Was it Heaven? or Hell?"—has been enacted in this household. Every day Clara & the nurses have lied about Jean to her mother, describing the fine times she is having outdoors in the winter sports.

That proved a hard, trying winter in the Clemens home, and the burden of it fell chiefly, indeed almost entirely, upon Clara Clemens. Mrs. Clemens became still more frail, and no other member of the family, not even her husband, was allowed to see her for longer than the briefest interval. Yet the patient was all the more anxious to know the news, and daily it had to be prepared—chiefly invented—for her comfort. In an account which Clemens once set down of the "Siege and Season of Unveracity," as he called it, he said:

Clara stood a daily watch of three or four hours, and hers was a hard office indeed. Daily she sealed up in her heart a dozen dangerous truths, and thus saved her mother's life and hope and happiness with holy lies. She had never told her mother a lie in her life before, and I may almost say that she never told her a truth afterward. It was fortunate for us all that Clara's reputation for truthfulness was so well established in her mother's mind. It was our daily protection from disaster. The mother never doubted Clara's word. Clara could tell her large improbabilities without exciting any suspicion, whereas if I tried to market even a small and simple one the case would have been different. I was never able to get a reputation like Clara's.

Mrs. Clemens questioned Clara every day concerning Jean's health, spirits, clothes, employments, and amusements, and how she was enjoying herself; and Clara furnished the information right along in minute detail—every word of it false, of course. Every day she had to tell how Jean dressed, and in time she got so tired of using Jean's existing clothes over and over again, and trying to get new effects out of them, that finally, as a relief to her hard-worked invention, she got to adding imaginary clothes to Jean's wardrobe, and probably would have doubled it and trebled it if a warning note in her mother's comments had not admonished her that she was spending more money on these spectral gowns and things than the family income justified.

Some portions of detailed accounts of Clara's busy days of this period, as written at the time by Clemens to Twichell and to Mrs. Crane, are eminently worth preserving. To Mrs. Crane:

Clara does not go to her Monday lesson in New York today [her mother having seemed not so well through the night], but forgets that fact and enters her mother's room (where she has no business to be) toward train-time *dressed in a wrapper*.

Livy. Why, Clara, aren't you going to your lesson?

Clara (almost caught). Yes.

L. In that costume?

Cl. Oh no.

L. Well, you can't make your train; it's impossible.

Cl. I know, but I'm going to take the other one.

L. Indeed *that* won't do—you'll be ever so much too late for your lesson.

Cl. No, the lesson-time has been put an hour later.

L. (satisfied, then suddenly). But, Clara, that train and the late lesson together will make you late to Mrs. Hapgood's luncheon.

CL. No, the train leaves fifteen minutes earlier than it used to.

L. (satisfied). Tell Mrs. Hapgood, etc., etc., etc. (which Clara promises to do). Clara, dear, after the luncheon—I hate to put this on you—but could you do two or three little shopping-errands for me?

CL. Oh, it won't trouble me a bit—I can do it. (Takes a list of the things she is to buy—a list which she will presently hand to another.)

At 3 or 4 P.M. Clara takes the things brought from New York, studies over her part a little, then goes to her mother's room.

LIVY. It's very good of you, dear. Of course, if I had known it was going to be so snowy and drizzly and sloppy I wouldn't have asked you to buy them. Did you get wet?

CL. Oh, nothing to hurt.

L. You took a cab both ways?

CL. Not from the station to the lesson—the weather was good enough till that was over.

L. Well, now, tell me everything Mrs. Hapgood said.

Clara tells her a long yarn—avoiding novelties and surprises and anything likely to inspire questions difficult to answer; and of course detailing the menu, for if it had been the feeding of the 5,000 Livy would have insisted on knowing what kind of bread it was and how the fishes were served. By and by, while talking of something else:

LIVY. Clams!—in the end of December. Are you sure it was clams?

CL. I didn't say cl— I meant Blue Points.

L. (tranquilized). It seemed odd. What is Jean·doing?

CL. She said she was going to do a little typewriting.

L. Has she been out to-day?

CL. Only a moment, right after luncheon. She was determined to go out again, but—

L. How did you know she was out?

CL. (saving herself in time). Katie told me. She was determined to go out again in the rain and snow, but I persuaded her to stay in.

L. (with moving and grateful admiration). Clara, you are

wonderful! the wise watch you keep over Jean, and the influence you have over her; it's so lovely of you, and I tied here and can't take care of her myself. (And she goes on with these undeserved praises till Clara is expiring with shame.)

To Twichell:

I am to see Livy a moment every afternoon until she has another bad night; and I stand in dread, for with all my practice I realize that in a sudden emergency I am but a poor, clumsy liar, whereas a fine alert and capable emergency liar is the only sort that is worth anything in a sick-chamber.

Now, Joe, just see what reputation can do. All Clara's life she has told Livy the truth and now the reward comes; Clara lies to her three and a half hours every day, and Livy takes it all at par, whereas even when I tell her a truth it isn't worth much without corroboration. . . .

Soon my brief visit is due. I've just been up listening at Livy's door.

5 P.M. A great disappointment. I was sitting outside Livy's door waiting. Clara came out a minute ago and said Livy is not so well, and the nurse can't let me see her to-day.

That pathetic drama was to continue in some degree for many a long month. All that winter and spring Mrs. Clemens kept but a frail hold on life. Clemens wrote little, and refused invitations everywhere he could. He spent his time largely in waiting for the two-minute period each day when he could stand at the bed-foot and say a few words to the invalid, and he confined his writing mainly to the comforting, affectionate messages which he was allowed to push under her door. He was always waiting there long before the moment he was permitted to enter. Her illness and her helplessness made manifest what Howells has fittingly characterized as his "beautiful and tender loyalty to her, which was the most moving quality of his most faithful soul."

THE SECOND RIVERDALE WINTER

MOST of Mark Twain's stories have been dramatized at one time or another, and with more or less success. He had two plays going that winter, one of them the little "Death Disk," which in story form had appeared a year before in *Harper's Magazine*. It was put on at the Carnegie Lyceum with considerable effect, but it was not of sufficient importance to warrant a long continuance.

Another play of that year was a dramatization of *Huckleberry Finn*, by Lee Arthur. This was played with a good deal of success in Baltimore, Philadelphia, and elsewhere, the receipts ranging from three hundred to twenty-one hundred dollars per night, according to the weather and locality. Why the play was discontinued is not altogether apparent; certainly many a dramatic enterprise has gone further, faring worse.

Huck in book form also had been having adventures a little earlier, in being tabooed on account of his morals by certain librarians of Denver and Omaha. It was years since Huck had been in trouble of that sort, and he acquired a good deal of newspaper notoriety in consequence.

Certain entries in Mark Twain's note-book reveal somewhat of his life and thought at this period. We find such entries as this:

Saturday, January 3, 1903. The offspring of riches: Pride, vanity, ostentation, arrogance, tyranny.

Sunday, January 4, 1903. The offspring of poverty: Greed, sordidness, envy, hate, malice, cruelty, meanness, lying, shirking, cheating, stealing, murder.

Monday, February 2, 1903. 33d wedding anniversary. I was allowed to see Livy 5 minutes this morning in honor of the day. She makes but little progress toward recovery, still there is certainly some, we are sure.

Sunday, March 1, 1903. We may not doubt that society in heaven consists mainly of undesirable persons.

Thursday, March 19, 1903. Susy's birthday. She would be 31 now.

The family illnesses, which presently included an allotment for himself, his old bronchitis, made him rage more than ever at the imperfections of the species which could be subject to such a variety of ills. Once he wrote:

Man was made at the end of the week's work when God was tired.

And again:

Adam, man's benefactor—he gave him all that he has ever received that was worth having—death.

The Riverdale home was in reality little more than a hospital that spring. Jean had scarcely recovered her physical strength when she was attacked by measles, and Clara also fell a victim to the infection. Fortunately Mrs. Clemens's health had somewhat improved.

It was during this period that Clemens formulated his eclectic therapeutic doctrine. Writing to Twichell April 4, 1903, he said:

Livy does make a little progress these past 3 or 4 days, progress which is visible to even the untrained eye. The physicians are doing good work for her, but *my* notion is, that no art of healing is the best for *all* ills. I should distribute the ailments around: surgery cases to the surgeon; lupus to the actinic-ray specialist; nervous prostration to the Christian Scientist; most ills to the allopath & the homeopath; & (in my own particular case) rheumatism, gout, & bronchial attack to the osteopathist.

He had plenty of time to think and to read during those weeks of confinement, and to rage, and to write when he felt the need of that expression, though he appears to have completed not much for print beyond his reply to Mrs. Eddy, already mentioned, and his burlesque, "Instructions in Art," with pictures by himself, published in the *Metropolitan* for April and May.

Howells called his attention to some military outrages in the Philippines, citing a case where a certain lieutenant[1] had tortured one of his men, a mild offender, to death out of pure deviltry, and had been tried but not punished for his fiendish crime.

Clemens undertook to give expression to his feelings on this subject, but he boiled so when he touched pen to paper to write of it that it was simply impossible for him to say anything within the bounds of print. Then his only relief was to rise and walk the floor, and curse out his fury at the race that had produced such a specimen.

Mrs. Clemens, who perhaps got some drift or the echo of these tempests, now and then sent him a little admonitory, affectionate note.

Among the books that Clemens read, or tried to read, during his confinement were certain of the novels of Sir Walter Scott. He had never been able to admire Scott, and determined now to try to understand this author's popularity and his standing with the critics; but after wading through the first volume of one novel, and beginning another one, he concluded to apply to one who

---

[1] The torture to death of Private Edward C. Richter, an American soldier, by orders of a commissioned officer of the United States army on the night of February 7, 1902. Private Richter was bound and gagged and the gag held in his mouth by means of a club while ice-water was slowly poured into his face, a dipper full at a time, for two hours and a half, until life became extinct.

could speak as having authority. He wrote to Brander Matthews:

DEAR BRANDER,—I haven't been out of my bed for 4 weeks, but—well, I have been reading a good deal, & it occurs to me to ask you to sit down, some time or other when you have 8 or 9 months to spare, & jot me down a certain few literary particulars for my help & elevation. Your time need not be thrown away, for at your further leisure you can make Columbian lectures out of the results & do your students a good turn.

1. Are there in Sir Walter's novels passages done in *good* English—English which is neither slovenly nor involved?

2. Are there passages whose English is not poor & thin & commonplace, but is of a quality above that?

3. Are there passages which burn with real fire—not punk, fox-fire, make-believe?

4. Has he heroes & heroines who are not cads and cadesses?

5. Has he personages whose acts & talk correspond with their characters as described by him?

6. Has he heroes & heroines whom the reader admires— admires and knows *why?*

7. Has he funny characters that are funny, and humorous passages that are humorous?

8. Does he ever chain the reader's interest & make him reluctant to lay the book down?

9. Are there pages where he ceases from posing, ceases from admiring the placid flood & flow of his own dilution, ceases from being artificial, & is for a time, long or short, recognizably sincere & in earnest?

10. Did he know how to write English, & didn't do it because he didn't want to?

11. Did he use the right word only when he couldn't think of another one, or did he run so much to wrong words because he didn't know the right one when he saw it?

12. Can you read him and keep your respect for him? Of course a person could in *his* day—an era of sentimentality & sloppy romantics—but land! can a body do it to-day?

Brander, I lie here dying, slowly dying, under the blight of Sir Walter. I have read the first volume of *Rob Roy*, & as far as Chapter XIX of *Guy Mannering*, & I can no longer hold my head up or take my nourishment. Lord, it's all so juvenile! so artificial, so shoddy; & *such* wax figures & skeletons & specters. Interest? Why, it is impossible to feel an interest in these bloodless shams, these milk-&-water humbugs. And oh, the poverty of invention! Not poverty in inventing situations, but poverty in furnishing reasons for them. Sir Walter usually gives himself away when he arranges for a situation—elaborates & elaborates & elaborates till, if you live to get to it, you don't believe in it when it happens.

I can't find the rest of *Rob Roy*, I can't stand any more *Mannering*—I do not know just what to do, but I will reflect, & not quit this great study rashly. . . .

My, I wish I could see you & Leigh Hunt!

Sincerely yours,
S. L. CLEMENS.

But a few days later he experienced a revelation. It came when he perseveringly attacked still a third work of Scott—*Quentin Durward*. Hastily he wrote to Matthews again:

I'm still in bed, but the days have lost their dullness since I broke into Sir Walter & lost my temper. I finished *Guy Mannering*—that curious, curious book, with its mob of squalid shadows gibbering around a single flesh-&-blood being—Dinmont; a book crazily put together out of the very refuse of the romance artist's stage properties—finished it & took up *Quentin Durward* & finished that.

It was like leaving the dead to mingle with the living; it was like withdrawing from the infant class in the college of journalism to sit under the lectures in English literature in Columbia University.

I wonder who wrote *Quentin Durward?* [1]

Among other books which he read that winter and spring was Helen Keller's *The Story of My Life*, then

---

[1] This letter, enveloped, addressed, and stamped, was evidently mislaid. It was found and mailed seven years later, June, 1910—a message from the dead.

recently published. That he finished it in a mood of sweet gentleness we gather from a long, lovely letter which he wrote her—a letter in which he said:

> I am charmed with your book—enchanted. You are a wonderful creature, the most wonderful in the world—you and your other half together—Miss Sullivan, I mean—for it took the pair of you to make a complete & perfect whole. How she stands out in her letters! her brilliancy, penetration, originality, wisdom, character, & the fine literary competencies of her pen—they are all there.

When reading and writing failed as diversion, Mark Twain often turned to mathematics. With no special talent for accuracy in the matter of figures, he had a curious fondness for calculations, scientific and financial, and he used to cover pages, ciphering at one thing and another, arriving pretty inevitably at the wrong results. When the problem was financial, and had to do with his own fortunes, his figures were as likely as not to leave him in a state of panic. The expenditures were naturally heavy that spring; and one night, when he had nothing better to do, he figured the relative proportion to his income. The result showed that they were headed straight for financial ruin. He put in the rest of the night fearfully rolling and tossing, and reconstructing his figures that grew always worse, and next morning summoned Jean and Clara and petrified them with the announcement that the cost of living was one hundred and twenty-five per cent. more than the money-supply.

Writing to MacAlister three days later he said:

> It was a mistake. When I came down in the morning, a gray and aged wreck, I found that in some unaccountable way (unaccountable to a business man, but not to me) I had multiplied the totals by two. By God, I dropped seventy-five years on the floor where I stood!

MARK TWAIN

Do you know it affected me as one is affected when one wakes out of a hideous dream & finds it was only a dream. It was a great comfort & satisfaction to me to call the daughters to a private meeting of the board again. Certainly there is a blistering & awful reality about a well-arranged unreality. It is quite within the possibilities that two or three nights like that of mine would drive a man to suicide. He would refuse to examine the figures, they would revolt him so, & he would go to his death unaware that there was nothing serious about them. I cannot get that night out of my head, it was so vivid, so real, so ghastly. In any other year of these thirty-three the relief would have been simple: go where you can, cut your cloth to fit your income. You can't do that when your wife *can't* be moved, even from one room to the next.

The doctor & a specialist met in conspiracy five days ago, & in their belief she will by and by come out of this as good as new, substantially. They ordered her to Italy for next winter—which seems to indicate that by autumn she will be able to undertake the voyage. So Clara is writing to a Florence friend to take a look around among the villas for us in the regions near that city.

CCXXVIII

PROFFERED HONORS

MARK TWAIN had been at home well on toward three years; but his popularity showed no signs of diminishing. So far from having waned, it had surged to a higher point than ever before. His crusade against public and private abuses had stirred readers, and had set them to thinking; the news of illness in his household; a report that he was contemplating another residence abroad —these things moved deeply the public heart, and a tide of letters flowed in, letters of every sort—of sympathy, of love, or hearty indorsement, whatever his attitude of reform.

When a writer in a New York newspaper said, "Let us go outside the realm of practical politics next time in choosing our candidates for the Presidency," and asked, "Who is our ablest and most conspicuous private citizen?" another editorial writer, Joseph Hollister, replied that Mark Twain was "the greatest man of his day in private life, and entitled to the fullest measure of recognition."

But Clemens was without political ambitions. He knew the way of such things too well. When Hollister sent him the editorial he replied only with a word of thanks, and did not, even in jest, encourage that tiny seed of a Presidential boom. One would like to publish many of the beautiful letters received during this period, for they are beautiful, most of them, however illiterate in form, however discouraging in length—beautiful in that they overflow with the writers' sincerity and gratitude.

So many of them came from children, usually without the hope of a reply, some signed only with initials, that the writers might not be open to the suspicion of being seekers for his autograph. Almost more than any other reward, Mark Twain valued this love of the children.

A department in the *St. Nicholas Magazine* offered a prize for a caricature drawing of some well-known man. There were one or two of certain prominent politicians and capitalists, and there was literally a wheelbarrow load of Mark Twain. When he was informed of this he wrote:

"No tribute could have pleased me more than that— the friendship of the children."

Tributes came to him in many forms. In his native State it was proposed to form a Mark Twain Association, with headquarters at Hannibal, with the immediate purpose of having a week set apart at the St. Louis World's Fair, to be called the Mark Twain week, with a special Mark Twain day, on which a national literary convention would be held. But when his consent was asked, and his co-operation invited, he wrote characteristically:

It is indeed a high compliment which you offer me, in naming an association after me and in proposing the setting apart of a Mark Twain day at the great St. Louis Fair, but such compliments are not proper for the living; they are proper and safe for the dead only. I value the impulse which moves you to tender me these honors. I value it as highly as any one can, and am grateful for it, but I should stand in a sort of terror of the honors themselves. So long as we remain alive we are not safe from doing things which, however righteously and honorably intended, can wreck our repute and extinguish our friendships.

I hope that no society will be named for me while I am still alive, for I might at some time or other do something which would cause its members to regret having done me that honor. After I shall have joined the dead I shall follow the custom of those people, and be guilty of no conduct that can wound any friend; but until that time shall come I shall be a doubtful quantity, like the rest of our race.

The committee, still hoping for his consent, again appealed to him. But again he wrote:

While I am deeply touched by the desire of my friends of Hannibal to confer these great honors upon me I must still forbear to accept them. Spontaneous and unpremeditated honors, like those which came to me at Hannibal, Columbia, St. Louis, and at the village stations all down the line, are beyond all price and are a treasure for life in the memory, for they are a free gift out of the heart and they come without solicitation; but I am a Missourian, and so I shrink from distinctions which have to be arranged beforehand and with my privity, for I then become a party to my own exalting. I am humanly fond of honors that happen, but chary of those that come by canvass and intention.

Somewhat later he suggested a different feature for the fair; one that was not practical, perhaps, but which certainly would have aroused interest—that is to say, an old-fashioned six-day steamboat-race from New Orleans to St. Louis, with the old-fashioned accessories, such as torch-baskets, forecastle crowds of negro singers, with a negro on the safety-valve. In his letter to President Francis he said:

As to particulars, I think that the race should be a genuine reproduction of the old-time race, not just an imitation of it, and that it should cover the whole course. I think the boats should begin the trip at New Orleans, and side by side (not an interval between), and end it at North St. Louis, a mile or two above the Big Mound.

In a subsequent letter to Governor Francis he wrote:

It has been a dear wish of mine to exhibit myself at the great Fair & get a prize, but circumstances beyond my control have interfered. . . .

I suppose you will get a prize, because you have created the most prodigious Fair the planet has ever seen. Very well, you have indeed earned it, and with it the gratitude of the State and the nation.

Newspaper men used every inducement to get interviews from him. They invited him to name a price for any time he could give them, long or short. One reporter offered him five hundred dollars for a two-hour talk. Another proposed to pay him one hundred dollars a week for a quarter of a day each week, allowing him to discuss any subject he pleased. One wrote asking him two questions: the first, "Your favorite method of escaping from Indians"; the second, "Your favorite method of escaping capture by the Indians when they were in pursuit of you." They inquired as to his favorite copy-book maxim; as to what he considered most important to a young man's success; his definition of a gentleman. They wished to know his plan for the settlement of labor troubles. But they did not awaken his interest, or his cupidity. To one applicant he wrote:

No, there are temptations against which we are fire-proof. Your proposition is one which comes to me with considerable frequency, but it never tempts me. The price isn't the objection; you offer plenty. It is the nature of the work that is the objection—a kind of work which I could not do well enough to satisfy me. To multiply the price by twenty would not enable me to do the work to my satisfaction, & by consequence would make no impression upon me.

Once he allowed himself to be interviewed for the *Herald*, when from Mr. Rogers's yacht he had watched Sir Thomas Lipton's *Shamrock* go down to defeat; but this was a subject which appealed to him—a kind of hot-weather subject—and he could be as light-minded about it as he chose.

CCXXIX

THE LAST SUMMER AT ELMIRA

THE Clemenses were preparing to take up residence in Florence, Italy. The Hartford house had been sold in May, ending forever the association with the city that so long had been a part of their lives. The Tarrytown place, which they had never occupied, they also agreed to sell, for it was the belief now that Mrs. Clemens's health would never greatly prosper there. Howells says, or at least implies, that they expected their removal to Florence to be final. He tells us, too, of one sunny afternoon when he and Clemens sat on the grass before the mansion at Riverdale, after Mrs. Clemens had somewhat improved, and how they "looked up toward a balcony where by and by that lovely presence made itself visible, as if it had stooped there from a cloud. A hand frailly waved a handkerchief; Clemens ran over the lawn toward it, calling tenderly." It was a greeting to Howells —the last he would ever receive from her.

Mrs. Clemens was able to make a trip to Elmira by the end of June, and on the 1st of July Mr. Rogers brought Clemens and his wife down the river on his yacht to the Lackawanna pier, and they reached Quarry Farm that evening. She improved in the quietude and restfulness of that beloved place. Three weeks later Clemens wrote to Twichell:

Livy is coming along: eats well, sleeps some, is mostly very gay, not very often depressed; spends all day on the porch, sleeps there a part of the night; makes excursions in carriage

& in wheel-chair; &, in the matter of superintending everything & everybody, has resumed business at the old stand.

During three peaceful months she spent most of her days reclining on the wide veranda, surrounded by those dearest to her, and looking out on the dreamlike land-scape—the long, grassy slope, the drowsy city, and the distant hills—getting strength for the far journey by sea. Clemens did some writing, occupying the old octagonal study—shut in now and overgrown with vines—where during the thirty years since it was built so many of his stories had been written. *A Dog's Tale*—that pathetic anti-vivisection story—appears to have been the last manuscript ever completed in the spot consecrated by Huck and Tom, and by Tom Canty the Pauper and the little wandering Prince.

It was October 5th when they left Elmira. Two days earlier Clemens had written in his note-book:

> To-day I placed flowers on Susy's grave—for the last time probably—& read words
> "Good-night, dear heart, good-night."

They did not return to Riverdale, but went to the Hotel Grosvenor for the intervening weeks. They had engaged passage for Italy on the *Princess Irene*, which would sail on the 24th. It was during the period of their waiting that Clemens concluded his final Harper contract. On that day, in his note-book, he wrote:

THE PROPHECY

In 1895 Cheiro the palmist examined my hand & said that in my 68th year (1903) I would become suddenly rich. I was a bankrupt & $94,000 in debt at the time through the failure of Charles L. Webster & Co. Two years later—in London—Cheiro repeated this long-distance prediction, & added that the riches would come from a quite unexpected source. I am superstitious. I kept the prediction in mind & often thought of it. When at last it came true, October 22, 1903, there was but a month & 9 days to spare.

The contract signed that day concentrates all my books in Harper's hands & now at last they are valuable; in fact they are a fortune. They *guarantee* me $25,000 a year for 5 years, and they will yield twice as much as that.[1]

During the conclusion of this contract Clemens made frequent visits to Fairhaven on the *Kanawha*. Joe Goodman came from the Pacific to pay him a good-by visit during this period. Goodman had translated the Mayan inscriptions, and his work had received recognition and publication by a group of British scientists. It was a fine achievement for a man in later life and Clemens admired it immensely. Goodman and Clemens enjoyed each other in the old way at quiet resorts where they could talk over the old tales. Another visitor of that summer was the son of an old friend, a Hannibal printer named Daulton. Young Daulton came with manuscripts seeking a hearing of the magazine editors, so Clemens wrote a letter which would insure that favor:

INTRODUCING MR. GEO. DAULTON

To GILDER, ALDEN, HARVEY, McCLURE, WALKER, PAGE, BOK, COLLIER, and such other members of the sacred guild as privilege me to call them friends—these:

Although I have no personal knowledge of the bearer of this, I have what is better: He comes recommended to me by his own father—a thing not likely to happen in any of your families, I reckon. I ask you, as a favor to me, to waive prejudice &

---

[1] In earlier note-books and letters Clemens more than once refers to this prophecy and wonders if it is to be realized. The Harper contract, which brought all of his books into the hands of one publisher (negotiated for him by Mr. Rogers), proved, in fact, a fortune. The books yielded always more than the guarantee; sometimes twice that amount, as he had foreseen.

superstition for this once & examine his work with an eye to its literary merit, instead of to the chastity of its spelling. I wish to God you cared less for that particular.

I set (or sat) type alongside of his father, in Hannibal, more than 50 years ago, when none but the pure in heart were in that business. A true man he was; and if I can be of any service to his son—and to you at the same time, let me hope—I am here heartily to try.

Yours by the sanctions of time & deserving,

Sincerely,

S. L. CLEMENS.

Among the kindly words which came to Mark Twain before leaving America was this one which Rudyard Kipling had written to his publisher, Frank Doubleday:

I love to think of the great and godlike Clemens. He is the biggest man you have on your side of the water by a damn sight, and don't you forget it. Cervantes was a relation of his.

It curiously happened that Clemens at the same moment was writing to Doubleday about Kipling:

I have been reading "The Bell Buoy" and "The Old Man" over and over again—my custom with Kipling's work—and saving up the rest for other leisurely and luxurious meals. A bell-buoy is a deeply impressive fellow-being. In these many recent trips up and down the Sound in the *Kanawha* he has talked to me nightly sometimes in his pathetic and melancholy way, sometimes with his strenuous and urgent note, and I got his meaning—now I have his words! No one but Kipling could do this strong and vivid thing. Some day I hope to hear the poem chanted or sung—with the bell-buoy breaking in out of the distance.

P. S.—Your letter has arrived. It makes me proud and glad—what Kipling says. I hope Fate will fetch him to Florence while we are there. I would rather see him than any other man.

THE RETURN TO FLORENCE

FROM the note-book:

Saturday, October 24, 1903. Sailed in the *Princess Irene* for Genoa at 11. Flowers & fruit from Mrs. Rogers & Mrs. Coe. We have with us Katie Leary (in our domestic service 23 years) & Miss Margaret Sherry (trained nurse).

Two days later he wrote:

Heavy storm all night. Only 3 stewardesses. Ours served 60 meals in rooms this morning.

On the 27th:

Livy is enduring the voyage marvelously well. As well as Clara & Jean, I think, & far better than the trained nurse. She has been out on deck an hour.
November 2. Due at Gibraltar 10 days from New York. 3 days to Naples, then 1 day to Genoa.
At supper the band played "Cavalleria Rusticana," which is forever associated in my mind with Susy. I love it better than any other, but it breaks my heart.

It was the "Intermezzo" he referred to, which had been Susy's favorite music, and whenever he heard it he remembered always one particular opera-night long ago, and Susy's face rose before him.

They were in Naples on the 5th; thence to Genoa, and to Florence, where presently they were installed in the Villa Reale di Quarto, a fine old Italian palace built by Cosimo more than four centuries ago. In later times it has been occupied and altered by royal families of Würtemberg and Russia. Now it was the property of the Countess Massiglia, from whom Clemens had leased it.

They had hoped to secure the Villa Papiniano, under Fiesole, near Professor Fiske, but negotiations for it had fallen through. The Villa Quarto, as it is usually called, was a more pretentious place and as beautifully located, standing as it does in an ancient garden looking out over Florence toward Vallombrosa and the Chianti hills. Yet now in the retrospect, it seems hardly to have been the retreat for an invalid. Its garden was supernaturally beautiful, all that one expects that a garden of Italy should be—such a garden as Maxfield Parrish might dream; but its beauty was that which comes of antiquity—the accumulation of dead years. Its funereal cypresses, its crumbling walls and arches, its clinging ivy and moldering marbles, and a clock that long ago forgot the hours, gave it a mortuary look. In a way it suggested Arnold Böcklin's "Todteninsel," and it might well have served as the allegorical setting for a gateway to the bourne of silence.

The house itself, one of the most picturesque of the old Florentine suburban palaces, was historically interesting, rather than cheerful. The rooms, in number more than sixty, though richly furnished, were vast and barnlike, and there were numbers of them wholly unused and never entered. There was a dearth of the modern improvements which Americans have learned to regard as a necessity, and the plumbing, such as it was, was not always in order. The place was approached by narrow streets, along which the more uninviting aspects of Italy were not infrequent. Youth and health and romance might easily have reveled in the place; but it seems now not to have been the best choice for that frail invalid, to whom cheer and brightness and freshness and the lovelier things of hope meant always so much.[1] Neither was the climate of Florence all that they had hoped for. Their former sunny winter had misled them. Tradition to the contrary, Italy—or at least Tuscany—is not one perpetual dream of sunlight. It is apt to be damp and cloudy; it is likely to be cold. Writing to MacAlister, Clemens said:

Florentine sunshine? Bless you, there isn't any. We have heavy fogs every morning & rain all day. This house is not merely large, it is vast—therefore I think it must always lack the home feeling.

His dissatisfaction in it began thus early, and it grew as one thing after another went wrong. With it all, however, Mrs. Clemens seemed to gain a little, and was glad to see company—a reasonable amount of company— to brighten her surroundings.

Clemens began to work and wrote a story or two, and those lively articles about the Italian language.

To Twichell he reported progress:

I have a handsome success in one way here. I left New York under a sort of half-promise to furnish to the Harper magazines 30,000 words this year. Magazining is difficult work because every third page represents two pages that you have put in the fire (you are nearly sure to start wrong twice), & so when you have finished an article & are willing to let it go to print it represents only 10 cents a word instead of 30.

But this time I had the curious (& unprecedented) luck to start right in each case. I turned out 37,000 words in 25 working days; & the reason I think I started right every time is, that not only have I approved and accepted the several articles, but the court of last resort (Livy) has done the same.

[1] Villa Quarto has recently been purchased by Signor P. de Ritter Lahony, and thoroughly restored and refreshed and beautified without the sacrifice of any of its romantic features.

On many of the between-days I did some work, but only of an idle & not necessarily necessary sort, since it will not see print until I am dead. I shall continue this (an hour per day), but the rest of the year I expect to put in on a couple of long books (half-completed ones). No more magazine work hanging over my head.

This secluded & silent solitude, this clean, soft air, & this enchanting view of Florence, the great valley & snow-mountains that frame it, are the right conditions for work. They are a persistent inspiration. To-day is very lovely; when the afternoon arrives there will be a new picture every hour till dark, & each of them divine—or progressing from divine to diviner & divinest. On this (second) floor Clara's room commands the finest; she keeps a window ten feet high wide open all the time & frames it in that. I go in from time to time every day & trade sass for a look. The central detail is a distant & stately snow-hump that rises above & behind black-forested hills, & its sloping vast buttresses, velvety & sun-polished, with purple shadows between, make the sort of picture we knew that time we walked in Switzerland in the days of our youth.

From this letter, which is of January 7, 1904, we gather that the weather had greatly improved, and with it Mrs. Clemens's health, notwithstanding she had an alarming attack in December. One of the stories he had finished was "The $30,000 Bequest." The work mentioned, which would not see print until after his death, was a continuation of those autobiographical chapters which for years he had been setting down as the mood seized him.

He experimented with dictation, which he had tried long before with Redpath, and for a time now found it quite to his liking. He dictated some of his copyright memories, and some anecdotes and episodes; but his amanuensis wrote only longhand, which perhaps hampered him, for he tired of it by and by and the dictations were discontinued.

Among these notes there is one elaborate description of the Villa di Quarto, dictated at the end of the winter, by which time we are not surprised to find he had become much attached to the place. The Italian spring was in the air, and it was his habit to grow fond of his surroundings. Some atmospheric paragraphs of these impressions invite us here:

We are in the extreme south end of the house, if there is any such thing as a south end to a house, whose orientation cannot be determined by me, because I am incompetent in all cases where an object does not point directly north & south. This one slants across between, & is therefore a confusion. This little private parlor is in one of the two corners of what I call the south end of the house. The sun rises in such a way that all the morning it is pouring its light through the 33 glass doors or windows which pierce the side of the house which looks upon the terrace & garden; the rest of the day the light floods this south end of the house, as I call it; at noon the sun is directly above Florence yonder in the distance in the plain, directly across those architectural features which have been so familiar to the world in pictures for some centuries, the Duomo, the Campanile, the Tomb of the Medici, & the beautiful tower of the Palazzo Vecchio; in this position it begins to reveal the secrets of the delicious blue mountains that circle around into the west, for its light discovers, uncovers, & exposes a white snowstorm of villas & cities that you cannot train yourself to have confidence in, they appear & disappear so mysteriously, as if they might not be villas & cities at all, but the ghosts of perished ones of the remote & dim Etruscan times; & late in the afternoon the sun sets down behind those mountains somewhere, at no particular time & at no particular place, so far as I can see.

Again at the end of March he wrote:

Now that we have lived in this house four and a half months my prejudices have fallen away one by one & the place has become very homelike to me. Under certain conditions I should like to go on living in it indefinitely. I should wish the Countess to move out of Italy, out of Europe, out of the planet. I should want her bonded to retire to her place in the next world &

inform me which of the two it was, so that I could arrange for my own hereafter.

Complications with their landlady had begun early, and in time, next to Mrs. Clemens's health, to which it bore such an intimate and vital relation, the indifference of the Countess Massiglia to their needs became the supreme and absorbing concern of life at the villa, and led to continued and almost continuous house-hunting.

Days when the weather permitted, Clemens drove over the hills looking for a villa which he could lease or buy— one with conveniences and just the right elevation and surroundings. There were plenty of villas; but some of them were badly situated as to altitude or view; some were falling to decay, and the search was rather a discouraging one. Still it was not abandoned, and the reports of these excursions furnished new interest and new hope always to the invalid at home.

"Even if we find it," he wrote Howells, "I am afraid it will be months before we can move Mrs. Clemens. Of course it will. But it comforts us to let on that we think otherwise, and these pretensions help to keep hope alive in her."

She had her bad days and her good days, days when it was believed she had passed the turning-point and was traveling the way to recovery; but the good days were always a little less hopeful, the bad days a little more discouraging. On February 22d Clemens wrote in his note-book:

At midnight Livy's pulse went to 192 & there was a collapse. Great alarm. Subcutaneous injection of brandy saved her.

And to MacAlister toward the end of March:

We are having quite perfect weather now & are hoping that it will bring effects for Mrs. Clemens.

But a few days later he added that he was watching the driving rain through the windows, and that it was bad weather for the invalid. "But it will not last," he said.

The invalid improved then, and there was a concert in Florence at which Clara Clemens sang. Clemens in his note-book says:

April 8. Clara's concert was a triumph. Livy woke up & sent for her to tell her all about it, near midnight.

But a day or two later she was worse again—then better. The hearts in that household were as pendulums, swinging always between hope and despair.

One familiar with the Clemens history might well have been filled with forebodings. Already in January a member of the family, Mollie Clemens, Orion's wife, died, news which was kept from Mrs. Clemens, as was the death of Aldrich's son, and that of Sir Henry M. Stanley, both of which occurred that spring.

Indeed, death harvested freely that year among the Clemens friendships. Clemens wrote Twichell:

Yours has just this moment arrived—just as I was finishing a note to poor Lady Stanley. I believe the last country-house visit we paid in England was to Stanley's. Lord! how my friends & acquaintances fall about me now in my gray-headed days! Vereshchagin, Mommsen, Dvorák, Lenbach, & Jókai, all so recently, & now Stanley. I have known Stanley 37 years. Goodness, who is there I haven't known?

CCXXXI

THE CLOSE OF A BEAUTIFUL LIFE

IN one of his notes near the end of April Clemens writes that once more, as at Riverdale, he has been excluded from Mrs. Clemens's room except for the briefest moment at a time. But on May 12th, to R. W. Gilder, he reported:

For two days now we have not been anxious about Mrs. Clemens (*unberufen*). After 20 months of bedridden solitude & bodily misery she all of a sudden ceases to be a pallid, shrunken shadow, & looks bright & young & pretty. She remains what she always was, the most wonderful creature of fortitude, patience, endurance, and recuperative power that ever was. But ah, dear! it won't last; this fiendish malady will play new treacheries upon her, and I shall go back to my prayers again—unutterable from any pulpit!

May 13, A.M. I have just paid one of my pair of permitted 2-minute visits per day to the sick-room. And found what I have learned to expect—retrogression.

There was a day when she was brought out on the terrace in a wheel-chair to see the wonder of the early Italian summer. She had been a prisoner so long that she was almost overcome with the delight of it all—the more so, perhaps, in the feeling that she might so soon be leaving it.

It was on Sunday, the 5th of June, that the end came. Clemens and Jean had driven out to make some calls, and had stopped at a villa which promised to fulfil most of the requirements. They came home full of enthusiasm concerning it, and Clemens, in his mind, had decided on the purchase. In the corridor Clara said:

"She is better to-day than she has been for three months."

Then quickly, under her breath, "Unberufen," which the others, too, added hastily—superstitiously.

Mrs. Clemens was, in fact, bright and cheerful, and anxious to hear all about the new property which was to become their home. She urged him to sit by her during the dinner-hour and tell her the details; but once, when the sense of her frailties came upon her, she said they must not mind if she could not go very soon, but be content where they were. He remained from half past seven until eight—a forbidden privilege, but permitted because she was so animated, feeling so well. Their talk was as it had been in the old days, and once during it he reproached himself, as he had so often done, and asked forgiveness for the tears he had brought into her life. When he was summoned to go at last he chided himself for remaining so long; but she said there was no harm, and kissed him, saying: "You will come back," and he answered, "Yes, to say good night," meaning at half past nine, as was the permitted custom. He stood a moment at the door throwing kisses to her, and she returning them, her face bright with smiles.

He was so hopeful and happy that it amounted to exaltation. He went to his room at first, then he was moved to do a thing which he had seldom done since Susy died. He went to the piano up-stairs and sang the old jubilee songs that Susy had liked to hear him sing. Jean came in presently, listening. She had not done this before, that he could remember. He sang "Swing Low, Sweet Chariot," and "My Lord He Calls Me." He noticed Jean then and stopped, but she asked him to go on.

Mrs. Clemens, in her room, heard the distant music, and said to her attendant:

"He is singing a good-night carol to me."

The music ceased presently, and then a moment later she asked to be lifted up. Almost in that instant life slipped away without a sound.

Clemens, coming to say good night, saw a little group about her bed, Clara and Jean standing as if dazed. He went and bent over and looked into her face, surprised that she did not greet him. He did not suspect what had happened until he heard one of the daughters ask:

"Katie, is it true? Oh, Katie, *is* it true?"

He realized then that she was gone.

In his note-book that night he wrote:

At a quarter past 9 this evening she that was the life of my life passed to the relief & the peace of death after 22 months of unjust & unearned suffering. I first saw her near 37 years ago, & now I have looked upon her face for the last time. Oh, so unexpected! . . . I was full of remorse for things done & said in these 34 years of married life that hurt Livy's heart.

He envied her lying there, so free from it all, with the great peace upon her face. He wrote to Howells and to Twichell, and to Mrs. Crane, those nearest and dearest ones. To Twichell he said:

How sweet she was in death, how young, how beautiful, how like her dear girlish self of thirty years ago, not a gray hair showing! This rejuvenescence was noticeable within two hours after her death; & when I went down again (2.30) it was complete. In all that night & all that day she never noticed my caressing hand—it seemed strange.

To Howells he recalled the closing scene:

I bent over her & looked in her face & I think I spoke—I was surprised & troubled that she did not notice me. Then we understood & our hearts broke. How poor we are to-day!

THE CLOSE OF A BEAUTIFUL LIFE

But how thankful I am that her persecutions are ended! I would not call her back if I could.

To-day, treasured in her worn, old Testament, I found a dear & gentle letter from you dated Far Rockaway, September 13, 1896, about our poor Susy's death. I am tired & old; I wish I were with Livy.

And in a few days:

It would break Livy's heart to see Clara. We excuse ourself from all the friends that call—though, of course, only intimates come. Intimates—but they are not the old, old friends, the friends of the old, old times when we laughed. Shall we ever laugh again? If I could only see a dog that I knew in the old times & could put my arms around his neck and tell him all, everything, & ease my heart!

CCXXXII

THE SAD JOURNEY HOME

A TIDAL wave of sympathy poured in. Noble and commoner, friend and stranger—humanity of every station—sent their messages of condolence to the friend of mankind. The cablegrams came first—bundles of them from every corner of the world—then the letters, a steady inflow. Howells, Twichell, Aldrich—those oldest friends who had themselves learned the meaning of grief —spoke such few and futile words as the language can supply to allay a heart's mourning, each recalling the rarity and beauty of the life that had slipped away. Twichell and his wife wrote:

DEAR, DEAR MARK,—There is nothing we can say. What is there *to* say? But here we are—with you all every hour and every minute—filled with unutterable thoughts; unutterable affection for the dead and for the living.

HARMONY AND JOE.

Howells in his letter said:

She hallowed what she touched far beyond priests. . . . What are you going to do, you poor soul?

A hundred letters crowd in for expression here, but must be denied—not, however, the beam of hope out of Helen Keller's illumined night:

Do try to reach through grief and feel the pressure of her hand, as I reach through darkness and feel the smile on my friends' lips and the light in their eyes though mine are closed.

THE SAD JOURNEY HOME

They were adrift again without plans for the future. They would return to America to lay Mrs. Clemens to rest by Susy and little Langdon, but beyond that they could not see. Then they remembered a quiet spot in Massachusetts, Tyringham, near Lee, where the Gilders lived, and so, on June 7th, he wrote:

DEAR GILDER FAMILY,—I have been worrying and worrying to know what to do; at last I went to the girls with an idea— to ask the Gilders to get us shelter near their summer home. It was the first time they have not shaken their heads. So to-morrow I will cable to you and shall hope to be in time.

An hour ago the best heart that ever beat for me and mine was carried silent out of this house, and I am as one who wanders and has lost his way. She who is gone was our head, she was our hands. We are now trying to make plans—*we:* we who have never made a plan before, nor ever needed to. If she could speak to us she would make it all simple and easy with a word, & our perplexities would vanish away. If she had known she was near to death she would have told us where to go and what to do, but she was not suspecting, neither were we. She was all our riches and she is gone; she was our breath, she was our life, and now we are nothing.

We send you our love—and with it the love of you that was in her heart when she died.

S. L. CLEMENS.

They arranged to sail on the *Prince Oscar* on the 29th of June. There was an earlier steamer, but it was the *Princess Irene*, which had brought them, and they felt they would not make the return voyage on that vessel. During the period of waiting a curious thing happened. Clemens one day got up in a chair in his room on the second floor to pull down the high window-sash. It did not move easily and his hand slipped. It was only by the merest chance that he saved himself from falling to the ground far below. He mentions this in his note-book, and once, speaking of it to Frederick Duneka, he said:

MARK TWAIN

"Had I fallen it would probably have killed me, and in my bereaved circumstances the world would have been convinced that it was suicide. It was one of those curious coincidences which are always happening and being misunderstood."

The homeward voyage and its sorrowful conclusion are pathetically conveyed in his notes:

June 29, 1904. Sailed last night at 10. The bugle-call to breakfast. I recognized the notes and was distressed. When I heard them last Livy heard them with me; now they fall upon her ear unheeded.

In my life there have been 68 Junes—but how vague & colorless 67 of them are contrasted with the deep blackness of this one!

July 1, 1904. I cannot reproduce Livy's face in my mind's eye—I was never in my life able to reproduce a face. It is a curious infirmity—& now at last I realize it is a calamity.

July 2, 1904. In these 34 years we have made many voyages together, Livy dear—& now we are making our last; you down below & lonely; I above with the crowd & lonely.

July 3, 1904. Ship-time, 8 A.M. In 13 hours & a quarter it will be 4 weeks since Livy died.

Thirty-one years ago we made our first voyage together—& this is our last one in company. Susy was a year old then. She died at 24 & had been in her grave 8 years.

July 10, 1904. To-night it will be 5 weeks. But to me it remains yesterday—as it has from the first. But this funeral march—how sad & long it is!

Two days more will end the second stage of it.

July 14, 1904 (ELMIRA). Funeral private in the house of Livy's young maidenhood. Where she stood as a bride 34 years ago there her coffin rested; & over it the same voice that had made her a wife then committed her departed spirit to God now.

It was Joseph Twichell who rendered that last service. Mr. Beecher was long since dead. It was a simple, touching utterance, closing with this tender word of farewell:

THE SAD JOURNEY HOME

Robert Browning, when he was nearing the end of his earthly days, said that death was the thing that we did not believe in. Nor do we believe in it. We who journeyed through the bygone years in companionship with the bright spirit now withdrawn are growing old. The way behind is long; the way before is short. The end cannot be far off. But what of that? Can we not say, each one:

"So long that power hath blessed me, sure it still
    Will lead me on;
O'er moor and fen; o'er crag and torrent, till
    The night is gone;
And with the morn, their angel faces smile,
Which I have loved long since, and lost awhile!"

And so good-by. Good-by, dear heart! Strong, tender, and true. Good-by until for us the morning break and these shadows fly away.

Dr. Samuel E. Eastman, who had succeeded Mr. Beecher, closed the service with a prayer, and so the last office we can render in this life for those we love was finished.

Clemens ordered that a simple marker should be placed at the grave, bearing, besides the name, the record of birth and death, followed by the German line:

Gott sei dir gnädig, O meine Wonne!

CCXXXIII

BEGINNING ANOTHER HOME

THERE was an extra cottage on the Gilder place at Tyringham, and this they occupied for the rest of that sad summer. Clemens, in his note-book, has preserved some of its aspects and incidents.

July 24, 1904. Rain—rain—rain. Cold. We built a fire in my room. Then clawed the logs out & threw water, remembering there was a brood of swallows in the chimney. The tragedy was averted.

July 31. LEE, MASSACHUSETTS (BERKSHIRE HILLS). Last night the young people out on a moonlight ride. Trolley frightened Jean's horse—collision—horse killed. Rodman Gilder picked Jean up, unconscious; she was taken to the doctor, per the car. Face, nose, side, back contused; tendon of left ankle broken.

August 10. NEW YORK. Clara here sick—never well since June 5. Jean is at the summer home in the Berkshire Hills crippled.

The next entry records the third death in the Clemens family within a period of eight months—that of Mrs. Moffett, who had been Pamela Clemens. Clemens writes:

September 1. Died at Greenwich, Connecticut, my sister, Pamela Moffett, aged about 73.
Death dates this year January 14, June 5, September 1.

That fall they took a house in New York City, on the corner of Ninth Street and Fifth Avenue, No. 21, remaining for a time at the Grosvenor while the new home was being set in order. The home furniture was brought from Hartford, unwrapped, and established in the light of strange environment. Clemens wrote:

We have not seen it for thirteen years. Katie Leary, our old housekeeper, who has been in our service more than twenty-four years, cried when she told me about it to-day. She said, "I had forgotten it was so beautiful, and it brought Mrs. Clemens right back to me—in that old time when she was so young and lovely."

Clara Clemens had not recovered from the strain of her mother's long illness and the shock of her death, and she was ordered into retirement with the care of a trained nurse. The life at 21 Fifth Avenue, therefore, began with only two remaining members of the broken family—Clemens and Jean.

Clemens had undertaken to divert himself with work at Tyringham, though without much success. He was not well; he was restless and disturbed; his heart bleak with a great loneliness. He prepared an article on Copyright for the *North American Review*,[1] and he began, or at least contemplated, that beautiful fancy, *Eve's Diary*, which in the widest and most reverential sense, from the first word to the last, conveys his love, his worship, and his tenderness for the one he had laid away. Adam's single comment at the end, "Wheresoever she was, *there* was Eden," was his own comment, and is perhaps the most tenderly beautiful line he ever wrote. These two books, *Adam's Diary* and *Eve's*—amusing and sometimes absurd as they are, and so far removed from the literal—are as autobiographic as anything he has done, and one of

[1] Published Jan., 1905. A dialogue presentation of copyright conditions, addressed to Thorwald Stolberg, Register of Copyrights, Washington, D. C. One of the best of Mark Twain's papers on the subject.

them as lovely in its truth.   Like the first Maker of men, Mark Twain created Adam in his own image; and his rare Eve is no less the companion with whom, half a lifetime before, he had begun the marriage journey.   Only here the likeness ceases.   No Serpent ever entered their Eden. And they never left it; it traveled with them so long as they remained together.

In the Christmas *Harper* for 1904 was published "Saint Joan of Arc"—the same being the *Joan* introduction prepared in London five years before.   Joan's proposed beatification had stirred a new interest in the martyred girl, and this most beautiful article became a sort of key-note of the public heart.   Those who read it were likely to go back and read the *Recollections*, and a new appreciation grew for that masterpiece.   In his later and wider acceptance by his own land, and by the world at large, the book came to be regarded with a fresh understanding.   Letters came from scores of readers, as if it were a newly issued volume.   A distinguished educator wrote:

I would rather have written your history of Joan of Arc than any other piece of literature in any language.

And this sentiment grew.   The demand for the book increased, and has continued to increase, steadily and rapidly.[1]   In the long and last analysis the good must prevail.   A day will come when there will be as many readers of *Joan* as of any other of Mark Twain's works.

[1] The growing appreciation of *Joan* is shown by the report of sales for the three years following 1904.   The sales for that year in America were 1,726; for 1905, 2,445; for 1906, 5,381; for 1907, 6,574.   At this point it passed *Pudd'nhead Wilson*, the *Yankee*, *The Gilded Age*, *Life on the Mississippi*, overtook the *Tramp Abroad*, and more than doubled *The American Claimant*.   Only *The Innocents Abroad*, *Huckleberry Finn*, *Tom Sawyer*, and *Roughing It* still ranged ahead of it, in the order named.

CCXXXIV

LIFE AT 21 FIFTH AVENUE

THE house at 21 Fifth Avenue, built by the architect who had designed Grace Church, had a distinctly ecclesiastical suggestion about its windows, and was of fine and stately proportions within. It was a proper residence for a venerable author and a sage, and with the handsome Hartford furnishings distributed through it, made a distinctly suitable setting for Mark Twain. But it was lonely for him. It lacked soul. He added, presently, a great Æolian Orchestrelle, with a variety of music for his different moods. He believed that he would play it himself when he needed the comfort of harmony, and that Jean, who had not received musical training, or his secretary could also play to him. He had a passion for music, or at least for melody and stately rhythmic measures, though his ear was not attuned to what are termed the more classical compositions. For Wagner, for instance, he cared little, though in a letter to Mrs. Crane he said:

Certainly nothing in the world is so solemn and impressive and so divinely beautiful as "Tannhäuser." It ought to be used as a religous service.

Beethoven's sonatas and symphonies also moved him deeply. Once, writing to Jean, he asked:

What is your favorite piece of music, dear? Mine is Beethoven's Fifth Symphony. I have found that out within a day or two.

It was the majestic movement and melodies of the second part that he found most satisfying; but he oftener inclined to the still tenderer themes of Chopin's nocturnes and one of Schubert's impromptus, while the "Lorelei" and the "Erlking" and the Scottish airs never wearied him. Music thus became a chief consolation during these lonely days—rich organ harmonies that filled the emptiness of his heart and beguiled from dull, material surroundings back into worlds and dreams that he had known and laid away.

He went out very little that winter—usually to the homes of old and intimate friends. Once he attended a small dinner given him by George Smalley at the Metropolitan Club; but it was a private affair, with only good friends present. Still, it formed the beginning of his return to social life, and it was not in his nature to retire from the brightness of human society, or to submerge himself in mourning. As the months wore on he appeared here and there, and took on something of his oldtime habit. Then his annual bronchitis appeared, and he was confined a good deal to his home, where he wrote or planned new reforms and enterprises.

The improvement of railway service, through which fewer persons should be maimed and destroyed each year, interested him. He estimated that the railroads and electric lines killed and wounded more than all of the wars combined, and he accumulated statistics and prepared articles on the subject, though he appears to have offered little of such matter for publication. Once, however, when his sympathy was awakened by the victim of a frightful trolley and train collision in Newark, New Jersey, he wrote a letter which promptly found its way into print.

DEAR MISS MADELINE,—Your good & admiring & affectionate brother has told me of your sorrowful share in the trolley disaster which brought unaccustomed tears to millions of eyes & fierce resentment against those whose criminal indifference to their responsibilities caused it, & the reminder has brought back to me a pang out of that bygone time. I wish I could take you sound & whole out of your bed & break the legs of those officials & put them in it—to stay there. For in my spirit I am merciful, and would not break their necks & backs also, as some would who have no feeling.

It is your brother who permits me to write this line—& so it is not an intrusion, you see.

May you get well—& soon! Sincerely yours,

S. L. CLEMENS.

A very little later he was writing another letter on a similar subject to St. Clair McKelway, who had narrowly escaped injury in a railway accident.

DEAR MCKELWAY,—Your innumerable friends are grateful, most grateful.

As I understand the telegrams, the engineers of your train had never seen a locomotive before. . . . The government's official report, showing that our railways killed twelve hundred persons last year & injured sixty thousand, convinces me that under present conditions one Providence is not enough properly & efficiently to take care of our railroad business. But it is characteristically American—always trying to get along short-handed & save wages.

A massacre of Jews in Moscow renewed his animosity for semi-barbaric Russia. Asked for a Christmas sentiment, he wrote:

It is my warm & world-embracing Christmas hope that all of us that deserve it may finally be gathered together in a heaven of rest & peace, & the others permitted to retire into the clutches of Satan, or the Emperor of Russia, according to preference—if they have a preference.

An article, "The Tsar's Soliloquy," written at this time, was published in the *North American Review* for March (1905). He wrote much more, but most of the other matter he put aside. On a subject like that he always discarded three times as much as he published, and it was usually about three times as terrific as that which found its way into type. "The Soliloquy," however, is severe enough. It represents the Tsar as contemplating himself without his clothes, and reflecting on what a poor human specimen he presents:

Is it this that 140,000,000 Russians kiss the dust before and worship?—manifestly not! No one could worship this spectacle which is Me. Then who is it, what is it, that they worship? Privately, none knows better than I: it is my clothes! Without my clothes I should be as destitute of authority as any other naked person. No one could tell me from a parson, a barber, a dude. Then who is the real Emperor of Russia! My clothes! There is no other.

The emperor continues this fancy, and reflects on the fierce cruelties that are done in his name. It was a withering satire on Russian imperialism, and it stirred a wide response. This encouraged Clemens to something even more pretentious and effective in the same line. He wrote "King Leopold's Soliloquy," the reflections of the fiendish sovereign who had maimed and slaughtered fifteen millions of African subjects in his greed—gentle, harmless blacks—men, women, and little children whom he had butchered and mutilated in his Congo rubber-fields. Seldom in the history of the world have there been such atrocious practices as those of King Leopold in the Congo, and Clemens spared nothing in his picture of them. The article was regarded as not quite suitable for magazine publication, and it was given to the Congo Reform Association and issued as a booklet for distribution, with no return to the author, who would gladly have written a hundred times as much if he could have saved that unhappy race and have sent Leopold to the electric chair.[1]

[1] The book was price-marked twenty-five cents, but the returns from such as were sold went to the cause. Thousands of them were

Various plans and movements were undertaken for Congo reform, and Clemens worked and wrote letters and gave his voice and his influence and exhausted his rage, at last, as one after another of the half-organized and altogether futile undertakings showed no results. His interest did not die, but it became inactive. Eventually he declared: "I have said all I can say on that terrible subject. I am heart and soul in any movement that will rescue the Congo and hang Leopold, but I cannot write any more."

His fires were likely to burn themselves out, they raged so fiercely. His final paragraph on the subject was a proposed epitaph for Leopold when time should have claimed him. It ran:

Here under this gilded tomb lies rotting the body of one the smell of whose name will still offend the nostrils of men ages upon ages after all the Cæsars and Washingtons & Napoleons shall have ceased to be praised or blamed & been forgotten— Leopold of Belgium.

Clemens had not yet lost interest in the American policy in the Philippines, and in his letters to Twichell he did not hesitate to criticize the President's attitude in this and related matters. Once, in a moment of irritation, he wrote:

DEAR JOE,—I knew I had in me somewhere a definite feeling about the President. If I could only find the words to define it with! Here they are, to a hair—from Leonard Jerome:

"For twenty years I have loved Roosevelt the man, and hated Roosevelt the statesman and politician."

It's mighty good. Every time in twenty-five years that I

distributed free. The Congo, a domain four times as large as the German empire, had been made the ward of Belgium at a convention in Berlin by the agreement of fourteen nations, America and thirteen European states. Leopold promptly seized the country for his personal advantage and the nations apparently found themselves powerless to depose him. No more terrible blunder was ever committed by an assemblage of civilized people.

have met Roosevelt the man a wave of welcome has streaked through me with the hand-grip; but whenever (as a rule) I meet Roosevelt the statesman & politician I find him destitute of morals & not respect-worthy. It is plain that where his political self & party self are concerned he has nothing resembling a conscience; that under those inspirations he is naïvely indifferent to the restraints of duty & even unaware of them; ready to kick the Constitution into the back yard whenever it gets in his way. . . .

But Roosevelt is excusable—I recognize it & (ought to) concede it. We are all insane, each in his own way, & with insanity goes irresponsibility. Theodore the man is sane; in fairness we ought to keep in mind that Theodore, as statesman & politician, is insane & irresponsible.

He wrote a great deal more from time to time on this subject; but that is the gist of his conclusions, and whether justified by time, or otherwise, it expresses today the deduction of a very large number of people. It is set down here, because it is a part of Mark Twain's history, and also because a little while after his death there happened to creep into print an incomplete and misleading note (since often reprinted), which he once made in a moment of anger, when he was in a less judicial frame of mind. It seems proper that a man's honest sentiments should be recorded concerning the nation's servants.

Clemens wrote an article at this period which he called the "War Prayer." It pictured the young recruits about to march away for war—the excitement and the celebration—the drum-beat and the heart-beat of patriotism—the final assembly in the church where the minister utters that tremendous invocation:

God the all-terrible! Thou who ordainest,
Thunder, Thy clarion, and lightning, Thy sword!

and the "long prayer" for victory to the nation's armies. As the prayer closes a white-robed stranger enters, moves up the aisle, and takes the preacher's place; then, after some moments of impressive silence, he begins:

"I come from the Throne—bearing a message from Almighty God! . . . He has heard the prayer of His servant, your shepherd, & will grant it if such shall be your desire after I His messenger shall have explained to you its import—that is to say its full import. For it is like unto many of the prayers of men in that it asks for more than he who utters it is aware of—except he pause & think.

"God's servant & yours has prayed his prayer. Has he paused & taken thought? Is it one prayer? No, it is two—one uttered, the other not. Both have reached the ear of Him who heareth all supplications, the spoken & the unspoken. . . .

"You have heard your servant's prayer—the uttered part of it. I am commissioned of God to put into words the other part of it—that part which the pastor—and also you in your hearts —fervently prayed, silently. And ignorantly & unthinkingly? God grant that it was so! You heard these words: 'Grant us the victory, O Lord our God!' That is sufficient. The *whole* of the uttered prayer is completed into those pregnant words.

"Upon the listening spirit of God the Father fell also the unspoken part of the prayer. He commandeth me to put it into words. Listen!

"O Lord our Father, our young patriots, idols of our hearts, go forth to battle—be Thou near them! With them—in spirit— we also go forth from the sweet peace of our beloved firesides to smite the foe.

"O Lord our God, help us to tear their soldiers to bloody shreds with our shells; help us to cover their smiling fields with the pale forms of their patriot dead; help us to drown the thunder of the guns with the wounded, writhing in pain; help us to lay waste their humble homes with a hurricane of fire; help us to wring the hearts of their unoffending widows with unavailing grief; help us to turn them out roofless with their little children to wander unfriended through wastes of their desolated land in rags & hunger & thirst, sport of the sun-flames of summer & the icy winds of winter, broken in spirit, worn with travail, imploring Thee for the refuge of the grave & denied it—for our sakes, who adore Thee, Lord, blast their hopes, blight their lives, protract their bitter pilgrimage, make heavy their steps, water their way with their tears, stain the white snow with the blood of their wounded feet! We ask of one who is the Spirit of love & who is the ever-faithful refuge & friend of all that are sore beset, & seek His aid with humble & contrite hearts. Grant our prayer, O Lord, & Thine shall be the praise & honor & glory now & ever, Amen."

(After a pause.) "Ye have prayed it; if ye still desire it, speak!—the messenger of the Most High waits."

.   .   .   .

It was believed, afterward, that the man was a lunatic, because there was no sense in what he said.

To Dan Beard, who dropped in to see him, Clemens read the "War Prayer," stating that he had read it to his daughter Jean, and others, who had told him he must not print it, for it would be regarded as sacrilege.

"Still you are going to publish it, are you not?"

Clemens, pacing up and down the room in his dressing-gown and slippers, shook his head.

"No," he said, "I have told the whole truth in that, and only dead men can tell the truth in this world. It can be published after I am dead."

He did not care to invite the public verdict that he was a lunatic, or even a fanatic with a mission to destroy the illusions and traditions and conclusions of mankind. To Twichell he wrote, playfully but sincerely:

Am I honest? I give you my word of honor (privately) I am not. For seven years I have suppressed a book which my conscience tells me I ought to publish. I hold it a duty to publish it. There are other difficult duties which I am equal to, but I am not equal to that one. Yes, even *I* am dishonest. Not in many ways, but in some. Forty-one, I think it is. We are certainly *all* honest in one or several ways—every man in the world—though I have a reason to think I am the only one whose black-list runs so light. Sometimes I feel lonely enough in this lofty solitude.

LIFE AT 21 FIFTH AVENUE

It was his *Gospel* he referred to as his unpublished book, his doctrine of Selfishness, and of Man the irresponsible Machine. To Twichell he pretended to favor war, which he declared, to his mind, was one of the very best methods known of diminishing the human race.

What a life it is!—this one! Everything we try to do, somebody intrudes & obstructs it. After years of thought & labor I have arrived within one little bit of a step of perfecting my invention for exhausting the oxygen in the globe's air during a stretch of two minutes, & of *course* along comes an obstructor who is inventing something to *protect* human life. Damn such a world anyway.

He generally wrote Twichell when he had things to say that were outside of the pale of print. He was sure of an attentive audience of one, and the audience, whether it agreed with him or not, would at least understand him and be honored by his confidence. In one letter of that year he said:

I have written you to-day, not to do you a service, but to do myself one. There was bile in me. I had to empty it or lose my day to-morrow. If I tried to empty it into the *North American Review*—oh, well, I couldn't afford the risk. No, the certainty! The certainty that I wouldn't be satisfied with the result; so I would burn it, & try again to-morrow; burn that and try again the next day. It happens so nearly every time. I have a family to support, & I can't afford this kind of dissipation. Last winter when I was sick I wrote a magazine article three times before I got it to suit me. I put $500 worth of work on it every day for ten days, & at last when I got it to suit me it contained but 3,000 words—$900. I burned it & said I would reform.

And I *have* reformed. I *have* to work my bile off whenever it gets to where I can't stand it, but I can work it off on you economically, because I don't have to make it suit me. It may not suit you, but that isn't any matter; I'm not writing it for that. I have used you as an equilibrium-restorer more than once in my time, & shall continue, I guess. I would like to use Mr. Rogers, & he is plenty good-natured enough, but it wouldn't be fair to keep him rescuing me from my leather-headed business snarls & make him read interminable bile-irruptions besides; I can't use Howells, he is busy & old & lazy, & won't stand it; I dasn't use Clara, there's things I have to say which she wouldn't put up with—a very dear little ashcat, but has claws.

And so—you're It.

I am writing from the grave. On these terms only can a man be approximately frank. He cannot be straitly & unqualifiedly frank either in the grave or out of it.

A MARK TWAIN NOTE CONCERNING CERTAIN WRITINGS INTENDED FOR PUBLICATION ONLY AFTER HIS LIFETIME

CCXXXV

A SUMMER IN NEW HAMPSHIRE

HE took for the summer a house at Dublin, New Hampshire, the home of Henry Copley Greene, Lone Tree Hill, on the Monadnock slope. It was in a lovely locality, and for neighbors there were artists, literary people, and those of kindred pursuits, among them a number of old friends. Colonel Higginson had a place near by, and Abbott H. Thayer, the painter, and George de Forest Brush, and the Raphael Pumpelly family, and many more.

Colonel Higginson wrote Clemens a letter of welcome as soon as the news got out that he was going to Dublin; and Clemens, answering, said:

I early learned that you would be my neighbor in the summer & I rejoiced, recognizing in you & your family a large asset. I hope for frequent intercourse between the two households. I shall have my youngest daughter with me. The other one will go from the rest-cure in this city to the rest-cure in Norfolk, Connecticut, & we shall not see her before autumn. We have not seen her since the middle of October.

Jean, the younger daughter, went to Dublin & saw the house & came back charmed with it. I know the Thayers of old— manifestly there is no lack of attractions up there. Mrs. Thayer and I were shipmates in a wild excursion perilously near 40 years ago.

Aldrich was here half an hour ago, like a breeze from over the fields, with the fragrance still upon his spirit. I am tired waiting for that man to get old.

They went to Dublin in May, and became at once a part of the summer colony which congregated there. There was much going to and fro among the different houses, pleasant afternoons in the woods, mountain-climbing for Jean, and everywhere a spirit of fine, unpretentious comradeship.

The Copley Greene house was romantically situated, with a charming outlook. Clemens wrote to Twichell:

We like it here in the mountains, in the shadows of Monadnock. It is a woody solitude. We have no near neighbors. We *have* neighbors and I can see their houses scattered in the forest distances, for we live on a hill. I am astonished to find that I have known 8 of these 14 neighbors a long time; 10 years is the shortest; then seven beginning with 25 years & running up to 37 years' friendship. It is the most remarkable thing I ever heard of.

This letter was written in July, and he states in it that he has turned out one hundred thousand words of a large manuscript. It was a fantastic tale entitled "3,000 Years among the Microbes," a sort of scientific revel—or revelry—the autobiography of a microbe that had been once a man, and through a failure in a biological experiment transformed into a cholera germ when the experimenter was trying to turn him into a bird. His habitat was the person of a disreputable tramp named Blitzowski, a human continent of vast areas, with seething microbic nations and fantastic life problems. It was a satire, of course—Gulliver's Lilliput outdone—a sort of scientific, socialistic, mathematical jamboree.

He tired of it before it reached completion, though not before it had attained the proportions of a book of size. As a whole it would hardly have added to his reputation, though it is not without fine and humorous passages, and certainly not without interest. Its chief mission was to divert him mentally that summer during those

A SUMMER IN NEW HAMPSHIRE

3,000 YEARS
AMONG ᵗʰᵉ MICROBES

By a microbe
=

WITH NOTES
added by the Same Hand

7,000 Years Later.

Translated from the Original
Microbic
by

Mark Twain

MARK TWAIN'S SUGGESTED TITLE-PAGE FOR HIS MICROBE BOOK

days and nights when he would otherwise have been alone and brooding upon his loneliness.[1]

His inability to reproduce faces in his mind's eye he mourned as an increasing calamity. Photographs were lifeless things, and when he tried to conjure up the faces of his dead they seemed to drift farther out of reach;

[1] For extracts from "3,000 Years among the Microbes" see Appendix V, at the end of this work.

but now and then kindly sleep brought to him something out of that treasure-house where all our realities are kept for us fresh and fair, perhaps for a day when we may claim them again. Once he wrote to Mrs. Crane:

SUSY DEAR,—I have had a lovely dream. Livy, dressed in black, was sitting up in my bed (here) at my right & looking as young & sweet as she used to when she was in health. She said, "What is the name of your sweet sister?" I said, "Pamela." "Oh yes, that is it, I thought it was—(naming a name which has escaped me) won't you write it down for me?" I reached eagerly for a pen & pad, laid my hands upon both, then said to myself, "It is only a dream," and turned back sorrowfully & there she was still. The conviction flamed through me that our lamented disaster was a dream, & this a reality. I said, "How blessed it is, how blessed it is, it was all a dream, only a dream!" She only smiled and did not ask what dream I meant, which surprised me. She leaned her head against mine & kept saying, "I was perfectly sure it was a dream; I never would have believed it wasn't." I think she said several things, but if so they are gone from my memory. I woke & did not know I had been dreaming. She was gone. I wondered how she could go without my knowing it, but I did not spend any thought upon that. I was too busy thinking of how vivid & real was the dream that we had lost her, & how unspeakably blessed it was to find that it was not true & that she was still ours & with us.

He had the orchestrelle moved to Dublin, although it was no small undertaking, for he needed the solace of its harmonies; and so the days passed along, and he grew stronger in body and courage as his grief drifted farther behind him. Sometimes, in the afternoon or in the evening, when the neighbors had come in for a little while, he would walk up and down and talk in his old, marvelous way of all the things on land and sea, of the past and of the future, "Of Providence, foreknowledge, will, and fate," of the friends he had known and of the things he had done, of the sorrow and absurdities of the world

It was the same old scintillating, incomparable talk of which Howells once said:

"We shall never know its like again. When he dies it will die with him."

It was during the summer at Dublin that Clemens and Rogers together made up a philanthropic ruse on Twichell. Twichell, through his own prodigal charities, had fallen into debt, a fact which Rogers knew. Rogers was a man who concealed his philanthropies when he could, and he performed many of them of which the world will never know. In this case he said:

"Clemens, I want to help Twichell out of his financial difficulty. I will supply the money and you will do the giving. Twichell must think it comes from you."

Clemens agreed to this on the condition that he be permitted to leave a record of the matter for his children, so that he would not appear in a false light to them, and that Twichell should learn the truth of the gift, sooner or later. So the deed was done, and Twichell and his wife lavished their thanks upon Clemens, who, with his wife, had more than once been their benefactors, making the deception easy enough now. Clemens writhed under these letters of gratitude, and forwarded them to Clara in Norfolk, and later to Rogers himself. He pretended to take great pleasure in this part of the conspiracy, but it was not an unmixed delight. To Rogers he wrote:

I wanted her [Clara] to see what a generous father she's got. I didn't tell her it was you, but by and by I want to tell her, when I have your consent; then I shall want her to remember the letters. I want a record there, for my Life when I am dead, & must be able to furnish the facts about the Relief-of-Lucknow-Twichell in case I fall suddenly, before I get those facts with your consent, before the Twichells themselves.

I read those letters with immense pride! I recognized that I had scored *one* good deed for sure on my halo account. I haven't had anything that tasted so good since the stolen watermelon.

P. S.—I am hurrying them off to you because I dasn't read them again! I should blush to my heels to fill up with this unearned gratitude again, pouring out of the thankful hearts of those poor swindled people who do not suspect you, but honestly believe I gave that money.

Mr. Rogers hastily replied:

MY DEAR CLEMENS,—The letters are lovely. Don't breathe. They are so happy! It would be a crime to let them think that you have in any way deceived them. I can keep still. You must. I am sending you all traces of the crime, so that you may look innocent and tell the truth, *as you usually do* when you think you can escape detection. Don't get rattled.

Seriously. You have done a kindness. You are proud of it, I know. You have made your friends happy, and you ought to be so glad as to cheerfully accept reproof from your conscience. Joe Wadsworth and I once stole a goose and gave it to a poor widow as a Christmas present. No crime in that. I always put my counterfeit money on the plate. "The passer of the sasser" always smiles at me and I get credit for doing generous things. But seriously again, if you do feel a little uncomfortable wait until I see you before you tell anybody. Avoid cultivating misery. I am trying to loaf ten solid days. We do hope to see you soon.

The secret was kept, and the matter presently (and characteristically) passed out of Clemens's mind altogether. He never remembered to tell Twichell, and it is revealed here, according to his wish.

The Russian-Japanese war was in progress that summer, and its settlement occurred in August. The terms of it did not please Mark Twain. When a newspaper correspondent asked him for an expression of opinion on the subject he wrote:

Russia was on the highroad to emancipation from an insane and intolerable slavery. I was hoping there would be no peace until Russian liberty was safe. I think that this was a holy war, in the best and noblest sense of that abused term, and that no war was ever charged with a higher mission.

I think there can be no doubt that that mission is now defeated and Russia's chain riveted; this time to stay. I think the Tsar will now withdraw the small humanities that have been forced from him, and resume his medieval barbarisms with a relieved spirit and an immeasurable joy. I think Russian liberty has had its last chance and has lost it.

I think nothing has been gained by the peace that is remotely comparable to what has been sacrificed by it. One more battle would have abolished the waiting chains of billions upon billions of unborn Russians, and I wish it could have been fought. I hope I am mistaken, yet in all sincerity I believe that this peace is entitled to rank as the most conspicuous disaster in political history.

It was the wisest public utterance on the subject—the deep, resonant note of truth sounding amid a clamor of foolish joy-bells. It was the message of a seer—the prophecy of a sage who sees with the clairvoyance of knowledge and human understanding. Clemens, a few days later, was invited by Colonel Harvey to dine with Baron Rosen and M. Sergius Witte; but an attack of his old malady—rheumatism—prevented his acceptance. His telegram of declination apparently pleased the Russian officials, for Witte asked permission to publish it, and declared that he was going to take it home to show to the Tsar. It was as follows:

To COLONEL HARVEY,—I am still a cripple, otherwise I should be more than glad of this opportunity to meet the illustrious magicians who came here equipped with nothing but a pen, & with it have divided the honors of the war with the sword. It is fair to presume that in thirty centuries history will not get done in admiring these men who attempted what the world regarded as the impossible & achieved it.   MARK TWAIN.

But this was a modified form. His original draft would perhaps have been less gratifying to that Russian embassy. It read:

To Colonel Harvey,—I am still a cripple, otherwise I should be more than glad of this opportunity to meet those illustrious magicians who with the pen have annulled, obliterated, & abolished every high achievement of the Japanese sword and turned the tragedy of a tremendous war into a gay & blithesome comedy. If I may, let me in all respect and honor salute them as my fellow-humorists, I taking third place, as becomes one who was not born to modesty, but by diligence & hard work is acquiring it. MARK.

There was still another form, brief and expressive:

DEAR COLONEL,—No, this is a love-feast; when you call a lodge of sorrow send for me. MARK.

Clemens's war sentiment was given the widest newspaper circulation, and brought him many letters, most of them applauding his words. Charles Francis Adams wrote him:

It attracted my attention because it so exactly expresses the views I have myself all along entertained.

And this was the gist of most of the expressed sentiments which came to him.

Clemens wrote a number of things that summer, among them a little essay entitled, "The Privilege of the Grave" —that is to say, free speech. He was looking forward, he said, to the time when he should inherit that privilege, when some of the things he had said, written and laid away, could be published without damage to his friends or family. An article entitled, "Interpreting the Deity," he counted as among the things to be uttered when he had entered into that last great privilege. It is an article on the reading of signs and auguries in all ages to discover the intentions of the Almighty, with historical examples of God's judgments and vindications. Here is a fair specimen. It refers to the chronicle of Henry Huntington:

A SUMMER IN NEW HAMPSHIRE

All through this book Henry exhibits his familiarity with the intentions of God and with the reasons for the intentions. Sometimes—very often, in fact—the act follows the intention after such a wide interval of time that one wonders how Henry could fit one act out of a hundred to one intention, and get the thing right every time, when there was such abundant choice among acts and intentions. Sometimes a man offends the Deity with a crime, and is punished for it thirty years later; meantime he has committed a million other crimes: no matter, Henry can pick out the one that brought the worms. Worms were generally used in those days for the slaying of particularly wicked people. This has gone out now, but in the old times it was a favorite. It always indicated a case of "wrath." For instance:

"The just God avenging Robert Fitzhildebrand's perfidity, a worm grew in his vitals which, gradually gnawing its way through his intestines, fattened on the abandoned man till, tortured with excruciating sufferings and venting himself in bitter moans, he was by a fitting punishment brought to his end" (p. 400).

It was probably an alligator, but we cannot tell; we only know it was a particular breed, and only used to convey wrath. Some authorities think it was an ichthyosaurus, but there is much doubt.

The entire article is in this amusing, satirical strain, and might well enough be printed to-day. It is not altogether clear why it was withheld, even then.

He finished his *Eve's Diary* that summer, and wrote a story which was originally planned to oblige Mrs. Minnie Maddern Fiske, to aid her in a crusade against bull-fighting in Spain. Mrs. Fiske wrote him that she had read his dog story, written against the cruelties of vivisection, and urged him to do something to save the horses that, after faithful service, were sacrificed in the bull-ring. Her letter closed:

I have lain awake nights very often wondering if I dare ask you to write a story of an old horse that is finally given over to the bull-ring. The story you would write would do more good than all the laws we are trying to have made and enforced for the prevention of cruelty to animals in Spain. We would translate and circulate the story in that country. I have wondered if you would ever write it.

With most devoted homage,   Sincerely yours,
          MINNIE MADDERN FISKE.

Clemens promptly replied:

DEAR MRS. FISKE,—I shall certainly write the story. But I may not get it to suit me, in which case it will go in the fire. Later I will try it again—& yet again—& again. I am used to this. It has taken me twelve years to write a short story—the shortest one I ever wrote, I think.[1] So do not be discouraged; I will stick to this one in the same way.

      Sincerely yours,
          S. L. CLEMENS.

It was an inspiring subject, and he began work on it immediately. Within a month from the time he received Mrs. Fiske's letter he had written that pathetic, heartbreaking little story, "A Horse's Tale," and sent it to *Harper's Magazine* for illustration. In a letter written to Mr. Duneka at the time, he tells of his interest in the narrative, and adds:

This strong interest is natural, for the heroine is my small daughter Susy, whom we lost. It was not intentional—it was a good while before I found it out, so I am sending you her picture to use—& to reproduce with photographic exactness the unsurpassable *expression* & all. May you find an artist who has lost an idol.

He explains how he had put in a good deal of work, with his secretary, on the orchestrelle to get the bugle-calls.

We are to do these theatricals this evening with a couple of neighbors for audience, and then pass the hat.

It is not one of Mark Twain's greatest stories, but its pathos brings the tears, and no one can read it without

[1] Probably "The Death Disk."

indignation toward the custom which it was intended to oppose. When it was published, a year later, Mrs. Fiske sent him her grateful acknowledgments, and asked permission to have it printed for pamphlet circulation in Spain.

A number of more or less notable things happened in this, Mark Twain's seventieth year. There was some kind of a reunion going on in California, and he was variously invited to attend. Robert Fulton, of Nevada, was appointed a committee of one to invite him to Reno for a great celebration which was to be held there. Clemens replied that he remembered, as if it were but yesterday, when he had disembarked from the Overland stage in front of the Ormsby Hotel, in Carson City, and told how he would like to accept the invitation.

If I were a few years younger I would accept it, and promptly, and I would go. I would let somebody else do the oration, but as for me I would talk—just talk. I would renew my youth; and talk—and talk—and talk—and have the time of my life! I would march the unforgotten and unforgetable antiques by, and name their names, and give them reverent hail and farewell as they passed—Goodman, McCarthy, Gillis, Curry, Baldwin, Winters, Howard, Nye, Stewart, Neely Johnson, Hal Clayton, North, Root—and my brother, upon whom be peace!—and then the desperadoes, who made life a joy, and the "slaughter-house," a precious possession: Sam Brown, Farmer Pete, Bill Mayfield, Six-fingered Jake, Jack Williams, and the rest of the crimson discipleship, and so on, and so on. Believe me, I would start a resurrection it would do you more good to look at than the next one will, if you go on the way you are going now.

Those were the days!—those old ones. They will come no more; youth will come no more. They were so full to the brim with the wine of life; there have been no others like them. It chokes me up to think of them. Would you like me to come out there and cry? It would not beseem my white head.

Good-by. I drink to you all. Have a good time—and take an old man's blessing.

MARK TWAIN

In reply to another invitation from H. H. Bancroft, of San Francisco, he wrote that his wandering days were over, and that it was his purpose to sit by the fire for the rest of his "remnant of life."

A man who, like me, is going to strike 70 on the 30th of next November has no business to be flitting around the way Howells does—that shameless old fictitious butterfly. (But if he comes don't tell him I said it, for it would hurt him & I wouldn't brush a flake of powder from his wing for anything. I only say it in envy of his indestructible youth anyway. Howells will be 88 in October.)

And it was either then or on a similar occasion that he replied after this fashion:

I have done more for San Francisco than any other of its old residents. Since I left there it has increased in population fully 300,000. I could have done more—I could have gone earlier—— it was suggested.

Which, by the way, is a perfect example of Mark Twain's humorous manner, the delicately timed pause, and the afterthought. Most humorists would have been contented to end with the statement, "I could have gone earlier." Only Mark Twain could have added that final exquisite touch—"it was suggested."

CCXXXVI

AT PIER 70

MARK TWAIN was nearing seventy, the scriptural limitation of life, and the returns were coming in. Some one of the old group was dying all the time. The roll-call returned only a scattering answer. Of his oldest friends, Charles Henry Webb, John Hay, and Sir Henry Irving, all died that year. When Hay died Clemens gave this message to the press:

I am deeply grieved, & I mourn with the nation this loss which is irreparable. My friendship with Mr. Hay & my admiration of him endured 38 years without impairment.

It was only a little earlier that he had written Hay an anonymous letter, a copy of which he preserved. It here follows:

DEAR & HONORED SIR,—I never hear any one speak of you & of your long roll of illustrious services in other than terms of pride & praise—& out of the heart. I think I am right in believing you to be the only man in the civil service of the country the cleanness of whose motives is never questioned by any citizen, & whose acts proceed always upon a broad & high plane, never by accident or pressure of circumstance upon a narrow or low one. There are majorities that are proud of more than one of the nation's great servants, but I believe, & I think I know, that you are the only one of whom the entire nation is proud. Proud & thankful.

Name & address are lacking here, & for a purpose: to leave you no chance to make my words a burden to you and a reproach to me, who would lighten your burdens if I could, not add to them.

Irving died in October, and Clemens ordered a wreath for his funeral. To MacAlister he wrote:

I profoundly grieve over Irving's death. It is another reminder. My section of the procession has but a little way to go. I could not be very sorry if I tried.

Mark Twain, nearing seventy, felt that there was not much left for him to celebrate; and when Colonel Harvey proposed a birthday gathering in his honor, Clemens suggested a bohemian assembly over beer and sandwiches in some snug place, with Howells, Henry Rogers, Twichell, Dr. Rice, Dr. Edward Quintard, Augustus Thomas, and such other kindred souls as were still left to answer the call. But Harvey had something different in view: something more splendid even than the sixty-seventh birthday feast, more pretentious, indeed, than any former literary gathering. He felt that the attainment of seventy years by America's most distinguished man of letters and private citizen was a circumstance which could not be moderately or even modestly observed. The date was set five days later than the actual birthday—that is to say, on December 5th, in order that it might not conflict with the various Thanksgiving holidays and occasions. Delmonico's great room was chosen for the celebration of it, and invitations were sent out to practically every writer of any distinction in America, and to many abroad. Of these nearly two hundred accepted, while such as could not come sent pathetic regrets.

What an occasion it was! The flower of American literature gathered to do honor to its chief. The whole atmosphere of the place seemed permeated with his presence, and when Colonel Harvey presented William Dean Howells, and when Howells had read another double-

barreled sonnet, and introduced the guest of the evening
with the words, "I will not say, 'O King, live forever,'
but, 'O King, live as long as you like!'" and Mark Twain
rose, his snow-white hair gleaming above that brilliant
assembly, it seemed that a world was speaking out in a
voice of applause and welcome. With a great tumult
the throng rose, a billow of life, the white handkerchiefs
flying foam-like on its crest. Those who had gathered
there realized that it was a mighty moment, not only in
his life but in theirs. They were there to see this supreme
embodiment of the American spirit as he scaled the
mountain-top. He, too, realized the drama of that moment—the marvel of it—and he must have flashed a swift
panoramic view backward over the long way he had come,
to stand, as he had himself once expressed it, "for a single,
splendid moment on the Alps of fame outlined against
the sun." He must have remembered; for when he came
to speak he went back to the very beginning, to his very
first banquet, as he called it, when, as he said, "I hadn't
any hair; I hadn't any teeth; I hadn't any clothes."
He sketched the meagerness of that little hamlet which
had seen his birth, sketched it playfully, delightfully, so
that his hearers laughed and shouted; but there was always a tenderness under it all, and often the tears were
not far beneath the surface. He told of his habits of life,
how he had attained seventy years by simply sticking
to a scheme of living which would kill anybody else;
how he smoked constantly, loathed exercise, and had no
other regularity of habits. Then, at last, he reached that
wonderful, unforgetable close:

Threescore years and ten!
It is the scriptural statute of limitations. After that you owe
no active duties; for you the strenuous life is over. You are a
time-expired man, to use Kipling's military phrase: You have
served your term, well or less well, and you are mustered out.
You are become an honorary member of the republic, you are

emancipated, compulsions are not for you, nor any bugle-call but "lights out." You pay the time-worn duty bills if you choose, or decline if you prefer—and without prejudice—for they are not legally collectable.

The previous-engagement plea, which in forty years has cost you so many twinges, you can lay aside forever; on this side of the grave you will never need it again. If you shrink at thought of night, and winter, and the late homecomings from the banquet and the lights and laughter through the deserted streets— a desolation which would not remind you now, as for a generation it did, that your friends are sleeping and you must creep in a-tiptoe and not disturb them, but would only remind you that you need not tiptoe, you can never disturb them more—if you shrink at the thought of these things you need only reply, "Your invitation honors me and pleases me because you still keep me in your remembrance, but I am seventy; seventy, and would nestle in the chimney-corner, and smoke my pipe, and read my book, and take my rest, wishing you well in all affection, and that when you in your turn shall arrive at Pier 70 you may step aboard your waiting ship with a reconciled spirit, and lay your course toward the sinking sun with a contented heart."

The tears that had been lying in wait were not restrained now. If there were any present who did not let them flow without shame, who did not shout their applause from throats choked with sobs, the writer of these lines failed to see them or to hear of them. There was not one who was ashamed to pay the great tribute of tears.

Many of his old friends, one after another, rose to tell their love for him—Brander Matthews, Cable, Kate Douglas Riggs, Gilder, Carnegie, Bangs, Bacheller— they kept it up far into the next morning. No other arrival at Pier 70 ever awoke a grander welcome.

CCXXXVII

AFTERMATH

THE announcement of the seventieth birthday dinner had precipitated a perfect avalanche of letters, which continued to flow in until the news accounts of it precipitated another avalanche. The carriers' bags were stuffed with greetings that came from every part of the world, from every class of humanity. They were all full of love and tender wishes. A card signed only with initials said: "God bless your old sweet soul for having lived."

Aldrich, who could not attend the dinner, declared that all through the evening he had been listening in his mind to a murmur of voices in the hall at Delmonico's. A group of English authors in London combined in a cable of congratulations. Anstey, Alfred Austin, Balfour, Barrie, Bryce, Chesterton, Dobson, Doyle, Gosse, Hardy, Hope, Jacobs, Kipling, Lang, Parker, Tenniel, Watson, and Zangwill were among the signatures.

Helen Keller wrote:

And you are seventy years old? Or is the report exaggerated, like that of your death? I remember, when I saw you last, at the house of dear Mr. Hutton, in Princeton, you said:

"If a man is a pessimist before he is forty-eight he knows too much. If he is an optimist after he is forty-eight he knows too little."

Now we *know* you are an optimist, and nobody would dare to accuse one on the "seven-terraced summit" of knowing little. So probably you are not seventy after all, but only forty-seven!

Helen Keller was right. Mark Twain was not a pessimist in his heart, but only by premeditation. It was his observation and his logic that led him to write those things that, even in their bitterness, somehow conveyed that spirit of human sympathy which is so closely linked to hope. To Miss Keller he wrote:

"Oh, thank you for your lovely words!"

He was given another birthday celebration that month —this time by the Society of Illustrators. Dan Beard, president, was also toast-master; and as he presented Mark Twain there was a trumpet-note, and a lovely girl, costumed as Joan of Arc, entered and, approaching him, presented him with a laurel wreath. It was planned and carried out as a surprise to him, and he hardly knew for the moment whether it was a vision or a reality. He was deeply affected, so much so that for several moments he could not find his voice to make any acknowledgments.

Clemens was more than ever sought now, and he responded when the cause was a worthy one. He spoke for the benefit of the Russian sufferers at the Casino on December 18th. Madame Sarah Bernhardt was also there, and spoke in French. He followed her, declaring that it seemed a sort of cruelty to inflict upon an audience our rude English after hearing that divine speech flowing in that lucid Gallic tongue.

It has always been a marvel to me—that French language; it has always been a puzzle to me. How beautiful that language is! How expressive it seems to be! How full of grace it is!

And when it comes from lips like those, how eloquent and how limpid it is! And, oh, I am always deceived—I always think I am going to understand it.

It is such a delight to me, *such* a delight to me, to meet Madame Bernhardt, and laugh hand to hand and heart to heart with her.

I have seen her play, as we all have, and, oh, that is divine;

but I have always wanted to know Madame Bernhardt herself
—her fiery self. I have wanted to know that beautiful character.

Why, she is the youngest person I ever saw, except myself—
for I always feel young when I come in the presence of young
people.

And truly, at seventy, Mark Twain was young, his
manner, his movement, his point of view—these were
all, and always, young.

A number of palmists about that time examined impressions of his hand without knowledge as to the owner,
and they all agreed that it was the hand of a man with
the characteristics of youth, with inspiration, and enthusiasm, and sympathy—a lover of justice and of the
sublime. They all agreed, too, that he was a deep
philosopher, though, alas! they likewise agreed that he
lacked the sense of humor, which is not as surprising as
it sounds, for with Mark Twain humor was never mere
fun-making nor the love of it; rather it was the flower
of his philosophy—its bloom and fragrance.

When the fanfare and drum-beat of his birthday honors
had passed by, and a moment of calm had followed, Mark
Twain set down some reflections on the new estate he
had achieved. The little paper, which forms a perfect
pendant to the "Seventieth Birthday Speech," here
follows:

OLD AGE

I think it likely that people who have not been here will be
interested to know what it is like. I arrived on the thirtieth
of November, fresh from carefree & frivolous 69, & was disappointed.

There is nothing novel about it, nothing striking, nothing to
thrill you & make your eye glitter & your tongue cry out, "Oh,
it *is* wonderful, perfectly wonderful!" Yes, it is disappointing.
You say, "Is *this* it?—this? after all this talk and fuss of a
thousand generations of travelers who have crossed this frontier

& looked about them & told what they saw & felt? Why, it looks just like 69."

And that is true. Also it is natural, for you have not come by the fast express; you have been lagging & dragging across the world's continents behind oxen; when that is your pace one country melts into the next one so gradually that you are not able to notice the change; 70 looks like 69; 69 looked like 68; 68 looked like 67—& so on back & back to the beginning. If you climb to a summit & look back—ah, then you see!

Down that far-reaching perspective you can make out each country & climate that you crossed, all the way up from the hot equator to the ice-summit where you are perched. You can make out where Infancy verged into Boyhood; Boyhood into down-lipped Youth; Youth into bearded, indefinite Young-Manhood; indefinite Young-Manhood into definite Manhood; definite Manhood, with large, aggressive ambitions, into sobered & heedful Husbandhood & Fatherhood; these into troubled & foreboding Age, with graying hair; this into Old Age, white-headed, the temple empty, the idols broken, the worshipers in their graves, nothing left but You, a remnant, a tradition, belated fag-end of a foolish dream, a dream that was so ingeniously dreamed that it seemed real all the time; nothing left but You, center of a snowy desolation, perched on the ice-summit, gazing out over the stages of that long *trek* & asking Yourself, "Would you do it again if you had the chance?"

CCXXXVIII

THE WRITER MEETS MARK TWAIN

WE have reached a point in this history where the narrative becomes mainly personal, and where, at the risk of inviting the charge of egotism, the form of the telling must change.

It was at the end of 1901 that I first met Mark Twain —at The Players Club on the night when he made the Founder's Address mentioned in an earlier chapter.

I was not able to arrive in time for the address, but as I reached the head of the stairs I saw him sitting on the couch at the dining-room entrance, talking earnestly to some one, who, as I remember it, did not enter into my consciousness at all. I saw only that crown of white hair, that familiar profile, and heard the slow modulations of his measured speech. I was surprised to see how frail and old he looked. From his pictures I had conceived him different. I did not realize that it was a temporary condition due to a period of poor health and a succession of social demands. I have no idea how long I stood there watching him. He had been my literary idol from childhood, as he had been of so many others; more than that, for the personality in his work had made him nothing less than a hero to his readers.

He rose presently to go, and came directly toward me. A year before I had done what new writers were always doing—I had sent him a book I had written, and he had done what he was always doing—acknowledged it with a kindly letter. I made my thanks now an excuse for addressing him. It warmed me to hear him say that he remembered the book, though at the time I confess I thought it doubtful. Then he was gone; but the mind and ear had photographed those vivid first impressions that remain always clear.

It was the following spring that I saw him again—at an afternoon gathering, and the memory of that occasion is chiefly important because I met Mrs. Clemens there for the only time, and like all who met her, however briefly, felt the gentleness and beauty of her spirit. I think I spoke with her at two or three different moments during the afternoon, and on each occasion was impressed with that feeling of acquaintanceship which we immediately experience with those rare beings whose souls are wells of human sympathy and free from guile. Bret Harte had just died, and during the afternoon Mr. Clemens asked me to obtain for him some item concerning the obsequies.

It was more than three years before I saw him again. Meantime, a sort of acquaintance had progressed. I had been engaged in writing the life of Thomas Nast, the cartoonist, and I had found among the material a number of letters to Nast from Mark Twain. I was naturally anxious to use those fine characteristic letters, and I wrote him for his consent. He wished to see the letters, and the permission that followed was kindness itself. His admiration of Nast was very great.

It was proper, under the circumstances, to send him a copy of the book when it appeared; but that was 1904, his year of sorrow and absence, and the matter was postponed. Then came the great night of his seventieth birthday dinner, with an opportunity to thank him in person for the use of the letters. There was only a brief exchange of words, and it was the next day, I think, that I sent him a copy of the book. It did not occur to me that I should hear of it again.

We step back a moment here. Something more than a year earlier, through a misunderstanding, Mark Twain's long association with The Players had been severed. It was a sorrow to him, and a still greater sorrow to the club. There was a movement among what is generally known as the "Round Table Group"—because its members have long had a habit of lunching at a large, round table in a certain window—to bring him back again. David Munro, associate editor of the *North American Review*—"David," a man well loved of men—and Robert Reid, the painter, prepared this simple document:

To
MARK TWAIN
from
THE CLANSMEN

Will ye no come back again?
Will ye no come back again?
Better lo'ed ye canna be,
Will ye no come back again?

It was signed by Munro and by Reid and about thirty others, and it touched Mark Twain deeply. The lines had always moved him. He wrote:

To ROBT. REID & THE OTHERS—

WELL-BELOVED,—Surely those lovely verses went to Prince Charlie's heart, if he had one, & certainly they have gone to mine. I shall be glad & proud to come back again after such a moving & beautiful compliment as this from comrades whom I have loved so long. I hope you can poll the necessary vote; I know you will try, at any rate. It will be many months before I can foregather with you, for this black border is not perfunctory, not a convention; it symbolizes the loss of one whose memory is the only thing I worship.

It is not necessary for me to thank you—& words could not deliver what I feel, anyway. I will put the contents of your envelope in the small casket where I keep the things which have become sacred to me. S. L. C.

So the matter was temporarily held in abeyance until he should return to social life. At the completion of his seventieth year the club had taken action, and Mark Twain had been brought back, not in the regular order of things, but as an honorary life member without dues or duties. There was only one other member of this class, Sir Henry Irving.

The Players, as a club, does not give dinners. Whatever is done in that way is done by one or more of the members in the private dining-room, where there is a single large table that holds twenty-five, even thirty when expanded to its limit. That room and that table have mingled with much distinguished entertainment, also with history. Henry James made his first after-dinner speech there, for one thing—at least he claimed it was his first, though this is by the way.

A letter came to me which said that those who had signed the plea for the Prince's return were going to welcome him in the private dining-room on the 3d of January. It was not an invitation, but a gracious privilege. I was in New York a day or two in advance of the date, and I think David Munro was the first person I met at The Players. As he greeted me his eyes were eager with something he knew I would wish to hear. He had been delegated to propose the dinner to Mark Twain, and had found him propped up in bed, and noticed on the table near him a copy of the Nast book. I suspect that Munro had led him to speak of it, and that the result had lost nothing, filtered through that radiant benevolence of his.

The night of January 3, 1906, remains a memory apart from other dinners. Brander Matthews presided, and Gilder was there, and Frank Millet and Willard Metcalf and Robert Reid, and a score of others; some of them are dead now, David Munro among them. It so happened that my seat was nearly facing the guest of the evening, who, by custom of The Players, is placed at the side and not at the end of the long table. He was no longer frail and thin, as when I had first met him. He had a robust, rested look; his complexion had the tints of a miniature painting. Lit by the glow of the shaded candles, relieved against the dusk richness of the walls, he made a picture of striking beauty. One could not take his eyes from it, and to one guest at least it stirred the farthest memories. I suddenly saw the interior of a farm-house sitting-room in the Middle West, where I had first heard uttered the name of Mark Twain, and where night after night a group gathered around the evening lamp to hear the tale of the first pilgrimage, which, to a boy of eight, had seemed only a wonderful poem and fairy tale. To Charles Harvey Genung, who sat next to me, I whispered something of this, and how, during the thirty-six years since then, no other human being to me had meant quite what Mark Twain had meant—in literature, in life, in the ineffable thing which means more than either, and which we call "inspiration," for lack of a truer word. Now here he was, just across the table. It was the fairy tale come true.

Genung said:

"You should write his life."

His remark seemed a pleasant courtesy, and was put aside as such. When he persisted I attributed it to the general bloom of the occasion, and a little to the wine, maybe, for the dinner was in its sweetest stage just then —that happy, early stage when the first glass of champagne, or the second, has proved its quality. He urged, in support of his idea, the word that Munro had brought concerning the Nast book, but nothing of what he said kindled any spark of hope. I could not but believe that some one with a larger equipment of experience, personal friendship, and abilities had already been selected for the task. By and by the speaking began—delightful, intimate speaking in that restricted circle—and the matter went out of my mind.

When the dinner had ended, and we were drifting about the table in general talk, I found an opportunity to say a word to the guest of the evening about his *Joan of Arc*, which I had recently re-read. To my happiness, he detained me while he told me the long-ago incident which had led to his interest, not only in the martyred girl, but in all literature. I think we broke up soon after, and descended to the lower rooms. At any rate, I presently found the faithful Charles Genung privately reasserting to me the proposition that I should undertake the biography of Mark Twain. Perhaps it was the brief sympathy established by the name of Joan of Arc, perhaps it was only Genung's insistent purpose—his faith, if I may be permitted the word. Whatever it was, there came an impulse, in the instant of bidding good-by to our guest of honor, which prompted me to say:

"May I call to see you, Mr. Clemens, some day?"

And something—dating from the primal atom, I suppose—prompted him to answer:

"Yes, come soon."

This was on Wednesday night, or rather on Thursday morning, for it was past midnight, and a day later I made an appointment with his secretary to call on Saturday.

I can say truly that I set out with no more than the barest hope of success, and wondering if I should have the courage, when I saw him, even to suggest the thought in my mind. I know I did not have the courage to confide in Genung that I had made the appointment—I was so sure it would fail. I arrived at 21 Fifth Avenue and was shown into that long library and drawing-room combined, and found a curious and deep interest in the books and ornaments along the shelves as I waited. Then I was summoned, and I remember ascending the stairs, wondering why I had come on so futile an errand, and trying to think of an excuse to offer for having come at all.

He was propped up in bed—in that stately bed—sitting, as was his habit, with his pillows placed at the foot, so that he might have always before him the rich, carved beauty of its headboard. He was delving through a copy of *Huckleberry Finn*, in search of a paragraph concerning which some random correspondent had asked explanation. He was commenting unfavorably on this correspondent and on miscellaneous letter-writing in general. He pushed the cigars toward me, and the talk of these matters ran along and blended into others more or less personal. By and by I told him what so many thousands had told him before: what he had meant to me, recalling the childhood impressions of that large, black-and-gilt-covered book with its wonderful pictures and adventures —the Mediterranean pilgrimage. Very likely it bored him —he had heard it so often—and he was willing enough, I dare say, to let me change the subject and thank him for the kindly word which David Munro had brought. I do not remember what he said then, but I suddenly found myself suggesting that out of his encouragement had grown a hope—though certainly it was something less—that I might some day undertake a book about himself. I expected the chapter to end at this point, and his silence which followed seemed long and ominous.

He said, at last, that at various times through his life he had been preparing some autobiographical matter, but that he had tired of the undertaking, and had put it aside. He added that he had hoped his daughters would one day collect his letters; but that a biography— a detailed story of personality and performance, of success and failure—was of course another matter, and that for such a work no arrangement had been made. He may have added one or two other general remarks; then, turning those piercing agate-blue eyes directly upon me, he said:

"When would you like to begin?"

There was a dresser with a large mirror behind him I happened to catch my reflection in it, and I vividly recollect saying to it mentally: "This is not true; it is only one of many similar dreams." But even in a dream one must answer, and I said:

"Whenever you like. I can begin now."

He was always eager in any new undertaking.

"Very good," he said. "The sooner, then, the better. Let's begin while we are in the humor. The longer you postpone a thing of this kind the less likely you are ever to get at it."

This was on Saturday, as I have stated. I mentioned that my family was still in the country, and that it would require a day or two to get established in the city. I asked if Tuesday, January 9th, would be too soon to begin. He agreed that Tuesday would do, and inquired something about my plan of work. Of course I had formed nothing definite, but I said that in similar undertakings a part of the work had been done with a stenographer, who had made the notes while I prompted the subject to recall a procession of incidents and episodes, to be supplemented with every variety of material obtainable—letters and other documentary accumulations. Then he said:

"I think I should enjoy dictating to a stenographer, with some one to prompt me and to act as audience. The room adjoining this was fitted up for my study. My manuscripts and notes and private books and many of my letters are there, and there are a trunkful or two of such things in the attic. I seldom use the room myself. I do my writing and reading in bed. I will turn that room over to you for this work. Whatever you need will be brought to you. We can have the dictation here in the morning, and you can put in the rest of the day to suit yourself. You can have a key and come and go as you please."

That was always his way. He did nothing by halves; nothing without unquestioning confidence and prodigality. He got up and showed me the lovely luxury of the study, with its treasures of material. I did not believe it true yet. It had all the atmosphere of a dream, and I have no distinct recollection of how I came away. When I returned to The Players and found Charles Harvey Genung there, and told him about it, it is quite certain that he perjured himself when he professed to believe it true and pretended that he was not surprised.

CCXXXIX

WORKING WITH MARK TWAIN

ON Tuesday, January 9, 1906, I was on hand with a capable stenographer—Miss Josephine Hobby, who had successively, and successfully, held secretarial positions with Charles Dudley Warner and Mrs. Mary Mapes Dodge, and was therefore peculiarly qualified for the work in hand.

Clemens, meantime, had been revolving our plans and adding some features of his own. He proposed to double the value and interest of our employment by letting his dictations continue the form of those earlier autobiographical chapters, begun with Redpath in 1885, and continued later in Vienna and at the Villa Quarto. He said he did not think he could follow a definite chronological program; that he would like to wander about, picking up this point and that, as memory or fancy prompted, without any particular biographical order. It was his purpose, he declared, that his dictations should not be published until he had been dead a hundred years or more—a prospect which seemed to give him an especial gratification.[1]

He wished to pay the stenographer, and to own these memoranda, he said, allowing me free access to them for

---

[1] As early as October, 1900, he had proposed to Harper & Brothers a contract for publishing his personal memoirs at the expiration of one hundred years from date, and letters covering the details were exchanged with Mr. Rogers. The document, however, was not completed.

any material I might find valuable. I could also suggest subjects for dictation, and ask particulars of any special episode or period. I believe this covered the whole arrangement, which did not require more than five minutes, and we set to work without further prologue.

I ought to state that he was in bed when we arrived, and that he remained there during almost all of these earlier dictations, clad in a handsome silk dressing-gown of rich Persian pattern, propped against great snowy pillows. He loved this loose luxury and ease, and found it conducive to thought. On the little table beside him, where lay his cigars, papers, pipes, and various knick-knacks, shone a reading-lamp, making more brilliant the rich coloring of his complexion and the gleam of his shining hair. There was daylight, too, but it was north light, and the winter days were dull. Also the walls of the room were a deep, unreflecting red, and his eyes were getting old. The outlines of that vast bed blending into the luxuriant background, the whole focusing to the striking central figure, remain in my mind to-day—a picture of classic value.

He dictated that morning some matters connected with the history of the Comstock mine; then he drifted back to his childhood, returning again to the more modern period, and closed, I think, with some comments on current affairs. It was absorbingly interesting; his quaint, unhurried fashion of speech, the unconscious movement of his hands, the play of his features as his fancies and phrases passed in mental review and were accepted or waved aside. We were watching one of the great literary creators of his time in the very process of his architecture. We constituted about the most select audience in the world enjoying what was, likely enough, its most remarkable entertainment. When he turned at last and inquired the time we were all amazed that two hours and more had slipped away.

"And how much I have enjoyed it!" he said. "It is the ideal plan for this kind of work. Narrative *w-iting* is always disappointing. The moment you pick up a pen you begin to lose the spontaneity of the personal relation, which contains the very essence of interest. With shorthand dictation one can talk as if he were at his own dinner-table—always a most inspiring place. I expect to dictate all the rest of my life, if you good people are willing to come and listen to it."

The dictations thus begun continued steadily from week to week, and always with increasing charm. We never knew what he was going to talk about, and it was seldom that *he* knew until the moment of beginning; then he went drifting among episodes, incidents, and periods in his irresponsible fashion; the fashion of table-conversation, as he said, the methodless method of the human mind. It was always delightful, and always amusing, tragic, or instructive, and it was likely to be one of these at one instant, and another the next. I felt myself the most fortunate biographer in the world, as undoubtedly I was, though not just in the way that I first imagined.

It was not for several weeks that I began to realize that these marvelous reminiscences bore only an atmospheric relation to history; that they were aspects of biography rather than its veritable narrative, and built largely—sometimes wholly—from an imagination that, with age, had dominated memory, creating details, even reversing them, yet with a perfect sincerity of purpose on the part of the narrator to set down the literal and unvarnished truth. It was his constant effort to be frank and faithful to fact, to record, to confess, and to condemn without stint. If you wanted to know the worst of Mark Twain you had only to ask him for it. He would give it, to the last syllable—worse than the worst, for his imagination would magnify it and adorn it with new iniquities, and if he gave it again, or a dozen times, he would improve upon it each time, until the thread of history was almost impossible to trace through the marvel of that fabric; and he would do the same for another person just as willingly. Those vividly real personalities that he marched and countermarched before us were the most convincing creatures in the world, the most entertaining, the most excruciatingly humorous, or wicked, or tragic; but, alas, they were not always safe to include in a record that must bear a certain semblance to history. They often disagreed in their performance, and even in their characters, with the documents in the next room, as I learned by and by when those records, disentangled, began to rebuild the structure of the years.

His gift of dramatization had been exercised too long to be discarded now. The things he told of Mrs. Clemens and of Susy were true—marvelously and beautifully true, in spirit and in aspect—and the actual detail of these mattered little in such a record. The rest was history only as *Roughing It* is history, or the *Tramp Abroad*; that is to say, it was fictional history, with fact as a starting-point. In a prefatory note to these volumes I have quoted Mark Twain's own lovely and whimsical admission, made once when he realized his deviations:

"When I was younger I could remember anything, whether it happened or not; but I am getting old, and soon I shall remember only the latter."

At another time he paraphrased one of Josh Billings's sayings in the remark: "It isn't so astonishing, the number of things that I can remember, as the number of things I can remember that aren't so."

I do not wish to say, by any means, that his so-called autobiography is a mere fairy tale. It is far from that. It is amazingly truthful in the character-picture it represents of the man himself. It is only not reliable—and it is sometimes even unjust—as detailed history. Yet, curiously enough, there were occasional chapters that were photographically exact, and fitted precisely with the more positive, if less picturesque, materials. It is also true that such chapters were likely to be episodes intrinsically so perfect as to not require the touch of art.

In the talks which we usually had, when the dictations were ended and Miss Hobby had gone, I gathered much that was of still greater value. Imagination was temporarily dispossessed, as it were, and, whether expounding some theory or summarizing some event, he cared little for literary effect, and only for the idea and the moment immediately present.

It was at such times that he allowed me to make those inquiries we had planned in the beginning, and which apparently had little place in the dictations themselves. Sometimes I led him to speak of the genesis of his various books, how he had come to write them, and I think there was not a single case where later I did not find his memory of these matters almost exactly in accord with the letters of the moment, written to Howells or Twichell, or to some member of his family. Such reminiscence was usually followed by some vigorous burst of human philosophy, often too vigorous for print, too human, but as dazzling as a search-light in its revelation.

It was during this earlier association that he propounded, one day, his theory of circumstance, already set down, that inevitable sequence of cause and effect, beginning with the first act of the primal atom. He had been dictating that morning his story of the clairvoyant dream which preceded his brother's death, and the talk of foreknowledge had continued. I said one might logically conclude from such a circumstance that the future was a fixed quantity.

"As absolutely fixed as the past," he said; and added the remark already quoted.[1] A little later he continued:

[1] Chap. lxxv, p. 397.

"Even the Almighty Himself cannot check or change that sequence of events once it is started. It is a fixed quantity, and a part of the scheme is a mental condition during certain moments—usually of sleep—when the mind may reach out and grasp some of the acts which are still to come."

It was a new angle to me—a line of logic so simple and so utterly convincing that I have remained unshaken in it to this day. I have never been able to find any answer to it, nor any one who could even attempt to show that the first act of the first created atom did not strike the key-note of eternity.

At another time, speaking of the idea that God works through man, he burst out:

"Yes, of course, just about as much as a man works through his microbes!"

He had a startling way of putting things like that, and it left not much to say.

I was at this period interested a good deal in mental healing, and had been treated for neurasthenia with gratifying results. Like most of the world, I had assumed, from his published articles, that he condemned Christian Science and its related practices out of hand. When I confessed, rather reluctantly, one day, the benefit I had received, he surprised me by answering:

"Of course you have been benefited. Christian Science is humanity's boon. Mother Eddy deserves a place in the Trinity as much as any member of it. She has organized and made available a healing principle that for two thousand years has never been employed, except as the merest kind of guesswork. She is the benefactor of the age."

It seemed strange, at the time, to hear him speak in this way concerning a practice of which he was generally regarded as the chief public antagonist. It was another angle of his many-sided character.

CCXL

THE DEFINITION OF A GENTLEMAN

THAT was a busy winter for him socially. He was constantly demanded for this thing and that—for public gatherings, dinners—everywhere he was a central figure. Once he presided at a Valentine dinner given by some Players to David Munro. He had never presided at a dinner before, he said, and he did it in his own way, which certainly was a taking one, suitable to that carefree company and occasion—a real Scotch occasion, with the Munro tartan everywhere, the table banked with heather, and a wild piper marching up and down in the anteroom, blowing savage airs in honor of Scotland's gentlest son.

An important meeting of that winter was at Carnegie Hall—a great gathering which had assembled for the purpose of aiding Booker T. Washington in his work for the welfare of his race. The stage and the auditorium were thronged with notables. Joseph H. Choate and Mark Twain presided, and both spoke; also Robert C. Ogden and Booker T. Washington himself. It was all fine and interesting. Choate's address was ably given, and Mark Twain was at his best. He talked of politics and of morals—public and private—how the average American citizen was true to his Christian principles three hundred and sixty-three days in the year, and how on the other two days of the year he left those principles at home and went to the tax-office and the voting-booths, and did his best to damage and undo his whole year's faithful and righteous work.

THE DEFINITION OF A GENTLEMAN

I used to be an honest man, but I am crumbling—no, I have crumbled. When they assessed me at $75,000 a fortnight ago I went out and tried to borrow the money and couldn't. Then when I found they were letting a whole crowd of millionaires live in New York at a third of the price they were charging me I was hurt, I was indignant, and said, this is the last feather. I am not going to run this town all by myself. In that moment—in that memorable moment, I began to crumble. In fifteen minutes the disintegration was complete. In fifteen minutes I was become just a mere moral sand-pile, and I lifted up my hand, along with those seasoned and experienced deacons, and swore off every rag of personal property I've got in the world.

I had never heard him address a miscellaneous audience. It was marvelous to see how he convulsed it, and silenced it, and controlled it at will. He did not undertake any special pleading for the negro cause; he only prepared the way with cheerfulness.

Clemens and Choate joined forces again, a few weeks later, at a great public meeting assembled in aid of the adult blind. Helen Keller was to be present, but she had fallen ill through overwork. She sent to Clemens one of her beautiful letters, in which she said:

I should be happy if I could have spelled into my hand the words as they fall from your lips, and receive, even as it is uttered, the eloquence of our newest ambassador to the blind.

Clemens, dictating the following morning, told of his first meeting with Helen Keller at a little gathering in Laurence Hutton's home, when she was about the age of fourteen. It was an incident that invited no elaboration, and probably received none.

Henry Rogers and I went together. The company had all assembled and had been waiting a while. The wonderful child arrived now with her about equally wonderful teacher, Miss Sullivan, and seemed quite well to recognize the character of her surroundings. She said, "Oh, the books, the books, so many, many books. How lovely!"

The guests were brought one after another. As she shook hands with each she took her hand away and laid her fingers lightly against Miss Sullivan's lips, who spoke against them the person's name.

Mr. Howells seated himself by Helen on the sofa, and she put her fingers against his lips and he told her a story of considerable length, and you could see each detail of it pass into her mind and strike fire there and throw the flash of it into her face.

After a couple of hours spent very pleasantly some one asked if Helen would remember the feel of the hands of the company after this considerable interval of time and be able to discriminate the hands and name the possessors of them. Miss Sullivan said, "Oh, she will have no difficulty about that." So the company filed past, shook hands in turn, and with each hand-shake Helen greeted the owner of the hand pleasantly and spoke the name that belonged to it without hesitation.

By and by the assemblage proceeded to the dining-room and sat down to the luncheon. I had to go away before it was over, and as I passed by Helen I patted her lightly on the head and passed on. Miss Sullivan called to me and said, "Stop, Mr. Clemens, Helen is distressed because she did not recognize your hand. Won't you come back and do that again?" I went back and patted her lightly on the head, and she said at once, "Oh, it's Mr. Clemens."

Perhaps some one can explain this miracle, but I have never been able to do it. Could she feel the wrinkles in my hand through her hair? Some one else must answer this.

It was three years following this dictation that the mystery received a very simple and rather amusing solution. Helen had come to pay a visit to Mark Twain's Connecticut home, Stormfield, then but just completed. He had met her, meantime, but it had not occurred to him before to ask her how she had recognized him that morning at Hutton's, in what had seemed such a marvelous way. She remembered, and with a smile said:

THE DEFINITION OF A GENTLEMAN

"I smelled you." Which, after all, did not make the incident seem much less marvelous.

On one of the mornings after Miss Hobby had gone Clemens said:

"A very curious thing has happened—a very large-sized—joke." He was shaving at the time, and this information came in brief and broken relays, suited to a performance of that sort. The reader may perhaps imagine the effect without further indication of it.

"I was going on a yachting trip once, with Henry Rogers, when a reporter stopped me with the statement that Mrs. Astor had said that there had never been a gentleman in the White House, and he wanted me to give him my definition of a gentleman. I didn't give him my definition; but he printed it, just the same, in the afternoon paper. I was angry at first, and wanted to bring a damage suit. When I came to read the definition it was a satisfactory one, and I let it go. Now to-day comes a letter and a telegram from a man who has made a will in Missouri, leaving ten thousand dollars to provide tablets for various libraries in the State, on which shall be inscribed Mark Twain's definition of a gentleman. He hasn't got the definition—he has only heard of it, and he wants me to tell him in which one of my books or speeches he can find it. I couldn't think, when I read that letter, what in the nation the man meant, but shaving somehow has a tendency to release thought, and just now it all came to me."

It was a situation full of amusing possibilities; but he reached no conclusion in the matter. Another telegram was brought in just then, which gave a sadder aspect to his thought, for it said that his old coachman, Patrick McAleer, who had begun in the Clemens service with the bride and groom of thirty-six years before, was very low, and could not survive more than a few days. This led him to speak of Patrick, his noble and faithful nature, and how he always claimed to be in their service, even during their long intervals of absence abroad. Clemens gave orders that everything possible should be done for Patrick's comfort. When the end came, a few days later, he traveled to Hartford to lay flowers on Patrick's bier, and to serve, with Patrick's friends— neighbor coachmen and John O'Neill, the gardener—as pall-bearer, taking his allotted place without distinction or favor.

It was the following Sunday, at the Majestic Theater, in New York, that Mark Twain spoke to the Young Men's Christian Association. For several reasons it proved an unusual meeting. A large number of free tickets had been given out, far more than the place would hold; and, further, it had been announced that when the ticket-holders had been seated the admission would be free to the public. The subject chosen for the talk was "Reminiscences."

When we arrived the streets were packed from side to side for a considerable distance and a riot was in progress. A great crowd had swarmed about the place, and the officials, instead of throwing the doors wide and letting the theater fill up, regardless of tickets, had locked them. As a result there was a shouting, surging human mass that presently dashed itself against the entrance. Windows and doors gave way, and there followed a wild struggle for entrance. A moment later the house was packed solid. A detachment of police had now arrived, and in time cleared the street. It was said that amid the tumult some had lost their footing and had been trampled and injured, but of this we did not learn until later. We had been taken somehow to a side entrance and smuggled into boxes.[1]

[1] The paper next morning bore the head-lines: " 10,000 Stampeded at the Mark Twain Meeting. Well-dressed Men and Women Clubbed by Police at Majestic Theater." In this account the paper stated that the crowd had collected an hour before the time for opening; that nothing of the kind had been anticipated and no police preparation had been made.

THE DEFINITION OF A GENTLEMAN

It was peaceful enough in the theater until Mark Twain appeared on the stage. He was wildly greeted, and when he said, slowly and seriously, "I thank you for this signal recognition of merit," there was a still noisier outburst. In the quiet that followed he began his memories, and went wandering along from one anecdote to another in the manner of his daily dictations.

At last it seemed to occur to him, in view of the character of his audience, that he ought to close with something in the nature of counsel suited to young men.

It is from experiences such as mine [he said] that we get our education of life. We string them into jewels or into tinware, as we may choose. I have received recently several letters asking for counsel or advice, the principal request being for some incident that may prove helpful to the young. It is my mission to teach, and I am always glad to furnish something. There have been a lot of incidents in my career to help me along—sometimes they helped me along faster than I wanted to go.

He took some papers from his pocket and started to unfold one of them; then, as if remembering, he asked how long he had been talking. The answer came, "Thirty-five minutes." He made as if to leave the stage, but the audience commanded him to go on.

"All right," he said, "I can stand more of my own talk than any one I ever knew." Opening one of the papers, a telegram, he read:

"In which one of your works can we find the definition of a gentleman?" Then he added:

I have not answered that telegram. I couldn't. I never wrote any such definition, though it seems to me that if a man has just, merciful, and kindly instincts he would be a gentleman, for he would need nothing else in this world.

He opened a letter. "From Howells," he said.

My old friend, William Dean Howells—Howells, the head of American literature. No one is able to stand with him. He is an old, old friend of mine, and he writes me, "'To-morrow I shall be sixty-nine years old." Why, I am surprised at Howells writing so. I have known him myself longer than that. I am sorry to see a man trying to appear so young. Let's see. Howells says now, "I see you have been burying Patrick. I suppose he was old, too."

The house became very still. Most of them had read an account of Mark Twain's journey to Hartford and his last service to his faithful servitor. The speaker's next words were not much above a whisper, but every syllable was distinct.

No, he was never old—Patrick. He came to us thirty-six years ago. He was our coachman from the day that I drove my young bride to our new home. He was a young Irishman, slender, tall, lithe, honest, truthful, and he never changed in all his life. He really was with us but twenty-five years, for he did not go with us to Europe; but he never regarded that a separation. As the children grew up he was their guide. He was all honor, honesty, and affection. He was with us in New Hampshire last summer, and his hair was just as black, his eyes were just as blue, his form just as straight, and his heart just as good as on the day we first met. In all the long years Patrick never made a mistake. He never needed an order; he never received a command. He knew. I have been asked for my idea of an ideal gentleman, and I give it to you —Patrick McAleer.

It was the sort of thing that no one but Mark Twain has quite been able to do, and it was the recognized quality behind it that had made crowds jam the street and stampede the entrance to be in his presence—to see him and to hear his voice.

CCXLI

GORKY, HOWELLS, AND MARK TWAIN

CLEMENS was now fairly back again in the wash of banquets and speech-making that had claimed him on his return from England, five years before. He made no less than a dozen speeches altogether that winter, and he was continually at some feasting or other, where he was sure to be called upon for remarks. He fell out of the habit of preparing his addresses, relying upon the inspiration of the moment, merely following the procedure of his daily dictations, which had doubtless given him confidence for this departure from his earlier method. There was seldom an afternoon or an evening that he was not required, and seldom a morning that the papers did not have some report of his doings. Once more, and in a larger fashion than ever, he had become "the belle of New York." But he was something further. An editorial in the *Evening Mail* said:

Mark Twain, in his "last and best of life for which the first was made," seems to be advancing rapidly to a position which makes him a kind of joint Aristides, Solon, and Themistocles of the American metropolis—an Aristides for justness and boldness as well as incessancy of opinion, a Solon for wisdom and cogency, and a Themistocles for the democracy of his views and the popularity of his person.

Things have reached the point where, if Mark Twain is not at a public meeting or banquet, he is expected to console it with one of his inimitable letters of advice and encouragement. If he deigns to make a public appearance there is a throng at the doors which overtaxes the energy and ability of the police. We must be glad that we have a public commentator like Mark Twain always at hand and his wit and wisdom continually on tap. His sound, breezy Mississippi Valley Americanism is a corrective to all sorts of snobbery. He cultivates respect for human rights by always making sure that he has his own.

He talked one afternoon to the Barnard girls, and another afternoon to the Women's University Club, illustrating his talk with what purported to be moral tales. He spoke at a dinner given to City Tax Commissioner Mr. Charles Putzel; and when he was introduced there as the man who had said, "When in doubt tell the truth," he replied that he had invented that maxim for others, but that when in doubt himself, he used more sagacity.

The speeches he made kept his hearers always in good humor; but he made them think, too, for there was always substance and sound reason and searching satire in the body of what he said.

It was natural that there should be reporters calling frequently at Mark Twain's home, and now and then the place became a veritable storm-center of news. Such a moment arrived when it became known that a public library in Brooklyn had banished *Huck Finn* and *Tom Sawyer* from the children's room, presided over by a young woman of rather severe morals. The incident had begun in November of the previous year. One of the librarians, Asa Don Dickinson, who had vigorously voted against the decree, wrote privately of the matter. Clemens had replied:

DEAR SIR,—I am greatly troubled by what you say. I wrote *Tom Sawyer* & *Huck Finn* for adults exclusively, & it always distresses me when I find that boys & girls have been allowed access to them. The mind that becomes soiled in youth can never again be washed clean. I know this by my own experience, & to this day I cherish an unappeasable bitterness against the unfaithful guardians of my young life, who not only permitted but compelled me to read an unexpurgated Bible through before I was 15 years old. None can do that and ever draw a clean, sweet breath again this side of the grave. Ask that young lady—she will tell you so.

Most honestly do I wish that I could say a softening word or two in defense of Huck's character since you wish it, but really, in my opinion, it is no better than those of Solomon, David, & the rest of the sacred brotherhood.

If there is an unexpurgated in the Children's Department, won't you please help that young woman remove *Tom & Huck* from that questionable companionship?

Sincerely yours,   S. L. CLEMENS.

I shall not show your letter to any one—it is safe with me.

Mr. Dickinson naturally kept this letter from the public, though he read it aloud to the assembled librarians, and the fact of its existence and its character eventually leaked out.[1] One of the librarians who had heard it mentioned it at a theater-party in hearing of an unrealized newspaper man. This was near the end of the following March.

The "tip" was sufficient. Telephone-bells began to jingle, and groups of newspaper men gathered simultaneously on Mr. Dickinson's and on Mark Twain's door-steps. At 21 Fifth Avenue you could hardly get in or out, for stepping on them. The evening papers surmised details, and *Huck* and *Tom* had a perfectly fresh crop of advertising, not only in America, but in distant lands. Dickinson wrote Clemens that he would not give out the letter without his authority, and Clemens replied:

Be wise as a serpent and wary as a dove! The newspaper boys want that letter—don't you let them get hold of it. They say you refuse to allow them to see it without my consent. Keep on refusing, and I'll take care of this end of the line.

[1] It has been supplied to the writer by Mr. Dickinson, and is published here with his consent.

In a recent letter to the writer Mr. Dickinson states that Mark Twain's solicitude was for the librarian, whom he was unwilling to involve in difficulties with his official superiors, and he adds:

There may be some doubt as to whether Mark Twain was or was not a *religious* man, for there are many definitions of the word *religion*. He was certainly a hater of conventions, had no patience with sanctimony and bibliolatry, and was perhaps irreverent. But any one who reads carefully the description of the conflict in Huck's soul, in regard to the betrayal of Jim, will credit the creator of the scene with deep and true moral feeling.

The reporters thinned out in the course of a few days when no result was forthcoming; but they were all back again presently when the Maxim Gorky fiasco came along. The distinguished revolutionist, Tchaykoffsky, as a sort of advance agent for Gorky, had already called upon Clemens to enlist his sympathy in their mission, which was to secure funds in the cause of Russian emancipation. Clemens gave his sympathy, and now promised his aid, though he did not hesitate to discourage the mission. He said that an American's enthusiasm in such matters stopped well above his pocket, and that this revolutionary would fail. Howells, too, was of this opinion. In his account of the episode he says:

I told a valued friend of his and mine that I did not believe he could get twenty-five hundred dollars, and I think now I set the figure too high.

Clemens's interest, however, grew. He attended a dinner given to Gorky at the "A Club," No. 3 Fifth Avenue, and introduced Gorky to the diners. Also he wrote a letter to be read by Tchaykoffsky at a meeting held at the Grand Central Palace, where three thousand people gathered to hear this great revolutionist recite the story of Russia's wrongs. The letter ran:

GORKY, HOWELLS, AND MARK TWAIN

Dear Mr. Tchaykoffsky,—My sympathies are with the Russian revolution, of course. It goes without saying. I hope it will succeed, and now that I have talked with you I take heart to believe it will. Government by falsified promises, by lies, by treachery, and by the butcher-knife, for the aggrandizement of a single family of drones and its idle and vicious kin has been borne quite long enough in Russia, I should think. And it is to be hoped that the roused nation, now rising in its strength, will presently put an end to it and set up the republic in its place. Some of us, even the white-headed, may live to see the blessed day when tsars and grand dukes will be as scarce there as I trust they are in heaven. Most sincerely yours,

Mark Twain.

Clemens and Howells called on Gorky and agreed to figure prominently in a literary dinner to be given in his honor. The movement was really assuming considerable proportions, when suddenly something happened which caused it to flatten permanently, and rather ridiculously.

Arriving at 21 Fifth Avenue, one afternoon, I met Howells coming out. I thought he had an unhappy, hunted look. I went up to the study, and on opening the door I found the atmosphere semi-opaque with cigar smoke, and Clemens among the drifting blue wreaths and layers, pacing up and down rather fiercely. He turned, inquiringly, as I entered. I had clipped a cartoon from a morning paper, which pictured him as upsetting the Tsar's throne—the kind of thing he was likely to enjoy. I said:

"Here is something perhaps you may wish to see, Mr. Clemens."

He shook his head violently.

"No, I can't see anything now," and in another moment had disappeared into his own room. Something extraordinary had happened. I wondered if, after all their lifelong friendship, he and Howells had quarreled. I was naturally curious, but it was not a good time to investigate. By and by I went down on the street, where the newsboys were calling extras. When I had bought one, and glanced at the first page, I knew. Gorky had been expelled from his hotel for having brought to America, as his wife, a woman not so recognized by the American laws. Madame Andreieva, a Russian actress, was a leader in the cause of freedom, and by Russian custom her relation with Gorky was recognized and condoned; but it was not sufficiently orthodox for American conventions, and it was certainly unfortunate that an apostle of high purpose should come handicapped in that way. Apparently the news had already reached Howells and Clemens, and they had been feverishly discussing what was best to do about the dinner.

Within a day or two Gorky and Madame Andreieva were evicted from a procession of hotels, and of course the papers rang with the head-lines. An army of reporters was chasing Clemens and Howells. The Russian revolution was entirely forgotten in this more lively, more intimate domestic interest. Howells came again, the reporters following and standing guard at the door below. In *My Mark Twain* he says:

That was the moment of the great Vesuvian eruption, and we figured ourselves in easy reach of a volcano which was every now and then "blowing a cone off," as the telegraphic phrase was. The roof of the great market in Naples had just broken in under its load of ashes and cinders, and crushed hundreds of people; and we asked each other if we were not sorry we had not been there, where the pressure would have been far less terrific than it was with us in Fifth Avenue. The forbidden butler came up with a message that there were some gentlemen below who wanted to see Clemens.

"How many?" he demanded.

"Five," the butler faltered.

"Reporters?"

The butler feigned uncertainty.

"What would you do?" he asked me.

"I wouldn't see them," I said, and then Clemens went directly down to them. How or by what means he appeased their voracity I cannot say, but I fancy it was by the confession of the exact truth, which was harmless enough. They went away joyfully, and he came back in radiant satisfaction with having seen them.

It is not quite clear at this time just what word was sent to Gorky; but the matter must have been settled that night, for Clemens was in a fine humor next morning. It was before dictation time, and he came drifting into the study and began at once to speak of the dinner and the impossibility of its being given now. Then he said:

"American public opinion is a delicate fabric. It shrivels like the webs of morning at the lightest touch."

Later in the day he made this memorandum:

Laws can be evaded and punishment escaped, but an openly transgressed custom brings sure punishment. The penalty may be unfair, unrighteous, illogical, and a cruelty; no matter, it will be inflicted just the same. Certainly, then, there can be but one wise thing for a visiting stranger to do—find out what the country's customs are and refrain from offending against them.

The efforts which have been made in Gorky's justification are entitled to all respect because of the magnanimity of the motive back of them, but I think that the ink was wasted. Custom is custom: it is built of brass, boiler-iron, granite; facts, reasonings, arguments have no more effect upon it than the idle winds have upon Gibraltar.[1]

The Gorky disturbance had hardly begun to subside when there came another upheaval that snuffed it out completely. On the afternoon of the 18th of April I heard, at The Players, a wandering telephonic rumor that a great earthquake was going on in San Francisco. Half

---

[1] To Dan Beard he said, "Gorky made an awful mistake, Dan. He might as well have come over here in his shirt-tail."

an hour later, perhaps, I met Clemens coming out of No. 21. He asked:

"Have you heard the news about San Francisco?"

I said I had heard a rumor of an earthquake, and had seen an extra with big scare-heads; but I supposed the matter was exaggerated.

"No," he said, "I am afraid it isn't. We have just had a telephone message that it is even worse than at first reported. A great fire is consuming the city. Come along to the news-stand and we'll see if there is a later edition."

We walked to Sixth Avenue and Eighth Street and got some fresh extras. The news was indeed worse than at first reported. San Francisco was going to destruction. Clemens was moved deeply, and began to recall this old friend and that whose lives and property might be in danger. He spoke of Joe Goodman and the Gillis families, and pictured conditions in the perishing city.

CCXLII

MARK TWAIN'S GOOD-BY TO THE PLATFORM

IT was on April 19, 1906, the day following the great earthquake, that Mark Twain gave a "Farewell Lecture" at Carnegie Hall for the benefit of the Robert Fulton Memorial Association. Some weeks earlier Gen. Frederick D. Grant, its president, had proposed to pay one thousand dollars for a Mark Twain lecture; but Clemens had replied that he was permanently out of the field, and would never again address any audience that had to pay to hear him.

"I always expect to talk as long as I can get people to listen to me," he said, "but I never again expect to charge for it." Later came one of his inspirations, and he wrote: "I will lecture for one thousand dollars, on one condition: that it will be understood to be my farewell lecture, and that I may contribute the thousand dollars to the Fulton Association."

It was a suggestion not to be discouraged, and the bills and notices, "Mark Twain's Farewell Lecture," were published without delay.

I first heard of the matter one afternoon when General Grant had called. Clemens came into the study where I was working; he often wandered in and out—sometimes without a word, sometimes to relieve himself concerning things in general. But this time he suddenly chilled me by saying:

"I'm going to deliver my farewell lecture, and I want you to appear on the stage and help me."

I feebly expressed my pleasure at the prospect. Then he said:

"I am going to lecture on Fulton—on the story of his achievements. It will be a burlesque, of course, and I

MARK TWAIN

Will Deliver His Farewell Lecture

CARNEGIE HALL

APRIL 19TH, 1906

FOR THE BENEFIT OF

THE

Robert Fulton Memorial Association

¶MILITARY ORGANIZATION OLD GUARD IN FULL DRESS UNIFORM WILL BE PRESENT

¶MUSIC BY OLD GUARD BAND

¶TICKETS AND BOXES ON SALE AT CARNEGIE HALL AND WALDORF-ASTORIA

SEATS $1.50, $1.00, 50 CENTS

HANDBILL OF MARK TWAIN'S "FAREWELL LECTURE"

am going to pretend to forget my facts, and I want you to sit there in a chair. Now and then, when I seem to get stuck, I'll lean over and pretend to ask you something, and I want you to pretend to prompt me. You don't need to laugh, or to pretend to be assisting in the performance any more than just that."

It was not likely that I should laugh. I had a sinking feeling in the cardiac region which does not go with mirth. It did not for the moment occur to me that the stage would be filled with eminent citizens and vice-presidents, and I had a vision of myself sitting there alone in the chair in that wide emptiness, with the chief performer directing attention to me every other moment or so, for perhaps an hour. Let me hurry on to say that it did not happen. I dare say he realized my unfitness for the work, and the far greater appropriateness of conferring the honor on General Grant, for in the end he gave him the assignment, to my immeasurable relief.

It was a magnificent occasion. That spacious hall was hung with bunting, the stage was banked and festooned with decoration of every sort. General Grant, surrounded by his splendidly uniformed staff, sat in the foreground, and behind was ranged a levee of foremost citizens of the republic. The band played "America" as Mark Twain entered, and the great audience rose and roared out its welcome. Some of those who knew him best had hoped that on this occasion of his last lecture he would tell of that first appearance in San Francisco, forty years before, when his fortunes had hung in the balance. Perhaps he did not think of it, and no one had had the courage to suggest it. At all events, he did a different thing. He began by making a strong plea for the smitten city where the flames were still raging, urging prompt help for those who had lost not only their homes, but the last shred of their belongings and their means of livelihood. Then followed his farcical history of Fulton, with General Grant to make the responses, and presently he drifted into the kind of lecture he had given so often in his long trip around the world—retelling the tales which had won him fortune and friends in many lands.

MARK TWAIN

I do not know whether the entertainment was long or short. I think few took account of time. To a letter of inquiry as to how long the entertainment would last, he had replied:

I cannot say for sure. It is my custom to keep on talking till I get the audience cowed. Sometimes it takes an hour and fifteen minutes, sometimes I can do it in an hour.

There was no indication at any time that the audience was cowed. The house was packed, and the applause was so recurrent and continuous that often his voice was lost to those in its remoter corners. It did not matter. The tales were familiar to his hearers; merely to see Mark Twain, in his old age and in that splendid setting, relating them was enough. The audience realized that it was witnessing the close of a heroic chapter in a unique career.

A PAGE OF MARK TWAIN'S LECTURE NOTES

CCXLIII

AN INVESTMENT IN REDDING

MANY of the less important happenings seem worth remembering now. Among them was the sale, at the Nast auction, of the Mark Twain letters, already mentioned. The fact that these letters brought higher prices than any others offered in this sale was gratifying. Roosevelt, Grant, and even Lincoln items were sold; but the Mark Twain letters led the list. One of them sold for forty-three dollars, which was said to be the highest price ever paid for the letter of a living man. It was the letter written in 1877, quoted earlier in this work, in which Clemens proposed the lecture tour to Nast. None of the Clemens-Nast letters brought less than twenty-seven dollars, and some of them were very brief. It was a new measurement of public sentiment. Clemens, when he heard of it, said:

"I can't rise to General Grant's lofty place in the estimation of this country; but it is a deep satisfaction to me to know that when it comes to letter-writing he can't sit in the front seat along with me. That forty-three-dollar letter ought to be worth as much as eighty-six dollars after I'm dead."

A perpetual string of callers came to 21 Fifth Avenue, and it kept the secretary busy explaining to most of them why Mark Twain could not entertain their propositions, or listen to their complaints, or allow them to express in person their views on public questions. He did see a great many of what might be called the milder type—

persons who were evidently sincere and not too heavily
freighted with eloquence. Of these there came one day
a very gentle-spoken woman who had promised that she
would stay but a moment, and say no more than a few
words, if only she might sit face to face with the great
man. It was in the morning hour before the dictations,
and he received her, quite correctly clad in his beautiful
dressing-robe and propped against his pillows. She kept
her contract to the letter; but when she rose to go she
said, in a voice of deepest reverence:

"May I kiss your hand?"

It was a delicate situation, and might easily have been
made ludicrous. Denial would have hurt her. As it was,
he lifted his hand, a small, exquisite hand it was, with
the gentle dignity and poise of a king, and she touched
her lips to it with what was certainly adoration. Then,
as she went, she said:

"How God must love you!"

"I hope so," he said, softly, and he did not even smile;
but after she had gone he could not help saying, in a quaint,
half-pathetic voice:

"I guess she hasn't heard of our strained relations."

Sitting in that royal bed, clad in that rich fashion, he
easily conveyed the impression of royalty, and watching
him through those marvelous mornings he seemed never
less than a king, as indeed he was—the king of a realm
without national boundaries. Some of those nearest to
him fell naturally into the habit of referring to him as
"the King," and in time the title crept out of the immediate household and was taken up by others who
loved him.

He had been more than once photographed in his bed;
but it was by those who had come and gone in a brief
time, with little chance to study his natural attitudes.
I had acquired some knowledge of the camera, and I
obtained his permission to let me photograph him—a

permission he seldom denied to any one. We had no dictations on Saturdays, and I took the pictures on one of these holiday mornings. He was so patient and tractable, and so natural in every attitude, that it was a delight to make the negatives. I was afraid he would become impatient, and made fewer exposures than I might otherwise have done. I think he expected very little from this amateur performance; but, by that happy element of accident which plays so large a part in photographic success, the results were better than I had hoped for. When I brought him the prints, a few days later, he expressed pleasure and asked, "Why didn't you make more?"

Among them was one in an attitude which had grown so familiar to us, that of leaning over to get his pipe from the smoking-table, and this seemed to give him particular satisfaction. It being a holiday, he had not donned his dressing-gown, which on the whole was well for the photographic result. He spoke of other pictures that had been made of him, especially denouncing one photograph, taken some twenty years before by Sarony, a picture, as he said, of a gorilla in an overcoat, which the papers and magazines had insisted on using ever since.

"Sarony was as enthusiastic about wild animals as he was about photography, and when Du Chaillu brought over the first gorilla he sent for me to look at it and see if our genealogy was straight. I said it was, and Sarony was so excited that I had recognized the resemblance between us, that he wanted to make it more complete, so he borrowed my overcoat and put it on the gorilla and photographed it, and spread that picture out over the world as mine. It turns up every week in some newspaper or magazine; but it's not my favorite; I have tried to get it suppressed."

Mark Twain made his first investment in Redding that spring. I had located there the autumn before, and bought a vacant old house, with a few acres of land, at what seemed a modest price. I was naturally enthusiastic over the bargain, and the beauty and salubrity of the situation. His interest was aroused, and when he learned that there was a place adjoining, equally reasonable and perhaps even more attractive, he suggested immediately that I buy it for him; and he wanted to write a check then for the purchase price, for fear the opportunity might be lost. I think there was then no purpose in his mind of building a country home; but he foresaw that such a site, at no great distance from New York, would become more valuable, and he had plenty of idle means. The purchase was made without difficulty—a tract of seventy-five acres, to which presently was added another tract of one hundred and ten acres, and subsequently still other parcels of land, to complete the ownership of the hilltop, for it was not long until he had conceived the idea of a home. He was getting weary of the heavy pressure of city life. He craved the retirement of solitude—one not too far from the maelstrom, so that he might mingle with it now and then when he chose. The country home would not be begun for another year yet, but the purpose of it was already in the air. No one of the family had at this time seen the location.

CCXLIV

TRAITS AND PHILOSOPHIES

I BROUGHT to the dictation one morning the Omar Khayyam card which Twichell had written him so long ago; I had found it among the letters. It furnished him a subject for that morning. He said:

How strange there was a time when I had never heard of Omar Khayyam! When that card arrived I had already read the dozen quatrains or so in the morning paper, and was still steeped in the ecstasy of delight which they occasioned. No poem had ever given me so much pleasure before, and none has given me so much pleasure since. It is the only poem I have ever carried about with me. It has not been from under my hand all these years.

He had no general fondness for poetry; but many poems appealed to him, and on occasion he liked to read them aloud. Once, during the dictation, some verses were sent up by a young authoress who was waiting below for his verdict. The lines pictured a phase of negro life, and she wished to know if he thought them worthy of being read at some Tuskegee ceremony. He did not fancy the idea of attending to the matter just then and said:

"Tell her she can read it. She has my permission. She may commit any crime she wishes in my name."

It was urged that the verses were of high merit and the author a very charming young lady.

"I'm very glad," he said, "and I am glad the Lord

made her; I hope He will make some more just like her.
I don't always approve of His handiwork, but in this case
I do."

Then suddenly he added:

"Well, let me see it—no time like the present to get
rid of these things."

He took the manuscript and gave such a rendition of
those really fine verses as I believe could not be improved
upon. We were held breathless by his dramatic fervor
and power. He returned a message to that young as-
pirant that must have made her heart sing. When the
dictation had ended that day, I mentioned his dramatic
gift.

"Yes," he said, "it is a gift, I suppose, like spelling and
punctuation and smoking. I seem to have inherited all
those." Continuing, he spoke of inherited traits in general.

"There was Paige," he said; "an ignorant man who
could not make a machine himself that would stand up,
nor draw the working plans for one; but he invented the
eighteen thousand details of the most wonderful machine
the world has ever known. He watched over the expert
draftsmen, and superintended the building of that marvel.
Pratt & Whitney built it; but it was Paige's machine,
nevertheless—the child of his marvelous gift. We don't
create any of our traits; we inherit all of them. They
have come down to us from what we impudently call the
lower animals. Man is the last expression, and combines
every attribute of the animal tribes that preceded him.
One or two conspicuous traits distinguish each family
of animals from the others, and those one or two traits
are found in every member of each family, and are so
prominent as to eternally and unchangeably establish
the character of that branch of the animal world. In
these cases we concede that the several temperaments
constitute a law of God, a command of God, and that

whatsoever is done in obedience to that law is blameless. Man, in his evolution, inherited the whole sum of these numerous traits, and with each trait its share of the law of God. He widely differs from them in this: that he possesses not a single characteristic that is equally prominent in each member of his race. You can say the house-fly is limitlessly brave, and in saying it you describe the whole house-fly tribe; you can say the rabbit is limitlessly timid, and by the phrase you describe the whole rabbit tribe; you can say the spider and the tiger are limitlessly murderous, and by that phrase you describe the whole spider and tiger tribes; you can say the lamb is limitlessly innocent and sweet and gentle, and by that phrase you describe all the lambs. There is hardly a creature that you cannot definitely and satisfactorily describe by one single trait—except man. Men are not all cowards like the rabbit, nor all brave like the house-fly, nor all sweet and innocent and gentle like the lamb, nor all murderous like the spider and the tiger and the wasp, nor all thieves like the fox and the bluejay, nor all vain like the peacock, nor all frisky like the monkey. These things are all in him somewhere, and they develop according to the proportion of each he received in his allotment. We describe a man by his vicious traits and condemn him; or by his fine traits and gifts, and praise him and accord him high merit for their possession. It is comical. He did not invent these things; he did not stock himself with them. God conferred them upon him in the first instant of creation. They constitute the law, and he could not escape obedience to the decree any more than Paige could have built the type-setter he invented, or the Pratt & Whitney machinists could have invented the machine which they built."

He liked to stride up and down, smoking as he talked, and generally his words were slowly measured, with varying pauses between them. He halted in the midst of his march, and without a suggestion of a smile added:

"What an amusing creature the human being is!"

It is absolutely impossible, of course, to preserve the atmosphere and personality of such talks as this—the delicacies of his speech and manner which carried an ineffable charm. It was difficult, indeed, to record the substance. I did not know shorthand, and I should not have taken notes at such times in any case; but I had trained myself in similar work to preserve, with a fair degree of accuracy, the form of phrase, and to some extent its wording, if I could get hold of pencil and paper soon enough afterward. In time I acquired a sort of phonographic faculty; though it always seemed to me that the bouquet, the subtleness of speech, was lacking in the result. Sometimes, indeed, he would dictate next morning the substance of these experimental reflections; or I would find among his papers memoranda and fragmentary manuscripts where he had set them down himself, either before or after he had tried them verbally. In these cases I have not hesitated to amend my notes where it seemed to lend reality to his utterance, though, even so, there is always lacking—and must be—the wonder of his personality.

CCXLV

A NUMBER of dictations of this period were about Susy, her childhood, and the biography she had `written of him, most of which he included in his chapters. More than once after such dictations he reproached himself bitterly for the misfortunes of his house. He consoled himself a little by saying that Susy had died at the right time, in the flower of youth and happiness; but he blamed himself for the lack of those things which might have made her childhood still more bright. Once he spoke of the biography she had begun, and added:

"Oh, I wish I had paid more attention to that little girl's work! If I had only encouraged her now and then, what it would have meant to her, and what a beautiful thing it would have been to have had her story of me told in her own way, year after year! If I had shown her that I cared, she might have gone on with it. We are always too busy for our children; we never give them the time nor the interest they deserve. We lavish gifts upon them; but the most precious gift—our personal association, which means so much to them—we give grudgingly and throw it away on those who care for it so little." Then, after a moment of silence: "But we are repaid for it at last. There comes a time when we want their company and their interest. We want it more than anything in the world, and we are likely to be starved for it, just as they were starved so long ago. There is no appreciation of my books that is so precious to me as appreciation

1299

from my children. Theirs is the praise we want, and the praise we are least likely to get."

His moods of remorse seemed to overwhelm him at times. He spoke of Henry's death and little Langdon's, and charged himself with both. He declared that for years he had filled Mrs. Clemens's life with privations, that the sorrow of Susy's death had hastened her own end. How darkly he painted it! One saw the jester, who for forty years had been making the world laugh, performing always before a background of tragedy.

But such moods were evanescent. He was oftener gay than somber. One morning before we settled down to work he related with apparent joy how he had made a failure of story-telling at a party the night before. An artist had told him a yarn, he said, which he had considered the most amusing thing in the world. But he had not been satisfied with it, and had attempted to improve on it at the party. He had told it with what he considered the nicest elaboration of detail and artistic effect, and when he had concluded and expected applause, only a sickening silence had followed.

"A crowd like that can make a good deal of silence when they combine," he said, "and it probably lasted as long as ten seconds, because it seemed an hour and a half. Then a lady said, with evident feeling, 'Lord, how pathetic!' For a moment I was stupefied. Then the fountains of my great deeps were broken up, and I rained laughter for forty days and forty nights during as much as three minutes. By that time I realized it was my fault. I had overdone the thing. I started in to deceive them with elaborate burlesque pathos, in order to magnify the humorous explosion at the end; but I had constructed such a fog of pathos that when I got to the humor you couldn't find it."

He was likely to begin the morning with some such incident which perhaps he did not think worth while to include in his dictations, and sometimes he interrupted his dictations to relate something aside, or to outline some plan or scheme which his thought had suggested.

Once, when he was telling of a magazine he had proposed to start, the *Back Number*, which was to contain reprints of exciting events from history—newspaper gleanings—eye-witness narrations, which he said never lost their freshness of interest—he suddenly interrupted himself to propose that we start such a magazine in the near future—he to be its publisher and I its editor. I think I assented, and the dictation proceeded, but the scheme disappeared permanently.

He usually had a number of clippings or slips among the many books on the bed beside him from which he proposed to dictate each day, but he seldom could find the one most needed. Once, after a feverishly impatient search for a few moments, he invited Miss Hobby to leave the room temporarily, so, as he said, that he might swear. He got up and we began to explore the bed, his profanity increasing amazingly with each moment. It was an enormously large bed, and he began to disparage the size of it.

"One could *lose a dog* in this bed," he declared.

Finally I suggested that he turn over the clipping which he had in his hand. He did so, and it proved to be the one he wanted. Its discovery was followed by a period of explosions, only half suppressed as to volume. Then he said:

"There ought to be a room in this house to swear in. It's dangerous to have to repress an emotion like that."

A moment later, when Miss Hobby returned, he was serene and happy again. He was usually gentle during the dictations, and patient with those around him—remarkably so, I thought, as a rule. But there were moments that involved risk. He had requested me to interrupt his dictation at any time that I found him repeating or contradicting himself, or misstating some fact known to me. At first I hesitated to do this, and cautiously mentioned the matter when he had finished. Then he was likely to say:

"Why didn't you stop me? Why did you let me go on making a jackass of myself when you could have saved me?"

So then I used to take the risk of getting struck by lightning, and nearly always stopped him at the time. But if it happened that I upset his thought the thunder-bolt was apt to fly. He would say:

"Now you've knocked everything out of my head."

Then, of course, I would apologize and say I was sorry, which would rectify matters, though half an hour later it might happen again. I became lightning-proof at last; also I learned better to select the psychological mo-ment for the correction.

There was a humorous complexion to the dictations which perhaps I have not conveyed to the reader at all; humor was his natural breath and life, and was not wholly absent in his most somber intervals.

But poetry was there as well. His presence was full of it: the grandeur of his figure; the grace of his movement; the music of his measured speech. Sometimes there were long pauses when he was wandering in distant valleys of thought and did not speak at all. At such times he had a habit of folding and refolding the sleeve of his dressing-gown around his wrist, regarding it intent-ly, as it seemed. His hands were so fair and shapely; the palms and finger-tips as pink as those of a child. Then when he spoke he was likely to fling back his great, white mane, his eyes half closed yet showing a gleam of fire between the lids, his clenched fist lifted, or his index-finger pointing, to give force and meaning to his words. I cannot recall the picture too often, or remind myself too frequently how precious it was to be there, and to see him and to hear him. I do not know why I have not said before that he smoked continually during these dictations—probably as an aid to thought—though he smoked at most other times, for that matter. His cigars were of that delicious fragrance which characterizes domestic tobacco; but I had learned early to take refuge in another brand when he offered me one. They were black and strong and inexpensive, and it was only his early training in the printing-office and on the river that had seasoned him to tobacco of that temper. Rich, admiring friends used to send him quantities of expensive imported cigars; but he seldom touched them, and they crumbled away or were smoked by visitors. Once, to a minister who proposed to send him something very special, he wrote:

I should accept your hospitable offer at once but for the fact that I couldn't do it and remain honest. That is to say, if I allowed you to send me what you believed to be good cigars it would distinctly mean that I meant to smoke them, whereas I should do nothing of the kind. I know a good cigar better than you do, for I have had 60 years' experience.

No, that is not what I mean; I mean I know a bad cigar better than anybody else. I judge by the price only; if it costs above 5 cents I know it to be either foreign or half foreign & unsmokable—by me. I have many boxes of Havana cigars, of all prices from 20 cents apiece up to $1.66 apiece; I bought none of them, they were all presents; they are an accumulation of several years. I have never smoked one of them & never shall; I work them off on the visitor. You shall have a chance when you come.

He smoked a pipe a good deal, and he preferred it to be old and violent; and once, when he had bought a new, expensive English brier-root he regarded it doubtfully for a time, and then handed it over to me, saying:

"I'd like to have you smoke that a year or two, and when it gets so you can't stand it, maybe it will suit me."

I am happy to add that subsequently he presented me with the pipe altogether, for it apparently never seemed to get qualified for his taste, perhaps because the tobacco used was too mild.

One day, after the dictation, word was brought up that a newspaper man was down-stairs who wished to see him concerning a report that Chauncey Depew was to resign his Senatorial seat and Mark Twain was to be nominated in his place. The fancy of this appealed to him, and the reporter was allowed to come up. He was a young man, and seemed rather nervous, and did not wish to state where the report had originated. His chief anxiety was apparently to have Mark Twain's comment on the matter. Clemens said very little at the time. He did not wish to be a Senator; he was too busy just now dictating biography, and added that he didn't think he would care for the job, anyway. When the reporter was gone, however, certain humorous possibilities developed. The Senatorship would be a stepping-stone to the Presidency, and with the combination of humorist, socialist, and peace-patriot in the Presidential chair the nation could expect an interesting time. Nothing further came of the matter. There was no such report. The young newspaper man had invented the whole idea to get a "story" out of Mark Twain. The item as printed next day invited a good deal of comment, and *Collier's Weekly* made it a text for an editorial on his mental vigor and general fitness for the place.

If it happened that he had no particular engagement for the afternoon, he liked to walk out, especially when the pleasant weather came. Sometimes we walked up Fifth Avenue, and I must admit that for a good while I could not get rid of a feeling of self-consciousness, for most people turned to look, though I was fully aware that

I did not in the least come into their scope of vision.
They saw only Mark Twain. The feeling was a more
comfortable one at The Players, where we sometimes
went for luncheon, for the acquaintance there and the
democracy of that institution had a tendency to eliminate contrasts and incongruities. We sat at the Round
Table among those good fellows who were always so glad
to welcome him.

Once we went to the "Music Master," that tender play
of Charles Klein's, given by that matchless interpreter,
David Warfield. Clemens was fascinated, and said more
than once:

"It is as permanent as 'Rip Van Winkle.' Warfield,
like Jefferson, can go on playing it all his life."

We went behind when it was over, and I could see that
Warfield glowed with Mark Twain's unstinted approval.
Later, when I saw him at The Players, he declared that
no former compliment had ever made him so happy.

There were some billiard games going on between the
champions Hoppe and Sutton, at the Madison Square
Garden, and Clemens, with his eager fondness for the
sport, was anxious to attend them. He did not like to go
anywhere alone, and one evening he invited me to ac-
company him. Just as he stepped into the auditorium
there was a vigorous round of applause. The players
stopped, somewhat puzzled, for no especially brilliant shot
had been made. Then they caught the figure of Mark
Twain and realized that the game, for the moment, was
not the chief attraction. The audience applauded again,
and waved their handkerchiefs. Such a tribute is not
often paid to a private citizen.

Clemens had a great admiration for the young champion Hoppe, which the billiardist's extreme youth and
brilliancy invited, and he watched his game with intense
eagerness. When it was over the referee said a few words
and invited Mark Twain to speak. He rose and told

them a story—probably invented on the instant. He said:

"Once in Nevada I dropped into a billiard-room casually, and picked up a cue and began to knock the balls around. The proprietor, who was a red-haired man, with such hair as I have never seen anywhere except on a torch, asked me if I would like to play. I said, 'Yes.' He said, 'Knock the balls around a little and let me see how you can shoot.' So I knocked them around, and thought I was doing pretty well, when he said, 'That's all right; I'll play you left-handed.' It hurt my pride, but I played him. We banked for the shot and he won it. Then he commenced to play, and I commenced to chalk my cue to get ready to play, and he went on playing, and I went on chalking my cue; and he played and I chalked all through that game. When he had run his string out I said:

"'That's wonderful! perfectly wonderful! If you can play that way left-handed what could you do right-handed?'

"'Couldn't do anything,' he said. 'I'm a left-handed man.'"

How it delighted them! I think it was the last speech of any sort he made that season. A week or two later he went to Dublin, New Hampshire, for the summer—this time to the Upton House, which had been engaged a year before, the Copley Greene place being now occupied by its owner.

CCXLVI

THE SECOND SUMMER AT DUBLIN

THE Upton House stands on the edge of a beautiful beech forest some two or three miles from Dublin, just under Monadnock—a good way up the slope. It is a handsome, roomy frame-house, and has a long colonnaded veranda overlooking one of the most beautiful landscape visions on the planet: lake, forest, hill, and a far range of blue mountains—all the handiwork of God is there. I had seen these things in paintings, but I had not dreamed that such a view really existed. The immediate foreground was a grassy slope, with ancient, blooming apple-trees; and just at the right hand Monadnock rose, superb and lofty, sloping down to the panorama below that stretched away, taking on an ever deeper blue, until it reached that remote range on which the sky rested and the world seemed to end. It was a masterpiece of the Greater Mind, and of the highest order, perhaps, for it had in it nothing of the touch of man. A church spire glinted here and there, but there was never a bit of field, or stone wall, or cultivated land. It was lonely; it was unfriendly; it cared nothing whatever for humankind; it was as if God, after creating all the world, had wrought His masterwork here, and had been so engrossed with the beauty of it that He had forgotten to give it a soul. In a sense this was true, for He had not made the place suitable for the habitation of men. It lacked the human touch, the human interest, and I could never quite believe in its reality.

The time of arrival heightened this first impression. It was mid-May and the lilacs were prodigally in bloom; but the bright sunlight was chill and unnatural, and there was a west wind that laid the grass flat and moaned through the house, and continued as steadily as if it must never stop from year's end to year's end. It seemed a spectral land, a place of supernatural beauty. Warm, still, languorous days would come, but that first feeling of unreality would remain permanent. I believe Jean Clemens was the only one who ever really loved the place. Something about it appealed to her elemental side and blended with her melancholy moods. She dressed always in white, and she was tall and pale and classically beautiful, and she was often silent, like a spirit. She had a little retreat for herself farther up the mountain-side, and spent most of her days there wood-carving, which was her chief diversion.

Clara Clemens did not come to the place at all. She was not yet strong, and went to Norfolk, Connecticut, where she could still be in quiet retirement and have her physician's care. Miss Hobby came, and on the 21st of May the dictations were resumed. We began in his bedroom, as before, but the feeling there was depressing—the absence of the great carved bed and other furnishings, which had been so much a part of the picture, was felt by all of us. Nothing of the old luxury and richness was there. It was a summer-furnished place, handsome but with the customary bareness. At the end of this first session he dressed in his snowy flannels, which he had adopted in the place of linen for summer wear, and we descended to the veranda and looked out over that wide, wonderful expanse of scenery.

"I think I shall like it," he said, "when I get acquainted with it, and get it classified and labeled, and I think we'll do our dictating out here hereafter. It ought to be an inspiring place."

So the dictations were transferred to the long veranda, and he was generally ready for them, a white figure pacing up and down before that panoramic background. During the earlier, cooler weeks he usually continued walking with measured step during the dictations, pausing now and then to look across the far-lying horizon. When it stormed we moved into the great living-room, where at one end there was a fireplace with blazing logs, and at the other the orchestrelle, which had once more been freighted up those mountain heights for the comfort of its harmonies. Sometimes, when the wind and rain were beating outside, and he was striding up and down the long room within, with only the blurred shapes of mountains and trees outlined through the trailing rain, the feeling of the unreality became so strong that it was hard to believe that somewhere down below, beyond the rain and the woods, there was a literal world—a commonplace world, where the ordinary things of life were going on in the usual way. When the dictation finished early, there would be music—the music that he loved most—Beethoven's symphonies, or the Schubert impromptu, or the nocturne by Chopin.[1] It is easy to understand that this carried one a remove farther from the customary things of life. It was a setting far out of the usual, though it became that unique white figure and his occupation. In my notes, made from day to day, I find that I have set down more than once an impression of the curious unreality of the place and its surroundings, which would show that it was not a mere passing fancy.

I had lodgings in the village, and drove out mornings for the dictations, but often came out again afoot on pleasant afternoons; for he was not much occupied with social matters, and there was opportunity for quiet, informing interviews. There was a woods path to the

---

[1] Schubert, Op. 142, No. 2; Chopin, Op. 37, No. 2.

Upton place, and it was a walk through a fairyland. A part of the way was through such a growth of beech timber as I have never seen elsewhere: tall, straight, mottled trees with an undergrowth of laurel, the sunlight sifting through; one found it easy to expect there story-book ladies, wearing crowns and green mantles, riding on white palfreys. Then came a more open way, an abandoned grass-grown road full of sunlight and perfume, and this led to a dim, religious place, a natural cathedral, where the columns were stately pine-trees branching and meeting at the top: a veritable temple in which it always seemed that music was about to play. You crossed a brook and climbed a little hill, and pushed through a hedge into a place more open, and the house stood there among the trees.

The days drifted along, one a good deal like another, except, as the summer deepened, the weather became warmer, the foliage changed, a drowsy haze gathered along the valleys and on the mountain-side. He sat more often now in a large rocking-chair, and generally seemed to be looking through half-closed lids toward the Monadnock heights, that were always changing in aspect—in color and in form—as cloud shapes drifted by or gathered in those lofty hollows. White and yellow butterflies hovered over the grass, and there were some curious, large black ants—the largest I have ever seen and quite harmless—that would slip in and out of the cracks on the veranda floor, wholly undisturbed by us. Now and then a light flutter of wind would come murmuring up from the trees below, and when the apple-bloom was falling there would be a whirl of white and pink petals that seemed a cloud of smaller butterflies.

On June 1st I find in my note-book this entry:

Warm and pleasant. The dictation about Grant continues; a great privilege to hear this foremost man of letters review his associations with that foremost man of arms. He remained seated to-day, dressed in white as usual, a large yellow pansy in his buttonhole, his white hair ruffled by the breeze. He wears his worn morocco slippers with black hose; sits in the rocker, smoking and looking out over the hazy hills, delivering his sentences with a measured accuracy that seldom calls for change. He is speaking just now of a Grant dinner which he attended where Depew spoke. One is impressed with the thought that we are looking at and listening to the war-worn veteran of a thousand dinners—the honored guest of many; an honored figure of all. Earlier, when he had been chastising some old offender, he added, "However, he's dead, and I forgive him." Then, after a moment's reflection, "No; strike that last sentence out." When we laughed, he added, "We can't forgive him yet."

A few days later—it was June 4th, the day before the second anniversary of the death of Mrs. Clemens—we found him at first in excellent humor from the long dictation of the day before. Then his mind reverted to the tragedy of the season, and he began trying to tell of it. It was hard work. He walked back and forth in the soft sunlight, saying almost nothing. He gave it up at last, remarking, "We will not work to-morrow." So we went away.

He did not dictate on the 5th or the 6th, but on the 7th he resumed the story of Mrs. Clemens's last days at Florence. The weather had changed: the sunlight and warmth had all gone; a chill, penetrating mist was on the mountains; Monadnock was blotted out. We expected him to go to the fire, but evidently he could not bear being shut in with that subject in his mind. A black cape was brought out and thrown about his shoulders, which seemed to fit exactly into the somberness of the picture. For two hours or more we sat there in the gloom and chill, while he paced up and down, detailing as graphically as might be that final chapter in the life of the woman he had loved.

It is hardly necessary to say that beyond the dictation Clemens did very little literary work during these months. He had brought his "manuscript trunk" as usual, thinking, perhaps, to finish the "microbe" story and other of the uncompleted things; but the dictation gave him sufficient mental exercise, and he did no more than look over his "stock in trade," as he called it, and incorporate a few of the finished manuscripts into "autobiography." Among these were the notes of his trip down the Rhone, made in 1891, and the old Stormfield story, which he had been treasuring and suppressing so long. He wrote Howells in June:

The dictating goes lazily and pleasantly on. With intervals. I find that I've been at it, off & on, nearly two hours for 155 days since January 9. To be exact, I've dictated 75 hours in 80 days & loafed 75 days. I've added 60,000 words in the month that I've been here; which indicates that I've dictated during 20 days of that time—40 hours, at an average of 1,500 words an hour. It's a plenty, & I'm satisfied.

There's a good deal of "fat." I've dictated (from January 9) 210,000 words, & the "fat" adds about 50,000 more.

The "fat" is old pigeonholed things of the years gone by which I or editors didn't das't to print. For instance, I am dumping in the little old book which I read to you in Hartford about 30 years ago & which you said "publish & ask Dean Stanley to furnish an introduction; he'll do it" (*Captain Stormfield's Visit to Heaven*). It reads quite to suit me without altering a word now that it isn't to see print until I am dead.

To-morrow I mean to dictate a chapter which will get my heirs & assigns burned alive if they venture to print it this side of A.D. 2006—which I judge they won't. There'll be lots of such chapters if I live 3 or 4 years longer. The edition of A.D. 2006 will make a stir when it comes out. I shall be hovering around taking notice, along with other dead pals. You are invited.

The chapter which was to invite death at the stake for his successors was naturally one of religious heresies—

a violent attack on the orthodox, scriptural God, but really an expression of the highest reverence for the God which, as he said, had created the earth and sky and the music of the constellations. Mark Twain once expressed himself concerning reverence and the lack of it:

"I was never consciously and purposely irreverent in my life, yet one person or another is always charging me with a lack of reverence. Reverence for what—for whom? Who is to decide what ought to command my reverence—my neighbor or I? I think I ought to do the electing myself. The Mohammedan reveres Mohammed—it is his privilege; the Christian doesn't—apparently that is his privilege; the account is square enough. They haven't any right to complain of the other, yet they do complain of each other, and that is where the unfairness comes in. Each says that the other is irreverent, and both are mistaken, for manifestly you can't have reverence for a thing that doesn't command it. If you could do that you could digest what you haven't eaten, and do other miracles and get a reputation."

He was not reading many books at this time—he was inclined rather to be lazy, as he said, and to loaf during the afternoons; but I remember that he read aloud *After the Wedding* and *The Mother*—those two beautiful word-pictures by Howells—which he declared sounded the depths of humanity with a deep-sea lead. Also he read a book by William Allen White, *In Our Town*, a collection of tales that he found most admirable. I think he took the trouble to send White a personal, hand-written letter concerning them, although, with the habit of dictation, he had begun, as he said, to "loathe the use of the pen."

There were usually some sort of mild social affairs going on in the neighborhood, luncheons and afternoon gatherings like those of the previous year, though he seems to have attended fewer of them, for he did not often leave the house. Once, at least, he assisted in an afternoon entertainment at the Dublin Club, where he introduced his invention of the art of making an impromptu speech, and was assisted in its demonstration by George de Forest Brush and Joseph Lindon Smith, to the very great amusement of a crowd of summer visitors. The "art" consisted mainly of having on hand a few reliable anecdotes and a set formula which would lead directly to them from any given subject.

Twice or more he collected the children of the neighborhood for charades and rehearsed them, and took part in the performance, as in the Hartford days. Sometimes he drove out or took an extended walk. But these things were seldom.

Now and then during the summer he made a trip to New York of a semi-business nature, usually going by the way of Fairhaven, where he would visit for a few days, journeying the rest of the way in Mr. Rogers's yacht. Once they made a cruise of considerable length to Bar Harbor and elsewhere. Here is an amusing letter which he wrote to Mrs. Rogers after such a visit:

DEAR MRS. ROGERS,—In packing my things in your house yesterday morning I inadvertently put in some articles that was laying around, I thinking about theollogy & not noticing, the way this family does in similar circumstances like these. Two books, Mr. Rogers' brown slippers, & a ham. I thought it was ourn, it looks like one we used to have. I am very sorry it happened, but it sha'n't occur again & don't you worry. He will temper the wind to the shorn lamb & I will send some of the things back anyway if there is some that won't keep.

CCXLVII

IN time Mark Twain became very lonely in Dublin. After the brilliant winter the contrast was too great. He was not yet ready for exile. In one of his dictations he said:

The skies are enchantingly blue. The world is a dazzle of sunshine. Monadnock is closer to us than usual by several hundred yards. The vast extent of spreading valley is intensely green—the lakes as intensely blue. And there is a new horizon, a remoter one than we have known before, for beyond the mighty half-circle of hazy mountains that form the usual frame of the picture rise certain shadowy great domes that are unfamiliar to our eyes. . . .

But there is a defect—only one, but it is a defect which almost entitles it to be spelled with a capital D. This is the defect of loneliness. We have not a single neighbor who is a neighbor. Nobody lives within two miles of us except Franklin MacVeagh, and he is the farthest off of any, because he is in Europe. . . .

I feel for Adam and Eve now, for I know how it was with them. I am existing, broken-hearted, in a Garden of Eden. . The Garden of Eden I now know was an unendurable solitude. I know that the advent of the serpent was a welcome change— anything for society. . . .

I never rose to the full appreciation of the utter solitude of this place until a symbol of it—a compact and visible allegory of it—furnished me the lacking lift three days ago. I was standing alone on this veranda, in the late afternoon, mourning over the stillness, the far-spreading, beautiful desolation, and the absence of visible life, when a couple of shapely and graceful deer came sauntering across the grounds and stopped, and at their leisure impudently looked me over, as if they had an idea of buying me as bric-à-brac. Then they seemed to conclude that they could do better for less money elsewhere, and they sauntered indolently away and disappeared among the trees. It sized up this solitude. It is so complete, so perfect, that even the wild animals are satisfied with it. Those dainty creatures were not in the least degree afraid of me.

This was no more than a mood—though real enough while it lasted—somber, and in its way regal. It was the loneliness of a king—King Lear. Yet he returned gladly enough to solitude after each absence.

It was just before one of his departures that I made another set of pictures of him, this time on the colonnaded veranda, where his figure had become so familiar. He had determined to have his hair cut when he reached New York, and I was anxious to get the pictures before this happened. When the proofs came—seven of them— he arranged them as a series to illustrate what he called "The Progress of a Moral Purpose." He ordered a number of sets of this series, and he wrote a legend on each photograph, numbering them from 1 to 7, laying each set in a sheet of letter-paper which formed a sort of wrapper, on which was written:

This series of 7 photographs registers with scientific precision, stage by stage, the progress of a moral purpose through the mind of the human race's Oldest Friend.   S. L. C.

He added a personal inscription, and sent one to each of his more intimate friends. One of the pictures amused him more than the others, because during the exposure a little kitten, unnoticed, had walked into it, and paused near his foot. He had never outgrown his love for cats, and he had rented this kitten and two others for the summer from a neighbor. He didn't wish to own them, he said, for then he would have to leave them behind uncared for, so he preferred to rent them and pay sufficiently to insure their subsequent care. These kittens he called Sackcloth and Ashes—Ashes being the joint name of the two that looked exactly alike, and so did not need distinctive titles. Their gambols always amused him. He would stop any time in the midst of dictation to enjoy them. Once, as he was about to enter the screen-door that led into the hall, two of the kittens ran up in front of him and stood waiting. With grave politeness he opened the door, made a low bow, and stepped back and said: "Walk in, gentlemen. I always give precedence to royalty." And the kittens marched in, tails in air. All summer long they played up and down the wide veranda, or chased grasshoppers and butterflies down the clover slope. It was a never-ending amusement to him to see them jump into the air after some insect, miss it and tumble back, and afterward jump up, with a surprised expression and a look of disappointment and disgust. I remember once, when he was walking up and down discussing some very serious subject—and one of the kittens was lying on the veranda asleep—a butterfly came drifting along three feet or so above the floor. The kitten must have got a glimpse of the insect out of the corner of its eye, and perhaps did not altogether realize its action. At all events, it suddenly shot straight up into the air, exactly like a bounding rubber ball, missed the butterfly, fell back on the porch floor with considerable force and with much surprise. Then it sprang to its feet, and, after spitting furiously once or twice, bounded away. Clemens had seen the performance, and it completely took his subject out of his mind. He laughed extravagantly, and evidently cared more for that moment's entertainment than for many philosophies.

In that remote solitude there was one important advantage—there was no procession of human beings with axes to grind, and few curious callers. Occasionally an automobile would find its way out there and make a circuit of the drive, but this happened too seldom to annoy him. Even newspaper men rarely made the long trip from Boston or New York to secure his opinions, and when they came it was by permission and appointment. Newspaper telegrams arrived now and then, asking for a sentiment on some public condition or event, and these he generally answered willingly enough. When the British Premier, Campbell-Bannerman, celebrated his seventieth birthday, the London *Tribune* and the New York *Herald* requested a tribute. He furnished it, for Bannerman was a very old friend. He had known him first at Marienbad in '91, and in Vienna in '98, in daily intercourse, when they had lived at the same hotel. His tribute ran:

To His Excellency the British Premier,—Congratulations, not condolences. Before seventy we are merely respected, at best, and we have to behave all the time, or we lose that asset; but after seventy we are respected, esteemed, admired, revered, and don't have to behave unless we want to. When I first knew you, Honored Sir, one of us was hardly even respected.   Mark Twain.

He had some misgivings concerning the telegram after it had gone, but he did not recall it.

Clemens became the victim of a very clever hoax that summer. One day a friend gave him two examples of the most deliciously illiterate letters, supposed to have been written by a woman who had contributed certain articles of clothing to the San Francisco sufferers, and later wished to recall them because of the protests of her household. He was so sure that the letters were genuine that he included them in his dictations, after reading them aloud with great effect. To tell the truth, they did seem the least bit too well done, too literary in their illiteracy; but his natural optimism refused to admit of any suspicion, and a little later he incorporated one of the Jennie Allen letters in a speech which he made at a Press Club dinner in New York on the subject of simplified spelling—offering it as an example of language with phonetic brevity exercising its supreme function, the direct conveyance of ideas. The letters, in the end, proved to be the clever work of Miss Grace Donworth, who has since published them serially and in book form. Clemens was not at all offended or disturbed by the exposure. He even agreed to aid the young author in securing a publisher, and wrote to Miss Stockbridge, through whom he had originally received the documents:

DEAR MISS STOCKBRIDGE (if she really exists),
    257 Benefit Street (if there is any such place):
    Yes, I should like a copy of that other letter. This whole fake is delightful, & I tremble with fear that you are a fake your-self & that I am your guileless prey. (But never mind, it isn't any matter.)
    Now as to publication—

He set forth his views and promised his assistance when enough of the letters should be completed.

Clemens allowed his name to be included with the list of spelling reformers, but he never employed any of the reforms in his letters or literature. His interest was mainly theoretical, and when he wrote or spoke on the subject his remarks were not likely to be testimonials in its favor. His own theory was that the alphabet needed reform, first of all, so that each letter or character should have one sound, and one sound only; and he offered as a solution of this an adaptation of shorthand. He wrote and dictated in favor of this idea to the end of his life. Once he said:

"Our alphabet is pure insanity. It can hardly spell any large word in the English language with any degree of certainty. Its sillinesses are quite beyond enumeration. English orthography may need reforming and simplifying, but the English alphabet needs it a good many times as much."

He would naturally favor simplicity in anything. I remember him reading, as an example of beautiful English, *The Death of King Arthur*, by Sir Thomas Malory, and his verdict:

"That is one of the most beautiful things ever written in English, and written when we had no vocabulary."

"A vocabulary, then, is sometimes a handicap?"

"It is indeed."

Still I think it was never a handicap with him, but rather the plumage of flight. Sometimes, when just the right word did not come, he would turn his head a little at different angles, as if looking about him for the precise term. He would find it directly, and it was invariably the word needed. Most writers employ, now and again, phrases that do not sharply present the idea—that blur the picture like a poor opera-glass. Mark Twain's English always focused exactly.

"WHAT IS MAN?" AND THE AUTOBIOGRAPHY

CLEMENS decided to publish anonymously, or, rather, to print privately, the *Gospel*, which he had written in Vienna some eight years before and added to from time to time. He arranged with Frank Double-day to take charge of the matter, and the De Vinne Press was engaged to do the work. The book was copyrighted in the name of J. W. Bothwell, the superintendent of the De Vinne company, and two hundred and fifty numbered copies were printed on hand-made paper, to be gradually distributed to intimate friends.[1] A number of the books were sent to newspaper reviewers, and so effectually had he concealed the personality of his work that no critic seems to have suspected the book's author-ship. It was not over-favorably received. It was generally characterized as a clever, and even brilliant, *exposé* of philosophies which were no longer startlingly new. The supremacy of self-interest and "man the ir-responsible machine" are the main features of *What Is Man?* and both of these and all the rest are compre-hended in his wider and more absolute doctrine of that inevitable life-sequence which began with the first created spark. There can be no training of the ideals, "upward

---

[1] In an introductory word (dated February, 1905) the author states that the studies for these papers had been made twenty-five or twenty-seven years before. He probably referred to the Mon-day Evening Club essay, "What Is Happiness?" (February, 1883). See chap. cxli.

and still upward," no selfishness and unselfishness, no atom of voluntary effort within the boundaries of that conclusion. Once admitting the postulate, that existence is merely a sequence of cause and effect beginning with the primal atom, and we have a theory that must stand or fall as a whole. We cannot say that man is a creature of circumstance and then leave him free to select his circumstance, even in the minutest fractional degree. It was selected for him with his disposition; in that first instant of created life. Clemens himself repeatedly emphasized this doctrine, and once, when it was suggested to him that it seemed to "surround everything, like the sky," he answered:,

"Yes, like the sky; you can't break through anywhere."

Colonel Harvey came to Dublin that summer and persuaded Clemens to let him print some selections from the dictations in the new volume of the *North American Review*, which he proposed to issue fortnightly. The matter was discussed a good deal, and it was believed that one hundred thousand words could be selected which would be usable forthwith, as well as in that long-deferred period for which it was planned. Colonel Harvey agreed to take a copy of the dictated matter and make the selections himself, and this plan was carried out. It may be said that most of the chapters were delightful enough; though, had it been possible to edit them with the more positive documents as a guide, certain complications might have been avoided. It does not matter now, and it was not a matter of very wide import then.

The payment of these chapters netted Clemens thirty thousand dollars—a comfortable sum, which he promptly proposed to spend in building on the property at Redding. He engaged John Mead Howells to prepare some preliminary plans.

Clara Clemens, at Norfolk, was written to of the matter.

A little later I joined her in Redding, and she was the first of the family to see that beautiful hilltop. She was well pleased with the situation, and that day selected the spot where the house should stand. Clemens wrote Howells that he proposed to call it "Autobiography House," as it was to be built out of the *Review* money, and he said:

"If you will build on my farm and live there it will set Mrs. Howells's health up for sure. Come and I'll sell you the site for twenty-five dollars. John will tell you it is a choice place."

The unusual summer was near its close. In my note-book, under date of September 16th, appears this entry:

Windy in valleys but not cold. This veranda is protected. It is peaceful here and perfect, but we are at the summer's end.

This is my last entry, and the dictations must have ceased a few days later. I do not remember the date of the return to New York, and apparently I made no record of it; but I do not think it could have been later than the 20th. It had been four months since the day of arrival, a long, marvelous summer such as I would hardly know again. When I think of that time I shall always hear the ceaseless slippered, shuffling walk, and see the white figure with its rocking, rolling movement passing up and down the long gallery, with that preternaturally beautiful landscape behind, and I shall hear his deliberate speech—always deliberate, save at rare intervals; always impressive, whatever the subject might be; whether recalling some old absurdity of youth, or denouncing orthodox creeds, or detailing the shortcomings of human-kind.

CCXLIX

BILLIARDS

THE return to New York marked the beginning of a new era in my relations with Mark Twain. I have not meant to convey that up to this time there was between us anything resembling a personal friendship. Our relations were friendly, certainly, but they were relations of convenience and mainly of a business, or at least of a literary nature. He was twenty-six years my senior, and the discrepancy of experience and attainments was not measurable. With such conditions friendship must be a deliberate growth; something there must be to bridge the dividing gulf. Truth requires the confession that, in this case, the bridge took a very solid, material form, it being, in fact, nothing less than a billiard-table.[1]

It was a present from Mrs. Henry H. Rogers, and had been intended for his Christmas; but when he heard of it he could not wait, and suggested delicately that if he had it "right now" he could begin using it sooner. So he went one day with Mr. Rogers to the Balke-Collender Company, and they selected a handsome combination table suitable to all games—the best that money could buy. He was greatly excited over the prospect, and his former bedroom was carefully measured, to be certain that it was large enough for billiard purposes. Then his bed was moved into the study, and the book-cases and certain appropriate pictures were placed and hung in the billiard-room to give it the proper feeling.

[1] Clemens had been without a billiard-table since 1891, the old one having been disposed of on the departure from Hartford.

BILLIARDS

The billiard-table arrived and was put in place, the brilliant green cloth in contrast with the rich red wall-paper and the bookbindings and pictures making the room wonderfully handsome and inviting.

Meantime, Clemens, with one of his sudden impulses, had conceived the notion of spending the winter in Egypt, on the Nile. He had gone so far, within a few hours after the idea developed, as to plan the time of his departure, and to partially engage a traveling secretary, so that he might continue his dictations. He was quite full of the idea just at the moment when the billiard-table was being installed. He had sent for a book on the subject—the letters of Lady Duff-Gordon, whose daughter, Janet Ross, had become a dear friend in Florence during the Viviani days. He spoke of this new purpose on the morning when we renewed the New York dictations, a month or more following the return from Dublin. When the dictation ended he said:

"Have you any special place to lunch to-day?"

I replied that I had not.

"Lunch here," he said, "and we'll try the new billiard-table."

I said what was eminently true—that I could not play —that I had never played more than a few games of pool, and those very long ago.

"No matter," he answered; "the poorer you play, the better I shall like it."

So I remained for luncheon and we began, November 2d, the first game ever played on the Christmas table. We played the English game, in which caroms and pockets both count. I had a beginner's luck, on the whole, and I remember it as a riotous, rollicking game, the beginning of a closer understanding between us—of a distinct epoch in our association. When it was ended he said:

"I'm not going to Egypt. There was a man here yesterday afternoon who said it was bad for bronchitis, and, besides, it's too far away from this billiard-table."

He suggested that I come back in the evening and play some more. I did so, and the game lasted until after midnight. He gave me odds, of course, and my "nigger luck," as he called it, continued. It kept him sweating and swearing feverishly to win. Finally, I made a great fluke—a carom, followed by most of the balls falling into the pockets.

"Well," he said, "when you pick up that cue this damn table drips at every pore."

After that the morning dictations became a secondary interest. Like a boy, he was looking forward to the afternoon of play, and it never seemed to come quick enough to suit him. I remained regularly for luncheon, and he was inclined to cut the courses short, that he might the sooner get up-stairs to the billiard-room. His earlier habit of not eating in the middle of the day continued; but he would get up and dress, and walk about the dining-room in his old fashion, talking that marvelous, marvelous talk which I was always trying to remember, and with only fractional success at best. To him it was only a method of killing time. I remember once, when he had been discussing with great earnestness the Japanese question, he suddenly noticed that the luncheon was about ending, and he said:

"Now we'll proceed to more serious matters—it's your—shot." And he was quite serious, for the green cloth and the rolling balls afforded him a much larger interest.

To the donor of his new possession Clemens wrote:

DEAR MRS. ROGERS,—The billiard-table is better than the doctors. I have a billiardist on the premises, & walk not less than ten miles every day with the cue in my hand. And the walking is not the whole of the exercise, nor the most health-giving part of it, I think. Through the multitude of the positions and attitudes it brings into play every muscle in the body & exercises them all.

The games begin right after luncheons, daily, & continue until midnight, with 2 hours' intermission for dinner & music. And so it is 9 hours' exercise per day & 10 or 12 on Sunday. Yesterday & last night it was 12—& I slept until 8 this morning without waking. The billiard-table as a Sabbath-breaker can beat any coal-breaker in Pennsylvania & give it 30 in the game. If Mr. Rogers will take to daily billiards he can do without the doctors & the massageur, I think.

We are really going to build a house on my farm, an hour & a half from New York. It is decided.

With love & many thanks.   S. L. C.

Naturally enough, with continued practice I improved my game, and he reduced my odds accordingly. He was willing to be beaten, but not too often. Like any other boy, he preferred to have the balance in his favor. We set down a record of the games, and he went to bed happier if the tally-sheet showed him winner.

It was natural, too, that an intimacy of association and of personal interest should grow under such conditions—to me a precious boon—and I wish here to record my own boundless gratitude to Mrs. Rogers for her gift, which, whatever it meant to him, meant so much more to me. The disparity of ages no longer existed; other discrepancies no longer mattered. The pleasant land of play is a democracy where such things do not count.

To recall all the humors and interesting happenings of those early billiard-days would be to fill a large volume. I can preserve no more than a few characteristic phases.

He was not an even-tempered player. When the balls were perverse in their movements and his aim unsteady, he was likely to become short with his opponent—critical and even faultfinding. Then presently a reaction would set in, and he would be seized with remorse. He would become unnecessarily gentle and kindly—even attentive—placing the balls as I knocked them into the pockets, hurrying the length of the table to render this service, endeavoring to show in every way except by actual confession in words that he was sorry for what seemed to him, no doubt, an unworthy display of temper, unjustified irritation.

Naturally, this was a mood that I enjoyed less than that which had induced it. I did not wish him to humble himself; I was willing that he should be severe, even harsh, if he felt so inclined; his age, his position, his genius entitled him to special privileges; yet I am glad, as I remember it now, that the other side revealed itself, for it completes the sum of his great humanity.

Indeed, he was always not only human, but superhuman; not only a man, but superman. Nor does this term apply only to his psychology. In no other human being have I ever seen such physical endurance. I was comparatively a young man, and by no means an invalid; but many a time, far in the night, when I was ready to drop with exhaustion, he was still as fresh and buoyant and eager for the game as at the moment of beginning. He smoked and smoked continually, and followed the endless track around the billiard-table with the light step of youth. At three or four o'clock in the morning he would urge just one more game, and would taunt me for my weariness. I can truthfully testify that never until the last year of his life did he willingly lay down the billiard-cue, or show the least suggestion of fatigue.

He played always at high pressure. Now and then, in periods of adversity, he would fly into a perfect passion with things in general. But, in the end, it was a sham battle, and he saw the uselessness and humor of it, even in the moment of his climax. Once, when he found it impossible to make any of his favorite shots, he became more and more restive, the lightning became vividly picturesque as the clouds blackened. Finally, with a regular thunder-blast, he seized the cue with both hands and literally mowed the balls across the table, landing one or two of them on the floor. I do not recall his exact remarks during the performance; I was chiefly concerned in getting out of the way, and those sublime utterances were lost. I gathered up the balls and we went on playing as if nothing had happened, only he was very gentle and sweet, like the sun on the meadows after the storm has passed by. After a little he said:

"This is a most amusing game. When you play badly it amuses me, and when I play badly and lose my temper it certainly must amuse you."

His enjoyment of his opponent's perplexities was very keen. When he had left the balls in some unfortunate position which made it almost impossible for me to score he would laugh boisterously. I used to affect to be injured and disturbed by this ridicule. Once, when he had made the conditions unusually hard for me, and was enjoying the situation accordingly, I was tempted to remark:

"Whenever I see you laugh at a thing like that I always doubt your sense of humor." Which seemed to add to his amusement.

Sometimes, when the balls were badly placed for me, he would offer ostensible advice, suggesting that I should shoot here and there—shots that were possible, perhaps, but not promising. Often I would follow his advice, and then when I failed to score his amusement broke out afresh.

Other billiardists came from time to time: Colonel Harvey, Mr. Duneka, and Major Leigh, of the Harper Company, and Peter Finley Dunne (Mr. Dooley); but they were handicapped by their business affairs, and were not dependable for daily and protracted sessions. Any number of his friends were willing, even eager, to come for his entertainment; but the percentage of them who could and would devote a number of hours each day to being beaten at billiards and enjoy the operation dwindled down to a single individual. Even I could not have done it—could not have afforded it, however much I might have enjoyed the diversion—had it not been contributory to my work. To me the association was invaluable; it drew from him a thousand long-forgotten incidents; it invited a stream of picturesque comments and philosophies; it furnished the most intimate insight into his character.

He was not always glad to see promiscuous callers, even some one that he might have met pleasantly elsewhere. One afternoon a young man whom he had casually invited to "drop in some day in town" happened to call in the midst of a very close series of afternoon games. It would all have been well enough if the visitor had been content to sit quietly on the couch and "bet on the game," as Clemens suggested, after the greetings were over; but he was a very young man, and he felt the necessity of being entertaining. He insisted on walking about the room and getting in the way, and on talking about the Mark Twain books he had read, and the people he had met from time to time who had known Mark Twain on the river, or on the Pacific coast, or elsewhere. I knew how fatal it was for him to talk to Clemens during his play, especially concerning matters most of which had been laid away. I trembled for our visitor. If I could have got his ear privately I should have said: "For heaven's sake sit down and keep still or go away! There's going to be a combination of earthquake and cyclone and avalanche if you keep this thing up."

I did what I could. I looked at my watch every other minute. At last, in desperation, I suggested that I retire from the game and let the visitor have my cue. I suppose I thought this would eliminate an element of danger. He declined on the ground that he seldom played, and con-

BILLIARDS

tinued his deadly visit. I have never been in an atmosphere so fraught with danger. I did not know how the game stood, and I played mechanically and forgot to count the score. Clemens's face was grim and set and savage. He no longer ventured even a word. By and by I noticed that he was getting white, and I said, privately, "Now, this young man's hour has come."

It was certainly by the mercy of God just then that the visitor said:

"I'm sorry, but I've got to go. I'd like to stay longer, but I've got an engagement for dinner."

I don't remember how he got out, but I know that tons lifted as the door closed behind him. Clemens made his shot, then very softly said:

"If he had stayed another five minutes I should have offered him twenty-five cents to go."

But a moment later he glared at me.

"Why in nation did you offer him your cue?"

"Wasn't that the courteous thing to do?" I asked.

"No!" he ripped out. "The courteous and proper thing would have been to strike him dead. Did you want to saddle that disaster upon us for life?"

He was blowing off steam, and I knew it and encouraged it. My impulse was to lie down on the couch and shout with hysterical laughter, but I suspected that would be indiscreet. He made some further comment on the propriety of offering a visitor a cue, and suddenly began to sing a travesty of an old hymn:

> "How tedious are they
> Who their sovereign obey,"

and so loudly that I said:

"Aren't you afraid he'll hear you and come back?" Whereupon he pretended alarm and sang under his breath, and for the rest of the evening was in boundless good-humor.

I have recalled this incident merely as a sample of things that were likely to happen at any time in his company, and to show the difficulty one might find in fitting himself to his varying moods. He was not to be learned in a day, or a week, or a month; some of those who knew him longest did not learn him at all.

We celebrated his seventy-first birthday by playing billiards all day. He invented a new game for the occasion; inventing rules for it with almost every shot.

It happened that no member of the family was at home on this birthday. Ill health had banished every one, even the secretary. Flowers, telegrams, and congratulations came, and there was a string of callers; but he saw no one beyond some intimate friends—the Gilders—late in the afternoon. When they had gone we went down to dinner. We were entirely alone, and I felt the great honor of being his only guest on such an occasion. Once between the courses, when he rose, as usual, to walk about, he wandered into the drawing-room, and seating himself at the orchestrelle began to play the beautiful flower-song from "Faust." It was a thing I had not seen him do before, and I never saw him do it again. When he came back to the table he said:

"Speaking of companions of the long ago, after fifty years they become only shadows and might as well be in the grave. Only those whom one has really loved mean anything at all. Of my playmates I recall John Briggs, John Garth, and Laura Hawkins—just those three; the rest I buried long ago, and memory cannot even find their graves."

He was in his loveliest humor all that day and evening; and that night, when he stopped playing, he said:

"I have never had a pleasanter day at this game."

I answered, "I hope ten years from to-night we shall still be playing it."

"Yes," he said, "still playing the best game on earth."

CCL

PHILOSOPHY AND PESSIMISM

IN a letter to MacAlister, written at this time, he said:

> The doctors banished Jean to the country 5 weeks ago; they
> banished my secretary to the country for a fortnight last Satur-
> day; they banished Clara to the country for a fortnight last
> Monday. . . . They banished me to Bermuda—to sail next
> Wednesday, but I struck and sha'n't go. My complaint is
> permanent bronchitis & is one of the very best assets I've got,
> for it excuses me from every public function this winter—& all
> other winters that may come.

If he had bronchitis when this letter was written, it
must have been of a very mild form, for it did not interfere with billiard games, which were more protracted and
strenuous than at almost any other period. I conclude,
therefore, that it was a convenient bronchitis, useful on
occasion.

For a full ten days we were alone in the big house with
the servants. It was a holiday most of the time. We
hurried through the mail in the morning and the telephone calls; then, while I answered such letters as required attention, he dictated for an hour or so to Miss
Hobby, after which, billiards for the rest of the day and
evening. When callers were reported by the butler, I went
down and got rid of them. Clara Clemens, before her departure, had pinned up a sign, "NO BILLIARDS AFTER 10
P.M.," which still hung on the wall, but it was outlawed.
Clemens occasionally planned excursions to Bermuda and

other places; but, remembering the billiard-table, which he could not handily take along, he abandoned these projects. He was a boy whose parents had been called away, left to his own devices, and bent on a good time.

There were likely to be irritations in his morning's mail, and more often he did not wish to see it until it had been pretty carefully sifted. So many people wrote who wanted things, so many others who made the claim of more or less distant acquaintanceship the excuse for long and trivial letters.

"I have stirred up three generations," he said; "first the grandparents, then the children, and now the grand-children; the great-grandchildren will begin to arrive soon."

His mail was always large; but often it did not look interesting. One could tell from the envelope and the superscription something of the contents. Going over one assortment he burst out:

"Look at them! Look how trivial they are! Every envelope looks as if it contained a trivial human soul."

Many letters were filled with fulsome praise and com-pliment, usually of one pattern. He was sated with such things, and seldom found it possible to bear more than a line or two of them. Yet a fresh, well-expressed note of appreciation always pleased him.

"I can live for two months on a good compliment," he once said.

Certain persistent correspondents, too self-centered to realize their lack of consideration, or the futility of their purpose, followed him relentlessly. Of one such he remarked:

"That woman intends to pursue me to the grave. I wish something could be done to appease her."

And again:

"Everybody in the world who wants something—something of no interest to me—writes to me to get it."

PHILOSOPHY AND PESSIMISM

These morning sessions were likely to be of great interest. Once a letter spoke of the desirability of being an optimist. "That word perfectly disgusts me," he said, and his features materialized the disgust, "just as that other word, pessimist, does; and the idea that one can, by any effort of will, be one or the other, any more than he can change the color of his hair. The reason why a man is a pessimist or an optimist is not because he wants to be, but because he was born so; and this man [a minister of the Gospel who was going to explain life to him] is going to tell me why he isn't a pessimist. Oh, he'll do it, but he won't tell the truth; he won't make it short enough."

Yet he was always patient with any one who came with spiritual messages, theological arguments, and consolations. He might have said to them: "Oh, dear friends, those things of which you speak are the toys that long ago I played with and set aside." He could have said it and spoken the truth; but I believe he did not even think it. He listened to any one for whom he had respect, and was grateful for any effort in his behalf.

One morning he read aloud a lecture given in London by George Bernard Shaw on religion, commenting as he read. He said:

"This lecture is a frank breath of expression [and his comments were equally frank]. There is no such thing as morality; it is not immoral for the tiger to eat the wolf, or the wolf the cat, or the cat the bird, and so on down; that is their business. There is always enough for each one to live on. It is not immoral for one nation to seize another nation by force of arms, or for one man to seize another man's property or life if he is strong enough and wants to take it. It is not immoral to create the human species—with or without ceremony; nature intended exactly these things."

At one place in the lecture Shaw had said: "No one

of good sense can accept any creed to-day without reservation."

"Certainly *not*," commented Clemens; "the reservation is that he is a d—d fool to accept it at all."

He was in one of his somber moods that morning. I had received a print of a large picture of Thomas Nast—the last one taken. The face had a pathetic expression which told the tragedy of his last years. Clemens looked at the picture several moments without speaking. Then he broke out:

"Why can't a man die when he's had his tragedy? I ought to have died long ago." And somewhat later: "Once Twichell heard me cussing the human race, and he said, 'Why, Mark, you are the last person in the world to do that—one selected and set apart as you are.' I said 'Joe, you don't know what you are talking about. I am not cussing altogether about my own little troubles. Any one can stand his own misfortunes; but when I read in the papers all about the rascalities and outrages going on I realize what a creature the human animal is. Don't you care more about the wretchedness of others than anything that happens to you?' Joe said he did, and shut up."

It occurred to me to suggest that he should not read the daily papers.

"No difference," he said. "I read books printed two hundred years ago, and they hurt just the same."

"Those people are all dead and gone," I objected.

"They hurt just the same," he maintained.

I sometimes thought of his inner consciousness as a pool darkened by his tragedies, its glassy surface, when calm, reflecting all the joy and sunlight and merriment of the world, but easily—so easily—troubled and stirred even to violence. Once following the dictation, when I came to the billiard-room he was shooting the balls about the table, apparently much depressed. He said:

"I have been thinking it out—if I live two years more I will put an end to it all. I will kill myself."

"You have much to live for—"

"But I am so tired of the eternal round," he interrupted; "so tired."

And I knew he meant that he was ill of the great loneliness that had come to him that day in Florence, and would never pass away.

I referred to the pressure of social demands in the city, and the relief he would find in his country home. He shook his head.

"The country home I need," he said, fiercely, "is a cemetery."

Yet the mood changed quickly enough when the play began. He was gay and hilarious presently, full of the humors and complexities of the game.

H. H. Rogers came in with a good deal of frequency, seldom making very long calls, but never seeming to have that air of being hurried which one might expect to find in a man whose day was only twenty-four hours long, and whose interests were so vast and innumerable. He would come in where we were playing, and sit down and watch the game, or perhaps would pick up a book and read, exchanging a remark now and then. More often, however, he sat in the bedroom, for his visits were likely to be in the morning. They were seldom business calls, or if they were, the business was quickly settled, and then followed gossip, humorous incident, or perhaps Clemens would read aloud something he had written. But once, after greetings, he began:

"Well, Rogers, I don't know what you think of it, but I think I have had about enough of this world, and I wish I were out of it."

Mr. Rogers replied, "I don't say much about it, but that expresses my view."

This from the foremost man of letters and one of the

foremost financiers of the time was impressive. Each at the mountain-top of his career, they agreed that the journey was not worth while—that what the world had still to give was not attractive enough to tempt them—to prevent a desire to experiment with the next stage. One could remember a thousand poor and obscure men who were perfectly willing to go on struggling and starving, postponing the day of settlement as long as possible; but perhaps, when one has had all the world has to give, when there are no new worlds in sight to conquer, one has a different feeling.

Well, the realization lay not so far ahead for either of them, though at that moment they both seemed full of life and vigor—full of youth. One could not imagine the day when for them it would all be over.

CCLI

A LOBBYING EXPEDITION

CLARA CLEMENS came home now and then to see how matters were progressing, and very properly, for Clemens was likely to become involved in social intricacies which required a directing hand. The daughter inherited no little of the father's characteristics of thought and phrase, and it was always a delight to see them together when one could be just out of range of the crossfire. I remember soon after her return, when she was making some searching inquiries concerning the billiard-room sign, and other suggested or instituted reforms, he said:

"Oh well, never mind, it doesn't matter. I'm boss in this house."

She replied, quickly: "Oh no, you're not. You're merely owner. I'm the captain—the commander-in-chief."

One night at dinner she mentioned the possibility of going abroad that year. During several previous summers she had planned to visit Vienna to see her old music-master, Leschetizky, once more before his death. She said:

"Leschetizky is getting so old. If I don't go soon I'm afraid I sha'n't be in time for his funeral."

"Yes," said her father, thoughtfully, "you keep rushing over to Leschetizky's funeral, and you'll miss mine."

He had made one or two social engagements without careful reflection, and the situation would require some delicacy of adjustment. During a moment between the courses, when he left the table and was taking his exercise in the farther room, she made some remark which suggested a doubt of her father's gift for social management. I said:

"Oh, well, he is a king, you know, and a king can do no wrong."

"Yes, I know," she answered. "The king can do no wrong; but he frightens me almost to death, sometimes, he comes so near it."

He came back and began to comment rather critically on some recent performance of Roosevelt's, which had stirred up a good deal of newspaper amusement—it was the Storer matter and those indiscreet letters which Roosevelt had written relative to the ambassadorship which Storer so much desired. Miss Clemens was inclined to defend the President, and spoke with considerable enthusiasm concerning his elements of popularity, which had won him such extraordinary admiration.

"Certainly he is popular," Clemens admitted, "and with the best of reasons. If the twelve apostles should call at the White House, he would say, 'Come in, come in! I am delighted to see you. I've been watching your progress, and I admired it very much.' Then if Satan should come, he would slap him on the shoulder and say 'Why, Satan, how *do* you do? I am so glad to meet you. I've read all your works and enjoyed every one of them.' Anybody could be popular with a gift like that."

It was that evening or the next, perhaps, that he said to her:

"Ben [one of his pet names for her], now that you are here to run the ranch, Paine and I are going to Washington on a vacation. You don't seem to admire our society much, anyhow."

There were still other reasons for the Washington expedition. There was an important bill up for the extension of the book royalty period, and the forces of copyright were going down in a body to use every possible means to get the measure through.

Clemens, during Cleveland's first administration, some nineteen years before, had accompanied such an expedition, and through S. S. ("Sunset") Cox had obtained the "privileges of the floor" of the House, which had enabled him to canvass the members individually. Cox assured the doorkeeper that Clemens had received the thanks of Congress for national literary service, and was therefore entitled to that privilege. This was not strictly true; but regulations were not very severe in those days, and the ruse had been regarded as a good joke, which had yielded excellent results. Clemens had a similar scheme in mind now, and believed that his friendship with Speaker Cannon—"Uncle Joe"—would obtain for him a similar privilege. The Copyright Association working in its regular way was very well, he said, but he felt he could do more as an individual than by acting merely as a unit of that body.

"I canvassed the entire House personally that other time," he said. "Cox introduced me to the Democrats, and John D. Long, afterward Secretary of the Navy, introduced me to the Republicans. I had a darling time converting those members, and I'd like to try the experiment again."

I should have mentioned earlier, perhaps, that at this time he had begun to wear white clothing regularly, regardless of the weather and season. On the return from Dublin he had said:

"I can't bear to put on black clothes again. I wish I could wear white all winter. I should prefer, of course, to wear colors, beautiful rainbow hues, such as the women have monopolized. Their clothing makes a great opera audience an enchanting spectacle, a delight to the eye and to the spirit—a garden of Eden for charm and color.

The men, clothed in odious black, are scattered here and there over the garden like so many charred stumps. If we are going to be gay in spirit, why be clad in funeral garments? I should like to dress in a loose and flowing costume made all of silks and velvets resplendent with stunning dyes, and so would every man I have ever known; but none of us dares to venture it. If I should appear on Fifth Avenue on a Sunday morning clothed as I would like to be clothed the churches would all be vacant and the congregation would come tagging after me. They would scoff, of course, but they would envy me, too. When I put on black it reminds me of my funerals. I could be satisfied with white all the year round."

It was not long after this that he said:

"I have made up my mind not to wear black any more, but white, and let the critics say what they will."

So his tailor was sent for, and six creamy flannel and serge suits were ordered, made with the short coats, which he preferred, with a gray suit or two for travel, and he did not wear black again, except for evening dress and on special occasions. It was a gratifying change, and though the newspapers made much of it, there was no one who was not gladdened by the beauty of his garments and their general harmony with his person. He had never worn anything so appropriate or so impressive.

This departure of costume came along a week or two before the Washington trip, and when his bags were being packed for the excursion he was somewhat in doubt as to the propriety of bursting upon Washington in December in that snowy plumage. I ventured:

"This is a lobbying expedition of a peculiar kind, and does not seem to invite any half-way measures. I should vote in favor of the white suit."

I think Miss Clemens was for it, too. She must have been or the vote wouldn't have carried, though it was clear he strongly favored the idea. At all events, the white suits came along.

We were off the following afternoon: Howells, Robert Underwood Johnson, one of the Appletons, one of the Putnams, George Bowker, and others were on the train. On the trip down in the dining-car there was a discussion concerning the copyrighting of ideas, which finally resolved itself into the possibility of originating a new one. Clemens said:

"There is no such thing as a new idea. It is impossible. We simply take a lot of old ideas and put them into a sort of mental kaleidoscope. We give them a turn and they make new and curious combinations. We keep on turning and making new combinations indefinitely; but they are the same old pieces of colored glass that have been in use through all the ages."

We put up at the Willard, and in the morning drove over to the Congressional Library, where the copyright hearing was in progress. There was a joint committee of the two Houses seated round a long table at work, and a number of spectators more or less interested in the bill, mainly, it would seem, men concerned with the protection of mechanical music-rolls. The fact that this feature was mixed up with literature was not viewed with favor by most of the writers. Clemens referred to the musical contingent as "those hand-organ men who ought to have a bill of their own."

I should mention that early that morning Clemens had written this letter to Speaker Cannon:

December 7, 1906.

DEAR UNCLE JOSEPH,—Please get me the thanks of the Congress—not next week, but right away. It is very necessary. Do accomplish this for your affectionate old friend *right away*; by persuasion, if you can; by violence, if you must, for it is imperatively necessary that I get on the floor for two or three hours and talk to the members, man by man, in behalf of the support, encouragement, and protection of one of the nation's most valuable assets and industries—its literature. I have arguments with me, also a barrel with liquid in it.

Give me a chance. Get me the thanks of Congress. Don't wait for others—there isn't time. I have stayed away and let Congress alone for seventy-one years and I am entitled to thanks. Congress knows it perfectly well, and I have long felt hurt that this quite proper and earned expression of gratitude has been merely felt by the House and never publicly uttered. Send me an order on the Sergeant-at-Arms quick. When shall I come? With love and a benediction, MARK TWAIN.

We went over to the Capitol now to deliver to "Uncle Joe" this characteristic letter. We had picked up Clemens's nephew, Samuel E. Moffett, at the Library, and he came along and led the way to the Speaker's room. Arriving there, Clemens laid off his dark overcoat and stood there, all in white, certainly a startling figure among those clerks, newspaper men, and incidental politicians. He had been noticed as he entered the Capitol, and a number of reporters had followed close behind. Within less than a minute word was being passed through the corridors that Mark Twain was at the Capitol in his white suit. The privileged ones began to gather, and a crowd assembled in the hall outside.

Speaker Cannon was not present at the moment; but a little later he "billowed" in—which seems to be the word to express it—he came with such a rush and tide of life. After greetings, Clemens produced the letter and read it to him solemnly, as if he were presenting a petition. Uncle Joe listened quite seriously, his head bowed a little, as if it were really a petition, as in fact it was. He smiled, but he said, quite seriously:

"That is a request that ought to be granted; but the time has gone by when I am permitted any such liberties. Tom Reed, when he was Speaker, inaugurated a strict precedent excluding all outsiders from the use of the floor of the House."

"I got in the other time," Clemens insisted.

"Yes," said Uncle Joe; "but that ain't now. Sunset Cox could let you in, but I can't. They'd hang *me*." He reflected a moment, and added: "I'll tell you what I'll do: I've got a private room down-stairs that I never use. It's all fitted up with table and desk, stationery, chinaware, and cutlery; you could keep house there, if you wanted to. I'll let you have it as long as you want to stay here, and I'll give you my private servant, Neal, who's been here all his life and knows every official, every Senator and Representative, and they all know him. He'll bring you whatever you want, and you can send in messages by him. You can have the members brought down singly or in bunches, and convert them as much as you please. I'd give you a key to the room, only I haven't got one myself. I never can get in when I want to, but Neal can get in, and he'll unlock it for you. You can have the room, and you can have Neal. Now, will that do you?"

Clemens said it would. It was, in fact, an offer without precedent. Probably never in the history of the country had a Speaker given up his private room to lobbyists. We went in to see the House open, and then went down with Neal and took possession of the room. The reporters had promptly seized upon the letter, and they now got hold of its author, led him to their own quarters, and, gathering around him, fired questions at him, and kept their note-books busy. He made a great figure, all in white there among them, and they didn't fail to realize the value of it as "copy." He talked about copyright, and about his white clothes, and about a silk hat which Howells wore.

Back in the Speaker's room, at last, he began laying out the campaign, which would begin next day. By and by he said:

"Look here! I believe I've got to speak over there in that committee-room to-day or to-morrow. I ought to know just when it is."

I had not heard of this before, and offered to go over and see about it, which I did at once. I hurried back faster than I had gone.

"Mr. Clemens, you are to speak in half an hour, and the room is crowded full; people waiting to hear you."

"The devil!" he said. "Well, all right; I'll just lie down here a few minutes and then we'll go over. Take paper and pencil and make a few headings."

There was a couch in the room. He lay down while I sat at the table with a pencil, making headings now and then, as he suggested, and presently he rose and, shoving the notes into his pocket, was ready. It was half past three when we entered the committee-room, which was packed with people and rather dimly lighted, for it was gloomy outside. Herbert Putnam, the librarian, led us to seats among the literary group, and Clemens, removing his overcoat, stood in that dim room clad as in white armor. There was a perceptible stir. Howells, startled for a moment, whispered:

"What in the world did he wear that white suit for?" though in his heart he admired it as much as the others.[1]

[1] Howells in his book *My Mark Twain* speaks of Clemens's white clothing as "an inspiration which few men would have had the courage to act upon." He adds:

"The first time I saw him wear it was at the author's hearing before the Congressional Committee on Copyright in Washington. Noth-could have been more dramatic than the gesture with which he flung off his long, loose, overcoat and stood forth in white from his feet to the crown of his silvery head. It was a magnificent coup, and he dearly loved a coup; but the magnificent speech which he made, tearing to shreds the venerable *farrago* of nonsense about non-property in ideas which had formed the basis of all copyright legislation, made you forget even his spectacularity."

A LOBBYING EXPEDITION

I don't remember who was speaking when we came in, but he was saying nothing important. Whoever it was, he was followed by Dr. Edward Everett Hale, whose age always commanded respect, and whose words always invited interest. Then it was Mark Twain's turn. He did not stand by his chair, as the others had done, but walked over to the Speaker's table, and, turning, faced his audience. I have never seen a more impressive sight than that snow-white figure in that dim-lit, crowded room. He never touched his notes; he didn't even remember them. He began in that even, quiet, deliberate voice of his—the most even, the most quiet, the most deliberate voice in the world—and, without a break or a hesitation for a word, he delivered a copyright argument, full of humor and serious reasoning, such a speech as no one in that room, I suppose, had ever heard. Certainly it was a fine and dramatic bit of impromptu pleading. The weary committee, which had been tortured all day with dull, statistical arguments made by the mechanical-device fiends, and dreary platitudes unloaded by men whose chief ambition was to shine as copyright champions, suddenly realized that they were being rewarded for the long waiting. They began to brighten and freshen, and uplift and smile, like flowers that have been wilted by a drought when comes the refreshing shower that means renewed life and vigor. Every listener was as if standing on tiptoe. When the last sentence was spoken the applause came like an explosion.

There came a universal rush of men and women to get near enough for a word and to shake his hand. But he was anxious to get away. We drove to the Willard and talked and smoked, and got ready for dinner. He was elated, and said the occasion required full-dress. We started down at last, fronted and frocked like penguins.

I did not realize then the fullness of his love for theatrical effect. I supposed he would want to go down with as

little ostentation as possible, so took him by the elevator
which enters the dining-room without passing through the
long corridor known as "Peacock Alley," because of its
being a favorite place for handsomely dressed fashion-
ables of the national capital. When we reached the entrance of the dining-room he said:

"Isn't there another entrance to this place?"

I said there was, but that it was very conspicuous.
We should have to go down the long corridor.

"Oh, well," he said, "I don't mind that. Let's go
back and try it over."

So we went back up the elevator, walked to the other
end of the hotel, and came down to the F Street entrance.
There is a fine, stately flight of steps—a really royal
stair—leading from this entrance down into "Peacock
Alley." To slowly descend that flight is an impressive
thing to do. It is like descending the steps of a throne-
room, or to some royal landing-place where Cleopatra's
barge might lie. I confess that I was somewhat nervous
at the awfulness of the occasion, but I reflected that I
was powerfully protected; so side by side, both in full-
dress, white ties, white-silk waistcoats, and all, we came
down that regal flight.

Of course he was seized upon at once by a lot of
feminine admirers, and the passage along the corridor
was a perpetual gantlet. I realize now that this gave
the dramatic finish to his day, and furnished him
with proper appetite for his dinner. I did not again
make the mistake of taking him around to the more
secluded elevator. I aided and abetted him every
evening in making that spectacular descent of the royal
stairway, and in running that fair and frivolous gantlet
the length of "Peacock Alley." The dinner was a continuous reception. No sooner was he seated than this
Congressman and that Senator came over to shake hands
with Mark Twain. Governor Francis of Missouri also

came. Eventually Howells drifted in, and Clemens reviewed the day, its humors and successes. Back in the rooms at last he summed up the progress thus far—smoked, laughed over "Uncle Joe's" surrender to the "copyright bandits," and turned in for the night.

We were at the Capitol headquarters in Speaker Cannon's private room about eleven o'clock next morning. Clemens was not in the best humor because I had allowed him to oversleep. He was inclined to be discouraged at the prospect, and did not believe many of the members would come down to see him. He expressed a wish for some person of influence and wide acquaintance, and walked up and down, smoking gloomily. I slipped out and found the Speaker's colored body-guard, Neal, and suggested that Mr. Clemens was ready now to receive the members.

That was enough. They began to arrive immediately. John Sharp Williams came first, then Boutell, from Illinois, Littlefield, of Maine, and after them a perfect procession, including all the leading lights—Dalzell, Champ Clark, McCall—one hundred and eighty or so in all during the next three or four hours.

Neal announced each name at the door, and in turn I announced it to Clemens when the press was not too great. He had provided boxes of cigars, and the room was presently blue with smoke, Clemens in his white suit in the midst of it, surrounded by those darker figures—shaking hands, dealing out copyright gospel and anecdotes—happy and wonderfully excited. There were chairs, but usually there was only standing room. He was on his feet for several hours and talked continually; but when at last it was over, and Champ Clark, who I believe remained longest and was most enthusiastic in the movement, had bade him good-by, he declared that he was not a particle tired, and added:

"I believe if our bill could be presented now it would pass."

He was highly elated, and pronounced everything a perfect success. Neal, who was largely responsible for the triumph, received a ten-dollar bill.

We drove to the hotel and dined that night with the Dodges, who had been neighbors at Riverdale. Later, the usual crowd of admirers gathered around him, among them I remember the minister from Costa Rica, the Italian minister, and others of the diplomatic service, most of whom he had known during his European residence. Some one told of traveling in India and China, and how a certain Hindu "god" who had exchanged autographs with Mark Twain during his sojourn there was familiar with only two other American names—George Washington and Chicago; while the King of Siam had read but three English books—the Bible, Bryce's *American Commonwealth*, and *The Innocents Abroad*.

We were at Thomas Nelson Page's for dinner next evening—a wonderfully beautiful home, full of art treasures. A number of guests had been invited. Clemens naturally led the dinner-talk, which eventually drifted to reading. He told of Mrs. Clemens's embarrassment when Stepniak had visited them and talked books, and asked her what her husband thought of Balzac, Thackeray, and the others. She had been obliged to say that he had not read them.

"'How interesting!' said Stepniak. But it wasn't interesting to Mrs. Clemens. It was torture."

He was light-spirited and gay; but recalling Mrs. Clemens saddened him, perhaps, for he was silent as we drove to the hotel, and after he was in bed he said, with a weary despair which even the words do not convey:

"If I had been there a minute earlier, it is possible—it is possible that she might have died in my arms. Sometimes I think that perhaps there was an instant—a single instant—when she realized that she was dying and that I was not there."

A LOBBYING EXPEDITION

In New York I had once brought him a print of the superb "Adams Memorial," by Saint-Gaudens—the bronze woman who sits in the still court in the Rock Creek Cemetery at Washington.

On the morning following the Page dinner at breakfast, he said:

"Engage a carriage and we will drive out and see the Saint-Gaudens bronze."

It was a bleak, dull December day, and as we walked down through the avenues of the dead there was a presence of realized sorrow that seemed exactly suited to such a visit. We entered the little inclosure of cedars where sits the dark figure which is art's supreme expression of the great human mystery of life and death. Instinctively we removed our hats, and neither spoke until after we had come away. Then:

"What does he call it?" he asked.

I did not know, though I had heard applied to it that great line of Shakespeare's—"the rest is silence."

"But that figure is not silent," he said.

And later, as we were driving home:

"It is in deep meditation on sorrowful things."

When we returned to New York he had the little print framed, and kept it always on his mantelpiece.

CCLII

THEOLOGY AND EVOLUTION

FROM the Washington trip dates a period of still closer association with Mark Twain. On the way to New York he suggested that I take up residence in his house — a privilege which I had no wish to refuse. There was room going to waste, he said, and it would be handier for the early and late billiard sessions. So, after that, most of the days and nights I was there.

Looking back on that time now, I see pretty vividly three quite distinct pictures. One of them, the rich, red interior of the billiard-room with the brilliant, green square in the center, on which the gay balls are rolling, and bending over it that luminous white figure in the instant of play. Then there is the long, lighted drawing-room with the same figure stretched on a couch in the corner, drowsily smoking, while the rich organ tones fill the place summoning for him scenes and faces which others do not see. This was the hour between dinner and billiards—the hour which he found most restful of the day. Sometimes he rose, walking the length of the parlors, his step timed to the music and his thought. Of medium height, he gave the impression of being tall—his head thrown up, and like a lion's, rather large for his body. But oftener he lay among the cushions, the light flooding his white hair and dress and heightening his brilliant coloring.

The third picture is that of the dinner-table—always beautifully laid, and always a shrine of wisdom when he was there. He did not always talk; but it was his habit to do so, and memory holds the clearer vision of him when, with eyes and face alive with interest, he presented some new angle of thought in fresh picturesqueness of speech. These are the pictures that have remained to me out of the days spent under his roof, and they will not fade while memory lasts.

Of Mark Twain's table philosophies it seems proper to make rather extended record. They were usually unpremeditated, and they presented the man as he was, and thought. I preserved as much of them as I could, and have verified phrase and idea, when possible, from his own notes and other unprinted writings.

This dinner-table talk naturally varied in character from that of the billiard-room. The latter was likely to be anecdotal and personal; the former was more often philosophical and commentative, ranging through a great variety of subjects scientific, political, sociological, and religious. His talk was often of infinity—the forces of creation—and it was likely to be satire of the orthodox conceptions, intermingled with heresies of his own devising.

Once, after a period of general silence, he said:

"No one who thinks can imagine the universe made by chance. It is too nicely assembled and regulated. There is, of course, a great Master Mind, but it cares nothing for our happiness or our unhappiness."

It was objected, by one of those present, that as the Infinite Mind suggested perfect harmony, sorrow and suffering were defects which that Mind must feel and eventually regulate.

"Yes," he said, "not a sparrow falls but He is noticing, if that is what you mean; but the human conception of it is that God is sitting up nights worrying over the individuals of this infinitesimal race."

Then he recalled a fancy which I have since found among his memoranda. In this note he had written:

The suns & planets that form the constellations of a billion billion solar systems & go pouring, a tossing flood of shining globes, through the viewless arteries of space are the blood-corpuscles in the veins of God; & the nations are the microbes that swarm and wiggle & brag in each, & think God can tell them apart at that distance & has nothing better to do than try. *This*—the entertainment of an eternity. Who so poor in his ambitions as to consent to be God on those terms? Blasphemy? No, it is not blasphemy. If God is as vast as that, He is above blasphemy; if He is as little as that, He is beneath it.

"The Bible," he said, "reveals the character of its God with minute exactness. It is a portrait of a man, if one can imagine a man with evil impulses far beyond the human limit. In the Old Testament He is pictured as unjust, ungenerous, pitiless, and revengeful, punishing innocent children for the misdeeds of their parents; punishing unoffending people for the sins of their rulers, even descending to bloody vengeance upon harmless calves and sheep as punishment for puny trespasses committed by their proprietors. It is the most damnatory biography that ever found its way into print. Its beginning is merely childish. Adam is forbidden to eat the fruit of a certain tree, and gravely informed that if he disobeys he shall die. How could that impress Adam? He could have no idea of what death meant. He had never seen a dead thing. He had never heard of one. If he had been told that if he ate the apples he would be turned into a meridian of longitude that threat would have meant just as much as the other one. The watery intellect that invented that notion could be depended on to go on and decree that all of Adam's descendants down to the latest day should be punished for that nursery trespass in the beginning.

"There is a curious poverty of invention in Bibles. Most of the great races each have one, and they all show this striking defect. Each pretends to originality, without possessing any. Each of them borrows from the other, confiscates old stage properties, puts them forth as fresh and new inspirations from on high. We borrowed the Golden Rule from Confucius, after it had seen service for centuries, and copyrighted it without a blush. We went back to Babylon for the Deluge, and are as proud of it and as satisfied with it as if it had been worth the trouble; whereas we know now that Noah's flood never happened, and couldn't have happened—not in that way. The flood is a favorite with Bible-makers. Another favorite with the founders of religions is the Immaculate Conception. It had been worn threadbare; but we adopted it as a new idea. It was old in Egypt several thousand years before Christ was born. The Hindus prized it ages ago. The Egyptians adopted it even for some of their kings. The Romans borrowed the idea from Greece. We got it straight from heaven by way of Rome. We are still charmed with it."

He would continue in this strain, rising occasionally and walking about the room. Once, considering the character of God—the Bible God—he said:

"We haven't been satisfied with God's character as it is given in the Old Testament; we have amended it. We have called Him a God of mercy and love and morals. He didn't have a single one of those qualities in the beginning. He didn't hesitate to send the plagues on Egypt, the most fiendish punishments that could be devised— not for the king, but for his innocent subjects, the women and the little children, and then only to exhibit His power —just to show off—and He kept hardening Pharaoh's heart so that He could send some further ingenuity of torture, new rivers of blood, and swarms of vermin and new pestilences, merely to exhibit samples of His workmanship. Now and then, during the forty years' wandering, Moses persuaded Him to be a little more lenient with the Israelites, which would show that Moses was the better character of the two. That Old Testament God never had an inspiration of His own."

He referred to the larger conception of God, that Infinite Mind which had projected the universe. He said:

"In some details that Old Bible God is probably a more correct picture than our conception of that Incomparable One that created the universe and flung upon its horizonless ocean of space those giant suns, whose signal-lights are so remote that we only catch their flash when it has been a myriad of years on its way. For that Supreme One is not a God of pity or mercy—not as we recognize these qualities. Think of a God of mercy who would create the typhus germ, or the house-fly, or the centipede, or the rattlesnake, yet these are all His handiwork. They are a part of the Infinite plan. The minister is careful to explain that all these tribulations are sent for a good purpose; but he hires a doctor to destroy the fever germ, and he kills the rattlesnake when he doesn't run from it, and he sets paper with molasses on it for the house-fly.

"Two things are quite certain: one is that God, the limitless God, manufactured those things, for no man could have done it. The man has never lived who could create even the humblest of God's creatures. The other conclusion is that God has no special consideration for man's welfare or comfort, or He wouldn't have created those things to disturb and destroy him. The human conception of pity and morality must be entirely unknown to that Infinite God, as much unknown as the conceptions of a microbe to man, or at least as little regarded.

"If God ever contemplates those qualities in man He probably admires them, as we always admire the thing which we do not possess ourselves; probably a little grain of pity in a man or a little atom of mercy would look as big to Him as a constellation. He could create a constellation with a thought; but He has been all the measureless ages, and He has never acquired those qualities that we have named—pity and mercy and morality. He goes on destroying a whole island of people with an earthquake, or a whole cityful with a plague, when we punish a man in the electric chair for merely killing the poorest of our race. The human being needs to revise his ideas again about God. Most of the scientists have done it already; but most of them don't dare to say so."

He pointed out that the moral idea was undergoing constant change; that what was considered justifiable in an earlier day was regarded as highly immoral now. He pointed out that even the Decalogue made no reference to lying, except in the matter of bearing false witness against a neighbor. Also, that there was a commandment against covetousness, though covetousness to-day was the basis of all commerce. The general conclusion being that the morals of the Lord had been the morals of the beginning; the morals of the first-created man, the morals of the troglodyte, the morals of necessity; and that the morals of mankind had kept pace with necessity, whereas those of the Lord had remained unchanged. It is hardly necessary to say that no one ever undertook to contradict any statements of this sort from him. In the first place, there was no desire to do so; and in the second place, any one attempting it would have cut a puny figure with his less substantial arguments and his less vigorous phrase. It was the part of wisdom and immeasurably the part of happiness to be silent and listen.

On another evening he began:

"The mental evolution of the species proceeds apparently by regular progress side by side with the physical development until it comes to man, then there is a long, unexplained gulf. Somewhere man acquired an asset which sets him immeasurably apart from the other animals—his imagination. Out of it he created for himself a conscience, and clothes, and immodesty, and a hereafter, and a soul. I wonder where he got that asset. It almost makes one agree with Alfred Russel Wallace that the world and the universe were created just for his benefit, that he is the chief love and delight of God. Wallace says that the whole universe was made to take care of and to keep steady this little floating mote in the center of it, which we call the world. It looks like a good deal of trouble for such a small result; but it's dangerous to dispute with a learned astronomer like Wallace. Still, I don't think we ought to decide too soon about it—not until the returns are all in. There is the geological evidence, for instance. Even after the universe was created, it took a long time to prepare the world for man. Some of the scientists, ciphering out the evidence furnished by geology, have arrived at the conviction that the world is prodigiously old. Lord Kelvin doesn't agree with them. He says that it isn't more than a hundred million years old, and he thinks the human race has inhabited it about thirty thousand years of that time. Even so, it was 99,970,000 years getting ready, impatient as the Creator doubtless was to see man and admire him. That was because God first had to make the oyster. You can't make an oyster out of nothing, nor you can't do it in a day. You've got to start with a vast variety of invertebrates, belemnites, trilobites, jebusites, amalekites, and that sort of fry, and put them into soak in a primary sea and observe and wait what will happen. Some of them will turn out a disappointment; the belemnites and the amalekites and such will be failures, and they will die out and become extinct in the course of the nineteen million years covered by the experiment; but all is not lost, for the amalekites will develop gradually into encrinites and stalactites and blatherskites, and one thing and another, as the mighty ages creep on and the periods pile their lofty crags in the primordial seas, and at last the first grand stage in the preparation of the world for man stands completed; the oyster is done. Now an oyster has hardly any more reasoning power than a man has, so it is probable this one jumped to the conclusion that the nineteen million years was a preparation for *him*. That would be just like an oyster, and, anyway, this one could not know at that early date that he was only an incident in a scheme, and that there was some more to the scheme yet.

"The oyster being finished, the next step in the preparation of the world for man was fish. So the old Silurian seas were opened up to breed the fish in. It took twenty million years to make the fish and to fossilize him so we'd have the evidence later.

"Then, the Paleozoic limit having been reached, it was necessary to start a new age to make the reptiles. Man would have to have some reptiles—not to eat, but to develop himself from. Thirty million years were required for the reptiles, and out of such material as was left were made those stupendous saurians that used to prowl about the steamy world in remote ages, with their snaky heads forty feet in the air and their sixty feet of body and tail racing and thrashing after them. They are all gone now, every one of them; just a few fossil remnants of them left on this far-flung fringe of time.

"It took all those years to get one of those creatures properly constructed to proceed to the next step. Then came the pterodactyl, who thought all that preparation all those millions of years had been intended to produce him, for there wasn't anything too foolish for a pterodactyl to imagine. I suppose he did attract a good deal of attention, for even the least observant could see that there was the making of a bird in him, also the making of a mammal, in the course of time. You can't say too much for the picturesqueness of the pterodactyl—he was the triumph of his period. He wore wings and had teeth.

and was a starchy-looking creature. But the progression went right along.

"During the next thirty million years the bird arrived, and the kangaroo, and by and by the mastodon, and the giant sloth, and the Irish elk, and the old Silurian ass, and some people thought that man was about due. But that was a mistake, for the next thing they knew there came a great ice-sheet, and those creatures all escaped across the Bering Strait and wandered around in Asia and died, all except a few to carry on the preparation with. There were six of those glacial periods, with two million years or so between each. They chased those poor orphans up and down the earth, from weather to weather, from tropic temperature to fifty degrees below. They never knew what kind of weather was going to turn up next, and if they settled any place the whole continent suddenly sank from under them, and they had to make a scramble for dry land. Sometimes a volcano would turn itself loose just as they got located. They led that uncertain, strenuous existence for about twenty-five million years, always wondering what was going to happen next, never suspecting that it was just a preparation for man, who had to be done just so or there wouldn't be any proper or harmonious place for him when he arrived, and then at last the monkey came, and everybody could see at a glance that man wasn't far off now, and that was true enough. The monkey went on developing for close upon five million years, and then he turned into a man—to all appearances.

"It does look like a lot of fuss and trouble to go through to build anything, especially a human being, and nowhere along the way is there any evidence of where he picked up that final asset—his imagination. It makes him different from the others—not any better, but certainly different. Those earlier animals didn't have it, and the monkey hasn't it or he wouldn't be so cheerful."

THEOLOGY AND EVOLUTION

He often held forth on the shortcomings of the human race—always a favorite subject—the incompetencies and imperfections of this final creation, in spite of, or because of, his great attribute—the imagination. Once (this was in the billiard-room) I started him by saying that whatever the conditions in other planets, there seemed no reason why life should not develop in each, adapted as perfectly to prevailing conditions as man is suited to conditions here. He said:

"Is it your idea, then, that man is perfectly adapted to the conditions of this planet?"

I began to qualify, rather weakly; but what I said did not matter. He was off on his favorite theme.

"Man adapted to the earth?" he said. "Why, he can't sleep out-of-doors without freezing to death or getting the rheumatism or the malaria; he can't keep his nose under water over a minute without being drowned; he can't climb a tree without falling out and breaking his neck. Why, he's the poorest, clumsiest excuse of all the creatures that inhabit this earth. He has got to be coddled and housed and swathed and bandaged and upholstered to be able to live at all. He is a rickety sort of a thing, anyway you take him, a regular British Museum of infirmities and inferiorities. He is always undergoing repairs. A machine that is as unreliable as he is would have no market. The higher animals get their teeth without pain or inconvenience. The original caveman, the troglodyte, may have got his that way. But now they come through months and months of cruel torture, and at a time of life when he is least able to bear it. As soon as he gets them they must all be pulled out again, for they were of no value in the first place, not worth the loss of a night's rest. The second set will answer for a while; but he will never get a set that can be depended on until the dentist makes one. The animals are not much troubled that way. In a wild state, a natural state, they have few diseases; their main one is old age. But man starts in as a child and lives on diseases to the end as a regular diet. He has mumps, measles, whooping-cough, croup, tonsilitis, diphtheria, scarlet-fever, as a matter of course. Afterward, as he goes along, his life continues to be threatened at every turn by colds, coughs, asthma, bronchitis, quinsy, consumption, yellow-fever, blindness, influenza, carbuncles, pneumonia, softening of the brain, diseases of the heart and bones, and a thousand other maladies of one sort and another. He's just a basketful of festering, pestilent corruption, provided for the support and entertainment of microbes. Look at the workmanship of him in some of its particulars. What are his tonsils for? They perform no useful function; they have no value. They are but a trap for tonsilitis and quinsy. And what is the appendix for? It has no value. Its sole interest is to lie and wait for stray grape-seeds and breed trouble. What is his beard for? It is just a nuisance. All nations persecute it with the razor. Nature, however, always keeps him supplied with it, instead of putting it on his head, where it ought to be. You seldom see a man bald-headed on his chin, but on his head. A man wants to keep his hair. It is a graceful ornament, a comfort, the best of all protections against weather, and he prizes it above emeralds and rubies, and Nature half the time puts it on so it won't stay.

"Man's sight and smell and hearing are all inferior. If he were suited to the conditions he could smell an enemy; he could hear him; he could see him, just as the animals can detect their enemies. The robin hears the earthworm burrowing his course under the ground; the bloodhound follows a scent that is two days old. Man isn't even handsome, as compared with the birds; and as for style, look at the Bengal tiger—that ideal of grace, physical perfection, and majesty. Think of the lion and the tiger and the leopard, and then think of man—that poor thing!—the animal of the wig, the ear-trumpet, the glass eye, the porcelain teeth, the wooden leg, the trepanned skull, the silver wind-pipe—a creature that is mended and patched all over from top to bottom. If he can't get renewals of his bric-à-brac in the next world what will he look like? He has just that one stupendous superiority—his imagination, his intellect. It makes him supreme—the higher animals can't match him there. It's very curious."

A letter which he wrote to J. Howard Moore concerning his book *The Universal Kinship* was of this period, and seems to belong here.

DEAR MR. MOORE,—The book has furnished me several days of deep pleasure & satisfaction; it has compelled my gratitude at the same time, since it saves me the labor of stating my own long-cherished opinions & reflections & resentments by doing it lucidly & fervently & irascibly for me.

There is one thing that always puzzles me: as inheritors of the mentality of our reptile ancestors we have improved the inheritance by a thousand grades; but in the matter of the morals which they left us we have gone backward as many grades. *That evolution* is strange & to me unaccountable & unnatural. Necessarily we started equipped with their perfect and blemishless morals; now we are wholly destitute; we have no *real* morals, but only artificial ones—morals created and preserved by the forced suppression of natural & healthy instincts. Yes, we are a sufficiently comical invention, we humans.

Sincerely yours,

S. L. CLEMENS.

CCLIII

I RECALL two pleasant social events of that winter: one a little party given at the Clemenses' home on New-Year's Eve, with charades and story-telling and music. It was the music feature of this party that was distinctive; it was supplied by wire through an invention known as the telharmonium which, it was believed, would revolutionize musical entertainment in such places as hotels, and to some extent in private houses. The music came over the regular telephone wire, and was delivered through a series of horns or megaphones—similar to those used for phonographs—the playing being done, meanwhile, by skilled performers at the central station. Just why the telharmonium has not made good its promises of popularity I do not know. Clemens was filled with enthusiasm over the idea. He made a speech a little before midnight, in which he told how he had generally been enthusiastic about inventions which had turned out more or less well in about equal proportions. He did not dwell on the failures, but he told how he had been the first to use a typewriter for manuscript work; how he had been one of the earliest users of the fountain-pen; how he had installed the first telephone ever used in a private house, and how the audience now would have a demonstration of the first telharmonium music so employed. It was just about the stroke of midnight when he finished, and a moment later the horns began to play chimes and "Auld Lang Syne" and "America."

AN EVENING WITH HELEN KELLER

The other pleasant evening referred to was a little company given in honor of Helen Keller. It was fascinating to watch her, and to realize with what a store of knowledge she had lighted the black silence of her physical life. To see Mark Twain and Helen Keller together was something not easily to be forgotten. When Mrs. Macy (who, as Miss Sullivan, had led her so marvelously out of the shadows) communicated his words to her with what seemed a lightning touch of the fingers her face radiated every shade of his meaning—humorous, serious, pathetic. Helen visited the various objects in the room, and seemed to enjoy them more than the usual observer of these things, and certainly in greater detail. Her sensitive fingers spread over articles of bric-à-brac, and the exclamations she uttered were always fitting, showing that she somehow visualized each thing in all its particulars. There was a bronze cat of handsome workmanship and happy expression, and when she had run those all-seeing fingers of hers over it she said: "It is smiling."

BILLIARD-ROOM NOTES

THE billiard games went along pretty steadily that winter. My play improved, and Clemens found it necessary to eliminate my odds altogether, and to change the game frequently in order to keep me in subjection. Frequently there were long and apparently violent arguments over the legitimacy of some particular shot or play—arguments to us quite as enjoyable as the rest of the game. Sometimes he would count a shot which was clearly out of the legal limits, and then it was always a delight to him to have a mock-serious discussion over the matter of conscience, and whether or not his conscience was in its usual state of repair. It would always end by him saying: "I don't wish even to *seem* to do anything which can invite suspicion. I refuse to count that shot," or something of like nature. Sometimes when I had let a questionable play pass without comment, he would watch anxiously until I had made a similar one and then insist on my scoring it to square accounts. His conscience was always repairing itself.

He had experimented, a great many years before, with what was in the nature of a trick on some unsuspecting player. It consisted in turning out twelve pool-balls on the table with one cue ball, and asking his guest how many caroms he thought he could make with all those twelve balls to play on. He had learned that the average player would seldom make more than thirty-one counts, and usually, before this number was reached, he would miss through some careless play or get himself into a position where he couldn't play at all. The thing looked absurdly easy. It looked as if one could go on playing all day long, and the victim was usually eager to bet that he could make fifty or perhaps a hundred; but for more than an hour I tried it patiently, and seldom succeeded in scoring more than fifteen or twenty without missing. Long after the play itself ceased to be amusing to me, he insisted on my going on and trying it some more, and he would throw himself back and roar with laughter, the tears streaming down his cheeks, to see me work and fume and fail.

It was very soon after that that Peter Dunne ("Mr. Dooley") came down for luncheon, and after several games of the usual sort, Clemens quietly—as if the idea had just occurred to him—rolled out the twelve balls and asked Dunne how many caroms he thought he could make without a miss. Dunne said he thought he could make a thousand. Clemens quite indifferently said that he didn't believe he could make fifty. Dunne offered to bet five dollars that he could, and the wager was made. Dunne scored about twenty-five the first time and missed; then he insisted on betting five dollars again, and his defeats continued until Clemens had twenty-five dollars of Dunne's money, and Dunne was sweating and swearing, and Mark Twain rocking with delight. Dunne went away still unsatisfied, promising that he would come back and try it again. Perhaps he practised in his absence, for when he returned he had learned something. He won his twenty-five dollars back, and I think something more added. Mark Twain was still ahead, for Dunne furnished him with a good five hundred dollars' worth of amusement.

Clemens never cared to talk and never wished to be talked to when the game was actually in progress. If there was anything to be said on either side, he would stop and rest his cue on the floor, or sit down on the couch, until the matter was concluded. Such interruptions happened pretty frequently, and many of the bits of personal comment and incident scattered along through this work are the result of those brief rests. Some shot, or situation, or word would strike back through the past and awaken a note long silent, and I generally kept a pad and pencil on the window-sill with the score-sheet, and later, during his play, I would scrawl some reminder that would be precious by and by.

On one of these I find a memorandum of what he called his three recurrent dreams. All of us have such things, but his seem worth remembering.

"There is never a month passes," he said, "that I do not dream of being in reduced circumstances, and obliged to go back to the river to earn a living. It is never a pleasant dream, either. I love to think about those days; but there's always something sickening about the thought that I have been obliged to go back to them; and usually in my dream I am just about to start into a black shadow without being able to tell whether it is Selma bluff, or Hat Island, or only a black wall of night.

"Another dream that I have of that kind is being compelled to go back to the lecture platform. I hate that dream worse than the other. In it I am always getting up before an audience with nothing to say, trying to be funny; trying to make the audience laugh, realizing that I am only making silly jokes. Then the audience realizes it, and pretty soon they commence to get up and leave. That dream always ends by my standing there in the semi-darkness talking to an empty house.

"My other dream is of being at a brilliant gathering in my night-garments. People don't seem to notice me there at first, and then pretty soon somebody points me out, and they all begin to look at me suspiciously, and I can see that they are wondering who I am and why I am there in that costume. Then it occurs to me that I can fix it by making myself known. I take hold of some man and whisper to him, 'I am Mark Twain'; but that does not improve it, for immediately I can hear him whispering to the others, 'He says he is Mark Twain,' and they all look at me a good deal more suspiciously than before, and I can see that they don't believe it, and that it was a mistake to make that confession. Sometimes, in that dream, I am dressed like a tramp instead of being in my night-clothes; but it all ends about the same—they go away and leave me standing there, ashamed. I generally enjoy my dreams, but not those three, and they are the ones I have oftenest."

Quite often some curious episode of the world's history would flash upon him—something amusing, or coarse, or tragic, and he would bring the game to a standstill and recount it with wonderful accuracy as to date and circumstance. He had a natural passion for historic events and a gift for mentally fixing them, but his memory in other ways was seldom reliable. He was likely to forget the names even of those he knew best and saw oftenest, and the small details of life seldom registered at all.

He had his breakfast served in his room, and once, on a slip of paper, he wrote, for his own reminder:

The accuracy of your forgetfulness is absolute—it seems never to fail. I prepare to pour my coffee so it can cool while I shave—and I always forget to pour it.

Yet, very curiously, he would sometimes single out a minute detail, something every one else had overlooked, and days or even weeks afterward would recall it vividly, and not always at an opportune moment. Perhaps this also was a part of his old pilot-training. Once Clara Clemens remarked:

"It always amazes me the things that father does

and does not remember. Some little trifle that nobody else would notice, and you are hoping that he didn't, will suddenly come back to him just when you least expect it or care for it."

My note-book contains the entry:

February 11, 1907. He said to-day:

"A blindfolded chess-player can remember every play and discuss the game afterward, while we can't remember from one shot to the next."

I mentioned his old pilot-memory as an example of what he could do if he wished.

"Yes," he answered, "those are special memories; a pilot will tell you the number of feet in every crossing at any time, but he can't remember what he had for breakfast."

"How long did you keep your pilot-memory?" I asked.

"Not long; it faded out right away, but the training served me, for when I went to report on a paper a year or two later I never had to make any notes."

"I suppose you still remember some of the river?"

"Not much. Hat Island, Helena. and here and there a place; but that is about all."

CCLV

FURTHER PERSONALITIES

LIKE every person living, Mark Twain had some peculiar and petty economies. Such things in great men are noticeable. He lived extravagantly. His household expenses at the time amounted to more than fifty dollars a day. In the matter of food, the choicest and most expensive the market could furnish was always served in lavish abundance. He had the best and highest-priced servants, ample as to number. His clothes he bought generously; he gave without stint to his children; his gratuities were always liberal. He never questioned pecuniary outgoes—seldom worried as to the state of his bank-account so long as there was plenty. He smoked cheap cigars because he preferred their flavor. Yet he had his economies. I have seen him, before leaving a room, go around and carefully lower the gas-jets, to provide against that waste. I have known him to examine into the cost of a cab, and object to an apparent overcharge of a few cents.

It seemed that his idea of economy might be expressed in these words: He abhorred extortion and visible waste.

Furthermore, he had exact ideas as to ownership. One evening, while we were playing billiards, I noticed a five-cent piece on the floor. I picked it up, saying:

"Here is five cents; I don't know whose it is."

He regarded the coin rather seriously, I thought, and said:

"I don't know, either."

I laid it on the top of the book-shelves which ran

around the room. The play went on, and I forgot the
circumstance. When the game ended that night I went
into his room with him, as usual, for a good-night word.
As he took his change and keys from the pocket of his
trousers, he looked the assortment over and said:

"That five-cent piece you found was mine."

I brought it to him at once, and he took it solemnly,
laid it with the rest of his change, and neither of us referred to it again. It may have been one of his jokes,
but I think it more likely that he remembered having
had a five-cent piece, probably reserved for car fare, and
that it was missing.

More than once, in Washington, he had said:

"Draw plenty of money for incidental expenses. Don't
bother to keep account of them."

So it was not miserliness; it was just a peculiarity,
a curious attention to a trifling detail.

He had a fondness for riding on the then newly completed Subway, which he called the Underground. Sometimes he would say:

"I'll pay your fare on the Underground if you want
to take a ride with me." And he always insisted on paying the fare; and once when I rode far up-town with him
to a place where he was going to luncheon, and had taken
him to the door, he turned and said, gravely:

"Here is five cents to pay your way home." And I
took it in the same spirit in which it had been offered.
It was probably this trait which caused some one occasionally to claim that Mark Twain was close in money
matters. Perhaps there may have been times in his life
when he was parsimonious; but, if so. I must believe
that it was when he was sorely pressed and exercising the
natural instinct of self-preservation. He wished to receive the full value (who does not?) of his labors and properties. He took a childish delight in piling up money;
but it became greed only when he believed some one with

whom he had dealings was trying to get an unfair division of profits. Then it became something besides greed. It became an indignation that amounted to malevolence. I was concerned in a number of dealings with Mark Twain, and at a period in his life when human traits are supposed to become exaggerated, which is to say old age, and if he had any natural tendency to be unfair, or small, or greedy in his money dealings I think I should have seen it. Personally, I found him liberal to excess, and I never observed in him anything less than generosity to those who were fair with him.

Once that winter, when a letter came from Steve Gillis saying that he was an invalid now, and would have plenty of time to read Sam's books if he owned them, Clemens ordered an expensive set from his publishers, and did what meant to him even more than the cost in money—he autographed each of those twenty-five volumes. Then he sent them, charges paid, to that far Californian retreat. It was hardly the act of a stingy man.

He had the human fondness for a compliment when it was genuine and from an authoritative source, and I remember how pleased he was that winter with Prof. William Lyon Phelps's widely published opinion, which ranked Mark Twain as the greatest American novelist, and declared that his fame would outlive any American of his time. Phelps had placed him above Holmes, Howells, James, and even Hawthorne. He had declared him to be more American than any of these—more American even than Whitman. Professor Phelps's position in Yale College gave this opinion a certain official weight; but I think the fact of Phelps himself being a writer of great force, with an American freshness of style, gave it a still greater value.

Among the pleasant things that winter was a meeting with Eugene F. Ware, of Kansas, with whose pen-name—"Ironquill"—Clemens had long been familiar.

Ware was a breezy Western genius of the finest type. If he had abandoned law for poetry, there is no telling how far his fame might have reached. There was in his work that same spirit of Americanism and humor and humanity that is found in Mark Twain's writings, and he had the added faculty of rhyme and rhythm, which would have set him in a place apart. I had known Ware personally during a period of Western residence, and later, when he was Commissioner of Pensions under Roosevelt. I usually saw him when he came to New York, and it was a great pleasure now to bring together the two men whose work I so admired. They met at a small private luncheon at The Players, and Peter Dunne was there, and Robert Collier, and it was such an afternoon as Howells has told of when he and Aldrich and Bret Harte and those others talked until the day faded into twilight, and twilight deepened into evening. Clemens had put in most of the day before reading Ware's book of poems, *The Rhymes of Ironquill*, and had declared his work to rank with the very greatest of American poetry—I think he called it the most truly American in flavor. I remember that at the luncheon he noted Ware's big, splendid physique and his Western liberties of syntax with a curious intentness. I believe he regarded him as being nearer his own type in mind and expression than any one he had met before.

Among Ware's poems he had been especially impressed with the "Fables," and with some verses entitled "Whist," which, though rather more optimistic, conformed to his own philosophy. They have a distinctly "Western" feeling.

WHIST

Hour after hour the cards were fairly shuffled,
  And fairly dealt, and still I got no hand;
The morning came; but I, with mind unruffled,
  Did simply say, "I do not understand."

FURTHER PERSONALITIES

Life is a game of whist. From unseen sources
  The cards are shuffled, and the hands are dealt.
Blind are our efforts to control the forces
  That, though unseen, are no less strongly felt.

I do not like the way the cards are shuffled,
  But still I like the game and want to play;
And through the long, long night will I, unruffled,
  Play what I get, until the break of day.

CCLVI

HONORS FROM OXFORD

CLEMENS made a brief trip to Bermuda during the winter, taking Twichell along; their first return to the island since the trip when they had promised to come back so soon—nearly thirty years before. They had been comparatively young men then. They were old now, but they found the green island as fresh and full of bloom as ever. They did not find their old landlady; they could not even remember her name at first, and then Twichell recalled that it was the same as an author of certain school-books in his youth, and Clemens promptly said, "Kirkham's Grammar." Kirkham was truly the name, and they went to find her; but she was dead, and the daughter, who had been a young girl in that earlier time, reigned in her stead and entertained the successors of her mother's guests. They walked and drove about the island, and it was like taking up again a long-discontinued book and reading another chapter of the same tale. It gave Mark Twain a fresh interest in Bermuda, one which he did not allow to fade again.

Later in the year (March, 1907) I also made a journey; it having been agreed that I should take a trip to the Mississippi and to the Pacific coast to see those old friends of Mark Twain's who were so rapidly passing away. John Briggs was still alive, and other Hannibal school-mates; also Joe Goodman and Steve Gillis, and a few more of the early pioneers—all eminently worth seeing in the matter of such work as I had in hand. The bil-

liard games would be interrupted; but whatever reluctance to the plan there may have been on that account
was put aside in view of prospective benefits. Clemens,
in fact, seemed to derive joy from the thought that he
was commissioning a kind of personal emissary to his
old comrades, and provided me with a letter of credentials.

It was a long, successful trip that I made, and it was
undertaken none too soon. John Briggs, a gentle-hearted
man, was already entering the valley of the shadow as
he talked to me by his fire one memorable afternoon, and
reviewed the pranks of those days along the river and in
the cave and on Holliday's Hill. I think it was six weeks
later that he died; and there were others of that scattering procession who did not reach the end of the year.
Joe Goodman, still full of vigor (in 1912), journeyed with
me to the green and dreamy solitudes of Jackass Hill
to see Steve and Jim Gillis, and that was an unforgetable
Sunday when Steve Gillis, an invalid, but with the fire
still in his eyes and speech, sat up on his couch in his little
cabin in that Arcadian stillness and told old tales and
adventures. When I left he said:

"Tell Sam I'm going to die pretty soon, but that I
love him; that I've loved him all my life, and I'll love
him till I die. This is the last word I'll ever send to
him." Jim Gillis, down in Sonora, was already lying at
the point of death, and so for him the visit was too late,
though he was able to receive a message from his ancient
mining partner, and to send back a parting word.

I returned by way of New Orleans and the Mississippi
River, for I wished to follow that abandoned water
highway, and to visit its presiding genius, Horace Bixby,
still alive and in service as pilot of the government snag-
boat, his headquarters at St. Louis.[1]

Coming up the river on one of the old passenger steam-

---

[1] He died August 2, 1912, at the age of 86.

boats that still exist, I noticed in a paper which came aboard that Mark Twain was to receive from Oxford University the literary doctor's degree. There had been no hint of this when I came away, and it seemed rather too sudden and too good to be true. That the little barefoot lad who had played along the river-banks at Hannibal, and received such meager advantages in the way of schooling—whose highest ambition had been to pilot such a craft as this one—was about to be crowned by the world's greatest institution of learning, to receive the highest recognition for achievement in the world of letters, was a thing which would not be likely to happen outside of a fairy tale.

Returning to New York, I ran out to Tuxedo, where he had taken a home for the summer (for it was already May), and walking along the shaded paths of that beautiful suburban park, he told me what he knew of the Oxford matter.

Moberly Bell, of the London *Times*, had been over in April, and soon after his return to England there had come word of the proposed honor. Clemens privately and openly (to Bell) attributed it largely to his influence. He wrote to him:

DEAR MR. BELL,—Your hand is in it & you have my best thanks. Although I wouldn't cross an ocean again for the price of the ship that carried me I am glad to do it for an Oxford degree. I shall plan to sail for England a shade before the middle of June, so that I can have a few days in London before the 26th.

A day or two later, when the time for sailing had been arranged, he overtook his letter with a cable:

I perceive your hand in it. You have my best thanks. Sail on *Minneapolis* June 8th. Due in Southampton ten days later.

Clemens said that his first word of the matter had been

a newspaper cablegram, and that he had been doubtful concerning it until a cablegram to himself had confirmed it.

"I never expected to cross the water again," he said; "but I would be willing to journey to Mars for that Oxford degree."

He put the matter aside then, and fell to talking of Jim Gillis and the others I had visited, dwelling especially on Gillis's astonishing faculty for improvising romances, recalling how he had stood with his back to the fire weaving his endless, grotesque yarns, with no other guide than his fancy. It was a long, happy walk we had, though rather a sad one in its memories; and he seemed that day, in a sense, to close the gate of those early scenes behind him, for he seldom referred to them afterward.

He was back at 21 Fifth Avenue presently, arranging for his voyage. Meantime, cable invitations of every sort were pouring in, from this and that society and dignitary; invitations to dinners and ceremonials, and what not, and it was clear enough that his English sojourn was to be a busy one. He had hoped to avoid this, and began by declining all but two invitations—a dinner-party given by Ambassador Whitelaw Reid and a luncheon proposed by the "Pilgrims." But it became clear that this would not do. England was not going to confer its greatest collegiate honor without being permitted to pay its wider and more popular tribute.

Clemens engaged a special secretary for the trip—Mr. Ralph W. Ashcroft, a young Englishman familiar with London life. They sailed on the 8th of June, by a curious coincidence exactly forty years from the day he had sailed on the *Quaker City* to win his great fame. I went with him to the ship. His first elation had passed by this time, and he seemed a little sad, remembering, I think, the wife who would have enjoyed this honor with him but could not share it now.

CCLVII

A TRUE ENGLISH WELCOME

MARK TWAIN'S trip across the Atlantic would seem to have been a pleasant one. The *Minneapolis* is a fine, big ship, and there was plenty of company. Prof. Archibald Henderson, Bernard Shaw's biographer, was aboard;[1] also President Patton, of the Princeton Theological Seminary; a well-known cartoonist, Richards, and some very attractive young people—school-girls in particular, such as all through his life had appealed to Mark Twain. Indeed, in his later life they made a stronger appeal than ever. The years had robbed him of his own little flock, and always he was trying to replace them. Once he said:

"During those years after my wife's death I was washing about on a forlorn sea of banquets and speech-making in high and holy causes, and these things furnished me intellectual cheer and entertainment; but they got at my heart for an evening only, then left it dry and dusty. I had reached the grandfather stage of life without grandchildren, so I began to adopt some."

He adopted several on that journey to England and on the return voyage, and he kept on adopting others during the rest of his life. These companionships became one of the happiest aspects of his final days, as we shall see by and by.

---

[1] Professor Henderson has since then published a volume on Mark Twain—an interesting commentary on his writings—mainly from the sociological point of view.

A TRUE ENGLISH WELCOME

There were entertainments on the ship, one of them given for the benefit of the Seamen's Orphanage. One of his adopted granddaughters—"Charley" he called her—played a violin solo and Clemens made a speech. Later his autographs were sold at auction. Dr. Patton was auctioneer, and one autographed postal card brought twenty-five dollars, which is perhaps the record price for a single Mark Twain signature. He wore his white suit on this occasion, and in the course of his speech referred to it. He told first of the many defects in his behavior, and how members of his household had always tried to keep him straight. The children, he said, had fallen into the habit of calling it "dusting papa off." Then he went on:

When my daughter came to see me off last Saturday at the boat she slipped a note in my hand and said, "Read it when you get aboard the ship." I didn't think of it again until day before yesterday, and it was a "dusting off." And if I carry out all the instructions that I got there I shall be more celebrated in England for my behavior than for anything else. I got instructions how to act on every occasion. She underscored "Now, don't you wear white clothes on ship or on shore until you get back," and I intended to obey. I have been used to obeying my family all my life, but I wore the white clothes to-night because the trunk that has the dark clothes in it is in the cellar. I am not apologizing for the white clothes; I am only apologizing to my daughter for not obeying her.

He received a great welcome when the ship arrived at Tilbury. A throng of rapid-fire reporters and photographers immediately surrounded him, and when he left the ship the stevedores gave him a round of cheers. It was the beginning of that almost unheard-of demonstration of affection and honor which never for a moment ceased, but augmented from day to day during the four weeks of his English sojourn.

MARK TWAIN

In a dictation following his return, Mark Twain said

Who began it? The very people of all people in the world whom I would have chosen: a hundred men of my own class— grimy sons of labor, the real builders of empires and civilizations, the stevedores! They stood in a body on the dock and charged their masculine lungs, and gave me a welcome which went to the marrow of me.

J. Y. W. MacAlister was at the St. Pancras railway station to meet him, and among others on the platform was Bernard Shaw, who had come down to meet Professor Henderson. Clemens and Shaw were presented, and met eagerly, for each greatly admired the other. A throng gathered. Mark Twain was extricated at last, and hurried away to his apartments at Brown's Hotel, "a placid, subdued, homelike, old-fashioned English inn," he called it, "well known to me years ago, a blessed retreat of a sort now rare in England, and becoming rarer every year."

But Brown's was not placid and subdued during his stay. The London newspapers declared that Mark Twain's arrival had turned Brown's not only into a royal court, but a post-office—that the procession of visitors and the bundles of mail fully warranted this statement. It was, in fact, an experience which surpassed in general magnitude and magnificence anything he had hitherto known. His former London visits, beginning with that of 1872, had been distinguished by high attentions, but all of them combined could not equal this. When England decides to get up an ovation, her people are not to be outdone even by the lavish Americans. An assistant secretary had to be engaged immediately, and it sometimes required from sixteen to twenty hours a day for two skilled and busy men to receive callers and reduce the pile of correspondence.

A pile of invitations had already accumulated, and

others flowed in. Lady Stanley, widow of Henry M. Stanley, wrote:

> You know I want to see you and join right hand to right hand. I must see your dear face again. . . . You will have no peace, rest, or leisure during your stay in London, and you will end by hating human beings. Let me come before you feel that way.

Mary Cholmondeley, the author of *Red Pottage*, niece of that lovable Reginald Cholmondeley, and herself an old friend, sent greetings and urgent invitations. Archdeacon Wilberforce wrote:

> I have just been preaching about your indictment of that *scoundrel* king of the Belgians and telling my people to buy the book. I am only a humble item among the very many who offer you a cordial welcome in England, but we long to see you again, and I should like to change hats with you again. Do you remember?

The Athenæum, the Garrick, and a dozen other London clubs had anticipated his arrival with cards of honorary membership for the period of his stay. Every leading photographer had put in a claim for sittings. It was such a reception as Charles Dickens had received in America in 1842, and again in 1867. A London paper likened it to Voltaire's return to Paris in 1778, when France went mad over him. There is simply no limit to English affection and hospitality once aroused. Clemens wrote:

> Surely such weeks as this must be very rare in this world: I had seen nothing like them before; I shall see nothing approaching them again!

Sir Thomas Lipton and Bram Stoker, old friends, were among the first to present themselves, and there was no break in the line of callers.

Clemens's resolutions for secluding himself were swept away. On the very next morning following his arrival he breakfasted with J. Henniker Heaton, father of International Penny Postage, at the Bath Club, just across Dover Street from Brown's. He lunched at the Ritz with Marjorie Bowen and Miss Bisland. In the afternoon he sat for photographs at Barnett's, and made one or two calls. He could no more resist these things than a débutante in her first season.

He was breakfasting again with Heaton next morning; lunching with "Toby, M.P.," and Mrs. Lucy; and having tea with Lady Stanley in the afternoon, and being elaborately dined next day at Dorchester House by Ambassador and Mrs. Reid. These were all old and tried friends. He was not a stranger among them, he said; he was at home. Alfred Austin, Conan Doyle, Anthony Hope, Alma Tadema, E. A. Abbey, Edmund Gosse, George Smalley, Sir Norman Lockyer, Henry W. Lucy, Sidney Brooks, and Bram Stoker were among those at Dorchester House —all old comrades, as were many of the other guests.

"I knew fully half of those present," he said afterward.

Mark Twain's bursting upon London society naturally was made the most of by the London papers, and all his movements were tabulated and elaborated, and when there was any opportunity for humor in the situation it was not left unimproved. The celebrated Ascot racing-cup was stolen just at the time of his arrival, and the papers suggestively mingled their head-lines, "Mark Twain Arrives: Ascot Cup Stolen," and kept the joke going in one form or another. Certain state jewels and other regalia also disappeared during his stay, and the news of these burglaries was reported in suspicious juxtaposition with the news of Mark Twain's doings.

English reporters adopted American habits for the occasion, and invented or embellished when the demand for a new sensation was urgent. Once, when following the custom of the place, he descended the hotel elevator in a perfectly proper and heavy brown bath robe, and stepped across narrow Dover Street to the Bath Club, the papers flamed next day with the story that Mark Twain had wandered about the lobby of Brown's and promenaded Dover Street in a sky-blue bath robe attracting wide attention.

Clara Clemens, across the ocean, was naturally a trifle disturbed by such reports, and cabled this delicate "dusting off":

"Much worried. Remember proprieties."

To which he answered:

"They all pattern after me," a reply to the last degree characteristic.

It was on the fourth day after his arrival, June 22d, that he attended the King's garden-party at Windsor Castle. There were eighty-five hundred guests at the King's party, and if we may judge from the London newspapers, Mark Twain was quite as much a figure in that great throng as any member of the royal family. His presentation to the King and the Queen is set down as an especially notable incident, and their conversation is quite fully given. Clemens himself reported:

His Majesty was very courteous. In the course of the conversation I reminded him of an episode of fifteen years ago, when I had the honor to walk a mile with him when he was taking the waters at Homburg, in Germany. I said that I had often told about that episode, and that whenever I was the historian I made good history of it and it was worth listening to, but that it had found its way into print once or twice in unauthentic ways and was badly damaged thereby. I said I should like to go on repeating this history, but that I should be quite fair and reasonably honest, and while I should probably never tell it twice in the same way I should at least never allow it to deteriorate in my hands. His Majesty intimated his willingness that I should continue to disseminate that piece of history; and he added a compliment, saying that he knew good and sound history would not suffer at my hands, and that if this good and sound history needed any improvement beyond the facts he would trust me to furnish that improvement.

I think it is not an exaggeration to say that the Queen looked as young and beautiful as she did thirty-five years ago when I saw her first. I did not say this to her, because I learned long ago never to say the obvious thing, but leave the obvious thing to commonplace and inexperienced people to say. That she still looked to me as young and beautiful as she did thirty-five years ago is good evidence that ten thousand people have already noticed this and have mentioned it to her. I could have said it and spoken the truth, but I was too wise for that. I kept the remark unuttered and saved her Majesty the vexation of hearing it the ten-thousand-and-oneth time.

All that report about my proposal to buy Windsor Castle and its grounds was a false rumor. I started it myself.

One newspaper said I patted his Majesty on the shoulder—an impertinence of which I was not guilty; I was reared in the most exclusive circles of Missouri and I know how to behave. The King rested his hand upon my arm a moment or two while we were chatting, but he did it of his own accord. The newspaper which said I talked with her Majesty with my hat on spoke the truth, but my reasons for doing it were good and sufficient—in fact unassailable. Rain was threatening, the temperature had cooled, and the Queen said, "Please put your hat on, Mr. Clemens." I begged her pardon and excused myself from doing it. After a moment or two she said, "Mr. Clemens, put your hat on"—with a slight emphasis on the word "on"—"I can't allow you to catch cold here." When a beautiful queen commands it is a pleasure to obey, and this time I obeyed—but I had already disobeyed once, which is more than a subject would have felt justified in doing; and so it is true, as charged; I did talk with the Queen of England with my hat on, but it wasn't fair in the newspaper man to charge it upon me as an impoliteness, since there were reasons for it which he could not know of.

Nearly all the members of the British royal family were there, and there were foreign visitors which included the King of Siam and a party of India princes in their gorgeous court costumes, which Clemens admired openly and said he would like to wear himself.

The English papers spoke of it as one of the largest and most distinguished parties ever given at Windsor. Clemens attended it in company with Mr. and Mrs. J. Henniker Heaton, and when it was over Sir Thomas Lipton joined them and motored with them back to Brown's.

He was at Archdeacon Wilberforce's next day, where a curious circumstance developed. When he arrived Wilberforce said to him, in an undertone:

"Come into my library. I have something to show you."

In the library Clemens was presented to a Mr. Pole, a plain-looking man, suggesting in dress and appearance the English tradesman. Wilberforce said:

"Mr. Pole, show to Mr. Clemens what you have brought here."

Mr. Pole unrolled a long strip of white linen and brought to view at last a curious, saucer-looking vessel of silver, very ancient in appearance, and cunningly overlaid with green glass. The archdeacon took it and handed it to Clemens as some precious jewel. Clemens said:

"What is it?"

Wilberforce impressively answered:

"It is the Holy Grail."

Clemens naturally started with surprise.

"You may well start," said Wilberforce; "but it's the truth. That is the Holy Grail."

Then he gave this explanation: Mr. Pole, a grain merchant of Bristol, had developed some sort of clairvoyant power, or at all events he had dreamed several times with great vividness the location of the true Grail. Another dreamer, a Dr. Goodchild, of Bath, was mixed up in the matter, and between them this peculiar vessel, which was not a cup, or a goblet, or any of the traditional things, had been discovered. Mr. Pole seemed a man of integrity, and it was clear that the churchman believed the discovery to be genuine and authentic. Of course there could be no positive proof. It was a thing that must be taken on trust. That the vessel itself was wholly different from anything that the generations had imagined, and was apparently of very ancient make, was opposed to the natural suggestion of fraud.

Clemens, to whom the whole idea of the Holy Grail was simply a poetic legend and myth, had the feeling that he had suddenly been transmigrated, like his own Connecticut Yankee, back into the Arthurian days; but he made no question, suggested no doubt. Whatever it was, it was to them the materialization of a symbol of faith which ranked only second to the cross itself, and he handled it reverently and felt the honor of having been one of the first permitted to see the relic. In a subsequent dictation he said:

I am glad I have lived to see that half-hour—that astonishing half-hour. In its way it stands alone in my life's experience. In the belief of two persons present this was the very vessel which was brought by night and secretly delivered to Nicodemus, nearly nineteen centuries ago, after the Creator of the universe had delivered up His life on the cross for the redemption of the human race; the very cup which the stainless Sir Galahad had sought with knightly devotion in far fields of peril and adventure in Arthur's time, fourteen hundred years ago; the same cup which princely knights of other bygone ages had laid down their lives in long and patient efforts to find, and had passed from life disappointed — and here it was at last, dug up by a grain-broker at no cost of blood or travel, and apparently no purity required of him above the average purity of the twentieth-century dealer in cereal futures; not even a stately name required—no Sir Galahad, no Sir Bors de Ganis, no Sir Lancelot of the Lake—nothing but a mere Mr. Pole.[1]

[1] From the New York *Sun* somewhat later:
"Mr. Pole communicated the discovery to a dignitary of the Church of England, who summoned a number of eminent persons,

A TRUE ENGLISH WELCOME

Clemens saw Mr. and Mrs. Rogers at Claridge's Hotel that evening; lunched with his old friends Sir Norman and Lady Lockyer next day; took tea with T. P. O'Connor at the House of Commons, and on the day following, which was June 25th, he was the guest of honor at one of the most elaborate occasions of his visit—a luncheon given by the Pilgrims at the Savoy Hotel. It would be impossible to set down here a report of the doings, or even a list of the guests, of that gathering. The Pilgrims is a club with branches on both sides of the ocean, and Mark Twain, on either side, was a favorite associate. At this luncheon the picture on the bill of fare represented him as a robed pilgrim, with a great pen for his staff, turning his back on the Mississippi River and being led along his literary way by a huge jumping frog, to which he is attached by a string. On a guest-card was printed:

Pilot of many Pilgrims since the shout
   "Mark Twain!"—that serves you for a deathless sign—
On Mississippi's waterway rang out
   Over the plummet's line—

Still where the countless ripples laugh above
   The blue of halcyon seas long may you keep
Your course unbroken, buoyed upon a love
   Ten thousand fathoms deep!
                —O. S. [Owen Seaman].

Augustine Birrell made the speech of introduction, closing with this paragraph:

Mark Twain is a man whom Englishmen and Americans do well to honor. He is a true consolidator of nations. His de-

including psychologists, to see and discuss it. Forty attended, including some peers with ecclesiastical interests, Ambassador Whitelaw Reid, Professor Crookes, and ministers of various religious bodies, including the Rev. R. J. Campbell. They heard Mr. Pole's story with deep attention, but he could not prove the genuineness of the relic."

lightful humor is of the kind which dissipates and destroys national prejudices. His truth and his honor—his love of truth and his love of honor—overflow all boundaries. He has made the world better by his presence, and we rejoice to see him here. Long may he live to reap a plentiful harvest of hearty honest human affection.

The toast was drunk standing. Then Clemens rose and made a speech which delighted all England. In his introduction Mr. Birrell had happened to say, "How I came here I will not ask!" Clemens remembered this, and looking down into Mr. Birrell's wine-glass, which was apparently unused, he said:

"Mr. Birrell doesn't know how he got here. But he will be able to get away all right—he has not drunk anything since he came."

He told stories about Howells and Twichell, and how Darwin had gone to sleep reading his books, and then he came down to personal things and company, and told them how, on the day of his arrival, he had been shocked to read on a great placard, "Mark Twain Arrives: Ascot Cup Stolen."

No doubt many a person was misled by those sentences joined together in that unkind way. I have no doubt my character has suffered from it. I suppose I ought to defend my character, but how can I defend it? I can say here and now that anybody can see by my face that I am sincere—that I speak the truth, and that I have never seen that Cup. I have not got the Cup, I did not have a chance to get it. I have always had a good character in that way. I have hardly ever stolen anything, and if I did steal anything I had discretion enough to know about the value of it first. I do not steal things that are likely to get myself into trouble. I do not think any of us do that. I know we all take things—that is to be expected; but really I have never taken anything, certainly in England, that amounts to any great thing. I do confess that when I was here seven years ago I stole a hat—but that did not amount to anything. It was not a good hat—it was only a clergyman's hat, anyway. I was at a luncheon-party and Archdeacon Wilberforce was there also. I dare say he is archdeacon now—he was a canon then—and he was serving in the Westminster Battery, if that is the proper term. I do not know, as you mix military and ecclesiastical things together so much.

He recounted the incident of the exchanged hats; then he spoke of graver things. He closed:

I cannot always be cheerful, and I cannot always be chaffing. I must sometimes lay the cap and bells aside and recognize that I am of the human race. I have my cares and griefs, and I therefore noticed what Mr. Birrell said—I was so glad to hear him say it—something that was in the nature of these verses here at the top of the program:

> He lit our life with shafts of sun
> And vanquished pain.
> Thus two great nations stand as one
> In honoring Twain.

I am very glad to have those verses. I am very glad and very grateful for what Mr. Birrell said in that connection. I have received since I have been here, in this one week, hundreds of letters from all conditions of people in England, men, women, and children, and there is compliment, praise, and, above all, and better than all, there is in them a note of affection.

Praise is well, compliment is well, but affection—that is the last and final and most precious reward that any man can win, whether by character or achievement, and I am very grateful to have that reward. All these letters make me feel that here in England, as in America, when I stand under the English or the American flag I am not a stranger, I am not an alien, but at home.

CCLVIII

DOCTOR OF LITERATURE, OXFORD

HE left, immediately following the Pilgrim luncheon, with Hon. Robert P. Porter, of the London *Times*, for Oxford, to remain his guest there during the various ceremonies. The encenia—the ceremony of conferring the degrees—occurred at the Sheldonian Theater the following morning, June 26, 1907.

It was a memorable affair. Among those who were to receive degrees that morning besides Samuel Clemens were: Prince Arthur of Connaught; Prime Minister Campbell-Bannerman; Whitelaw Reid; Rudyard Kipling; Sidney Lee; Sidney Colvin; Lord Archbishop of Armagh, Primate of Ireland; Sir Norman Lockyer; Auguste Rodin, the sculptor; Saint-Saëns, and Gen. William Booth, of the Salvation Army—something more than thirty, in all, of the world's distinguished citizens.

The candidates assembled at Magdalen College, and led by Lord Curzon, the Chancellor, and clad in their academic plumage, filed in radiant procession to the Sheldonian Theater, a group of men such as the world seldom sees collected together. The London *Standard* said of it:

So brilliant and so interesting was the list of those who had been selected by Oxford University on Convocation to receive degrees, *honoris causa*, in this first year of Lord Curzon's chancellorship, that it is small wonder that the Sheldonian Theater was besieged to-day at an early hour.

Shortly after 11 o'clock the organ started playing the strains

1392

of "God Save the King," and at once a great volume of sound arose as the anthem was taken up by the undergraduates and the rest of the assemblage. Every one stood up as, headed by the mace of office, the procession slowly filed into the theater, under the leadership of Lord Curzon, in all the glory of his robes of office, the long black gown heavily embroidered with gold, the gold-tasseled mortar-board, and the medals on his breast forming an admirable setting, thoroughly in keeping with the dignity and bearing of the late Viceroy of India. Following him came the members of Convocation, a goodly number consisting of doctors of divinity, whose robes of scarlet and black enhanced the brilliance of the scene. Robes of salmon and scarlet—which proclaim the wearer to be a doctor of civil law—were also seen in numbers, while here and there was a gown of gray and scarlet, emblematic of the doctorate of science or of letters.

The encenia is an impressive occasion; but it is not a silent one. There is a splendid dignity about it; but there goes with it all a sort of Greek chorus of hilarity, the time-honored prerogative of the Oxford undergraduate, who insists on having his joke and his merriment at the expense of those honored guests. The degrees of doctor of law were conferred first. Prince Arthur was treated with proper dignity by the gallery; but when Whitelaw Reid stepped forth a voice shouted, "Where's your Star-spangled Banner?" and when England's Prime Minister—Campbell-Bannerman—came forward some one shouted, "What about the House of Lords?" and so they kept it up, cheering and chaffing, until General Booth was introduced as the "Passionate advocate of the dregs of the people, leader of the 'submerged tenth," and general of the Salvation Army," when the place broke into a perfect storm of applause, a storm that a few minutes later became, according to the *Daily News*, "a veritable cyclone," for Mark Twain, clad in his robe of scarlet and gray, had been summoned forward to receive the highest academic honors which the world has to give. The undergraduates went wild then. There was such a mingling of yells and calls and questions, such as, "Have you brought the Jumping Frog with you?" "Where is the Ascot Cup?" "Where are the rest of the Innocents?" that it seemed as if it would not be possible to present him at all; but, finally, Chancellor Curzon addressed him (in Latin), "Most amiable and charming sir, you shake the sides of the whole world with your merriment," and the great degree was conferred.

If only Tom Sawyer could have seen him then! If only Olivia Clemens could have sat among those who gave him welcome! But life is not like that. There is always an incompleteness somewhere, and the shadow across the path.

Rudyard Kipling followed—another supreme favorite, who was hailed with the chorus, "For he's a jolly good fellow," and then came Saint-Saëns. The prize poems and essays followed, and then the procession of newly created doctors left the theater with Lord Curzon at their head. So it was all over—that for which, as he said, he would have made the journey to Mars. The world had nothing more to give him now except that which he had already long possessed—its honor and its love.

The newly made doctors were to be the guests of Lord Curzon at All Souls College for luncheon. As they left the theater (according to Sidney Lee):

The people in the streets singled out Mark Twain, formed a vast and cheering body-guard around him and escorted him to the college gates. But before and after the lunch it was Mark Twain again whom everybody seemed most of all to want to meet. The Maharajah of Bikanir, for instance, finding himself seated at lunch next to Mrs. Riggs (Kate Douglas Wiggin), and hearing that she knew Mark Twain, asked her to present him— a ceremony duly performed later on the quadrangle. At the garden-party given the same afternoon in the beautiful grounds of St. John's, where the indefatigable Mark put in an appearance, it was just the same—every one pressed forward for an exchange of greetings and a hand-shake. On the following day, when the Oxford pageant took place, it was even more so. "Mark Twain's Pageant," it was called by one of the papers.[1]

Clemens remained the guest of Robert Porter, whose house was besieged with those desiring a glimpse of their new doctor of letters. If he went on the streets he was instantly recognized by some newsboy or cabman or butcher-boy, and the word ran along like a cry of fire, while the crowds assembled.

At a luncheon which the Porters gave him the proprietor of the catering establishment garbed himself as a waiter in order to have the distinction of serving Mark Twain, and declared it to have been the greatest moment of his life. This gentleman—for he was no less than that —was a man well-read, and his tribute was not inspired by mere snobbery. Clemens, learning of the situation, later withdrew from the drawing-room for a talk with him.

"I found," he said, "that he knew about ten or fifteen times as much about my books as I knew about them myself."

Mark Twain viewed the Oxford pageant from a box with Rudyard Kipling and Lord Curzon, and as they sat there some one passed up a folded slip of paper, on the outside of which was written, "Not true." Opening it, they read—

> East is East and West is West,
> And never the *Twain* shall meet,

—a quotation from Kipling.

They saw the panorama of history file by, a wonderful spectacle which made Oxford a veritable dream of the

---

[1] There was a dinner that evening at one of the colleges where, through mistaken information, Clemens wore black evening dress when he should have worn his scarlet gown. "When I arrived," he said, "the place was just a conflagration—a kind of human prairie-fire. I looked as out of place as a Presbyterian in hell."

Middle Ages. The lanes and streets and meadows were thronged with such costumes as Oxford had seen in its long history. History was realized in a manner which no one could appreciate more fully than Mark Twain.

"I was particularly anxious to see this pageant," he said, "so that I could get ideas for my funeral procession, which I am planning on a large scale."

He was not disappointed; it was a realization to him of all the gorgeous spectacles that his soul had dreamed from youth up.

He easily recognized the great characters of history as they passed by, and he was recognized by them in turn; for they waved to him and bowed and sometimes called his name, and when he went down out of his box, by and by, Henry VIII. shook hands with him, a monarch he had always detested, though he was full of friendship for him now; and Charles I. took off his broad, velvet-plumed hat when they met, and Henry II. and Rosamond and Queen Elizabeth all saluted him—ghosts of the dead centuries.

CCLIX

LONDON SOCIAL HONORS

WE may not detail all the story of that English visit;
even the path of glory leads to monotony at last.
We may only mention a few more of the great honors
paid to our unofficial ambassador to the world: among
them a dinner given to members of the Savage Club by
the Lord Mayor of London at the Mansion House, also a
dinner given by the American Society at the Hotel Cecil in
honor of the Fourth of July. Clemens was the guest of
honor, and responded to the toast given by Ambassador
Reid, "The Day we Celebrate." He made an amusing
and not altogether unserious reference to the American
habit of exploding enthusiasm in dangerous fireworks.
To English colonists he gave credit for having established American independence, and closed:

We have, however, one Fourth of July which is absolutely
our own, and that is the memorable proclamation issued forty
years ago by that great American to whom Sir Mortimer Durand
paid that just and beautiful tribute—Abraham Lincoln: a
proclamation which not only set the black slave free, but set his
white owner free also. The owner was set free from that burden
and offense, that sad condition of things where he was in so
many instances a master and owner of slaves when he did not
want to be. That proclamation set them all free. But even
in this matter England led the way, for she had set her slaves
free thirty years before, and we but followed her example. We
always follow her example, whether it is good or bad. And it
was an English judge, a century ago, that issued that other

great proclamation, and established that great principle, that
when a slave, let him belong to whom he may, and let him come
whence he may, sets his foot upon English soil his fetters, by
that act, fall away and he is a free man before the world!

It is true, then, that all our Fourths of July, and we have five
of them, England gave to us, except that one that I have mentioned—the Emancipation Proclamation; and let us not forget
that we owe this debt to her. Let us be able to say to old
England, this great-hearted, venerable old mother of the race,
you gave us our Fourths of July, that we love and that we honor
and revere; you gave us the Declaration of Independence, which
is the charter of our rights; you, the venerable Mother of Liberties, the Champion and Protector of Anglo-Saxon Freedom—
you gave us these things, and we do most honestly thank you
for them.

It was at this dinner that he characteristically confessed, at last, to having stolen the Ascot Cup.

He lunched one day with Bernard Shaw, and the two
discussed the philosophies in which they were mutually
interested. Shaw regarded Clemens as a sociologist before all else, and gave it out with great frankness that
America had produced just two great geniuses—Edgar
Allan Poe and Mark Twain. Later Shaw wrote him a
note, in which he said:

I am persuaded that the future historian of America will find
your works as indispensable to him as a French historian finds
the political tracts of Voltaire. I tell you so because I am the
author of a play in which a priest says, "Telling the truth's the
funniest joke in the world," a piece of wisdom which you helped
to teach me.

Clemens saw a great deal of Moberly Bell. The
two lunched and dined privately together when there
was opportunity, and often met at the public gatherings.

The bare memorandum of the week following July

Fourth will convey something of Mark Twain's London activities:

Friday, July 5. Dined with Lord and Lady Portsmouth.

Saturday, July 6. Breakfasted at Lord Avebury's. Lord Kelvin, Sir Charles Lyell, and Sir Archibald Geikie were there. Sat 22 times for photos, 16 at Histed's. Savage Club dinner in the evening. White suit. Ascot Cup.

Sunday, July 7. Called on Lady Langattock and others. Lunched with Sir Norman Lockyer.

Monday, July 8. Lunched with Plasmon directors at Bath Club. Dined privately at C. F. Moberly Bell's.

Tuesday, July 9. Lunched at the House with Sir Benjamin Stone. Balfour and Komura were the other guests of honor. *Punch* dinner in the evening. Joy Agnew and the cartoon.

Wednesday, July 10. Went to Liverpool with Tay Pay. Attended banquet in the Town Hall in the evening.

Thursday, July 11. Returned to London with Tay Pay. Calls in the afternoon.

The Savage Club would inevitably want to entertain him on its own account, and their dinner of July 6th was a handsome affair. He felt at home with the Savages, and put on white for the only time publicly in England. He made them one of his reminiscent speeches, recalling his association with them on his first visit to London, thirty-seven years before. Then he said:

That is a long time ago, and as I had come into a very strange land, and was with friends, as I could see, that has always remained in my mind as a peculiarly blessed evening, since it brought me into contact with men of my own kind and my own feelings. I am glad to be here, and to see you all, because it is very likely that I shall not see you again. I have been received, as you know, in the most delightfully generous way in England ever since I came here. It keeps me choked up all the time. Everybody is so generous, and they do seem to give you such a hearty welcome. Nobody in the world can appreciate it higher than I do.

The club gave him a surprise in the course of the evening. A note was sent to him accompanied by a parcel, which, when opened, proved to contain a gilded plaster replica of the Ascot Gold Cup. The note said:

Dere Mark, i return the Cup. You couldn't keep your mouth shut about it. 'Tis 2 pretty 2 melt, as you want me 2; next time I work a pinch ile have a pard who don't make after-dinner speeches.

There was a postcript which said: "I changed the acorn atop for another nut with my knife." The acorn was, in fact, replaced by a well-modeled head of Mark Twain.

So, after all, the Ascot Cup would be one of the trophies which he would bear home with him across the Atlantic.

Probably the most valued of his London honors was the dinner given to him by the staff of *Punch*. *Punch* had already saluted him with a front-page cartoon by Bernard Partridge, a picture in which the presiding genius of that paper, Mr. Punch himself, presents him with a glass of the patronymic beverage with the words, "Sir, I honor myself by drinking your health. Long life to you—and happiness—and perpetual youth!"

Mr. Agnew, chief editor; Linley Sambourne, Francis Burnand, Henry Lucy, and others of the staff welcomed him at the *Punch* offices at 10 Bouverie Street, in the historic *Punch* dining-room where Thackeray had sat, and Douglas Jerrold, and so many of the great departed. Mark Twain was the first foreign visitor to be so honored —in fifty years the first stranger to sit at the sacred board —a mighty distinction. In the course of the dinner they gave him a pretty surprise, when little Joy Agnew presented him with the original drawing of Partridge's cartoon.

Nothing could have appealed to him more, and the *Punch* dinner, with its associations and that dainty presentation, remained apart in his memory from all other feastings.

Clemens had intended to return early in July, but so much was happening that he postponed his sailing until the 13th. Before leaving America he had declined a dinner offered by the Lord Mayor of Liverpool.

Repeatedly urged to let Liverpool share in his visit, he had reconsidered now, and on the day following the *Punch* dinner, on July 10th, they carried him, with T. P. O'Connor (Tay Pay) in the Prince of Wales's special coach to Liverpool, to be guest of honor at the reception and banquet which Lord Mayor Japp tendered him at the Town Hall. Clemens was too tired to be present while the courses were being served, but arrived rested and fresh to respond to his toast. Perhaps because it was his farewell speech in England, he made that night the most effective address of his four weeks' visit—one of the most effective of his whole career. He began with some light reference to the stealing of the Ascot Cup and the Dublin Jewels, and to other disappearances that had been laid to his charge, to amuse his hearers, and spoke at greater length than usual, and with even greater variety. Then laying all levity aside, he told them, like the Queen of Sheba, all that was in his heart.

. . . Home is dear to us all, and now I am departing to my own home beyond the ocean. Oxford has conferred upon me the highest honor that has ever fallen to my share of this life's prizes. It is the very one I would have chosen, as outranking all and any others, the one more precious to me than any and all others within the gift of man or state. During my four weeks' sojourn in England I have had another lofty honor, a continuous honor, an honor which has flowed serenely along, without halt or obstruction, through all these twenty-six days, a most moving and pulse-stirring honor—the heartfelt grip of the hand, and the welcome that does not descend from the pale-gray matter of the brain, but rushes up with the red blood from the heart. It makes me proud and sometimes it makes me humble, too. Many and many a year ago I gathered an incident from Dana's *Two Years Before the Mast*. It was like this: There was a presumptuous little self-important skipper in a coasting sloop engaged in the dried-apple and kitchen-furniture trade, and he was always hailing every ship that came in sight. He did it just to hear himself talk and to air his small grandeur. One day a majestic Indiaman came plowing by with course on course of canvas towering into the sky, her decks and yards swarming with sailors, her hull burdened to the Plimsoll line with a rich freightage of precious spices, lading the breezes with gracious and mysterious odors of the Orient. It was a noble spectacle, a sublime spectacle! *Of* course the little skipper popped into the shrouds and squeaked out a hail, "Ship ahoy! What ship is that? And whence and whither?" In a deep and thunderous bass the answer came back through the speaking-trumpet, "The *Begum*, of Bengal—142 days out from Canton—homeward bound! What ship is that?" Well, it just crushed that poor little creature's vanity flat, and he squeaked back most humbly, "Only the *Mary Ann*, fourteen hours out from Boston, bound for Kittery Point—with nothing to speak of!" Oh, what an eloquent word that "only," to express the depths of his humbleness! That is just my case. During just one hour in the twenty-four—not more—I pause and reflect in the stillness of the night with the echoes of your English welcome still lingering in my ears, and then I am humble. Then I am properly meek, and for that little while I am only the *Mary Ann*, fourteen hours out, cargoed with vegetables and tinware; but during all the other twenty-three hours my vain self-complacency rides high on the white crests of your approval, and then I am a stately Indiaman, plowing the great seas under a cloud of canvas and laden with the kindest words that have ever been vouchsafed to any wandering alien in this world, I think; then my twenty-six fortunate days on this old mother soil seem to be multiplied by six, and *I* am the *Begum*, of Bengal, 142 days out from Canton—homeward bound!

He returned to London, and with one of his young acquaintances, an American—he called her Francesca—paid many calls. It took the dreariness out of that social function to perform it in that way. With a list of the calls they were to make they drove forth each day to cancel the social debt. They paid calls in every walk of life. His young companion was privileged to see the inside of London homes of almost every class, for he showed no partiality; he went to the homes of the poor and the rich alike. One day they visited the home of an old bookkeeper whom he had known in 1872 as a clerk in a large establishment, earning a salary of perhaps a pound a week, who now had risen mightily, for he had become head bookkeeper in that establishment on a salary of six pounds a week, and thought it great prosperity and fortune for his old age.

He sailed on July 13th for home, besought to the last moment by a crowd of autograph-seekers and reporters and photographers, and a multitude who only wished to see him and to shout and wave good-by. He was sailing away from them for the last time. They hoped he would make a speech, but that would not have been possible. To the reporters he gave a farewell message: "It has been the most enjoyable holiday I have ever had, and I am sorry the end of it has come. I have met a hundred old friends, and I have made a hundred new ones. It is a good kind of riches to have; there is none better, I think." And the London *Tribune* declared that "the ship that bore him away had difficulty in getting clear. so thickly was the water strewn with the bay-leaves of his triumph. For Mark Twain has triumphed, and in his all-too-brief stay of a month has done more for the cause of the world's peace than will be accomplished by the Hague Conference. He has made the world laugh again."

His ship was the *Minnetonka*, and there were some little folks aboard to be adopted as grandchildren. On July 15th, in a fog, the *Minnetonka* collided with the bark *Sterling*, and narrowly escaped sinking her. On the whole, however, the homeward way was clear, and the vessel ~eached New York nearly a day in advance of their schedule. Some ceremonies of welcome had been prepared for him; but they were upset by the early arrival, so that when he descended the gang-plank to his native soil only a few who had received special information were there to greet him. But perhaps he did not notice it. He seldom took account of the absence of such things. By early afternoon, however, the papers rang with the announcement that Mark Twain was home again.

It is a sorrow to me that I was not at the dock to welcome him. I had been visiting in Elmira, and timed my return for the evening of the 22d, to be on hand the following morning, when the ship was due. When I saw the announcement that he had already arrived I called a greeting over the telephone, and was told to come down and play billiards. I confess I went with a certain degree of awe, for one could not but be overwhelmed with the echoes of the great splendor he had so recently achieved, and I prepared to sit a good way off in silence, and hear something of the tale of this returning conqueror; but when I arrived he was already in the billiard-room knocking the balls about—his coat off, for it was a hot night. As I entered he said:

"Get your cue. I have been inventing a new game." And I think there were scarcely ten words exchanged before we were at it. The pageant was over; the curtain was rung down. Business was resumed at the old stand.

MATTERS PSYCHIC AND OTHERWISE

HE returned to Tuxedo and took up his dictations, and mingled freely with the social life; but the contrast between his recent London experience and his semi-retirement must have been very great. When I visited him now and then, he seemed to me lonely—not especially for companionship, but rather for the life that lay behind him—the great career which in a sense now had been completed since he had touched its highest point. There was no billiard-table at Tuxedo, and he spoke expectantly of getting back to town and the games there, also of the new home which was then building in Redding, and which would have a billiard-room where we could assemble daily—my own habitation being not far away. Various diversions were planned for Redding; among them was discussed a possible school of philosophy, such as Hawthorne and Emerson and Alcott had established at Concord.

He spoke quite freely of his English experiences, but usually of the more amusing phases. He almost never referred to the honors that had been paid to him, yet he must have thought of them sometimes, and cherished them, for it had been the greatest national tribute ever paid to a private citizen; he must have known that, in his heart. He spoke amusingly of his visit to Marie Corelli, in Stratford, and of the Holy Grail incident, ending the latter by questioning—in words at least—all psychic manifestations. I said to him:

"But remember your own dream, Mr. Clemens, which presaged the death of your brother."

He answered: "I ask nobody to believe that it ever happened. To me it is true; but it has no logical right to be true, and I do not expect belief in it." Which I thought a peculiar point of view, but on the whole characteristic.

He was invited to be a special guest at the Jamestown Exposition on Fulton Day, in September, and Mr. Rogers lent him his yacht in which to make the trip. It was a break in the summer's monotonies, and the Jamestown honors must have reminded him of those in London. When he entered the auditorium where the services were to be held there was a demonstration which lasted more than five minutes. Every person in the hall rose and cheered, waving handkerchiefs and umbrellas. He made them a brief, amusing talk on Fulton and other matters, then introduced Admiral Harrington, who delivered a masterly address and was followed by Martin W. Littleton, the real orator of the day. Littleton acquitted himself so notably that Mark Twain conceived for him a deep admiration, and the two men quickly became friends. They saw each other often during the remainder of the Jamestown stay, and Clemens, learning that Littleton lived just across Ninth Street from him in New York, invited him to come over when he had an evening to spare and join the billiard games.

So it happened, somewhat later, when every one was back in town, Mr. and Mrs. Littleton frequently came over for billiards, and the games became three-handed with an audience—very pleasant games played in that way. Clemens sometimes set himself up as umpire, and became critic and gave advice, while Littleton and I played. He had a favorite shot that he frequently used himself and was always wanting us to try, which was to drive the ball to the cushion at the beginning of the shot.

He played it with a good deal of success, and achieved unexpected results with it. He was even inspired to write a poem on the subject.

"CUSHION FIRST"

When all your days are dark with doubt,
   And dying hope is at its worst;
When all life's balls are scattered wide,
With not a shot in sight, to left or right,
Don't give it up;
Advance your cue and shut your eyes,
   And take the cushion first.

The Harry Thaw trial was in progress just then, and Littleton was Thaw's chief attorney. It was most interesting to hear from him direct the day's proceedings and his views of the situation and of Thaw.

Littleton and billiards recall a curious thing which happened one afternoon. I had been absent the evening before, and Littleton had been over. It was after luncheon now, and Clemens and I began preparing for the customary games. We were playing then a game with four balls, two white and two red. I began by placing the red balls on the table, and then went around looking in the pockets for the two white cue-balls. When I had made the round of the table I had found but one white ball. I thought I must have overlooked the other, and made the round again. Then I said:

"There is one white ball missing."

Clemens, to satisfy himself, also made the round of the pockets, and said:

"It was here last night." He felt in the pockets of the little white-silk coat which he usually wore, thinking that he might unconsciously have placed it there at the end of the last game, but his coat pockets were empty.

He said: "I'll bet Littleton carried that ball home with him."

Then I suggested that near the end of the game it might have jumped off the table, and I looked carefully under the furniture and in the various corners, but without success. There was another set of balls, and out of it I selected a white one for our play, and the game began. It went along in the usual way, the balls constantly falling into the pockets, and as constantly being replaced on the table. This had continued for perhaps half an hour, there being no pocket that had not been frequently occupied and emptied during that time; but then it happened that Clemens reached into the middle pocket, and taking out a white ball laid it in place, whereupon we made the discovery that *three white balls* lay upon the table. The one just taken from the pocket was the missing ball. We looked at each other, both at first too astonished to say anything at all. No one had been in the room since we began to play, and at no time during the play had there been more than two white balls in evidence, though the pockets had been emptied at the end of each shot. The pocket from which the missing ball had been taken had been filled and emptied again and again. Then Clemens said:

"We must be dreaming."

We stopped the game for a while to discuss it, but we could devise no material explanation. I suggested the kobold — that mischievous invisible which is supposed to play pranks by carrying off such things as pencils, letters, and the like, and suddenly restoring them almost before one's eyes. Clemens, who, in spite of his material logic, was always a mystic at heart, said:

"But that, so far as I know, has never happened to more than one person at a time, and has been explained by a sort of temporary mental blindness. This thing has happened to two of us, and there can be no question as to the positive absence of the object."

"How about dematerialization?"

"Yes, if one of us were a medium that might be considered an explanation."

He went on to recall that Sir Alfred Russel Wallace had written of such things, and cited instances which Wallace had recorded. In the end he said:

"Well, it happened, that's all we can say, and nobody can ever convince me that it didn't."

We went on playing, and the ball remained solid and substantial ever after, so far as I know.

I am reminded of two more or less related incidents of this period. Clemens was, one morning, dictating something about his *Christian Union* article concerning Mrs. Clemens's government of children, published in 1885. I had discovered no copy of it among the materials, and he was wishing very much that he could see one. Somewhat later, as he was walking down Fifth Avenue, the thought of this article and his desire for it suddenly entered his mind. Reaching the corner of Forty-second Street, he stopped a moment to let a jam of vehicles pass. As he did so a stranger crossed the street, noticed him, and came dodging his way through the blockade and thrust some clippings into his hand.

"Mr. Clemens," he said, "you don't know me, but here is something you may wish to have. I have been saving them for more than twenty years, and this morning it occurred to me to send them to you. I was going to mail them from my office, but now I will give them to you," and with a word or two he disappeared. The clippings were from the *Christian Union* of 1885, and were the much-desired article. Clemens regarded it as a remarkable case of mental telegraphy.

"Or, if it wasn't that," he said, "it was a most remarkable coincidence."

The other circumstance has been thought amusing. I had gone to Redding for a few days, and while there, one afternoon about five o'clock, fell over a coal-scuttle and scarified myself a good deal between the ankle and the knee. I mention the hour because it seems important. Next morning I received a note, prompted by Mr. Clemens, in which he said:

Tell Paine I am sorry he fell and skinned his shin at five o'clock yesterday afternoon.

I was naturally astonished, and immediately wrote:

I did fall and skin my shin at five o'clock yesterday afternoon, but how did you find it out?

I followed the letter in person next day, and learned that at the same hour on the same afternoon Clemens himself had fallen up the front steps and, as he said, "peeled from his starboard shin a ribbon of skin three inches long." The disaster was still uppermost in his mind at the time of writing, and the suggestion of my own mishap had flashed out for no particular reason.

Clemens was always having his fortune told, in one way or another, being superstitious, as he readily confessed, though at times professing little faith in these prognostics. Once when a clairvoyant, of whom he had never even heard, and who, he had reason to believe, was ignorant of his family history, told him more about it than he knew himself, besides reading a list of names from a piece of paper which Clemens had concealed in his vest pocket, he came home deeply impressed. The clairvoyant added that he would probably live to a great age and die in a foreign land—a prophecy which did not comfort him.

CCLXI

MINOR EVENTS AND DIVERSIONS

MARK TWAIN was deeply interested during the autumn of 1907 in the Children's Theater of the Jewish Educational Alliance, on the lower East Side—a most worthy institution which ought to have survived. A Miss Alice M. Herts, who developed and directed it, gave her strength and health to build up an institution through which the minds of the children could be diverted from less fortunate amusements. She had interested a great body of Jewish children in the plays of Shakespeare, and of more modern dramatists, and these they had performed from time to time with great success. The admission fee to the performance was ten cents, and the theater was always crowded with other children—certainly a better diversion for them than the amusements of the street, though of course, as a business enterprise, the theater could not pay. It required patrons. Miss Herts obtained permission to play "The Prince and the Pauper," and Mark Twain agreed to become a sort of chief patron in using his influence to bring together an audience who might be willing to assist financially in this worthy work.

"The Prince and the Pauper" evening turned out a distinguished affair. On the night of November 19, 1907, the hall of the Educational Alliance was crowded with such an audience as perhaps never before assembled on the East Side; the finance and the fashion of New York were there. It was a gala night for the little East Side per-

1411

formers. Behind the curtain they whispered to each other that they were to play before queens. The performance they gave was an astonishing one. So fully did they enter into the spirit of Tom Canty's rise to royalty that they seemed absolutely to forget that they were lowly-born children of the Ghetto. They had become little princesses and lords and maids-in-waiting, and they moved through their pretty tinsel parts as if all their ornaments were gems and their raiment cloth of gold. There was no hesitation, no awkwardness of speech or gesture, and they rose really to sublime heights in the barn scene where the little Prince is in the hands of the mob. Never in the history of the stage has there been assembled a mob more wonderful than that. These children knew mobs! A mob to them was a daily sight, and their reproduction of it was a thing to startle you with its realism. Never was it absurd; never was there a single note of artificiality in it. It was Hogarthian in its bigness.

Both Mark Twain and Miss Herts made brief addresses, and the audience shouted approval of their words. It seems a pity that such a project as that must fail, and I do not know why it happened. Wealthy men and women manifested an interest; but there was some hitch somewhere, and the Children's Theater exists to-day only as history.[1]

It was at a dinner at The Players—a small, private dinner given by Mr. George C. Riggs—that I saw Edward L. Burlingame and Mark Twain for the only time to-

[1] In a letter to a Mrs. Amelia Dunne Hookway, who had conducted some children's plays at the Howland School, Chicago, Mark Twain once wrote: "If I were going to begin life over again I would have a children's theater and watch it, and work for it, and see it grow and blossom and bear its rich moral and intellectual fruitage; and I should get more pleasure and a saner and healthier profit out of my vocation than I should ever be able to get out of any other, constituted as I am. Yes, you are easily the most fortunate of women, I think."

gether. They had often met during the forty-two years that had passed since their long-ago Sandwich Island friendship; but only incidentally, for Mr. Burlingame cared not much for great public occasions, and as editor of *Scribner's Magazine* he had been somewhat out of the line of Mark Twain's literary doings.

Howells was there, and Gen. Stewart L. Woodford, David Bispham, John Finley, Louis Evan Shipman, Nicholas Biddle, and David Munro. Clemens told that night, for the first time, the story of General Miles and the three-dollar dog, inventing it, I believe, as he went along, though for the moment it certainly did sound like history. He told it often after that, and it has been included in his book of speeches.

Later, in the cab, he said:

"That was a mighty good dinner. Riggs knows how to do that sort of thing. I enjoyed it ever so much. Now we'll go home and play billiards."

We began about eleven o'clock, and played until after midnight. I happened to be too strong for him, and he swore amazingly. He vowed that it was not a gentleman's game at all, that Riggs's wine had demoralized the play. But at the end, when we were putting up the cues, he said:

"Well, those were good games. There is nothing like billiards after all."

We did not play billiards on his birthday that year. He went to the theater in the afternoon; and it happened that, with Jesse Lynch Williams, I attended the same performance—the "Toy-Maker of Nuremburg"—written by Austin Strong. It proved to be a charming play, and I could see that Clemens was enjoying it. He sat in a box next to the stage, and the actors clearly were doing their very prettiest for his benefit.

When later I mentioned having seen him at the play, he spoke freely of his pleasure in it.

"It is a fine, delicate piece of work," he said. "I wish I could do such things as that."

"I believe you are too literary for play-writing."

"Yes, no doubt. There was never any question with the managers about my plays. They always said they wouldn't *act*. Howells has come pretty near to something once or twice. I judge the trouble is that the literary man is thinking of the style and quality of the thing, while the playwright thinks only of how it will play. One is thinking of how it will sound, the other of how it will look."

"I suppose," I said, "the literary man should have a collaborator with a genius for stage mechanism. John Luther Long's exquisite plays would hardly have been successful without David Belasco to stage them. Belasco cannot write a play himself, but in the matter of acting construction his genius is supreme."

"Yes, so it is; it was Belasco who made it possible to play "The Prince and the Pauper"—a collection of literary garbage before he got hold of it."

Clemens attended few public functions now. He was beset with invitations, but he declined most of them. He told the dog story one night to the Pleiades Club, assembled at the Brevoort; but that was only a step away, and we went in after the dining was ended and came away before the exercises were concluded.

He also spoke at a banquet given to Andrew Carnegie—Saint Andrew, as he called him—by the Engineers Club, and had his usual fun at the chief guest's expense.

I have been chief guest at a good many banquets myself, and I know what brother Andrew is feeling like now. He has been receiving compliments and nothing but compliments, but he knows that there is another side to him that needs censure.

I am going to vary the complimentary monotony. While we have all been listening to the complimentary talk Mr. Carnegie's face has scintillated with fictitious innocence. You'd think he never committed a crime in his life. But he has.

Look at his pestiferous simplified spelling. Imagine the calamity on two sides of the ocean when he foisted his simplified spelling on the whole human race. We've got it all now so that nobody could spell. . . .

If Mr. Carnegie had left spelling alone we wouldn't have had any spots on the sun, or any San Francisco quake, or any business depression.

There, I trust he feels better now and that he has enjoyed my abuse more than he did his compliments. And now that I think I have him smoothed down and feeling comfortable I just want to say one thing more—that his simplified spelling is all right enough, but, like chastity, you can carry it too far.

As he was about to go, Carnegie called his attention to the beautiful souvenir bronze and gold-plated goblets that stood at each guest's plate. Carnegie said:

"The club had those especially made at Tiffany's for this occasion. They cost ten dollars apiece."

Clemens said: "Is that so? Well, I only meant to take my own; but if that's the case I'll load my cab with them."

We made an attempt to reform on the matter of billiards. The continued strain of late hours was doing neither of us any particular good. More than once I journeyed into the country on one errand and another, mainly for rest; but a card saying that he was lonely and upset, for lack of his evening games, quickly brought me back again. It was my wish only to serve him; it was a privilege and an honor to give him happiness.

Billiards, however, was not his only recreation just then. He walked out a good deal, and especially of a pleasant Sunday morning he liked the stroll up Fifth Avenue. Sometimes we went as high as Carnegie's, on Ninety-second Street, and rode home on top of the electric stage—always one of Mark Twain's favorite diversions.

From that high seat he liked to look down on the panorama of the streets, and in that free, open air he could smoke without interference. Oftener, however, we turned at Fifty-ninth Street, walking both ways.

When it was pleasant we sometimes sat on a bench in Central Park; and once he must have left a handkerchief there, for a few days later one of his handkerchiefs came to him accompanied by a note. Its finder, a Mr. Lockwood, received a reward, for Mark Twain wrote him:

There is more rejoicing in this house over that one handkerchief that was lost and is found again than over the ninety and nine that never went to the wash at all. Heaven will reward you, I know it will.

On Sunday mornings the return walk would be timed for about the hour that the churches would be dismissed. On the first Sunday morning we had started a little early, and I thoughtlessly suggested, when we reached Fifty-ninth Street, that if we returned at once we would avoid the throng. He said, quietly:

"I like the throng."

So we rested in the Plaza Hotel until the appointed hour. Men and women noticed him, and came over to shake his hand. The gigantic man in uniform, in charge of the carriages at the door, came in for a word. He had opened carriages for Mr. Clemens at the Twenty-third Street station, and now wanted to recall that honor. I think he received the most cordial welcome of any one who came. I am sure he did. It was Mark Twain's way to warm to the man of a lower social rank. He was never too busy, never too preoccupied, to grasp the hand of such a man, to listen to his story, and to say just the words that would make that man happy remembering them.

We left the Plaza Hotel and presently were amid the throng of outpouring congregations. Of course he was the object on which every passing eye turned; the presence to which every hat was lifted. I realized that this open and eagerly paid homage of the multitude was still dear to him, not in any small and petty way, but as the tribute of a nation, the expression of that affection which in his London and Liverpool speeches he had declared to be the last and final and most precious reward that any man can win, whether by character or achievement. It was his final harvest, and he had the courage to claim it —the aftermath of all his years of honorable labor and noble living.

THE "CRIME" OF SIMPLIFIED SPELLING. (BY CESARE)

CCLXII

FROM MARK TWAIN'S MAIL

IF the reader has any curiosity as to some of the less usual letters which a man of wide public note may inspire, perhaps he will find a certain interest in a few selected from the thousands which yearly came to Mark Twain.

For one thing, he was constantly receiving prescriptions and remedies whenever the papers reported one of his bronchial or rheumatic attacks. It is hardly necessary to quote examples of these, but only a form of his occasional reply, which was likely to be in this wise:

DEAR SIR [or MADAM],—I try every remedy sent to me. I am now on No. 87. Yours is 2,653. I am looking forward to its beneficial results.

Of course a large number of the nostrums and palliatives offered were preparations made by the wildest and longest-haired medical cranks. One of these sent an advertisement of a certain Elixir of Life, which was guaranteed to cure everything—to "wash and cleanse the human molecules, and so restore youth and preserve life everlasting."

Anonymous letters are not usually popular or to be encouraged, but Mark Twain had an especial weakness for compliments that came in that way. They were not mercenary compliments. The writer had nothing to gain. Two such letters follow—both written in England just at the time of his return.

FROM MARK TWAIN'S MAIL

Mark Twain.

Dear Sir,—Please accept a poor widow's good-by and kindest wishes. I have had some of your books sent to me; have enjoyed them very much—only wish I could afford to buy some.

I should very much like to have seen you. I have many photos of you which I have cut from several papers which I read. I have one where you are writing in bed, which I cut from the *Daily News*. Like myself, you believe in lots of sleep and rest. I am 70 and I find I need plenty. Please forgive the liberty I have taken in writing to you. If I can't come to your funeral may we meet beyond the river.

May God guard you, is the wish of a lonely old widow.

Yours sincerely,

The other letter also tells its own story:

Dear, kind Mark Twain,—For years I have wanted to write and thank you for the comfort you were to me once, only I never quite knew where you were, and besides I did not want to bother you; but to-day I was told by some one who saw you going into the lift at the Savoy that you looked sad and I thought it might cheer you a little tiny bit to hear how you kept a poor lonely girl from ruining her eyes with crying every night for long months.

Ten years ago I had to leave home and earn my living as a governess and Fate sent me to spend a winter with a very dull old country family in the depths of Staffordshire. According to the genial English custom, after my five charges had gone to bed, I took my evening meal alone in the school-room, where "Henry Tudor had supped the night before Bosworth," and there I had to stay without a soul to speak to till I went to bed. At first I used to cry every night, but a friend sent me a copy of your *Huckleberry Finn* and I never cried any more. I kept him handy under the copy-books and maps, and when Henry Tudor commenced to stretch out his chilly hands toward me I grabbed my dear *Huck* and he never once failed me; I opened him at random and in two minutes I was in another world. That's why I am so grateful to you and so fond of you, and I thought you might like to know; for it is yourself that has the kind heart, as is easily seen from the way you wrote about the poor old nigger. I am a stenographer now and live at home, but I shall never forget how you helped me. God bless you and spare you long to those you are dear to.

A letter which came to him soon after his return from England contained a clipping which reported the good work done by Christian missionaries in the Congo, especially among natives afflicted by the terrible sleeping sickness. The letter itself consisted merely of a line, which said:

Won't you give your friends, the missionaries, a good mark for this?

The writer's name was signed, and Mark Twain answered:

In China the missionaries are not wanted, & so they ought to be decent & go away. But I have not heard that in the Congo the missionary servants of God are unwelcome to the native.

Evidently those missionaries are pitying, compassionate, kind. How it would improve God to take a lesson from them! He invented & distributed the germ of that awful disease among those helpless, poor savages, & now He sits with His elbows on the balusters & looks down & enjoys this wanton crime. Confidently, & between you & me—well, never mind, I might get struck by lightning if I said it.

Those are good and kindly men, those missionaries, but they are a measureless satire upon their Master.

To which the writer answered:

O wicked Mr. Clemens! I have to ask Saint Joan of Arc to pray for you; then one of these days, when we all stand before the Golden Gates and we no longer "see through a glass darkly and know only in part," there will be a struggle at the heavenly portals between Joan of Arc and St. Peter, but your blessed Joan will conquer and she'll lead Mr. Clemens through the gates of pearl and apologize and plead for him.

FROM MARK TWAIN'S MAIL

Of the letters that irritated him, perhaps the following is as fair a sample as any, and it has additional interest in its sequel.

DEAR SIR,—I have written a book—naturally—which fact, however, since I am not your enemy, need give you no occasion to rejoice. Nor need you grieve, though I am sending you a copy. If I knew of any way of compelling you to read it I would do so, but unless the first few pages have that effect I can do nothing. Try the first few pages. I have done a great deal more than that with your books, so perhaps you owe me something—say ten pages. If after that attempt you put it aside I shall be sorry—for you.

I am afraid that the above looks flippant—but think of the twitterings of the soul of him who brings in his hand an unbidden book, written by himself. To such a one much is due in the way of indulgence. Will you remember that? Have you forgotten early twitterings of your own?

In a memorandum made on this letter Mark Twain wrote:

Another one of those peculiarly depressing letters—a letter cast in artificially humorous form, whilst no art could make the subject humorous—to me.

Commenting further, he said:

As I have remarked before about one thousand times the coat of arms of the human race ought to consist of a man with an ax on his shoulder proceeding toward a grindstone, or it ought to represent the several members of the human race holding out the hat to one another; for we are all beggars, each in his own way. One beggar is too proud to beg for pennies, but will beg for an introduction into society; another does not care for society, but he wants a postmastership; another will inveigle a lawyer into conversation and then sponge on him for free advice. The man who wouldn't do any of these things will beg for the Presidency. Each admires his own dignity and greatly guards it, but in his opinion the others haven't any.

MARK TWAIN

Mendicancy is a matter of taste and temperament, no doubt, but no human being is without some form of it. I know my own form, you know yours. Let us conceal them from view and abuse the others. There is no man so poor but what at intervals some man comes to him with an ax to grind. By and by the ax's aspect becomes familiar to the proprietor of the grindstone. He perceives that it is the same old ax. If you are a governor you know that the stranger wants an office. The first time he arrives you are deceived; he pours out such noble praises of you and your political record that you are moved to tears; there's a lump in your throat and you are thankful that you have lived for this happiness. Then the stranger discloses his ax, and you are ashamed of yourself and your race. Six repetitions will cure you. After that you interrupt the compliments and say, "Yes, yes, that's all right; never mind about that. What is it you want?"

But you and I are in the business ourselves. Every now and then we carry our ax to somebody and ask a whet. I don't carry mine to strangers—I draw the line there; perhaps that is your way. This is bound to set us up on a high and holy pinnacle and make us look down in cold rebuke on persons who carry their axes to strangers.

I do not know how to answer that stranger's letter. I wish he had spared me. Never mind about him—I am thinking about myself. I wish he had spared *me*. The book has not arrived yet; but no matter, I am prejudiced against it.

It was a few days later that he added:

I wrote to that man. I fell back upon the old overworked, polite lie, and thanked him for his book and said I was promising myself the pleasure of reading it. Of course that set me free; I was not obliged to read it now at all, and, being free, my prejudice was gone, and as soon as the book came I opened it to see what it was like. I was not able to put it down until I had finished. It was an embarrassing thing to have to write to that man and confess that fact, but I had to do it. That first letter was merely a lie. Do you think I wrote the second one to give that man pleasure? Well, I did, but it was second-hand pleasure. I wrote it first to give myself comfort, to make myself forget the original lie.

Mark Twain's interest was once aroused by the following:

DEAR SIR,—I have had more or less of your works on my shelves for years, and believe I have practically a complete set now. This is nothing unusual, of course, but I presume it will seem to you unusual for any one to keep books constantly in sight which the owner regrets ever having read.

Every time my glance rests on the books I do regret having read them, and do not hesitate to tell you so to your face, and care not who may know my feelings. You, who must be kept busy attending to your correspondence, will probably pay little or no attention to this small fraction of it, yet my reasons, I believe, are sound and are probably shared by more people than you are aware of.

Probably you will not read far enough through this to see who has signed it, but if you do, and care to know why I wish I had left your work unread, I will tell you as briefly as possible if you will ask me. GEORGE B. LAUDER.

Clemens did not answer the letter, but put it in his pocket, perhaps intending to do so, and a few days later, in Boston, when a reporter called, he happened to remember it. The reporter asked permission to print the queer document, and it appeared in his Mark Twain interview next morning. A few days later the writer of it sent a second letter, this time explaining:

MY DEAR SIR,—I saw in to-day's paper a copy of the letter which I wrote you October 26th.

I have read and re-read your works until I can almost recall some of them word for word. My familiarity with them is a constant source of pleasure which I would not have missed, and therefore the regret which I have expressed is more than offset by thankfulness.

Believe me, the regret which I feel for having read your works is entirely due to the unalterable fact that I can never again have the pleasure of reading them for the first time.

Your sincere admirer,

GEORGE B. LAUDER.

Mark Twain promptly replied this time:

DEAR SIR,—You fooled me completely; I didn't divine what the letter was concealing, neither did the newspaper men, so you are a very competent deceiver.

Truly yours,

S. L. CLEMENS.

It was about the end of 1907 that the new St. Louis Harbor boat was completed. The editor of the St. Louis Republic reported that it has been christened "Mark Twain," and asked for a word of comment. Clemens sent this line:

May my namesake follow in my righteous footsteps, then neither of us will need any fire insurance.

Editor Republic —
St. Louis, Mo.

May my namesake follow
in my righteous footsteps,
then neither of us will need
any fire insurance —

Mark Twain

CCLXIII

SOME LITERARY LUNCHEONS

HOWELLS, in his book, refers to the Human Race Luncheon Club, which Clemens once organized for the particular purpose of damning the species in concert. It was to consist, beside Clemens himself, of Howells, Colonel Harvey, and Peter Dunne; but it somehow never happened that even this small membership could be assembled while the idea was still fresh, and therefore potent.

Out of it, however, grew a number of those private social gatherings which Clemens so dearly loved—small luncheons and dinners given at his own table. The first of these came along toward the end of 1907, when Howells was planning to spend the winter in Italy.

"Howells is going away," he said, "and I should like to give him a stag-party. We'll enlarge the Human Race Club for the occasion."

So Howells, Colonel Harvey, Martin Littleton, Augustus Thomas, Robert Porter, and Paderewski were invited. Paderewski was unable to come, and seven in all assembled.

Howells was first to arrive.

"Here comes Howells," Clemens said. "Old Howells—a thousand years old."

But Howells didn't look it. His face was full of good-nature and apparent health, and he was by no means venerable, either in speech or action. Thomas, Porter, Littleton, and Harvey drifted in. Cocktails were served and luncheon was announced.

Claude, the butler, had prepared the table with fine artistry—its center a mass of roses. There was to be no woman in the neighborhood—Clemens announced this fact as a sort of warrant for general freedom of expression.

Thomas's play, "The Witching Hour," was then at the height of its great acceptance, and the talk naturally began there. Thomas told something of the difficulty which he found in being able to convince a manager that it would succeed, and declared it to be his own favorite work. I believe there was no dissenting opinion as to its artistic value, or concerning its purpose and psychology, though these had been the stumbling-blocks from a managerial point of view.

When the subject was concluded, and there had come a lull, Colonel Harvey, who was seated at Clemens's left, said:

"Uncle Mark"—he often called him that—"Major Leigh handed me a report of the year's sales just as I was leaving. It shows your royalty returns this year to be very close to fifty thousand dollars. I don't believe there is another such return from old books on record."

This was said in an undertone, to Clemens only, but was overheard by one or two of those who sat nearest. Clemens was not unwilling to repeat it for the benefit of all, and did so. Howells said:

"A statement like that arouses my basest passions. The books are no good; it's just the advertising they get."

Clemens said: "Yes, my contract compels the publisher to advertise. It costs them two hundred dollars every time they leave the advertisement out of the magazines."

"And three hundred every time we put it in," said Harvey. "We often debate whether it is more profitable to put in the advertisement or to leave it out."

The talk switched back to plays and acting. Thomas recalled an incident of Beerbohm Tree's performance of

"Hamlet." W. S. Gilbert, of light-opera celebrity, was present at a performance, and when the play ended Mrs. Tree hurried over to him and said:

"Oh, Mr. Gilbert, what did you think of Mr. Tree's rendition of Hamlet?"

"Remarkable," said Gilbert. "Funny without being vulgar."

It was with such idle tales and talk-play that the afternoon passed. Not much of it all is left to me, but I remember Howells saying, "Did it ever occur to you that the newspapers abolished hell? Well, they did —it was never done by the church. There was a consensus of newspaper opinion that the old hell with its lake of fire and brimstone was an antiquated institution; in fact a dead letter." And again, "I was coming down Broadway last night, and I stopped to look at one of the street-venders selling those little toy fighting roosters. It was a bleak, desolate evening; nobody was buying anything, and as he pulled the string and kept those little roosters dancing and fighting his remarks grew more and more cheerless and sardonic.

"'Japanese game chickens,' he said; 'pretty toys, amuse the children with their antics. Child of three can operate it. Take them home for Christmas. Chicken-fight at your own fireside.' I tried to catch his eye to show him that I understood his desolation and sorrow, but it was no use. He went on dancing his toy chickens, and saying, over and over, 'Chicken-fight at your own fireside.'"

The luncheon over, we wandered back into the drawing-room, and presently all left but Colonel Harvey. Clemens and the Colonel went up to the billiard-room and engaged in a game of cushion caroms, at twenty-five cents a game. I was umpire and stakeholder, and it was a most interesting occupation, for the series was close and a very cheerful one. It ended the day much to

Mark Twain's satisfaction, for he was oftenest winner. That evening he said:

"We will repeat that luncheon; we ought to repeat it once a month. Howells will be gone, but we must have the others. We cannot have a thing like that too often."

There was, in fact, a second stag-luncheon very soon after, at which George Riggs was present and that rare Irish musician, Denis O'Sullivan. It was another choice afternoon, with a mystical quality which came of the music made by O'Sullivan on some Hindu reeds—pipes of Pan. But we shall have more of O'Sullivan presently —all too little, for his days were few and fleeting.

Howells could not get away just yet. Colonel Harvey, who, like James Osgood, would not fail to find excuse for entertainment, chartered two drawing-room cars, and with Mrs. Harvey took a party of fifty-five or sixty congenial men and women to Lakewood for a good-by luncheon to Howells. It was a day borrowed from June, warm and beautiful.

The trip down was a sort of reception. Most of the guests were acquainted, but many of them did not often meet. There was constant visiting back and forth the full length of the two coaches. Denis O'Sullivan was among the guests. He looked in the bloom of health, and he had his pipes and played his mystic airs; then he brought out the tin-whistle of Ireland, and blew such rollicking melodies as capering fairies invented a long time ago. This was on the train going down.

There was a brief program following the light-hearted feasting—an informal program fitting to that sunny day. It opened with some recitations by Miss Kitty Cheatham; then Colonel Harvey introduced Howells, with mention of his coming journey. As a rule, Howells does not enjoy speaking. He is willing to read an address on occasion, but he has owned that the prospect of talking without his notes terrifies him. This time, however, there was no reluctance, though he had prepared no speech. He was among friends. He looked even happy when he got on his feet, and he spoke like a happy man. He talked about Mark Twain. It was all delicate, delicious chaffing which showed Howells at his very best—all too short for his listeners.

Clemens, replying, returned the chaff, and rambled amusingly among his fancies, closing with a few beautiful words of "Godspeed and safe return" to his old comrade and friend.

Then once more came Denis and his pipes. No one will ever forget his part of the program. The little samples we had heard on the train were expanded and multiplied and elaborated in a way that fairly swept his listeners out of themselves into that land where perhaps Denis himself wanders playing now; for a month later, strong and lusty and beautiful as he seemed that day, he suddenly vanished from among us and his reeds were silent. It never occurred to us then that Denis could die; and as he finished each melody and song there was a shout for a repetition, and I think we could have sat there and let the days and years slip away unheeded, for time is banished by music like that, and one wonders if it might not even divert death.

It was dark when we crossed the river homeward; the myriad lights from heaven-climbing windows made an enchanted city in the sky. The evening, like the day, was warm, and some of the party left the ferry-cabin to lean over and watch the magic spectacle, the like of which is not to be found elsewhere on the earth.

CCLXIV

"CAPTAIN STORMFIELD" IN PRINT

DURING the forty years or so that had elapsed since the publication of the "Gates Ajar" and the perpetration of Mark Twain's intended burlesque, built on Captain Ned Wakeman's dream, the Christian religion in its more orthodox aspects had undergone some large modifications. It was no longer regarded as dangerous to speak lightly of hell, or even to suggest that the golden streets and jeweled architecture of the sky might be regarded as symbols of hope rather than exhibits of actual bullion and lapidary construction. Clemens re-read his extravaganza, *Captain Stormfield's Visit to Heaven*, gave it a modernizing touch here and there, and handed it to his publishers, who must have agreed that it was no longer dangerous, for it was promptly accepted and appeared in the December and January numbers (1907–8) of *Harper's Magazine*, and was also issued as a small book. If there were any readers who still found it blasphemous, or even irreverent, they did not say so; the letters that came—and they were a good many—expressed enjoyment and approval, also (some of them) a good deal of satisfaction that Mark Twain "had returned to his earlier form."

The publication of this story recalled to Clemens's mind another heresy somewhat similar which he had written during the winter of 1891 and 1892 in Berlin. This was a dream of his own, in which he had set out on a train with the evangelist Sam Jones and the Archbishop of Canterbury for the other world. He had noticed that his ticket was to a different destination than the Archbishop's, and so, when the prelate nodded and finally went to sleep, he changed the tickets in their hats with disturbing results. Clemens thought a good deal of this fancy when he wrote it, and when Mrs. Clemens had refused to allow it to be printed he had laboriously translated it into German, with some idea of publishing it surreptitiously; but his conscience had been too much for him. He had confessed, and even the German version had been suppressed.

Clemens often allowed his fancy to play with the idea of the orthodox heaven, its curiosities of architecture, and its employments of continuous prayer, psalm-singing, and harpistry.

"What a childish notion it was," he said, "and how curious that only a little while ago human beings were so willing to accept such fragile evidences about a place of so much importance. If we should find somewhere to-day an ancient book containing an account of a beautiful and blooming tropical Paradise secreted in the center of eternal icebergs—an account written by men who did not even claim to have seen it themselves—no geographical society on earth would take any stock in that book, yet that account would be quite as authentic as any we have of heaven. If God has such a place prepared for us, and really wanted us to know it, He could have found some better way than a book so liable to alterations and misinterpretation. God has had no trouble to prove to man the laws of the constellations and the construction of the world, and such things as that, none of which agree with His so-called book. As to a hereafter, we have not the slightest evidence that there is any—*no* evidence that appeals to logic and reason. I have never seen what to me seemed an atom of proof that there is a future life."

Then, after a long pause, he added:

"And yet—I am strongly inclined to expect one."

CCLXV

LOTOS CLUB HONORS

IT was on January 11, 1908, that Mark Twain was
given his last great banquet by the Lotos Club. The
club was about to move again, into splendid new quarters,
and it wished to entertain him once more in its old rooms.

He wore white, and amid the throng of black-clad men
was like a white moth among a horde of beetles. The
room fairly swarmed with them, and they seemed likely
to overwhelm him.

President Lawrence was toast-master of the evening,
and he ended his customary address by introducing
Robert Porter, who had been Mark Twain's host at
Oxford. Porter told something of the great Oxford
week, and ended by introducing Mark Twain. It had
been expected that Clemens would tell of his London
experiences. Instead of doing this, he said he had started
a new kind of collection, a collection of compliments.
He had picked up a number of valuable ones abroad and
some at home. He read selections from them, and kept
the company going with cheers and merriment until
just before the close of his speech. Then he repeated,
in his most impressive manner, that stately conclusion
of his Liverpool speech, and the room became still and
the eyes of his hearers grew dim. It may have been even
more moving than when originally given, for now the closing
words, "homeward bound," had only the deeper meaning.

Dr. John MacArthur followed with a speech that was
as good a sermon as any he ever delivered, and closed it
by saying:

"I do not want men to prepare for heaven, but to prepare to remain on earth, and it is such men as Mark Twain who make other men not fit to die, but fit to live."

Andrew Carnegie also spoke, and Colonel Harvey, and as the speaking ended Robert Porter stepped up behind Clemens and threw over his shoulders the scarlet Oxford robe which had been surreptitiously brought, and placed the mortar-board cap upon his head, while the diners vociferated their approval. Clemens was quite calm.

"I like this," he said, when the noise had subsided. "I like its splendid color. I would dress that way all the time, if I dared."

In the cab going home I mentioned the success of his speech, how well it had been received.

"Yes," he said; "but then I have the advantage of knowing now that I am likely to be favorably received, whatever I say. I know that my audiences are warm and responseful. It is an immense advantage to feel that. There are cold places in almost every speech, and if your audience notices them and becomes cool, you get a chill yourself in those zones, and it is hard to warm up again. Perhaps there haven't been so many lately; but I have been acquainted with them more than once." And then I could not help remembering that deadly Whittier birthday speech of more than thirty years before—that bleak, arctic experience from beginning to end.

"We have just time for four games," he said, as we reached the billiard-room; but there was no sign of stopping when the four games were over. We were winning alternately, and neither noted the time. I was leaving by an early train, and was willing to play all night. The milk-wagons were rattling outside when he said:

"Well, perhaps we'd better quit now. It seems pretty early, though." I looked at my watch. It was quarter to four, and we said good night.

CCLXVI

A WINTER IN BERMUDA

EDMUND CLARENCE STEDMAN died suddenly at his desk, January 18, 1908, and Clemens, in response to telegrams, sent this message:

I do not wish to talk about it. He was a valued friend from days that date back thirty-five years. His loss stuns me and unfits me to speak.

He recalled the New England dinners which he used to attend, and where he had often met Stedman.

"Those were great affairs," he said. "They began early, and they ended early. I used to go down from Hartford with the feeling that it wasn't an all-night supper, and that it was going to be an enjoyable time. Choate and Depew and Stedman were in their prime then —we were all young men together. Their speeches were always worth listening to. Stedman was a prominent figure there. There don't seem to be any such men now—or any such occasions."

Stedman was one of the last of the old literary group. Aldrich had died the year before. Howells and Clemens were the lingering "last leaves."

Clemens gave some further luncheon entertainments to his friends, and added the feature of "doe" luncheons —pretty affairs where, with Clara Clemens as hostess, were entertained a group of brilliant women, such as Mrs. Kate Douglas Riggs, Geraldine Farrar, Mrs. Robert Collier, Mrs. Frank Doubleday, and others. I cannot

report those luncheons, for I was not present, and the drift
of the proceedings came to me later in too fragmentary
a form to be used as history; but I gathered from Clemens
himself that he had done all of the talking, and I think
they must have been very pleasant afternoons. Among
the acknowledgments that followed one of these affairs
is this characteristic word-play from Mrs. Riggs:

N. B.—A lady who is invited to and attends a *doe luncheon*
is, of course, a doe. The question is, if she attends *two* doe
luncheons in succession is she a doe-doe? If so is she extinct
and can never attend a third?

Luncheons and billiards, however, failed to give sufficient brightness to the dull winter days, or to insure him
against an impending bronchial attack, and toward the
end of January he sailed away to Bermuda, where skies
were bluer and roadsides gay with bloom. His sojourn
was brief this time, but long enough to cure him, he said,
and he came back full of happiness. He had been driving about over the island with a newly adopted granddaughter, little Margaret Blackmer, whom he had met
one morning in the hotel dining-room. A part of his
dictated story will convey here this pretty experience.

My first day in Bermuda paid a dividend—in fact a double
dividend: it broke the back of my cold and it added a jewel
to my collection. As I entered the breakfast-room the first
object I saw in that spacious and far-reaching place was a little
girl seated solitary at a table for two. I bent down over her and
patted her cheek and said:

"I don't seem to remember your name; what is it?"
By the sparkle in her brown eyes it amused her. She said:
"Why, you've never known it, Mr. Clemens, because you've
never seen me before."
"Why, that is true, now that I come to think; it certainly is
true, and it must be one of the reasons why I have forgotten
your name. But I remember it now perfectly—it's Mary."

She was amused again; amused beyond smiling; amused to a chuckle, and she said:

"Oh no, it isn't; it's Margaret."

I feigned to be ashamed of my mistake and said:

"Ah, well, I couldn't have made that mistake a few years ago; but I am old, and one of age's earliest infirmities is a damaged memory; but I am clearer now—clearer-headed—it all comes back to me just as if it were yesterday. It's Margaret Holcomb."

She was surprised into a laugh this time, the rippling laugh that a happy brook makes when it breaks out of the shade into the sunshine, and she said:

"Oh, you are wrong again; you don't get anything right. It isn't Holcomb, it's Blackmer."

I was ashamed again, and confessed it; then:

"How old are you, dear?"

"Twelve, New-Year's. Twelve and a month."

We were close comrades—inseparables, in fact—for eight days. Every day we made pedestrian excursions—called them that anyway, and honestly they were intended for that, and that is what they would have been but for the persistent intrusion of a gray and grave and rough-coated donkey by the name of Maud. Maud was four feet long; she was mounted on four slender little stilts, and had ears that doubled her altitude when she stood them up straight. Her tender was a little bit of a cart with seat room for two in it, and you could fall out of it without knowing it, it was so close to the ground. This battery was in command of a nice, grave, dignified, gentle-faced little black boy whose age was about twelve, and whose name, for some reason or other, was Reginald. Reginald and Maud—I shall not easily forget those names, nor the combination they stood for. The trips going and coming were five or six miles, and it generally took us three hours to make it. This was because Maud set the pace. Whenever she detected an ascending grade she respected it; she stopped and said with her ears:

"This is getting unsatisfactory. We will camp here."

The whole idea of these excursions was that Margaret and I should employ them for the gathering of strength, by walking, yet we were oftener in the cart than out of it. She drove and I superintended. In the course of the first excursions I found a beautiful little shell on the beach at Spanish Point; its hinge was old and dry, and the two halves came apart in my hand. I gave one of them to Margaret and said:

"Now dear, sometime or other in the future I shall run across you somewhere, and it may turn out that it is not you at all, but will be some girl that only resembles you. I shall be saying to myself 'I know that this is a Margaret by the look of her, but I don't know for sure whether this is my Margaret or somebody else's'; but, no matter, I can soon find out, for I shall take my half shell out of my pocket and say, 'I think you are my Margaret, but I am not certain; if you are my Margaret you can produce the other half of this shell.'"

Next morning when I entered the breakfast-room and saw the child I approached and scanned her searchingly all over, then said, sadly:

"No, I am mistaken; it looks like my Margaret, but it isn't, and I am so sorry. I shall go away and cry now."

Her eyes danced triumphantly, and she cried out:

"No, you don't have to. There!" and she fetched out the identifying shell.

I was beside myself with gratitude and joyful surprise, and revealed it from every pore. The child could not have enjoyed this thrilling little drama more if we had been playing it on the stage. Many times afterward she played the chief part herself, pretending to be in doubt as to my identity and challenging me to produce my half of the shell. She was always hoping to catch me without it, but I always defeated that game—wherefore she came to recognize at last that I was not only old, but very smart.

Sometimes, when they were not walking or driving, they sat on the veranda, and he prepared history-lessons for little Margaret by making grotesque figures on cards with numerous legs and arms and other fantastic symbols and features to fix the length of some king's reign. For William the Conqueror, for instance, who reigned twenty-one years, he drew a figure of eleven legs and ten arms. It was the proper method of impressing facts upon the mind of a child. It carried him back to those days at Elmira when he had arranged for his own little girls the

MARK TWAIN

game of kings. A Miss Wallace, a friend of Margaret's,
and usually one of the pedestrian party, has written a
dainty book of those Bermudian days.[1]

Miss Wallace says:

Margaret felt for him the deep affection that children have
for an older person who understands them and treats them
with respect. Mr. Clemens never talked down to her, but
considered her opinions with a sweet dignity.

There were some pretty sequels to the shell incident.
After Mark Twain had returned to New York, and Margaret was there, she called one day with her mother, and
sent up her card. He sent back word, saying:

"I seem to remember the name; but if this is really the
person whom I think it is she can identify herself by a
certain shell I once gave her, of which I have the other
half. If the two halves fit, I shall know that this is
the same little Margaret that I remember."

The message went down, and the other half of the shell
was promptly sent up. Mark Twain had the two half-
shells incased firmly in gold, and one of these he wore
on his watch-fob, and sent the other to Margaret.

He afterward corresponded with Margaret, and once
wrote her:

I'm already making mistakes. When I was in New York,
six weeks ago, I was on a corner of Fifth Avenue and I saw a
small girl—not a big one—start across from the opposite corner,
and I exclaimed to myself joyfully, "That is certainly my Margaret!" so I rushed to meet her. But as she came nearer I
began to doubt, and said to myself, "It's a Margaret—that is
plain enough—but I'm afraid it is somebody else's." So when
I was passing her I held my shell so she couldn't help but see it.
Dear, she only glanced at it and passed on! I wondered if she
could have overlooked it. It seemed best to find out; so I
turned and followed and caught up with her, and said, deferen-

---

[1] *Mark Twain and the Happy Islands*, by Elizabeth Wallace.

tially, "Dear Miss, I already know your first name by the look of you, but would you mind telling me your other one?" She was vexed and said pretty sharply, "It's Douglas, if you're so anxious to know. I know *your* name by your looks, and I'd advise you to shut yourself up with your pen and ink and write some more rubbish. I am surprised that they allow you to run at large. You are likely to get run over by a baby-carriage any time. Run along now and don't let the cows bite you."

What an idea! There aren't any cows in Fifth Avenue. But I didn't smile; I didn't let on to perceive how uncultured she was. She was from the country, of course, and didn't know what a comical blunder she was making.

Mr. Rogers's health was very poor that winter, and Clemens urged him to try Bermuda, and offered to go back with him; so they sailed away to the summer island, and though Margaret was gone, there was other entertaining company—other granddaughters to be adopted, and new friends and old friends, and diversions of many sorts. Mr. Rogers's son-in-law, William Evarts Benjamin, came down and joined the little group. It was one of Mark Twain's real holidays. Mr. Rogers's health improved rapidly, and Mark Twain was in fine trim. To Mrs. Rogers, at the end of the first week, he wrote:

DEAR MRS. ROGERS,—He is getting along splendidly! This was the very place for him. He enjoys himself & is as quarrelsome as a cat.

But he will get a backset if Benjamin goes home. Benjamin is the brightest man in these regions, & the best company. Bright? He is much more than that, he is brilliant. He keeps the crowd intensely alive.

With love & all good wishes.   S. L. C.

Mark Twain and Henry Rogers were much together and much observed. They were often referred to as "the King" and "the Rajah," and it was always a question whether it was "the King" who took care of "the Rajah," or *vice versa.* There was generally a group to gather around them, and Clemens was sure of an attentive audience, whether he wanted to air his philosophies, his views of the human race, or to read aloud from the verses of Kipling.

"I am not fond of all poetry," he would say; "but there's something in Kipling that appeals to me. I guess he's just about my level."

Miss Wallace recalls certain Kipling readings in his room, when his friends gathered to listen.

On those Kipling evenings the *mise-en-scène* was a striking one. The bare hotel room, the pine woodwork and pine furniture, loose windows which rattled in the sea-wind. Once in a while a gust of asthmatic music from the spiritless orchestra downstairs came up the hallway. Yellow, unprotected gas-lights burned uncertainly, and Mark Twain in the midst of this lay on his bed (there was no couch) still in his white serge suit, with the light from the jet shining down on the crown of his silver hair, making it gleam and glisten like frosted threads.

In one hand he held his book, in the other he had his pipe, which he used principally to gesture with in the most dramatic passages.

Margaret's small successors became the earliest members of the Angel Fish Club, which Clemens concluded to organize after a visit to the spectacular Bermuda aquarium. The pretty angel-fish suggested youth and feminine beauty to him, and his adopted granddaughters became angel-fish to him from that time forward. He bought little enamel angel-fish pins, and carried a number of them with him most of the time, so that he could create membership on short notice. It was just another of the harmless and happy diversions of his gentler side. He was always fond of youth and freshness. He regarded the decrepitude of old age as an unnecessary part of life. Often he said:

"If I had been helping the Almighty when He created

man, I would have had Him begin at the other end, and
start human beings with old age. How much better it
would have been to start old and have all the bitterness
and blindness of age in the beginning! One would not
mind then if he were looking forward to a joyful youth.
Think of the joyous prospect of growing young instead
of old! Think of looking forward to eighteen instead of
eighty! Yes, the Almighty made a poor job of it. I
wish He had invited my assistance."

To one of the angel-fish he wrote, just after his return:

I miss you, dear. I miss Bermuda, too, but not so much as
I miss you; for you were rare, and occasional and select, and
Ltd., whereas Bermuda's charms and graciousnesses were free
and common and unrestricted—like the rain, you know, which
falls upon the just and the unjust alike; a thing which would
not happen if I were superintending the rain's affairs. No, I
would rain softly and sweetly upon the just, but whenever I
caught a sample of the unjust outdoors I would drown him.

CCLXVII

[AS I am beginning this chapter, April 16, 1912, the news comes of the loss, on her first trip, of the great White Star Line steamer *Titanic*, with the destruction of many passengers, among them Frank D. Millet, William T. Stead, Isadore Straus, John Jacob Astor, and other distinguished men. They died as heroes, remaining with the ship in order that the women and children might be saved.

It was the kind of death Frank Millet would have wished to die. He was always a soldier—a knight. He has appeared from time to time in these pages, for he was a dear friend of the Clemens household. One of America's foremost painters, at the time of his death he was head of the American Academy of Arts in Rome.]

Mark Twain made a number of addresses during the spring of 1908. He spoke at the Cartoonists' dinner, very soon after his return from Bermuda; he spoke at the Booksellers' banquet, expressing his debt of obligation to those who had published and sold his books; he delivered a fine address at the dinner given by the British Schools and University Club at Delmonico's, May 25th, in honor of Queen Victoria's birthday. In that speech he paid high tribute to the Queen for her attitude toward America during the crisis of the Civil War, and to her royal consort, Prince Albert.

What she did for us in America in our time of storm and stress we shall not forget, and whenever we call it to mind we shall always gratefully remember the wise and righteous mind that guided her in it and sustained and supported her—Prince Albert's. We need not talk any idle talk here to-night about either possible or impossible war between two countries; there will be no war while we remain sane and the son of Victoria and Albert sits upon the throne. In conclusion, I believe I may justly claim to utter the voice of my country in saying that we hold him in deep honor, and also in cordially wishing him a long life and a happy reign.

But perhaps his most impressive appearance was at the dedication of the great City College (May 14, 1908), where President John Finley, who had been struggling along with insufficient room, was to have space at last for his freer and fuller educational undertakings. A great number of honored scholars, statesmen, and diplomats assembled on the college campus, a spacious open court surrounded by stately college architecture of medieval design. These distinguished guests were clad in their academic robes, and the procession could not have been widely different from that one at Oxford of a year before. But there was something rather fearsome about it, too. A kind of scaffolding had been reared in the center of the campus for the ceremonies, and when those grave men in their robes of state stood grouped upon it the picture was strikingly suggestive of one of George Cruikshank's drawings of an execution scene at the Tower of London. Many of the robes were black—these would be the priests—and the few scarlet ones would be the cardinals who might have assembled for some royal martyrdom. There was a bright May sunlight over it all, one of those still, cool brightnesses which served to heighten the weird effect. I am sure that others felt it besides myself, for everybody seemed wordless and awed, even at times when there was no occasion for silence. There was something of another age about the whole setting, to say the least.

We left the place in a motor-car, a crowd of boys following after. As Clemens got in they gathered around the car and gave the college yell, ending with "Twain! Twain! Twain!" and added three cheers for Tom Sawyer, Huck Finn, and Pudd'nhead Wilson. They called for a speech, but he only said a few words in apology for not granting their request. He made a speech to them that night at the Waldorf—where he proposed for the City College a chair of citizenship, an idea which met with hearty applause.

In the same address he referred to the "God Trust" motto on the coins, and spoke approvingly of the President's order for its removal.

We do not trust in God, in the important matters of life, and not even a minister of the Gospel will take any coin for a cent more than its accepted value because of that motto. If cholera should ever reach these shores we should probably pray to be delivered from the plague, but we would put our main trust in the Board of Health.

Next morning, commenting on the report of this speech, he said:

"If only the reporters would not try to improve on what I say. They seem to miss the fact that the very art of saying a thing effectively is in its delicacy, and as they can't reproduce the manner and intonation in type they make it emphatic and clumsy in trying to convey it to the reader."

I pleaded that the reporters were often young men, eager, and unmellowed in their sense of literary art.

"Yes," he agreed, "they are so afraid their readers won't see my good points that they set up red flags to mark them and beat a gong. They mean well, but I wish they wouldn't do it."

He referred to the portion of his speech concerning the motto on the coins. He had freely expressed similar sentiments on other public occasions, and he had received a letter criticizing him for saying that we do not really trust in God in any financial matter.

"I wanted to answer it," he said; "but I destroyed it. It didn't seem worth noticing."

I asked how the motto had originated.

"About 1853 some idiot in Congress wanted to announce to the world that this was a religious nation, and proposed putting it there, and no other Congressman had courage enough to oppose it, of course. It took courage in those days to do a thing like that; but I think the same thing would happen to-day."

"Still the country has become broader. It took a brave man before the Civil War to confess he had read the *Age of Reason*."

"So it did, and yet that seems a mild book now. I read it first when I was a cub pilot, read it with fear and hesitation, but marveling at its fearlessness and wonderful power. I read it again a year or two ago, for some reason, and was amazed to see how tame it had become. It seemed that Paine was apologizing everywhere for hurting the feelings of the reader."

He drifted, naturally, into a discussion of the Knickerbocker Trust Company's suspension, which had tied up some fifty-five thousand dollars of his capital, and wondered how many were trusting in God for the return of these imperiled sums. Clemens himself, at this time, did not expect to come out whole from that disaster. He had said very little when the news came, though it meant that his immediate fortunes were locked up, and it came near stopping the building activities at Redding. It was only the smaller things of life that irritated him. He often met large calamities with a serenity which almost resembled indifference. In the Knickerbocker situation he even found humor as time passed, and wrote a number of gay letters, some of which found their way into print.

It should be added that in the end there was no loss to any of the Knickerbocker depositors.

CCLXVIII

THE building of the new home at Redding had been going steadily forward for something more than a year. John Mead Howells had made the plans; W. W. Sunderland and his son Philip, of Danbury, Connecticut, were the builders, and in the absence of Miss Clemens, then on a concert tour, Mark Twain's secretary, Miss I. V. Lyon, had superintended the furnishing.

"Innocence at Home," as the place was originally named, was to be ready for its occupant in June, with every detail in place, as he desired. He had never visited Redding; he had scarcely even glanced at the plans or discussed any of the decorations of the new home. He had required only that there should be one great living-room for the orchestrelle, and another big room for the billiard-table, with plenty of accommodations for guests. He had required that the billiard-room be red, for something in his nature answered to the warm luxury of that color, particularly in moments of diversion. Besides, his other billiard-rooms had been red, and such association may not be lightly disregarded. His one other requirement was that the place should be complete.

"I don't want to see it," he said, "until the cat is purring on the hearth."

Howells says:

"He had grown so weary of change, and so indifferent to it, that he was without interest."

But it was rather, I think, that he was afraid of *losing*

1446

interest by becoming wearied with details which were likely to exasperate him; also, he wanted the dramatic surprise of walking into a home that had been conjured into existence as with a word.

It was expected that the move would be made early in the month; but there were delays, and it was not until the 18th of June that he took possession.

The plan, at this time, was only to use the Redding place as a summer residence, and the Fifth Avenue house was not dismantled. A few days before the 18th the servants, with one exception, were taken up to the new house, Clemens and myself remaining in the loneliness of No. 21, attending to the letters in the morning and playing billiards the rest of the time, waiting for the appointed day and train. It was really a pleasant three days. He invented a new game, and we were riotous and laughed as loudly as we pleased. I think he talked very little of the new home which he was so soon to see. It was referred to no oftener than once or twice a day, and then I believe only in connection with certain of the billiard-room arrangements. I have wondered since what picture of it he could have had in his mind, for he had never seen a photograph. He had a general idea that it was built upon a hill, and that its architecture was of the Italian villa order. I confess I had moments of anxiety, for I had selected the land for him, and had been more or less accessory otherwise. I did not really worry, for I knew how beautiful and peaceful it all was; also something of his taste and needs.

It had been a dry spring, and country roads were dusty, so that those who were responsible had been praying for rain, to be followed by a pleasant day for his arrival. Both petitions were granted; June 18th would fall on Thursday, and Monday night there came a good, thorough, and refreshing shower that washed the vegetation clean and laid the dust. The morning of the 18th was bright and sunny and cool. Clemens was up and shaved by six o'clock in order to be in time, though the train did not leave until four in the afternoon—an express newly timed to stop at Redding—its first trip scheduled for the day of Mark Twain's arrival.

We were still playing billiards when word was brought up that the cab was waiting. My daughter, Louise, whose school on Long Island had closed that day, was with us. Clemens wore his white flannels and a Panama hat, and at the station a group quickly collected, reporters and others, to interview him and speed him to his new home. He was cordial and talkative, and quite evidently full of pleasant anticipation. A reporter or two and a special photographer came along, to be present at his arrival.

The new, quick train, the green, flying landscape, with glimpses of the Sound and white sails, the hillsides and clear streams becoming rapidly steeper and clearer as we turned northward: all seemed to gratify him, and when he spoke at all it was approvingly. The hour and a half required to cover the sixty miles of distance seemed very short. As the train slowed down for the Redding station, he said:

"We'll leave this box of candy"—he had bought a large box on the way—"those colored porters sometimes like candy, and we can get some more."

He drew out a great handful of silver.

"Give them something—give everybody liberally that does any service."

There was a sort of open-air reception in waiting. Redding had recognized the occasion as historic. A varied assemblage of vehicles festooned with flowers had gathered to offer a gallant country welcome.

It was now a little before six o'clock of that long June day, still and dreamlike, and to the people assembled there may have been something which was not quite

reality in the scene. There was a tendency to be very
still. They nodded, waved their hands to him, smiled,
and looked their fill; but a spell lay upon them, and they
did not cheer. It would have been a pity if they had done
so. A noise, and the illusion would have been shattered.

His carriage led away on the three-mile drive to the
house on the hilltop, and the floral turnout fell in behind.
No first impression of a fair land could have come at a
sweeter time. Hillsides were green, fields were white
with daisies, dog-wood and laurel shone among the
trees. And over all was the blue sky, and everywhere
the fragrance of June.

He was very quiet as we drove along. Once with gentle
humor, looking over a white daisy field, he said:

"That is buckwheat. I always recognize buckwheat
when I see it. I wish I knew as much about other things
as I know about buckwheat. It seems to be very plentiful here; it even grows by the roadside." And a little
later: "This is the kind of a road I like; a good country
road through the woods."

The water was flowing over the mill-dam where the
road crosses the Saugatuck, and he expressed approval
of that clear, picturesque little river, one of those charming Connecticut streams. A little farther on a brook
cascaded down the hillside, and he compared it with
some of the tiny streams of Switzerland, I believe the
Giessbach. The lane that led to the new home opened
just above, and as he entered the leafy way he said, "This
is just the kind of a lane I like," thus completing his
acceptance of everything but the house and the location.

The last of the procession had dropped away at the
entrance of the lane, and he was alone with those who
had most anxiety for his verdict. They had not long to
wait. As the carriage ascended higher to the open view
he looked away, across the Saugatuck Valley to the nest•
ling village and church-spire and farm-houses, and to the

distant hills, and declared the land to be a good land and beautiful—a spot to satisfy one's soul. Then came the house—simple and severe in its architecture—an Italian villa, such as he had known in Florence, adapted now to American climate and needs. The scars of building had not all healed yet, but close to the house waved green grass and blooming flowers that might have been there always. Neither did the house itself look new. The soft, gray stucco had taken on a tone that melted into the sky and foliage of its background. At the entrance his domestic staff waited to greet him, and then he stepped across the threshold into the wide hall and stood in his own home for the first time in seventeen years. It was an anxious moment, and no one spoke immediately. But presently his eye had taken in the satisfying harmony of the place and followed on through the wide doors that led to the dining-room—on through the open French windows to an enchanting vista of tree-tops and distant farmside and blue hills. He said, very gently:

"How beautiful it all is! I did not think it could be as beautiful as this."

He was taken through the rooms; the great living-room at one end of the hall—a room on the walls of which there was no picture, but only color-harmony—and at the other end of the hall, the splendid, glowing billiard-room, where hung all the pictures in which he took delight. Then to the floor above, with its spacious apartments and a continuation of color-welcome and concord, the windows open to the pleasant evening hills. When he had seen it all—the natural Italian garden below the terraces; the loggia, whose arches framed landscape vistas and formed a rare picture-gallery; when he had completed the round and stood in the billiard-room—his especial domain—once more he said, as a final verdict:

"It is a perfect house—perfect, so far as I can see, in every detail. It might have been here always."

He was at home there from that moment—absolutely, marvelously at home, for he fitted the setting perfectly, and there was not a hitch or flaw in his adaptation. To see him over the billiard-table, five minutes later, one could easily fancy that Mark Twain, as well as the house, had "been there always." Only the presence of his daughters was needed now to complete his satisfaction in everything.

There were guests that first evening—a small home dinner-party—and so perfect were the appointments and service, that one not knowing would scarcely have imagined it to be the first dinner served in that lovely room. A little later, at the foot of the garden of bay and cedar, neighbors, inspired by Dan Beard, who had recently located near by, set off some fireworks. Clemens stepped out on the terrace and saw rockets climbing through the summer sky to announce his arrival.

"I wonder why they all go to so much trouble for me," he said, softly. "I never go to any trouble for anybody" —a statement which all who heard it, and all his multitude of readers in every land, stood ready to deny.

That first evening closed with billiards—boisterous, triumphant billiards—and when with midnight the day ended and the cues were set in the rack, there was none to say that Mark Twain's first day in his new home had not been a happy one.

CCLXIX

FIRST DAYS AT STORMFIELD

I WENT up next afternoon, for I knew how he dreaded loneliness. We played billiards for a time, then set out for a walk, following the long drive to the leafy lane that led to my own property. Presently he said:

"In one way I am sorry I did not see this place sooner. I never want to leave it again. If I had known it was so beautiful I should have vacated the house in town and moved up here permanently."

I suggested that he could still do so, if he chose, and he entered immediately into the idea. By and by we turned down a deserted road, grassy and beautiful, that ran along his land. At one side was a slope facing the west, and dotted with the slender, cypress-like cedars of New England. He asked if that belonged to his land, and on being told it did he said:

"I would like Howells to have a house there. We must try to give that to Howells."

At the foot of the hill we came to a brook and followed it into a meadow. I told him that I had often caught fine trout there, and that soon I would bring in some for breakfast. He answered:

"Yes, I should like that. I don't care to catch them any more myself. I like them very hot."

We passed through some woods and came out near my own ancient little house. He noticed it and said:

"The man who built that had some memory of Greece in his mind when he put on that little porch with those columns."

My second daughter, Frances, was coming from a distant school on the evening train, and the carriage was starting just then to bring her. I suggested that perhaps he would find it pleasant to make the drive.

"Yes," he agreed, "I should enjoy that."

So I took the reins, and he picked up little Joy, who came running out just then, and climbed into the back seat. It was another beautiful evening, and he was in a talkative humor. Joy pointed out a small turtle in the road, and he said:

"That is a wild turtle. Do you think you could teach it arithmetic?"

Joy was uncertain.

"Well," he went on, "you ought to get an arithmetic —a little ten-cent arithmetic—and teach that turtle."

We passed some swampy woods, rather dim and jungle-like.

"Those," he said, "are elephant woods."

But Joy answered:

"They are fairy woods. The fairies are there, but you can't see them because they wear magic cloaks."

He said: "I wish I had one of those magic cloaks, sometimes. I had one once, but it is worn out now."

Joy looked at him reverently, as one who had once been the owner of a piece of fairyland.

It was a sweet drive to and from the village. There are none too many such evenings in a lifetime. Colonel Harvey's little daughter, Dorothy, came up a day or two later, and with my daughter Louise spent the first week with him in the new home. They were created "Angel-Fishes"— the first in the new aquarium; that is to say, the billiard-room, where he followed out the idea by hanging a row of colored prints of Bermuda fishes in a sort of frieze around the walls. Each visiting member was required to select one as her particular patron fish and he wrote her name upon it. It was his delight to gather his juvenile guests in this room and teach them the science of billiard angles; but it was so difficult to resist taking the cue and making plays himself that he was required to stand on a little platform and give instruction just out of reach. His snowy flannels and gleaming white hair, against those rich red walls, with those small, summer-clad players, made a pretty picture.

The place did not retain its original name. He declared that it would always be "Innocence at Home" to the angel-fish visitors, but that the title didn't remain continuously appropriate. The money which he had derived from *Captain Stormfield's Visit to Heaven* had been used to build the loggia wing, and he considered the name of "Stormfield" as a substitute. When, presently, the summer storms gathered on that rock-bound, open hill, with its wide reaches of vine and shrub—wild, fierce storms that bent the birch and cedar, and strained at the bay and huckleberry, with lightning and turbulent wind and thunder, followed by the charging rain—the name seemed to become peculiarly appropriate. Standing with his head bared to the tumult, his white hair tossing in the blast, and looking out upon the wide splendor of the spectacle, he rechristened the place, and "Stormfield" it became and remained.

The last day of Mark Twain's first week in Redding, June 25th, was saddened by the news of the death of Grover Cleveland at his home in Princeton, New Jersey. Clemens had always been an ardent Cleveland admirer, and to Mrs. Cleveland now he sent this word of condolence:

Your husband was a man I knew and loved and honored for twenty-five years. I mourn with you.

And once during the evening he said:

"He was one of our two or three real Presidents. There is none to take his place."

CCLXX

THE ALDRICH MEMORIAL

AT the end of June came the dedication at Portsmouth, New Hampshire, of the Thomas Bailey Aldrich Memorial Museum, which the poet's wife had established there in the old Aldrich homestead. It was hot weather. We were obliged to take a rather poor train from South Norwalk, and Clemens was silent and gloomy most of the way to Boston. Once there, however, lodged in a cool and comfortable hotel, matters improved. He had brought along for reading the old copy of Sir Thomas Malory's Arthur Tales, and after dinner he took off his clothes and climbed into bed and sat up and read aloud from those stately legends, with comments that I wish I could remember now, only stopping at last when overpowered with sleep.

We went on a special train to Portsmouth next morning through the summer heat, and assembled, with those who were to speak, in the back portion of the opera-house, behind the scenes. Clemens was genial and good-natured with all the discomfort of it; and he liked to fancy, with Howells, who had come over from Kittery Point, how Aldrich must be amused at the whole circumstance if he could see them punishing themselves to do honor to his memory. Richard Watson Gilder was there, and Hamilton Mabie; also Governor Floyd of New Hampshire; Colonel Higginson, Robert Bridges, and other distinguished men. We got to the more open atmosphere of the stage presently, and the exercises began. Clemens was last on the program.

The others had all said handsome, serious things, and Clemens himself had mentally prepared something of the sort; but when his turn came, and he rose to speak, a sudden reaction must have set in, for he delivered an address that certainly would have delighted Aldrich living, and must have delighted him dead, if he could hear it. It was full of the most charming humor, delicate, refreshing, and spontaneous. The audience, that had been maintaining a proper gravity throughout, showed its appreciation in ripples of merriment that grew presently into genuine waves of laughter. He spoke out his regret for having worn black clothes. It was a mistake, he said, to consider this a solemn time—Aldrich would not have wished it to be so considered. He had been a man who loved humor and brightness and wit, and had helped to make life merry and delightful. Certainly, if he could know, he would not wish this dedication of his own home to be a lugubrious, smileless occasion.

Outside, when the services were ended, the venerable juvenile writer, J. T. Trowbridge, came up to Clemens with extended hand. Clemens said:

"Trowbridge, are you still alive? You must be a thousand years old. Why, I listened to your stories while I was being rocked in the cradle."

Trowbridge said:

"Mark, there's some mistake. My earliest infant smile was wakened with one of your jokes."

They stood side by side against a fence in the blazing sun and were photographed—an interesting picture.

We returned to Boston that evening. Clemens did not wish to hurry in the summer heat, and we remained another day quietly sight-seeing, and driving around and around Commonwealth Avenue in a victoria in the cool of the evening. Once, remembering Aldrich, he said:

"I was just planning *Tom Sawyer* when he was beginning the *Story of a Bad Boy*. When I heard that he was writing that I thought of giving up mine, but Aldrich insisted that it would be a foolish thing to do. He thought my Missouri boy could not by any chance conflict with his boy of New England, and of course he was right." [1]

He spoke of how great literary minds usually came along in company. He said:

"Now and then, on the stream of time, small gobs of that thing which we call genius drift down, and a few of these lodge at some particular point, and others collect about them and make a sort of intellectual island—a towhead, as they say on the river—such an accumulation of intellect we call a group, or school, and name it.

"Thirty years ago there was the Cambridge group. Now there's been still another, which included Aldrich and Howells and Stedman and Cable. It will soon be gone. I suppose they will have to name it by and by."

He pointed out houses here and there of people he had known and visited in other days. The driver was very anxious to go farther, to other and more distinguished sights. Clemens mildly but firmly refused any variation of the program, and so we kept on driving around and around the shaded loop of Commonwealth Avenue until dusk fell and the lights began to twinkle among the trees.

[1] Mr. Clemens's memory tricked him here, as it was likely to do. Aldrich's *Bad Boy* was published in 1868, several years before *Tom Sawyer* was planned. It is likely, however, that the book did not come to Mark Twain's notice until he began discussing his own boy story.

CCLXXI

DEATH OF "SAM" MOFFETT

CLEMENS'S next absence from Redding came on August 1, 1908, when the sudden and shocking news was received of the drowning of his nephew, Samuel E. Moffett, in the surf of the Jersey shore. Moffett was his nearest male relative, and a man of fine intellect and talents. He was superior in those qualities which men love—he was large-minded and large-hearted, and of noble ideals. With much of the same sense of humor which had made his uncle's fame, he had what was really an abnormal faculty of acquiring and retaining encyclopedic data. Once as a child he had visited Hartford when Clemens was laboring over his history game. The boy was much interested, and asked permission to help. His uncle willingly consented, and referred him to the library for his facts. But he did not need to consult the books: he already had English history stored away, and knew where to find every detail of it. At the time of his death Moffett held an important editorial position on *Collier's Weekly.*

Clemens was fond and proud of his nephew. Returning from the funeral, he was much depressed, and a day or two later became really ill. He was in bed for a few days, resting, he said, after the intense heat of the journey. Then he was about again and proposed billiards as a diversion. We were all alone one very still, warm August afternoon playing, when he suddenly said:

"I feel a little dizzy; I will sit down a moment."

DEATH OF "SAM" MOFFETT

I brought him a glass of water and he seemed to recover, but when he rose and started to play I thought he had a dazed look. He said:

"I have lost my memory. I don't know which is my ball. I don't know what game we are playing."

But immediately this condition passed, and we thought little of it, considering it merely a phase of biliousness due to his recent journey. I have been told since, by eminent practitioners, that it was the first indication of a more serious malady.

He became apparently quite himself again and showed his usual vigor—light of step and movement, able to skip up and down stairs as heretofore. In a letter to Mrs. Crane, August 12th, he spoke of recent happenings:

DEAR AUNT SUE,—It was a most moving, a most heart-breaking sight, the spectacle of that stunned & crushed & inconsolable family. I came back here in bad shape, & had a bilious collapse, but I am all right again, though the doctor from New York has given peremptory orders that I am not to stir from here before frost. O fortunate Sam Moffett! fortunate Livy Clemens! doubly fortunate Susy! Those swords go through & through my heart, but there is never a moment that I am not glad, for the sake of the dead, that they have escaped.

How Livy would love this place! How her very soul would steep itself thankfully in this peace, this tranquillity, this deep stillness, this dreamy expanse of woodsy hill & valley! You must come, Aunt Sue, & stay with us a real good visit. Since June 26 we have had 21 guests, & they have all liked it and said they would come again.

To Howells, on the same day, he wrote:

Won't you & Mrs. Howells & Mildred come & give us as many days as you can spare & examine John's triumph? It is the most satisfactory house I am acquainted with, & the most satisfactorily situated. . . . I have dismissed my stenographer, & have entered upon a holiday whose other end is the cemetery.

CCLXXII

STORMFIELD ADVENTURES

CLEMENS had fully decided, by this time, to live the year round in the retirement at Stormfield, and the house at 21 Fifth Avenue was being dismantled. He had also, as he said, given up his dictations for the time, at least, after continuing them, with more or less regularity, for a period of two and a half years, during which he had piled up about half a million words of comment and reminiscence. His general idea had been to add portions of this matter to his earlier books as the copyrights expired, to give them new life and interest, and he felt that he had plenty now for any such purpose.

He gave his time mainly to his guests, his billiards, and his reading, though of course he could not keep from writing on this subject and that as the fancy moved him, and a drawer in one of his dressers began to accumulate fresh though usually fragmentary manuscripts. He read the daily paper, but he no longer took the keen, restless interest in public affairs. New York politics did not concern him any more, and national politics not much. When the *Evening Post* wrote him concerning the advisability of renominating Governor Hughes he replied:

If you had asked me two months ago my answer would have been prompt & loud & strong: yes, I want Governor Hughes renominated. But it is too late, & my mouth is closed. I have become a citizen & taxpayer of Connecticut, & could not now, without impertinence, meddle in matters which are none of my business. I could not do it with impertinence without trespassing on the monopoly of another.

STORMFIELD ADVENTURES

Howells speaks of Mark Twain's "absolute content" with his new home, and these are the proper words to express it. He was like a storm-beaten ship that had drifted at last into a serene South Sea haven.

The days began and ended in tranquillity. There were no special morning regulations. One could have his breakfast at any time and at almost any place. He could have it in bed if he liked, or in the loggia or living-room, or billiard-room. He might even have it in the dining-room, or on the terrace, just outside. Guests—there were usually guests—might suit their convenience in this matter—also as to the forenoons. The afternoon brought games — that is, billiards, provided the guest knew billiards, otherwise hearts. Those two games were his safety-valves, and while there were no printed requirements relating to them the unwritten code of Stormfield provided that guests, of whatever age or previous faith, should engage in one or both of these diversions.

Clemens, who usually spent his forenoon in bed with his reading and his letters, came to the green table of skill and chance eager for the onset; if the fates were kindly, he approved of them openly. If not—well, the fates were old enough to know better, and, as heretofore, had to take the consequences. Sometimes, when the weather was fine and there were no games (this was likely to be on Sunday afternoons), there were drives among the hills and along the Saugatuck through the Redding Glen.

The cat was always "purring on the hearth" at Stormfield—several cats—for Mark Twain's fondness for this clean, intelligent domestic animal remained, to the end, one of his happiest characteristics. There were never too many cats at Stormfield, and the "hearth" included the entire house, even the billiard-table. When, as was likely to happen at any time during the game, the kittens Sinbad, or Danbury, or Billiards would decide to hop up and play with the balls, or sit in the pockets and grab at

1461

them as they went by, the game simply added this element of chance, and the uninvited player was not disturbed. The cats really owned Stormfield; any one could tell that from their deportment. Mark Twain held the title deeds; but it was Danbury and Sinbad and the others that possessed the premises. They occupied any portion of the house or its furnishings at will, and they never failed to attract attention. Mark Twain might be pre-occupied and indifferent to the comings and goings of other members of the household; but no matter what he was doing, let Danbury appear in the offing and he was observed and greeted with due deference, and complimented and made comfortable. Clemens would arise from the table and carry certain choice food out on the terrace to Tammany, and be satisfied with almost no acknowledgment by way of appreciation. One could not imagine any home of Mark Twain where the cats were not supreme. In the evening, as at 21 Fifth Avenue, there was music—the stately measures of the orchestrelle—while Mark Twain smoked and mingled unusual speculation with long, long backward dreams.

It was three months from the day of arrival in Redding that some guests came to Stormfield without invitation —two burglars, who were carrying off some bundles of silver when they were discovered. Claude, the butler, fired a pistol after them to hasten their departure, and Clemens, wakened by the shots, thought the family was opening champagne and went to sleep again.

It was far in the night; but neighbor H. A. Lounsbury and Deputy-Sheriff Banks were notified, and by morning the thieves were captured, though only after a pretty desperate encounter, during which the officer received a bullet-wound. Lounsbury and a Stormfield guest had tracked them in the dark with a lantern to Bethel, a distance of some seven miles. The thieves, also their pursuers, had boarded the train there. Sheriff Banks was waiting at the West Redding station when the train came down, and there the capture was made. It was a remarkably prompt and shrewd piece of work. Clemens gave credit for its success chiefly to Lounsbury, whose talents in many fields always impressed him. The thieves were taken to the Redding Town Hall for a preliminary hearing. Subsequently they received severe sentences.

Clemens tacked this notice on his front door:

NOTICE

TO THE NEXT BURGLAR

There is nothing but plated ware in this house now and henceforth.

You will find it in that brass thing in the dining-room over in the corner by the basket of kittens.

If you want the basket put the kittens in the brass thing. Do not make a noise—it disturbs the family.

You will find rubbers in the front hall by that thing which has the umbrellas in it, chiffonnier, I think they call it, or pergola, or something like that.

Please close the door when you go away!

Very truly yours,
S. L. CLEMENS.

CCLXXIII

STORMFIELD PHILOSOPHIES

NOW came the tranquil days of the Connecticut autumn. The change of the landscape colors was a constant delight to Mark Twain. There were several large windows in his room, and he called them his picture-gallery. The window-panes were small, and each formed a separate picture of its own that was changing almost hourly. The red tones that began to run through the foliage: the red berry bushes; the fading grass, and the little touches of sparkling frost that came every now and then at early morning; the background of distant blue hills and changing skies—these things gave his gallery a multitude of variation that no art-museums could furnish. He loved it all, and he loved to walk out in it, pacing up and down the terrace, or the long path that led to the pergola at the foot of a natural garden. If a friend came, he was willing to walk much farther; and we often descended the hill in one direction or another, though usually going toward the "gorge," a romantic spot where a clear brook found its way through a deep and rather dangerous-looking chasm. Once he was persuaded to descend into this fairy-like place, for it was well worth exploring; but his footing was no longer sure and he did not go far.

He liked better to sit on the grass-grown, rocky arch above and look down into it, and let his talk follow his mood. He liked to contemplate the geology of his surroundings, the record of the ageless periods of construction required to build the world. The marvels of science always appealed to him. He reveled in the thought of the almost limitless stretches of time, the millions upon millions of years that had been required for this stratum and that—he liked to amaze himself with the sounding figures. I remember him expressing a wish to see the Grand Cañon of Arizona, where, on perpendicular walls six thousand feet high, the long story of geological creation is written. I had stopped there during my Western trip of the previous year, and I told him something of its wonders. I urged him to see them for himself, offering to go with him. He said:

"I should enjoy that; but the railroad journey is so far and I should have no peace. The papers would get hold of it, and I would have to make speeches and be interviewed, and I never want to do any of those things again."

I suggested that the railroads would probably be glad to place a private car at his service, so that he might travel in comfort; but he shook his head.

"That would only make me more conspicuous."

"How about a disguise?"

"Yes," he said, "I might put on a red wig and false whiskers and change my name, but I couldn't disguise my drawling speech and they'd find me out."

It was amusing, but it was rather sad, too. His fame had deprived him of valued privileges.

He talked of many things during these little excursions. Once he told how he had successfully advised his nephew, Moffett, in the matter of obtaining a desirable position. Moffett had wanted to become a reporter. Clemens devised a characteristic scheme. He said:

"I will get you a place on any newspaper you may select if you promise faithfully to follow out my instructions."

The applicant agreed, eagerly enough. Clemens said:

"Go to the newspaper of your choice. Say that you are idle and want work, that you are pining for work—longing for it, and that you ask no wages, and will support yourself. All that you ask is work. That you will do anything, sweep, fill the inkstands, mucilage-bottles, run errands, and be generally useful. You must never ask for wages. You must wait until the offer of wages comes to you. You must work just as faithfully and just as eagerly as if you were being paid for it. Then see what happens."

The scheme had worked perfectly. Young Moffett had followed his instructions to the letter. By and by he attracted attention. He was employed in a variety of ways that earned him the gratitude and the confidence of the office. In obedience to further instructions, he began to make short, brief, unadorned notices of small news matters that came under his eye and laid them on the city editor's desk. No pay was asked; none was expected. Occasionally one of the items was used. Then, of course, it happened, as it must sooner or later at a busy time, that he was given a small news assignment. There was no trouble about his progress after that. He had won the confidence of the management and shown that he was not afraid to work.

The plan had been variously tried since, Clemens said, and he could not remember any case in which it had failed. The idea may have grown out of his own pilot apprenticeship on the river, when cub pilots not only received no salary, but paid for the privilege of learning.

Clemens discussed public matters less often than formerly, but they were not altogether out of his mind. He thought our republic was in a fair way to become a monarchy — that the signs were already evident. He referred to the letter which he had written so long ago in Boston, with its amusing fancy of the Archbishop of Dublin and his Grace of Ponkapog, and declared that, after all, it contained something of prophecy.[1] He would not live to see the actual monarchy, he said, but it was coming.

"I'm not expecting it in my time nor in my children's time, though it may be sooner than we think. There are two special reasons for it and one condition. The first reason is, that it is in the nature of man to want a definite something to love, honor, reverently look up to and obey; a God and King, for example. The second reason is, that while little republics have lasted long, protected by their poverty and insignificance, great ones have not. And the condition is, vast power and wealth, which breed commercial and political corruptions, and incite public favorites to dangerous ambitions."

He repeated what I had heard him say before, that in one sense we already had a monarchy; that is to say, a ruling public and political aristocracy which could create a Presidential succession. He did not say these things bitterly now, but reflectively and rather indifferently.

He was inclined to speak unhopefully of the international plans for universal peace, which were being agitated rather persistently.

"The gospel of peace," he said, "is always making a deal of noise, always rejoicing in its progress but always neglecting to furnish statistics. There are no peaceful nations now. All Christendom is a soldier-camp. The poor have been taxed in some nations to the starvation point to support the giant armaments which Christian governments have built up, each to protect itself from the rest of the Christian brotherhood, and incidentally to snatch any scrap of real estate left exposed by a weaker owner. King Leopold II. of Belgium, the most intensely Christian monarch, since Alexander VI., that has escaped hell thus far, has stolen an entire kingdom in Africa, and

---

[1] See chap. xcvii; also Appendix M.

in fourteen years of Christian endeavor there has reduced the population from thirty millions to fifteen by murder and mutilation and overwork, confiscating the labor of the helpless natives, and giving them nothing in return but salvation and a home in heaven, furnished at the last moment by the Christian priest.

"Within the last generation each Christian power has turned the bulk of its attention to finding out newer and still newer and more and more effective ways of killing Christians, and, incidentally, a pagan now and then; and the surest way to get rich quickly in Christ's earthly kingdom is to invent a kind of gun that can kill more Christians at one shot than any other existing kind. All the Christian nations are at it. The more advanced they are, the bigger and more destructive engines of war they create."

Once, speaking of battles great and small, and how important even a small battle must seem to a soldier who had fought in no other, he said:

"To him it is a mighty achievement, an achievement with a big A, when to a war-worn veteran it would be a mere incident. For instance, to the soldier of one battle, San Juan Hill was an Achievement with an A as big as the Pyramids of Cheops; whereas, if Napoleon had fought it, he would have set it down on his cuff at the time to keep from forgetting it had happened. But that is all natural and human enough. We are all like that."

The curiosities and absurdities of religious superstitions never failed to furnish him with themes more or less amusing. I remember one Sunday, when he walked down to have luncheon at my house, he sat under the shade and fell to talking of Herod's slaughter of the innocents, which he said could not have happened.

"Tacitus makes no mention of it," he said, "and he would hardly have overlooked a sweeping order like that, issued by a petty ruler like Herod. Just consider a little king of a corner of the Roman Empire ordering the slaughter of the first-born of a lot of Roman subjects. Why, the Emperor would have reached out that long arm of his and dismissed Herod. That tradition is probably about as authentic as those connected with a number of old bridges in Europe which are said to have been built by Satan. The inhabitants used to go to Satan to build bridges for them, promising him the soul of the first one that crossed the bridge; then, when Satan had the bridge done, they would send over a rooster or a jackass—a cheap jackass; that was for Satan, and of course they could fool him that way every time. Satan must have been pretty simple, even according to the New Testament, or he wouldn't have led Christ up on a high mountain and offered him the world if he would fall down and worship him. That was a manifestly absurd proposition, because Christ, as the Son of God, already owned the world; and, besides, what Satan showed him was only a few rocky acres of Palestine. It is just as if some one should try to buy Rockefeller, the owner of all the Standard Oil Company, with a gallon of kerosene."

He often spoke of the unseen forces of creation, the immutable laws that hold the planet in exact course and bring the years and the seasons always exactly on schedule time. "The Great Law" was a phrase often on his lips. The exquisite foliage, the cloud shapes, the varieties of color everywhere: these were for him outward manifestations of the Great Law, whose principle I understood to be unity—exact relations throughout all nature; and in this I failed to find any suggestion of pessimism, but only of justice. Once he wrote on a card for preservation:

From everlasting to everlasting, this is the law: the *sum* of wrong & misery shall always keep exact step with the *sum* of human blessedness.

No "civilization," no "advance," has ever modified these proportions by even the shadow of a shade, nor ever can, while our race endures.

CCLXXIV

CITIZEN AND FARMER

THE procession of guests at Stormfield continued pretty steadily. Clemens kept a book in which visitors set down their names and the dates of arrival and departure, and when they failed to attend to these matters he diligently did it himself after they were gone.

Members of the Harper Company came up with their wives; "angel-fish" swam in and out of the aquarium; Bermuda friends came to see the new home; Robert Collier, the publisher, and his wife—"Mrs. Sally," as Clemens liked to call her—paid their visits; Lord Northcliffe, who was visiting America, came with Colonel Harvey, and was so impressed with the architecture of Stormfield that he adopted its plans for a country-place he was about to build in Newfoundland. Helen Keller, with Mr. and Mrs. Macy, came up for a week-end visit. Mrs. Crane came over from Elmira; and, behold! one day came the long-ago sweetheart of his childhood, little Laura Hawkins—Laura Frazer now, widowed and in the seventies, with a granddaughter already a young lady quite grown up.

That Mark Twain was not wearying of the new conditions we may gather from a letter written to Mrs. Rogers in October:

I've grown young in these months of dissipation here. And I have left off drinking—it isn't necessary now. Society & theology are sufficient for me.

CITIZEN AND FARMER

To Helen Allen, a Bermuda "Angel-Fish," he wrote:

We have good times here in this soundless solitude on the hilltop. The moment I saw the house I was glad I built it, & now I am gladder & gladder all the time. I was not dreaming of living here except in the summer-time—that was before I saw this region & the house, you see—but that is all changed now; I shall stay here winter & summer both & not go back to New York at all. My child, it's as tranquil & contenting as Bermuda. You will be very welcome here, dear.

He interested himself in the affairs and in the people of Redding. Not long after his arrival he had gathered in all the inhabitants of the country-side, neighbors of every quality, for closer acquaintance, and threw open to them for inspection every part of the new house. He appointed Mrs. Lounsbury, whose acquaintance was very wide, a sort of committee on reception, and stood at the entrance with her to welcome each visitor in person.

It was a sort of gala day, and the rooms and the grounds were filled with the visitors. In the dining-room there were generous refreshments. Again, not long afterward, he issued a special invitation to all of those—architects, builders, and workmen—who had taken any part, however great or small, in the building of his home. Mr. and Mrs. Littleton were visiting Stormfield at this time, and both Clemens and Littleton spoke to these assembled guests from the terrace, and made them feel that their efforts had been worth while.

Presently the idea developed to establish something that would be of benefit to his neighbors, especially to those who did not have access to much reading-matter. He had been for years flooded with books by authors and publishers, and there was a heavy surplus at his home in the city. When these began to arrive he had a large number of volumes set aside as the nucleus of a public library. An unused chapel not far away—it could be seen from one of his windows—was obtained for the purpose; officers were elected; a librarian was appointed, and so the Mark Twain Library of Redding was duly established. Clemens himself was elected its first president, with the resident physician, Dr. Ernest H. Smith, vice-president, and another resident, William E. Grumman, librarian. On the afternoon of its opening the president made a brief address. He said:

I am here to speak a few instructive words to my fellow-farmers. I suppose you are all farmers. I am going to put in a crop next year, when I have been here long enough and know how. I couldn't make a turnip stay on a tree now after I had grown it. I like to talk. It would take more than the Redding air to make me keep still, and I like to instruct people. It's noble to be good, and it's nobler to teach others to be good, and less trouble. I am glad to help this library. We get our morals from books. I didn't get mine from books, but I know that morals do come from books—theoretically at least. Mr. Beard or Mr. Adams will give some land, and by and by we are going to have a building of our own.

This statement was news to both Mr. Beard and Mr. Adams and an inspiration of the moment; but Mr. Theodore Adams, who owned a most desirable site, did in fact promptly resolve to donate it for library purposes. Clemens continued:

I am going to help build that library with contributions—from my visitors. Every male guest who comes to my house will have to contribute a dollar or go away without his baggage.[1] If those burglars that broke into my house recently had done that they would have been happier now, or if they'd have broken into this library they would have read a few books and led a better life. Now they are in jail, and if they keep on they will go to Congress. When a person starts downhill you can

[1] A characteristic notice to guests requiring them to contribute a dollar to the Library Building Fund was later placed on the billiard-room mantel at Stormfield with good results.

never tell where he's going to stop. I am sorry for those burglars. They got nothing that they wanted and scared away most of my servants. Now we are putting in a burglar-alarm instead of a dog. Some advised the dog, but it costs even more to entertain a dog than a burglar. I am having the ground electrified, so that for a mile around any one who puts his foot across the line sets off an alarm that will be heard in Europe. Now I will introduce the real president to you, a man whom you know already—Dr. Smith.

So a new and important benefit was conferred upon the community, and there was a feeling that Redding, besides having a literary colony, was to be literary in fact.

It might have been mentioned earlier that Redding already had literary associations when Mark Twain arrived. As far back as Revolutionary days Joel Barlow, a poet of distinction, and once Minister to France, had been a resident of Redding, and there were still Barlow descendants in the township.

William Edgar Grumman, the librarian, had written the story of Redding's share in the Revolutionary War— no small share, for Gen. Israel Putnam's army had been quartered there during at least one long, trying winter. Charles Burr Todd, of one of the oldest Redding families, himself still a resident, was also the author of a Redding history.

Of literary folk not native to Redding, Dora Reed Goodale and her sister Elaine, the wife of Dr. Charles A. Eastman, had long been residents of Redding Center; Jeanette L. Gilder and Ida M. Tarbell had summer homes on Redding Ridge; Dan Beard, as already mentioned, owned a place near the banks of the Saugatuck, while Kate V. St. Maur, also two of Nathaniel Hawthorne's granddaughters had recently located adjoining the Stormfield lands. By which it will be seen that Redding was in no way unsuitable as a home for Mark Twain.

CCLXXV

A MANTEL AND A BABY ELEPHANT

MARK TWAIN was the receiver of two notable presents that year. The first of these, a mantel from Hawaii, presented to him by the Hawaiian Promotion Committee, was set in place in the billiard-room on the morning of his seventy-third birthday. This committee had written, proposing to build for his new home either a mantel or a chair, as he might prefer, the same to be carved from the native woods. Clemens decided on a billiard-room mantel, and John Howells forwarded the proper measurements. So, in due time, the mantel arrived, a beautiful piece of work and in fine condition, with the Hawaiian word, "Aloha," one of the sweetest forms of greeting in any tongue, carved as its central ornament.

To the donors of the gift Clemens wrote:

The beautiful mantel was put in its place an hour ago, & its friendly "Aloha" was the first uttered greeting received on my 73d birthday. It is rich in color, rich in quality, & rich in decoration; therefore it exactly harmonized with the taste for such things which was born in me & which I have seldom been able to indulge to my content. It will be a great pleasure to me, daily renewed, to have under my eye this lovely reminder of the loveliest fleet of islands that lies anchored in any ocean, & I beg to thank the committee for providing me that pleasure.

To F. N. Otremba, who had carved the mantel, he sent this word:

A MANTEL AND A BABY ELEPHANT

I am grateful to you for the valued compliment to me in the labor of heart and hand and brain which you have put upon it. It is worthy of the choicest place in the house and it has it.

It was the second beautiful mantel in Stormfield—the Hartford library mantel, removed when that house was sold, having been installed in the Stormfield living-room.

Altogether the seventy-third birthday was a pleasant one. Clemens, in the morning, drove down to see the library lot which Mr. Theodore Adams had presented, and the rest of the day there were fine, close billiard games, during which he was in the gentlest and happiest moods. He recalled the games of two years before, and as we stopped playing I said:

"I hope a year from now we shall be here, still playing the great game."

And he answered, as then:

"Yes, it *is* a great game—the best game on earth." And he held out his hand and thanked me for coming, as he never failed to do when we parted, though it always hurt me a little, for the debt was so largely mine.

Mark Twain's second present came at Christmas-time. About ten days earlier, a letter came from Robert J. Collier, saying that he had bought a baby elephant which he intended to present to Mark Twain as a Christmas gift. He added that it would be sent as soon as he could get a car for it, and the loan of a keeper from Barnum & Bailey's headquarters at Bridgeport.

The news created a disturbance in Stormfield. One could not refuse, discourteously and abruptly, a costly present like that; but it seemed a disaster to accept it. An elephant would require a roomy and warm place, also a variety of attention which Stormfield was not prepared to supply. The telephone was set going and certain timid excuses were offered by the secretary. There was no good place to put an elephant in Stormfield, but Mr. Collier said, quite confidently:

"Oh, put him in the garage."

"But there's no heat in the garage."

"Well, put him in the loggia, then. That's closed in, isn't it, for the winter? Plenty of sunlight—just the place for a young elephant."

"But we play cards in the loggia. We use it for a sort of sun-parlor."

"But that wouldn't matter. He's a kindly, playful little thing. He'll be just like a kitten. I'll send the man up to look over the place and tell you just how to take care of him, and I'll send up several bales of hay in advance. It isn't a large elephant, you know: just a little one—a regular plaything."

There was nothing further to be done; only to wait and dread until the Christmas present's arrival.

A few days before Christmas ten bales of hay arrived and several bushels of carrots. This store of provender aroused no enthusiasm at Stormfield. It would seem there was no escape now.

On Christmas morning Mr. Lounsbury telephoned up that there was a man at the station who said he was an elephant-trainer from Barnum & Bailey's, sent by Mr. Collier to look at the elephant's quarters and get him settled when he should arrive. Orders were given to bring the man over. The day of doom was at hand.

But Lounsbury's detective instinct came once more into play. He had seen a good many elephant-trainers at Bridgeport, and he thought this one had a doubtful look.

"Where is the elephant?" he asked, as they drove along.

"He will arrive at noon."

"Where are you going to put him?"

"In the loggia."

"How big is he?"

"About the size of a cow."

"How long have you been with Barnum and Bailey?"

"Six years."

"Then you must know some friends of mine" (naming two that had no existence until that moment).

"Oh yes, indeed. I know them well."

Lounsbury didn't say any more just then, but he had a feeling that perhaps the dread at Stormfield had grown unnecessarily large. Something told him that this man seemed rather more like a butler, or a valet, than an elephant-trainer. They drove to Stormfield, and the trainer looked over the place. It would do perfectly, he said. He gave a few instructions as to the care of this new household feature, and was driven back to the station to bring it.

Lounsbury came back by and by, bringing the elephant but not the trainer. It didn't need a trainer. It was a beautiful specimen; with soft, smooth coat and handsome trappings, perfectly quiet, well-behaved and small—suited to the loggia, as Collier had said—for it was only two feet long and beautifully made of cloth and cotton— one of the finest toy elephants ever seen anywhere.

It was a good joke, such as Mark Twain loved—a carefully prepared, harmless bit of foolery. He wrote Robert Collier, threatening him with all sorts of revenge, declaring that the elephant was devastating Stormfield.

"To send an elephant in a trance, under pretense that it was dead or stuffed!" he said. "The animal came to life, as you knew it would, and began to observe Christmas, and we now have no furniture left and no servants and no visitors, no friends, no photographs, no burglars —nothing but the elephant. Be kind, be merciful, be generous; take him away and send us what is left of the earthquake."

Collier wrote that he thought it unkind of him to look a gift-elephant in the trunk. And with such chaffing and gaiety the year came to an end.

SHAKESPEARE-BACON TALK

WHEN the bad weather came there was not much company at Stormfield, and I went up regularly each afternoon, for it was lonely on that bleak hill, and after his forenoon of reading or writing he craved diversion. My own home was a little more than a half-mile away, and I enjoyed the walk, whatever the weather. I usually managed to arrive about three o'clock. He would watch from his high windows until he saw me raise the hilltop, and he would be at the door when I arrived, so that there might be no delay in getting at the games. Or, if it happened that he wished to show me something in his room, I would hear his rich voice sounding down the stair. Once, when I arrived, I heard him calling, and going up I found him highly pleased with the arrangement of two pictures on a chair, placed so that the glasses of them reflected the sunlight on the ceiling. He said:

"They seem to catch the reflection of the sky and the winter colors. Sometimes the hues are wonderfully iridescent."

He pointed to a bunch of wild red berries on the mantel with the sun on them.

"How beautifully they light up!" he said; "some of them in the sunlight, some still in the shadow."

He walked to the window and stood looking out on the somber fields.

"The lights and colors are always changing there," he said. "I never tire of it."

To see him then so full of the interest and delight of the moment, one might easily believe he had never known tragedy and shipwreck. More than any one I ever knew, he lived in the present. Most of us are either dreaming of the past or anticipating the future—forever beating the dirge of yesterday or the tattoo of to-morrow. Mark Twain's step was timed to the march of the moment. There were days when he recalled the past and grieved over it, and when he speculated concerning the future; but his greater interest was always of the now, and of the particular locality where he found it. The thing which caught his fancy, however slight or however important, possessed him fully for the time, even if never afterward.

He was especially interested that winter in the Shakespeare-Bacon problem. He had long been unable to believe that the actor-manager from Stratford had written those great plays, and now a book just published, *The Shakespeare Problem Restated*, by George Greenwood, and another one in press, *Some Characteristic Signatures of Francis Bacon*, by William Stone Booth, had added the last touch of conviction that Francis Bacon, and Bacon only, had written the Shakespeare dramas. I was ardently opposed to this idea. The romance of the boy, Will Shakespeare, who had come up to London and began by holding horses outside of the theater, and ended by winning the proudest place in the world of letters, was something I did not wish to let perish. I produced all the stock testimony—Ben Jonson's sonnet, the internal evidence of the plays themselves, the actors who had published them—but he refused to accept any of it. He declared that there was not a single proof to show that Shakespeare had written one of them.

"Is there any evidence that he didn't?" I asked.

"There's evidence that he couldn't," he said. "It required a man with the fullest legal equipment to have written them. When you have read Greenwood's book you will see how untenable is any argument for Shakespeare's authorship."

I was willing to concede something, and offered a compromise.

"Perhaps," I said, "Shakespeare was the Belasco of that day—the managerial genius, unable to write plays himself, but with the supreme gift of making effective drama from the plays of others. In that case it is not unlikely that the plays would be known as Shakespeare's. Even in this day John Luther Long's "Madam Butterfly" is sometimes called Belasco's play, though it is doubtful if Belasco ever wrote a line of it."

He considered this view, but not very favorably. The Booth book was at this time a secret, and he had not told me anything concerning it; but he had it in his mind when he said, with an air of the greatest conviction:

"I *know* that Shakespeare did not write those plays, and I have reason to believe he did not touch the text in any way."

"How can you be so positive?" I asked.

He replied:

"I have private knowledge from a source that cannot be questioned."

I now suspected that he was joking, and asked if he had been consulting a spiritual medium; but he was clearly in earnest.

"It is the great discovery of the age," he said, quite seriously. "The world will soon ring with it. I wish I could tell you about it, but I have passed my word. You will not have long to wait."

I was going to sail for the Mediterranean in February, and I asked if it would be likely that I would know this great secret before I sailed. He thought not; but he said that more than likely the startling news would be given to the world while I was on the water, and it might come to me on the ship by wireless. I confess I was amazed and intensely curious by this time. I conjectured the discovery of some document—some Bacon or Shakespeare private paper which dispelled all the mystery of the authorship. I hinted that he might write me a letter which I could open on the ship; but he was firm in his refusal. He had passed his word, he repeated, and the news might not be given out as soon as that; but he assured me more than once that wherever I might be, in whatever remote locality, it would come by cable, and the world would quake with it. I was tempted to give up my trip, to be with him at Stormfield at the time of the upheaval.

Naturally the Shakespeare theme was uppermost during the remaining days that we were together. He had engaged another stenographer, and was now dictating, forenoons, his own views on the subject—views co-ordinated with those of Mr. Greenwood, whom he liberally quoted, but embellished and decorated in his own gay manner. These were chapters for his autobiography, he said, and I think he had then no intention of making a book of them. I could not quite see why he should take all this argumentary trouble if he had, as he said, positive evidence that Bacon, and not Shakespeare, had written the plays. I thought the whole matter very curious.

The Shakespeare interest had diverging by-paths. One evening, when we were alone at dinner, he said:

"There is only one other illustrious man in history about whom there is so little known," and he added, "Jesus Christ."

He reviewed the statements of the Gospels concerning Christ, though he declared them to be mainly traditional and of no value. I agreed that they contained confusing statements, and conflicted more or less with justice and reason; but I said I thought there was truth in them, too.

"Why do you think so?" he asked.

"Because they contain matters that are self-evident—things eternally and essentially just."

"Then you make your own Bible?"

"Yes, from those materials combined with human reason."

"Then it does not matter where the truth, as you call it, comes from?"

I admitted that the source did not matter; that truth from Shakespeare, Epictetus, or Aristotle was quite as valuable as from the Scriptures. We were on common ground now. He mentioned Marcus Aurelius, the Stoics, and their blameless lives. I, still pursuing the thought of Jesus, asked:

"Do you not think it strange that in that day when Christ came, admitting that there was a Christ, such a character could have come at all—in the time of the Pharisees and the Sadducees, when all was ceremony and unbelief?"

"I remember," he said, "the Sadducees didn't believe in hell. He brought them one."

"Nor the resurrection. He brought them that, also."

He did not admit that there had been a Christ with the character and mission related by the Gospels.

"It is all a myth," he said. "There have been Saviours in every age of the world. It is all just a fairy tale, like the idea of Santa Claus."

"But," I argued, "even the spirit of Christmas is real when it is genuine. Suppose that we admit there was no physical Saviour—that it is only an idea—a spiritual embodiment which humanity has made for itself and is willing to improve upon as its own spirituality improves, wouldn't that make it worthy?"

"But then the fairy story of the atonement dissolves, and with it crumbles the very foundations of any established church. You can create your own Testament, your own Scripture, and your own Christ, but you've got to give up your atonement."

"As related to the crucifixion, yes, and good riddance to it; but the death of the old order and the growth of spirituality comes to a sort of atonement, doesn't it?"

He said:

"A conclusion like that has about as much to do with the Gospels and Christianity as Shakespeare had to do with Bacon's plays. You are preaching a doctrine that would have sent a man to the stake a few centuries ago. I have preached that in my own *Gospel*."

I remembered then, and realized that, by my own clumsy ladder, I had merely mounted from dogma and superstition to his platform of training the ideals to a higher contentment of soul.

"IS SHAKESPEARE DEAD?"

I SET out on my long journey with much reluctance. However, a series of guests with various diversions had been planned, and it seemed a good time to go. Clemens gave me letters of introduction, and bade me Godspeed. It would be near the end of April before I should see him again.

Now and then on the ship, and in the course of my travels, I remembered the great news I was to hear coⁿ-cerning Shakespeare. In Cairo, at Shepheard's, I looked eagerly through English newspapers, expecting any moment to come upon great head-lines; but I was always disappointed. Even on the return voyage there was no one I could find who had heard any particular Shakespeare news.

Arriving in New York, I found that Clemens himself had published his Shakespeare dictations in a little volume of his own, entitled, *Is Shakespeare Dead?* The title certainly suggested spiritistic matters, and I got a volume at Harpers', and read it going up on the train, hoping to find somewhere in it a solution of the great mystery. But it was only matter I had already known; the secret was still unrevealed.

At Redding I lost not much time in getting up to Stormfield. There had been changes in my absence. Clara Clemens had returned from her travels, and Jean, whose health seemed improved, was coming home to be her father's secretary. He was greatly pleased with these things, and declared he was going to have a home once more with his children about him.

He was quite alone that day, and we walked up and down the great living-room for an hour, perhaps, while he discussed his new plans. For one thing, he had incorporated his pen-name, Mark Twain, in order that the protection of his copyrights and the conduct of his literary business in general should not require his personal attention. He seemed to find a relief in this, as he always did in dismissing any kind of responsibility. When we went in for billiards I spoke of his book, which I had read on the way up, and of the great Shakespearian secret which was to astonish the world. Then he told me that the matter had been delayed, but that he was no longer required to suppress it; that the revelation was in the form of a book—a book which revealed conclusively to any one who would take the trouble to follow the directions that the acrostic name of Francis Bacon in a great variety of forms ran through many—probably through all —of the so-called Shakespeare plays. He said it was far and away beyond anything of the kind ever published; that Ignatius Donnelly and others had merely glimpsed the truth, but that the author of this book, William Stone Booth, had demonstrated, beyond any doubt or question, that the Bacon signatures were there. The book would be issued in a few days, he said. He had seen a set of proofs of it, and while it had not been published in the best way to clearly demonstrate its great revelation, it must settle the matter with every reasoning mind. He confessed that his faculties had been more or less defeated in. attempting to follow the ciphers, and he complained bitterly that the evidence had not been set forth so that he who merely skims a book might grasp it.

He had failed on the acrostics at first; but more recently he had understood the rule, and had been able to work out several Bacon signatures. He complimented me by saying that he felt sure that when the book came I would have no trouble with it.

Without going further with this matter, I may say here that the book arrived presently, and between us we did work out a considerable number of the claimed acrostics by following the rules laid down. It was certainly an interesting if not wholly convincing occupation, and it would be a difficult task for any one to prove that the ciphers are not there. Just why this pretentious volume created so little agitation it would be hard to say. Certainly it did not cause any great upheaval in the literary world, and the name of William Shakespeare still continues to be printed on the title-page of those marvelous dramas so long associated with his name.

Mark Twain's own book on the subject—*Is Shakespeare Dead?*—found a wide acceptance, and probably convinced as many readers. It contained no new arguments; but it gave a convincing touch to the old ones, and it was certainly readable.[1]

Among the visitors who had come to Stormfield was Howells. Clemens had called a meeting of the Human Race Club, but only Howells was able to attend. We will let him tell of his visit:

We got on very well without the absentees, after finding them in the wrong, as usual, and the visit was like those I used to have with him so many years before in Hartford, but there was not the old ferment of subjects. Many things had been discussed and put away for good, but we had our old fondness for nature and for each other, who were so differently parts of it. He showed his absolute content with his house, and that was the greater

---

[1] Mark Twain had the fullest conviction as to the Bacon authorship of the Shakespeare plays. One evening, with Mr. Edward Loomis, we attended a fine performance of "Romeo and Juliet" given by Sothern and Marlowe. At the close of one splendid scene he said, quite earnestly, "That is about the best play that Lord Bacon ever wrote."

pleasure for me because it was my son who designed it. The architect had been so fortunate as to be able to plan it where a natural avenue of savins, the close-knit, slender, cypress-like cedars of New England, led away from the rear of the villa to the little level of a pergola, meant some day to be wreathed and roofed with vines. But in the early spring days all the landscape was in the beautiful nakedness of the Northern winter. It opened in the surpassing loveliness of wooded and meadowed uplands, under skies that were the first days blue, and the last gray over a rainy and then a snowy floor. We walked up and down, up and down, between the villa terrace and the pergola, and talked with the melancholy amusement, the sad tolerance of age for the sort of men and things that used to excite us or enrage us; now we were far past turbulence or anger. Once we took a walk together across the yellow pastures to a chasmal creek on his grounds, where the ice still knit the clayey banks together like crystal mosses; and the stream far down clashed through and over the stones and the shards of ice. Clemens pointed out the scenery he had bought to give himself elbow-room, and showed me the lot he was going to have me build on. The next day we came again with the geologist he had asked up to Stormfield to analyze its rocks. Truly he loved the place. . . .

My visit at Stormfield came to an end with tender relucting on his part and on mine. Every morning before I dressed I heard him sounding my name through the house for the fun of it and I know for the fondness, and if I looked out of my door there he was in his long nightgown swaying up and down the corridor, and wagging his great white head like a boy that leaves his bed and comes out in the hope of frolic with some one. The last morning a soft sugar-snow had fallen and was falling, and I drove through it down to the station in the carriage which had been given him by his wife's father when they were first married, and had been kept all those intervening years in honorable retirement for this final use.[1] Its springs had not grown yielding with time, it had rather the stiffness and severity

---

[1] This carriage—a finely built coupé—had been presented to Mrs. Crane when the Hartford house was closed. When Stormfield was built she returned it to its original owner.

of age; but for him it must have swung low like the sweet chariot
of the negro "spiritual" which I heard him sing with such
fervor when those wonderful hymns of the slaves began to make
their way northward.

Howells's visit resulted in a new inspiration. Clemens
started to write him one night when he could not sleep,
and had been reading the volume of letters of James Russell Lowell. Then, next morning, he was seized with the
notion of writing a series of letters to such friends as
Howells, Twichell, and Rogers—letters not to be mailed,
but to be laid away for some future public. He wrote
two of these immediately—to Howells and to Twichell.
The Howells letter (or letters, for it was really double)
is both pathetic and amusing. The first part ran:

3 in the morning, April 17, 1909.

My pen has gone dry and the ink is out of reach. Howells,
did you write me day-before-day-before yesterday or did I
dream it? In my mind's eye I most vividly see your hand-
write on a square blue envelope in the mail-pile. I have hunted
the house over, but there is no such letter. *Was* it an illusion?

I am reading Lowell's letters & smoking. I woke an hour
ago & am reading to keep from wasting the time. On page 305,
Vol. I, I have just margined a note:

"*Young* friend! I like *that!* You ought to see him *now.*"

It seemed startlingly strange to hear a person call you young.
It was a brick out of a blue sky, & knocked me groggy for a
moment. Ah me, the pathos of it is that we *were* young then.
And he—why, so was he, but he didn't know it. He didn't even
know it 9 years later, when we saw him approaching and you
warned me, saying:

"Don't say anything about age—he has just turned 50 &
thinks he is old, & broods over it."

Well, Clara *did* sing! And you wrote her a dear letter.
Time to go to sleep.

Yours ever,

MARK.

The second letter, begun at 10 A.M., outlines the plan by which he is to write on the subject uppermost in his mind without restraint, knowing that the letter is not to be mailed.

. . . The *scheme* furnishes a definite target for each letter, & you can choose the target that's going to be the most sympathetic for what you are hungering & thirsting to say at that particular moment. And you can talk with a quite unallowable frankness & freedom because you are not going to send the letter. When you are on fire with theology you'll not write it to Rogers, who wouldn't be an inspiration; you'll write it to Twichell, because it will make him writhe and squirm & break the furniture. When you are on fire with a good thing that's indecent you won't waste it on Twichell; you'll save it for Howells, who will love it. As he will never see it you can make it really indecenter than he could stand; & so no harm is done, yet a vast advantage is gained.

The letter was not finished, and the scheme perished there. The Twichell letter concerned missionaries, and added nothing to what he had already said on the subject.

He wrote no letter to Mr. Rogers—perhaps never wrote to him again.

CCLXXVIII

THE DEATH OF HENRY ROGERS

CLEMENS, a little before my return, had been on a trip to Norfolk, Virginia, to attend the opening ceremonies of the Virginia Railway. He had made a speech on that occasion, in which he had paid a public tribute to Henry Rogers, and told something of his personal obligation to the financier.

He began by telling what Mr. Rogers had done for Helen Keller, whom he called "the most marvelous person of her sex that has existed on this earth since Joan of Arc." Then he said:

That is not all Mr. Rogers has done, but you never see that side of his character because it is never protruding; but he lends a helping hand daily out of that generous heart of his. You never hear of it. He is supposed to be a moon which has one side dark and the other bright. But the other side, though you don't see it, is not dark; it is bright, and its rays penetrate, and others do see it who are not God.

I would take this opportunity to tell something that I have never been allowed to tell by Mr. Rogers, either by my mouth or in print, and if I don't look at him I can tell it now. In 1894, when the publishing company of Charles L. Webster, of which I was financial agent, failed, it left me heavily in debt. If you will remember what commerce was at that time you will recall that you could not sell anything, and could not buy anything, and I was on my back; my books were not worth anything at all, and I could not give away my copyrights. Mr. Rogers had long-enough vision ahead to say, "Your books have supported you before, and after the panic is over they will support you again," and that was a correct proposition. He saved my copyrights, and saved me from financial ruin. He it was who arranged with my creditors to allow me to roam the face of the earth and persecute the nations thereof with lectures, promising at the end of four years I would pay dollar for dollar. That arrangement was made, otherwise I would now be living out-of-doors under an umbrella, and a borrowed one at that.

You see his white mustache and his hair trying to get white (he is always trying to look like me—I don't blame him for that). These are only emblematic of his character, and that is all. I say, without exception, hair and all, he is the whitest man I have ever known.

This had been early in April. Something more than a month later Clemens was making a business trip to New York to see Mr. Rogers. I was telephoned early to go up and look over some matters with him before he started. I do not remember why I was not to go along that day, for I usually made such trips with him. I think it was planned that Miss Clemens, who was in the city, was to meet him at the Grand Central Station. At all events, she did meet him there, with the news that during the night Mr. Rogers had suddenly died. This was May 20, 1909. The news had already come to the house, and I had lost no time in preparations to follow by the next train. I joined him at the Grosvenor Hotel, on Fifth Avenue and Tenth Street. He was upset and deeply troubled by the loss of his stanch adviser and friend. He had a helpless look, and he said his friends were dying away from him and leaving him adrift.

"And how I hate to do anything," he added, "that requires the least modicum of intelligence!"

We remained at the Grosvenor for Mr. Rogers's funeral. Clemens served as one of the pall-bearers, but he did not feel equal to the trip to Fairhaven. He wanted to be very quiet, he said. He could not undertake to travel that distance among those whom he knew so well, and with whom he must of necessity join in conversation; so we remained in the hotel apartment, reading and saying very little until bedtime. Once he asked me to write a letter to Jean: "Say, 'Your father says every little while, "How glad I am that Jean is at home again!"'" for that is true and I think of it all the time."

But by and by, after a long period of silence, he said: "Mr. Rogers is under the ground now."

And so passed out of earthly affairs the man who had contributed so largely to the comfort of Mark Twain's old age. He was a man of fine sensibilities and generous impulses; withal a keen sense of humor.

One Christmas, when he presented Mark Twain with a watch and a match-case, he wrote:

MY DEAR CLEMENS,—For many years your friends have been complaining of your use of tobacco, both as to quantity and quality. Complaints are now coming in of your use of time. Most of your friends think that you are using your supply somewhat lavishly, but the chief complaint is in regard to the quality.

I have been appealed to in the mean time, and have concluded that it is impossible to get the right kind of time from a blacking-box.

Therefore, I take the liberty of sending you herewith a machine that will furnish only the best. Please use it with the kind wishes of   Yours truly,   H. H. ROGERS.

P. S.—Complaint has also been made in regard to the furrows you make in your trousers in scratching matches. You will find a furrow on the bottom of the article inclosed. Please use it. Compliments of the season to the family.

He was a man too busy to write many letters, but when he did write (to Clemens at least) they were always playful and unhurried. One reading them would not find it easy to believe that the writer was a man on whose shoulders lay the burdens of stupendous finance—burdens so heavy that at last he was crushed beneath their weight.

CCLXXIX

AN EXTENSION OF COPYRIGHT

ONE of the pleasant things that came to Mark Twain that year was the passage of a copyright bill, which added to the royalty period an extension of fourteen years. Champ Clark had been largely instrumental in the success of this measure, and had been fighting for it steadily since Mark Twain's visit to Washington in 1906. Following that visit, Clark wrote:

. . . It [the original bill] would never pass because the bill had literature and music all mixed together. Being a Missourian of course it would give me great pleasure to be of service to you. What I want to say is this: you have prepared a simple bill relating only to the copyright of books; send it to me and I will try to have it passed.

Clemens replied that he might have something more to say on the copyright question by and by—that he had in hand a dialogue[1] which would instruct Congress, but this he did not complete. Meantime a simple bill was proposed and early in 1909 it became a law. In June Clark wrote:

DR. SAMUEL L. CLEMENS,
    Stormfield, Redding, Conn.
MY DEAR DOCTOR,—I am gradually becoming myself again, after a period of exhaustion that almost approximated prostra-

---

[1] Similar to the "Open Letter to the Register of Copyrights," *North American Review*, January, 1905.

tion. After a long lecture tour last summer I went immediately into a hard campaign; as soon as the election was over, and I had recovered my disposition, I came here and went into those tariff hearings, which began shortly after breakfast each day, and sometimes lasted until midnight. Listening patiently and meekly, withal, to the lying of tariff barons for many days and nights was followed by the work of the long session; that was followed by a hot campaign to take Uncle Joe's rules away from him; on the heels of that "Campaign that Failed" came the tariff fight in the House. I am now getting time to breathe regularly and I am writing to ask you if the copyright law is acceptable to you. If it is not acceptable to you I want to ask you to write and tell me how it should be changed and I will give my best endeavors to the work. I believe that your ideas and wishes in the matter constitute the best guide we have as to what should be done in the case.

Your friend,   CHAMP CLARK.

To this Clemens replied:

STORMFIELD, REDDING, CONN., *June 5, 1909.*

DEAR CHAMP CLARK,—Is the new copyright law acceptable to me? Emphatically yes! Clark, it is the only sane & clearly defined & just & righteous copyright law that has ever existed in the United States. Whosoever will compare it with its predecessors will have no trouble in arriving at that decision.

The bill which was before the committee two years ago when I was down there was the most stupefying jumble of conflicting & apparently irreconcilable interests that was ever seen; and we all said "the case is hopeless, absolutely hopeless—out of this chaos nothing can be built." But we were in error; out of that chaotic mass this excellent bill has been constructed, the warring interests have been reconciled, and the result is as comely and substantial a legislative edifice as lifts its domes and towers and protective lightning-rods out of the statute-book I think. When I think of that other bill, which even the Deity couldn't understand, and of this one, which even I can understand, I take off my hat to the man or men who devised this one. Was it R. U. Johnson? Was it the Authors' League? Was it both together? I don't know, but I take off my hat,

AN EXTENSION OF COPYRIGHT

anyway. Johnson has written a valuable article about the new law—I inclose it.

At last—at last and for the first time in copyright history—we are ahead of England! Ahead of her in two ways: by length of time and by fairness to all interests concerned. Does this sound like shouting? Then I must modify it: all we possessed of copyright justice before the 4th of last March we owed to England's initiative.

Truly yours,
S. L. CLEMENS.

Clemens had prepared what was the final word on the subject of copyright just before this bill was passed—a petition for a law which he believed would regulate the whole matter. It was a generous, even if a somewhat Utopian, plan, eminently characteristic of its author. The new fourteen-year extension, with the prospect of more, made this or any other compromise seem inadvisable.[1]

[1] The reader may consider this last copyright document by Mark Twain under Appendix N, at the end of this volume.

CCLXXX

A WARNING

CLEMENS had promised to go to Baltimore for the graduation of "Francesca" of his London visit in 1907—and to make a short address to her class.

It was the eighth of June when we set out on this journey,[1] but the day was rather bleak and there was a chilly rain. Clemens had a number of errands to do in New York, and we drove from one place to another, attending to them. Finally, in the afternoon, the rain ceased, and while I was arranging some matters for him he concluded to take a ride on the top of a Fifth Avenue stage. It was fine and pleasant when he started, but the weather thickened again and when he returned he complained that he had felt a little chilly. He seemed in fine condition, however, next morning and was in good spirits all the way to Baltimore. Chauncey Depew was on the train and they met in the dining-car—the last time, I think, they ever saw each other. He was tired when we reached the Belvedere Hotel in Baltimore and did not wish to see the newspaper men. It happened that the reporters had a

[1] The reader may remember that it was the 8th of June, 1867, that Mark Twain sailed for the Holy Land. It was the 8th of June, 1907, that he sailed for England to take his Oxford degree. This 8th of June, 1909, was at least slightly connected with both events, for he was keeping an engagement made with Francesca in London, and my notes show that he discussed, on the way to the station, some incidents of his Holy Land trip and his attitude at that time toward Christian traditions. As he rarely mentioned the Quaker City trip, the coincidence seems rather curious. It is most unlikely that Clemens himself in any way associated the two dates.

special purpose in coming just at this time, for it had suddenly developed that in his Shakespeare book, through an oversight, due to haste in publication, full credit had not been given to Mr. Greenwood for the long extracts quoted from his work. The sensational head-lines in a morning paper, "Is Mark Twain a Plagiarist?" had naturally prompted the newspaper men to see what he would have to say on the subject. It was a simple matter, easily explained, and Clemens himself was less disturbed about it than anybody. He felt no sense of guilt, he said; and the fact that he had been stealing and caught at it would give Mr. Greenwood's book far more advertising than if he had given him the full credit which he had intended. He found a good deal of amusement in the situation, his only worry being that Clara and Jean would see the paper and be troubled.

He had taken off his clothes and was lying down, reading. After a little he got up and began walking up and down the room. Presently he stopped and, facing me, placed his hand upon his breast. He said:

"I think I must have caught a little cold yesterday on that Fifth Avenue stage. I have a curious pain in my breast."

I suggested that he lie down again and I would fill his hot-water bag. The pain passed away presently, and he seemed to be dozing. I stepped into the next room and busied myself with some writing. By and by I heard him stirring again and went in where he was. He was walking up and down and began talking of some recent ethnological discoveries — something relating to prehistoric man.

"What a fine boy that prehistoric man must have been," he said—"the very first one! Think of the gaudy style of him, how he must have lorded it over those other creatures, walking on his hind legs, waving his arms, practising and getting ready for the pulpit."

The fancy amused him, but presently he paused in his walk and again put his hand on his breast, saying:

"That pain has come back. It's a curious, sickening, deadly kind of pain. I never had anything just like it."

It seemed to me that his face had become rather gray. I said:

"Where is it, exactly, Mr. Clemens?"

He laid his hand in the center of his breast and said:

"It is here, and it is very peculiar indeed."

Remotely in my mind occurred the thought that he had located his heart, and the "peculiar deadly pain" he had mentioned seemed ominous. I suggested, however, that it was probably some rheumatic touch, and this opinion seemed warranted when, a few moments later, the hot water had again relieved it. This time the pain had apparently gone to stay, for it did not return while we were in Baltimore. It was the first positive manifestation of the angina which eventually would take him from us.

The weather was pleasant in Baltimore, and his visit to St. Timothy's School and his address there were the kind of diversions that meant most to him. The flock of girls, all in their pretty commencement dresses, assembled and rejoicing at his playfully given advice: not to smoke—to excess; not to drink—to excess; not to marry—to excess; he standing there in a garb as white as their own —it made a rare picture—a sweet memory—and it was the last time he ever gave advice from the platform to any one.

Edward S. Martin also spoke to the school, and then there was a great feasting in the big assembly-hall.

It was on the lawn that a reporter approached him with the news of the death of Edward Everett Hale— another of the old group. Clemens said thoughtfully, after a moment:

"I had the greatest respect and esteem for Edward Everett Hale, the greatest admiration for his work. I

A WARNING

am as grieved to hear of his death as I can ever be to hear of the death of any friend, though my grief is always tempered with the satisfaction of knowing that for the one that goes, the hard, bitter struggle of life is ended."

We were leaving the Belvedere next morning, and when the subject of breakfast came up for discussion he said:

"That was the most delicious Baltimore fried chicken we had yesterday morning. I think we'll just repeat that order. It reminds me of John Quarles's farm."

We had been having our meals served in the rooms, but we had breakfast that morning down in the dining-room, and "Francesca" and her mother were there.

As he stood on the railway platform waiting for the train, he told me how once, fifty-five years before, as a boy of eighteen, he had changed cars there for Washington and had barely caught his train—the crowd yelling at him as he ran.

We remained overnight in New York, and that evening, at the Grosvenor, he read aloud a poem of his own which I had not seen before. He had brought it along with some intention of reading it at St. Timothy's, he said, but had not found the occasion suitable.

"I wrote it a long time ago in Paris. I'd been reading aloud to Mrs. Clemens and Susy—in '93, I think—about Lord Clive and Warren Hastings, from Macaulay— how great they were and how far they fell. Then I took an imaginary case—that of some old demented man mumbling of his former state. I described him, and re-peated some of his mumblings. Susy and Mrs. Clemens said, 'Write it'—so I did, by and by, and this is it. I call it 'The Derelict.'"

He read in his effective manner that fine poem, the opening stanza of which follows:

You sneer, you ships that pass me by,
　Your snow-pure canvas towering proud!
You *traders* base!—why, once such fry
　Paid reverence, when like a cloud

MARK TWAIN

Storm-swept I drove along,
  My Admiral at post, his pennon blue
Faint in the wilderness of sky, my long
  Yards bristling with my gallant crew,
My ports flung wide, my guns displayed,
  My tall spars hid in bellying sail!
—You struck your topsails then, and made
  Obeisance—*now* your manners fail.

He had employed rhyme with more facility than was
usual for him, and the figure and phrasing were full of
vigor.

"It is strong and fine," I said, when he had finished.

"Yes," he assented. "It seems so as I read it now.
It is so long since I have seen it that it is like reading
another man's work. I should call it good, I believe."

He put the manuscript in his bag and walked up and
down the floor talking.

"There is no figure for the human being like the ship,"
he said; "no such figure for the storm-beaten human
drift as the derelict—such men as Clive and Hastings
could only be imagined as derelicts adrift, helpless,
tossed by every wind and tide."

We returned to Redding next day. On the train going
home he fell to talking of books and authors, mainly of
the things he had never been able to read.

"When I take up one of Jane Austen's books," he said,
"such as *Pride and Prejudice*, I feel like a barkeeper entering the kingdom of heaven. I know what his sensation would be and his private comments. He would not
find the place to his taste, and he would probably say so."

He recalled again how Stepniak had come to Hartford,
and how humiliated Mrs. Clemens had been to confess
that her husband was not familiar with the writings of
Thackeray and others.

"I don't know anything about anything," he said,
mournfully, "and never did. My brother used to try

A WARNING

to get me to read Dickens, long ago. I couldn't do it—
I was ashamed; but I couldn't do it. Yes, I have read
The Tale of Two Cities, and could do it again. I have
read it a good many times; but I never could stand
Meredith and most of the other celebrities."

By and by he handed me the *Saturday Times Review*,
saying:

"Here is a fine poem, a great poem, I think. I can
stand that."

It was "The Palatine (in the 'Dark Ages')," by Willa
Sibert Cather, reprinted from *McClure's*. The reader
will understand better than I can express why these
lofty opening stanzas appealed to Mark Twain:

THE PALATINE

"Have you been with the King to Rome,
    Brother, big brother?"
"I've been there and I've come home,
    Back to your play, little brother."

"Oh, how high is Cæsar's house,
    Brother, big brother?"
"Goats about the doorways browse;
Night-hawks nest in the burnt roof-tree,
Home of the wild bird and home of the bee.
    A thousand chambers of marble lie
    Wide to the sun and the wind and the sky.
    Poppies we find amongst our wheat
    Grow on Cæsar's banquet seat.
    Cattle crop and neatherds drowse
    On the floors of Cæsar's house."

"But what has become of Cæsar's gold,
    Brother, big brother?"
"The times are bad and the world is old—
    Who knows the where of the Cæsar's gold?
    Night comes black on the Cæsar's hill;
    The wells are deep and the tales are ill.

1501

Fireflies gleam in the damp and mold,
All that is left of the Cæsar's gold.
Back to your play, little brother."

Farther along in our journey he handed me the paper
again, pointing to these lines of Kipling:

How is it not good for the Christian's health
To hurry the Aryan brown,
For the Christian riles and the Aryan smiles,
And he weareth the Christian down;
And the end of the fight is a tombstone white
And the name of the late deceased:
And the epitaph drear: "A fool lies here
Who tried to hustle the East."

"I could stand any amount of that," he said, and presently: "Life is too long and too short. Too long for
the weariness of it; too short for the work to be done.
At the very most, the average mind can only master a
few languages and a little history."

I said: "Still, we need not worry. If death ends all
it does not matter; and if life is eternal there will be
time enough."

"Yes," he assented, rather grimly, "that optimism of
yours is always ready to turn hell's back yard into a
playground."

I said that, old as I was, I had taken up the study of
French, and mentioned Bayard Taylor's having begun
Greek at fifty, expecting to need it in heaven.

Clemens said, reflectively: "Yes—but you see—that
was *Greek*."

CCLXXXI

THE LAST SUMMER AT STORMFIELD

I WAS at Stormfield pretty constantly during the rest of that year. At first I went up only for the day; but later, when his health did not improve, and when he expressed a wish for companionship evenings, I remained most of the nights as well. Our rooms were separated only by a bath-room; and as neither of us was much given to sleep, there was likely to be talk or reading aloud at almost any hour when both were awake. In the very early morning I would usually slip in, softly, sometimes to find him propped up against his pillows sound asleep, his glasses on, the reading-lamp blazing away as it usually did, day or night; but as often as not he was awake, and would have some new plan or idea of which he was eager to be delivered, and there was always interest, and nearly always amusement in it, even if it happened to be three in the morning or earlier.

Sometimes, when he thought it time for me to be stirring, he would call softly, but loudly enough for me to hear if awake; and I would go in, and we would settle again problems of life and death and science, or, rather, he would settle them while I dropped in a remark here and there, merely to hold the matter a little longer in solution.

The pains in his breast came back, and with a good deal of frequency as the summer advanced; also, they became more severe. Dr. Edward Quintard came up from New York, and did not hesitate to say that the trouble proceeded chiefly from the heart, and counseled diminished smoking, with less active exercise, advising particularly against Clemens's lifetime habit of lightly skipping up and down stairs.

There was no prohibition as to billiards, however, or leisurely walking, and we played pretty steadily through those peaceful summer days, and often took a walk down into the meadows or perhaps in the other direction, when it was not too warm or windy. Once we went as far as the river, and I showed him a part of his land he had not seen before—a beautiful cedar hillside, remote and secluded, a place of enchantment. On the way I pointed out a little corner of land which earlier he had given me to straighten our division line. I told him I was going to build a study on it, and call it "Markland." He thought it an admirable building-site, and I think he was pleased with the name. Later he said:

"If you had a place for that extra billiard-table of mine [the Rogers table, which had been left in New York] I would turn it over to you."

I replied that I could adapt the size of my proposed study to fit a billiard-table, and he said:

"Now that will be very good. Then, when I want exercise, I can walk down and play billiards with you, and when you want exercise you can walk up and play billiards with me. You must build that study."

So it was we planned, and by and by Mr. Lounsbury had undertaken the work.

During the walks Clemens rested a good deal. There were the New England hills to climb, and then he found that he tired easily, and that weariness sometimes brought on the pain. As I remember now, I think how bravely he bore it. It must have been a deadly, sickening, numbing pain, for I have seen it crumple him, and his face become colorless while his hand dug at his breast; but he never complained, he never bewailed, and at billiards he would persist in going on and playing in his turn, even while he was bowed with the anguish of the attack.

We had found that a glass of very hot water relieved it, and we kept always a thermos bottle or two filled and ready. At the first hint from him I would pour out a glass and another, and sometimes the relief came quickly; but there were times, and alas! they came oftener, when that deadly gripping did not soon release him. Yet there would come a week or a fortnight when he was apparently perfectly well, and at such times we dismissed the thought of any heart malady, and attributed the whole trouble to acute indigestion, from which he had always suffered more or less.

We were alone together most of the time. He did not appear to care for company that summer. Clara Clemens had a concert tour in prospect, and her father, eager for her success, encouraged her to devote a large part of her time to study. For Jean, who was in love with every form of outdoor and animal life, he had established headquarters in a vacant farm-house on one corner of the estate, where she had collected some stock and poultry, and was overflowingly happy. Ossip Gabrilowitsch was a guest in the house a good portion of the summer, but had been invalided through severe surgical operations, and for a long time rarely appeared, even at meal-times. So it came about that there could hardly have been a closer daily companionship than was ours during this the last year of Mark Twain's life. For me, of course, nothing can ever be like it again in this world. One is not likely to associate twice with a being from another star.

CCLXXXII

PERSONAL MEMORANDA

IN the notes I made of this period I caught a little drift of personality and utterance, and I do not know better how to preserve these things than to give them here, as nearly as may be, in the sequence and form in which they were set down.

One of the first of these entries occurs in June, when Clemens was re-reading with great interest and relish Andrew D. White's *Science and Theology*, which he called a lovely book.[1]

June 21. A peaceful afternoon, and we walked farther than usual, resting at last in the shade of a tree in the lane that leads to Jean's farm-house. I picked a dandelion-ball, with some remark about its being one of the evidences of the intelligent principle in nature—the seeds winged for a wider distribution.

"Yes," he said, "those are the great evidences; no one who reasons can doubt them."

And presently he added:

"That is a most amusing book of White's. When you read it you see how those old theologians never reasoned at all. White tells of an old bishop who figured out that God created the world in an instant on a certain day in October exactly so many years before Christ, and proved it. And I knew a preacher myself once who declared that the fossils in the rocks proved nothing as to the age of the world. He said that God could create the rocks with those fossils in them for ornaments if He wanted to. Why, it takes twenty years to build a little island in the Mississippi River, and that man actually believed that

[1] A History of the Warfare of Science with Theology in Christendom.

God created the whole world and all that's in it in six days. White tells of another bishop who gave two new reasons for thunder; one being that God wanted to show the world His power, and another that He wished to frighten sinners to repent. Now consider the proportions of that conception, even in the pettiest way you can think of it. Consider the idea of God thinking of all that. Consider the President of the United States wanting to impress the flies and fleas and mosquitoes, getting up on the dome of the Capitol and beating a bass-drum and setting off red fire."

He followed the theme a little further, then we made our way slowly back up the long hill, he holding to my arm, and resting here and there, but arriving at the house seemingly fresh and ready for billiards.

June 23. I came up this morning with a basket of strawberries. He was walking up and down, looking like an ancient Roman. He said:

"Consider the case of Elsie Sigel [1]—what a ghastly ending to any life!"

Then turning upon me fiercely, he continued:

"Anybody that knows anything knows that there was not a single life that was ever lived that was worth living. Not a single child ever begotten that the begetting of it was not a crime. Suppose a community of people to be living on the slope of a volcano, directly under the crater and in the path of lava-flow; that volcano has been breaking out right along for ages and is certain to break out again. They do not know when it will break out, but they know it will do it—*that* much can be counted on. Suppose those people go to a community in a far neighborhood and say, 'We'd like to change places with you. Come take our homes and let us have yours.' Those people would say, 'Never mind, we are not interested in your country. We know what has happened there, and what will happen again.' We don't care to live under the blow that is likely to fall at any moment; and yet every time we bring a child into the world we are bringing it to a country, to a community gathered under

[1] Granddaughter of Gen. Franz Sigel. She was mysteriously murdered while engaged in settlement work among the Chinese.

the crater of a volcano, knowing that sooner or later death will come, and that before death there will be catastrophes infinitely worse. Formerly it was much worse than now, for before the ministers abolished hell a man knew, when he was begetting a child, that he was begetting a soul that had only one chance in a hundred of escaping the eternal fires of damnation. He knew that in all probability that child would be brought to damnation—one of the ninety-nine black sheep. But since hell has been abolished death has become more welcome. I wrote a fairy story once. It was published somewhere. I don't remember just what it was now, but the substance of it was that a fairy gave a man the customary wishes. I was interested in seeing what he would take. First he chose wealth and went away with it, but it did not bring him happiness. Then he came back for the second selection, and chose fame, and that did not bring happiness either. Finally he went to the fairy and chose death, and the fairy said, in substance, 'If you hadn't been a fool you'd have chosen that in the first place.'

"The papers called me a pessimist for writing that story. Pessimist ——! the man who *isn't* a pessimist is a d—d fool."

But this was one of his savage humors, stirred by tragic circumstance. Under date of July 5th I find this happier entry:

We have invented a new game, three-ball carom billiards, each player continuing until he has made five, counting the number of his shots as in golf, the one who finishes in the fewer shots wins. It is a game we play with almost exactly equal skill, and he is highly pleased with it. He said this afternoon:

"I have never enjoyed billiards as I do now. I look forward to it every afternoon as my reward at the end of a good day's work."[1]

We went out in the loggia by and by and Clemens read aloud from a book which Professor Zubelin left here a few days ago—

[1] His work at this time was an article on Marjorie Fleming, the "wonder child," whose quaint writings and brief little life had been published to the world by Dr. John Brown. Clemens always adored the thought of Marjorie, and in this article one can see that she ranked almost next to Joan of Arc in his affections.

The Religion of a Democrat. Something in it must have suggested to Clemens his favorite science, for presently he said:

"I have been reading an old astronomy; it speaks of the perfect line of curvature of the earth in spite of mountains and abysses, and I have imagined a man three hundred thousand miles high picking up a ball like the earth and looking at it and holding it in his hand. It would be about like a billiard-ball to him, and he would turn it over in his hand and rub it with his thumb, and where he rubbed over the mountain ranges he might say, 'There seems to be some slight roughness here, but I can't detect it with my eye; it seems perfectly smooth to look at.' The Himalayas to him, the highest peak, would be one-sixty-thousandth of his height, or about the one-thousandth part of an inch as compared with the average man."

I spoke of having somewhere read of some very tiny satellites, one as small, perhaps, as six miles in diameter, yet a genuine world.

"Could a man live on a world so small as that?" I asked.

"Oh yes," he said. "The gravitation that holds it together would hold him on, and he would always seem upright, the same as here. His horizon would be smaller, but even if he were six feet tall he would only have one foot for each mile of that world's diameter, so you see he would be little enough, even for a world that he could walk around in half a day."

He talked astronomy a great deal—marvel astronomy. He had no real knowledge of the subject, and I had none of any kind, which made its ungraspable facts all the more thrilling. He was always thrown into a sort of ecstasy by the unthinkable distances of space—the supreme drama of the universe. The fact that Alpha Centauri was twenty-five trillions of miles away—two hundred and fifty thousand times the distance of our own remote sun, and that our solar system was traveling, as a whole, toward the bright star Vega, in the constellation of Lyra, at the rate of forty-four miles a second, yet would be thousands upon thousands of years reaching its destination, fairly enraptured him.

The astronomical light-year—that is to say, the distance

light-year, p 45

```
                    93,000,000
                          63,000
          279,000,000,000,000
        5580,000,00
        ────────────────────────
        5,859,000,000,000
```

.000 times 100,000,000 is

100,000,000,000

Is it about 6,000,000,000,000 miles, a light-year?   000 (six thousand billion)

Alpha Centauri's distance, 24 or 25,000,000,000 miles?   (one 4 light-years)   000

p.45

From one star to its nearest neighbor 8 light-years.

PART OF MARK TWAIN'S "LIGHT-YEAR" CALCULATION

which light travels in a year—was one of the things which he loved to contemplate; but he declared that no two authorities ever figured it alike, and that he was going to figure it for himself. I came in one morning, to find that he had covered several sheets of paper with almost interminable rows of ciphers, and with a result, to him at least, entirely satisfactory. I am quite certain that he was prouder of those figures and their enormous aggregate than if he had just completed an immortal tale; and when he added that the nearest fixed star—Alpha Centauri—was between four and five light-years distant from the earth, and that there was no possible way to think that distance in miles or even any calculable fraction of it, his glasses shone and his hair was roached up as with the stimulation of these stupendous facts.

By and by he said:

PERSONAL MEMORANDA

"I came in with Halley's comet in 1835. It is coming again next year, and I expect to go out with it. It will be the greatest disappointment of my life if I don't go out with Halley's comet. The Almighty has said, no doubt: 'Now here are these two unaccountable freaks; they came in together, they must go out together.' Oh! I am looking forward to that." And a little later he added:

"I've got some kind of a heart disease, and Quintard won't tell me whether it is the kind that carries a man off in an instant or keeps him lingering along and suffering for twenty years or so. I was in hopes that Quintard would tell me that I was likely to drop dead any minute; but he didn't. He only told me that my blood-pressure was too strong. He didn't give me any schedule; but I expect to go with Halley's comet."

I seem to have omitted making any entries for a few days; but among his notes I find this entry, which seems to refer to some discussion of a favorite philosophy, and has a special interest of its own:

July 14, 1909. Yesterday's dispute resumed, I still maintaining that, whereas we *can* think, we generally don't *do* it. Don't do it, & don't have to do it: we are automatic machines which act unconsciously. From morning till sleeping-time, all day long. All day long our machinery is doing things from *habit & instinct*, & without requiring any help or attention from our poor little 7-by-9 thinking apparatus. This reminded me of something: thirty years ago, in Hartford, the billiard-room was my study, & I wrote my letters there the first thing every morning. My table lay two points off the starboard bow of the billiard-table, & the door of exit and entrance bore northeast-&-by-east-half-east from that position, consequently you could see the door across the length of the billiard-table, but you couldn't see the floor *by* the said table. I found I was always forgetting to ask intruders to carry my letters down-stairs for the mail, so I concluded to lay them on the floor by the door; then the intruder would have to walk over them, & that would indicate to him what they were there for. Did it? No, it didn't. He was a machine, & had *habits*. Habits take precedence of thought.

Now consider this: a stamped & addressed letter lying on the floor—lying aggressively & conspicuously on the floor—is an unusual spectacle; so unusual a spectacle that you would think an intruder couldn't see it there without immediately divining that it was not there by accident, but had been deliberately *placed* there & for a definite purpose. Very well; it may surprise you to learn that that most simple & most natural & obvious thought would never occur to any intruder on this planet, whether he be fool, half-fool, or the most brilliant of thinkers. For he is always an automatic machine & has habits, & his habits will act before his thinking apparatus can get a chance to exert its powers. My scheme failed because every human being has the habit of picking up any apparently misplaced thing & placing it where it won't be stepped on.

My first intruder was George. He went and came without saying anything. Presently I found the letters neatly piled up on the billiard-table. I was astonished. I put them on the floor again. The next intruder piled them on the billiard-table without a word. I was profoundly moved, profoundly interested. So I set the trap again. Also again, & again, & yet again —all day long. I caught every member of the family, & every servant; also I caught the three finest intellects in the town. In every instance old, time-worn automatic habit got in its work so promptly that the thinking apparatus never got a chance.

I do not remember this particular discussion, but I do distinctly recall being one of those whose intelligence was not sufficient to prevent my picking up the letter he had thrown on the floor in front of his bed, and being properly classified for doing it.

Clemens no longer kept note-books, as in an earlier time, but set down innumerable memoranda—comments, stray reminders, and the like—on small pads, and bunches of these tiny sheets accumulated on his table and about his room. I gathered up many of them then and afterward, and a few of these characteristic bits may be offered here.

PERSONAL MEMORANDA

KNEE

It is at our mother's knee that we acquire our noblest & truest & highest ideals, but there is seldom any money in them.

JEHOVAH

He is all-good.   He made man for hell or hell for man, one or the other—take your choice.   He made it hard to get into heaven and easy to get into hell.

He commended man to multiply & replenish—what?   Hell.

ONE OF MARK TWAIN'S MEMORANDA
1513

MARK TWAIN

HISTORY

A historian who would convey the truth has got to lie. Often he must enlarge the truth by diameters, otherwise his reader would not be able to see it.

MORALS

are not the important thing—nor enlightenment—nor civilization. A man can do absolutely well without them, but he can't do without *something to eat*. The supremest thing is the *needs of the body*, not of the mind & spirit.

SUGGESTION

There is conscious suggestion & there is unconscious suggestion—both come from outside—whence all ideas come.

DUELS

I think I could wipe out a dishonor by crippling the other man, but I don't see how I could do it by letting him cripple me.

I have no feeling of animosity toward people who do not believe as I do; I merely do not respect 'em. In some serious matters (relig.) I would have them burnt.

I am old now and once was a sinner. I often think of it with a kind of soft regret. I trust my days are numbered. I would not have that detail overlooked.

She was always a girl, she was always young because her heart was young; & I was young because she lived in my heart & preserved its youth from decay.

He often busied himself working out more extensively some of the ideas that came to him—moral ideas, he called them. One fancy which he followed in several forms (some of them not within the privilege of print) was that of an inquisitive little girl, Bessie, who pursues her mother with difficult questionings.[1] He read these aloud as he finished them, and it is certain that they lacked neither logic nor humor.

Sometimes he went to a big drawer in his dresser, where he kept his finished manuscripts, and took them out and looked over them, and read parts of them aloud, and talked of the plans he had had for them, and how one idea after another had been followed for a time and had failed to satisfy him in the end.

Two fiction schemes that had always possessèd him he had been unable to bring to any conclusion. Both of these have been mentioned in former chapters; one being the notion of a long period of dream-existence during a brief moment of sleep, and the other being the story of a mysterious visitant from another realm. He had experimented with each of these ideas in no less than three forms, and there was fine writing and dramatic narrative in all; but his literary architecture had somehow fallen short of his conception. "The Mysterious Stranger" in one of its forms I thought might be satisfactorily concluded, and he admitted that he could probably end it without much labor. He discussed something of his plans, and later I found the notes for its conclusion. But I suppose he was beyond the place where he could take up those old threads, though he contemplated, fondly enough, the possibility, and recalled how he had read at least one form of the dream tale to Howells, who had urged him to complete it.[2]

---

[1] Under Appendix W, at the end of this volume, the reader will find one of the "Bessie" dialogues.

[2] The above was written in 1912. About a year later I found among some loose papers that startling closing chapter of "The Mysterious Stranger," probably written about the time of our conversation. The story, thus completed, was published serially in *Harper's Magazine*, and later in book form. By many it is regarded as the author's high-water mark.

CCLXXXIII

ASTRONOMY AND DREAMS

AUGUST 5, 1909. This morning I noticed on a chair a copy of Flaubert's *Salâmmbo* which I recently lent him. I asked if he liked it.

"No," he said, "I didn't like any of it."

"But you read it?"

"Yes, I read every line of it."

"You admitted its literary art?"

"Well, it's like this: If I should go to the Chicago stockyards and they should kill a beef and cut it up and the blood should splash all over everything, and then they should take me to another pen and kill another beef and the blood should splash over everything again, and so on to pen after pen, I should care for it about as much as I do for that book."

"But those were bloody days, and you care very much for that period in history."

"Yes, that is so. But when I read Tacitus and know that I am reading history I can accept it as such and supply the imaginary details and enjoy it, but this thing is such a continuous procession of blood and slaughter and stench it worries me. It has great art—I can see that. That scene of the crucified lions and the death cañon and the tent scene are marvelous, but I wouldn't read that book again without a salary."

August 16. He is reading Suetonius, which he already knows by heart—so full of the cruelties and licentiousness of imperial Rome.

This afternoon he began talking about Claudius.

"They called Claudius a lunatic," he said, "but just see what nice fancies he had. He would go to the arena between times and have captives and wild beasts brought out and turned in

1516

together for his special enjoyment. Sometimes when there were no captives on hand he would say, 'Well, never mind; bring out a carpenter.' Carpentering around the arena wasn't a popular job in those days. He went visiting once to a province and thought it would be pleasant to see how they disposed of criminals and captives in their crude, old-fashioned way, but there was no executioner on hand. No matter; the Emperor of Rome was in no hurry—he would wait. So he sat down and stayed there until an executioner came."

I said, "How do you account for the changed attitude toward these things? We are filled with pity to-day at the thought of torture and suffering."

"Ah! but that is because we have drifted that way and exercised the quality of compassion. Relax a muscle and it soon loses its vigor; relax that quality and in two generations—in one generation—we should be gloating over the spectacle of blood and torture just the same. Why, I read somewhere a letter written just before the Lisbon catastrophe in 1755 about a scene on the public square of Lisbon: A lot of stakes with the fagots piled for burning and heretics chained for burning. The square was crowded with men and women and children, and when those fires were lighted, and the heretics began to shriek and writhe, those men and women and children laughed so they were fairly beside themselves with the enjoyment of the scene. The Greeks don't seem to have done these things. I suppose that indicates earlier advancement in compassion."

Colonel Harvey and Mr. Duneka came up to spend the night. Mr. Clemens had one of his seizures during the evening. They come oftener and last longer. One last night continued for an hour and a half. I slept there.

September 7. To-day news of the North Pole discovered by Peary. Five days ago the same discovery was reported by Cook. Clemens's comment: "It's the greatest joke of the ages." But a moment later he referred to the stupendous fact of Arcturus being fifty thousand times as big as the sun.

September 21. This morning he told me, with great glee, the dream he had had just before wakening. He said:

"I was in an automobile going slowly, with a little girl beside me, and some uniformed person walking along by us. I said, 'I'll get out and walk, too'; but the officer replied, 'This is only one of the smallest of our fleet.'

"Then I noticed that the automobile had no front, and there were two cannons mounted where the front should be. I noticed, too, that we were traveling very low, almost down on the ground. Presently we got to the bottom of a hill and started up another, and I found myself walking ahead of the 'mobile. I turned around to look for the little girl, and instead of her I found a kitten capering beside me, and when we reached the top of the hill we were looking out over a most barren and desolate waste of sand-heaps without a speck of vegetation anywhere, and the kitten said, 'This view beggars all admiration.' Then all at once we were in a great group of people and I undertook to repeat to them the kitten's remark, but when I tried to do it the words were so touching that I broke down and cried, and all the group cried, too, over the kitten's moving remark."

The joy with which he told this absurd sleep fancy made it supremely ridiculous and we laughed until tears really came.

One morning he said: "I was awake a good deal in the night, and I tried to think of interesting things. I got to working out geological periods, trying to think of some way to comprehend them, and then astronomical periods. Of course it's impossible, but I thought of a plan that seemed to mean something to me. I remembered that Neptune is two billion eight hundred million miles away. That, of course, is incomprehensible, but then there is the nearest fixed star with its twenty-five trillion miles—*twenty-five trillion*—or nearly ten thousand times as far, and then I took this book and counted the lines on a page and I found that there was an average of thirty-two lines to the page and two hundred and forty pages, and I figured out that, counting the distance to Neptune as *one line*, there were still not enough lines in the book by nearly two thousand to reach the nearest fixed star, and somehow that gave me a sort of dim idea of the vastness of the distance and kind of a journey into space."

ASTRONOMY AND DREAMS

Later I figured out another method of comprehending a little of that great distance by estimating the existence of the human race at thirty thousand years (Lord Kelvin's figures) and the average generation to have been thirty-three years with a world population of 1,500,000,000 souls. I assumed the nearest fixed star to be the first station in Paradise and the first soul to have started thirty thousand years ago. Traveling at the rate of about thirty miles a second, it would just now be arriving in Alpha Centauri with all the rest of that buried multitude stringing out behind at an average distance of twenty miles apart.

Few things gave him more pleasure than the contemplation of such figures as these. We made occasional business trips to New York, and during one of them visited the Museum of Natural History to look at the brontosaur and the meteorites and the astronomical model in the entrance hall. To him these were the most fascinating things in the world. He contemplated the meteorites and the brontosaur, and lost himself in strange and marvelous imaginings concerning the far reaches of time and space whence they had come down to us.

Mark Twain lived curiously apart from the actualities of life. Dwelling mainly among his philosophies and speculations, he observed vaguely, or minutely, what went on about him; but in either case the fact took a place, not in the actual world, but in a world within his consciousness, or subconsciousness, a place where facts were likely to assume new and altogether different relations from those they had borne in the physical occurrence. It not infrequently happened, therefore, when he recounted some incident, even the most recent, that history took on fresh and startling forms. More than once I have known him to relate an occurrence of the day before with a reality of circumstance that carried absolute conviction, when the details themselves were precisely reversed. If his attention were called to the discrepancy, his face would take on a blank look, as of one suddenly aroused from dreamland, to be followed by an almost childish interest in your revelation and ready acknowledgment of his mistake. I do not think such mistakes humiliated him; but they often surprised and, I think, amused him.

Insubstantial and deceptive as was this inner world of his, to him it must have been much more real than the world of flitting physical shapes about him. He would fix you keenly with his attention, but you realized, at last, that he was placing you and seeing you not as a part of the material landscape, but as an item of his own inner world—a world in which philosophies and morals stood upright—a very good world indeed, but certainly a topsyturvy world when viewed with the eye of mere literal scrutiny. And this was, mainly, of course, because the routine of life did not appeal to him. Even members of his household did not always stir his consciousness.

He knew they were there; he could call them by name; he relied upon them; but his knowledge of them always suggested the knowledge that Mount Everest might have of the forests and caves and boulders upon its slopes, useful, perhaps, but hardly necessary to the giant's existence, and in no important matter a part of its greater life.

CCLXXXIV

A LIBRARY CONCERT

IN a letter which Clemens wrote to Miss Wallace at this time, he tells of a concert given at Stormfield on September 21st for the benefit of the new Redding Library. Gabrilowitsch had so far recovered that he was up and about and able to play. David Bispham, the great barytone, always genial and generous, agreed to take part, and Clara Clemens, already accustomed to public singing, was to join in the program. The letter to Miss Wallace supplies the rest of the history.

We had a grand time here yesterday. Concert in aid of the little library.

TEAM

Gabrilowitsch, pianist.
David Bispham, vocalist.
Clara Clemens, ditto.
Mark Twain, introducer of team.

Detachments and squads and groups and singles came from everywhere—Danbury, New Haven, Norwalk, Redding, Redding Ridge, Ridgefield, and even from New York: some in 60-h.p. motor-cars, some in buggies and carriages, and a swarm of farmer-young-folk on foot from miles around—525 altogether.

If we hadn't stopped the sale of tickets a day and a half before the performance we should have been swamped. We jammed 160 into the library (not quite all had seats), we filled the loggia, the dining-room, the hall, clear into the billiard-room, the stairs, and the brick-paved square outside the dining-room door.

The artists were received with a great welcome, and it woke

them up, and I tell you they performed to the Queen's taste! The program was an hour and three-quarters long and the encores added a half-hour to it. The enthusiasm of the house was hair-lifting. They all stayed an hour after the close to shake hands and congratulate.

We had no dollar seats except in the library, but we accumulated $372 for the Building Fund. We had tea at half past six for a dozen—the Hawthornes, Jeannette Gilder, and her niece, etc.; and after 8-o'clock dinner we had a private concert and a ball in the bare-stripped library until 10; nobody present but the team and Mr. and Mrs. Paine and Jean and her dog. And me. Bispham did "Danny Deever" and the "Erlkönig" in his majestic, great organ-tones and artillery, and Gabrilowitsch played the accompaniments as they were never played before, I do suppose.

There is not much to add to that account. Clemens, introducing the performers, was the gay feature of the occasion. He spoke of the great reputation of Bispham and Gabrilowitsch; then he said:

"My daughter is not as famous as these gentlemen, but she is ever so much better-looking."

The music of the evening that followed, with Gabrilowitsch at the piano and David Bispham to sing, was something not likely ever to be repeated. Bispham sang the "Erlkönig" and "Killiecrankie," the "Grenadiers" and several other songs. He spoke of having sung Wagner's "Grenadiers" at the composer's home following his death, and how none of the family had heard it before.

There followed dancing, and Jean Clemens, fine and handsome, apparently full of life and health, danced down that great living-room as care-free as if there was no shadow upon her life. And the evening was distinguished in another way, for before it ended Clara Clemens had promised Ossip Gabrilowitsch to become his wife.

CCLXXXV

A WEDDING AT STORMFIELD

THE wedding of Ossip Gabrilowitsch and Clara Clemens was not delayed. Gabrilowitsch had signed for a concert tour in Europe, and unless the marriage took place forthwith it must be postponed many months. It followed, therefore, fifteen days after the engagement. They were busy days. Clemens, enormously excited and pleased over the prospect of the first wedding in his family, personally attended to the selection of those who were to have announcement-cards, employing a stenographer to make the list.

October 6th was a perfect wedding-day. It was one of those quiet, lovely fall days when the whole world seems at peace. Claude, the butler, with his usual skill in such matters, had decorated the great living-room with gay autumn foliage and flowers, brought in mainly from the woods and fields. They blended perfectly with the warm tones of the walls and furnishings, and I do not remember ever having seen a more beautiful room. Only relatives and a few of the nearest friends were invited to the ceremony. The Twichells came over a day ahead, for Twichell, who had assisted in the marriage rites between Samuel Clemens and Olivia Langdon, was to perform that ceremony for their daughter now. A fellow-student of the bride and groom when they had been pupils of Leschetizky, in Vienna—Miss Ethel Newcomb—was at the piano and played softly the Wedding March from "Tannhäuser." Jean Clemens was

1523

the only bridesmaid, and she was stately and classically beautiful, with a proud dignity in her office. Jervis Langdon, the bride's cousin and childhood playmate, acted as best man, and Clemens, of course, gave the bride away. By request he wore his scarlet Oxford gown over his snowy flannels, and was splendid beyond words. I do not write of the appearance of the bride and groom, for brides and grooms are always handsome and always happy, and certainly these were no exception. It was all so soon over, the feasting ended, and the principals whirling away into the future. I have a picture in my mind of them seated together in the automobile, with Richard Watson Gilder standing on the step for a last good-by, and before them a wide expanse of autumn foliage and distant hills. I remember Gilder's voice saying, when the car was on the turn, and they were waving back to us:

"Over the hills and far away,
  Beyond the utmost purple rim,
Beyond the night, across the day,
  Through all the world she followed him."

The matter of the wedding had been kept from the newspapers until the eve of the wedding, when the Associated Press had been notified. A representative was there; but Clemens had characteristically interviewed himself on the subject, and it was only necessary to hand the reporter a typewritten copy. Replying to the question (put to himself), "Are you pleased with the marriage?" he answered:

Yes, fully as much as any marriage could please me or any other father. There are two or three solemn things in life and a happy marriage is one of them, for the terrors of life are all to come. I am glad of this marriage, and Mrs. Clemens would be glad, for she always had a warm affection for Gabrilowitsch.

A WEDDING AT STORMFIELD

There was another wedding at Stormfield on the following afternoon—an imitation wedding. Little Joy came up with me, and wished she could stand in just the spot where she had seen the bride stand, and she expressed a wish that she could get married like that. Clemens said:

"Frankness is a jewel; only the young can afford it."

Then he happened to remember a ridiculous boy-doll —a white-haired creature with red coat and green trousers, a souvenir imitation of himself from one of the Rogers Christmas trees. He knew where it was, and he got it out. Then he said:

"Now, Joy, we will have another wedding. This is Mr. Colonel Williams, and you are to become his wedded wife."

So Joy stood up very gravely and Clemens performed the ceremony, and I gave the bride away, and Joy to him became Mrs. Colonel Williams thereafter, and entered happily into her new estate.

CCLXXXVI

AUTUMN DAYS

A HARVEST of letters followed the wedding: a general congratulatory expression, mingled with admiration, affection, and good-will. In his interview Clemens had referred to the pain in his breast; and many begged him to deny that there was anything serious the matter with him, urging him to try this relief or that, pathetically eager for his continued life and health. They cited the comfort he had brought to world-weary humanity and his unfailing stand for human justice as reasons why he should live. Such letters could not fail to cheer him.

A letter of this period, from John Bigelow, gave him a pleasure of its own. Clemens had written Bigelow, apropos of some adverse expression on the tariff:

Thank you for any hard word you can say about the tariff. I guess the government that robs its own people earns the future it is preparing for itself.

Bigelow was just then declining an invitation to the annual dinner of the Chamber of Commerce. In sending his regrets he said:

The sentiment I would propose if I dared to be present would be the words of Mark Twain, the statesman:

"The government that robs its own people earns the future it is preparing for itself."

Now to Clemens himself he wrote:

Rochefoucault never said a cleverer thing, nor Dr. Franklin a wiser one. . . . Be careful, or the Demos will be running you for President when you are not on your guard.

Yours more than ever,

JOHN BIGELOW.

Among the tributes that came, was a sermon by the Rev. Fred Winslow Adams, of Schenectady, New York, with Mark Twain as its subject. Mr. Adams chose for his text, "Take Mark and bring him with thee; for he is profitable for the ministry," and he placed the two Marks, St. Mark and Mark Twain, side by side as ministers to humanity, and characterized him as "a fearless knight of righteousness." A few weeks later Mr. Adams himself came to Stormfield, and, like all open-minded ministers of the Gospel, he found that he could get on very well indeed with Mark Twain.

In spite of the good-will and the good wishes Clemens's malady did not improve. As the days grew chillier he found that he must remain closer indoors. The cold air seemed to bring on the pains, and they were gradually becoming more severe; then, too, he did not follow the doctor's orders in the matter of smoking, nor altogether as to exercise.

To Miss Wallace he wrote:

I can't walk, I can't drive, I'm not down-stairs much, and I don't see company, but I drink barrels of water to keep the pain quiet; I read, and read, and read, and smoke, and smoke, and smoke all the time (as formerly), and it's a contented and comfortable life.

But this was not altogether accurate as to details. He did come down-stairs many times daily, and he persisted in billiards regardless of the paroxysms. We found, too, that the seizures were induced by mental agitation. One night he read aloud to Jean and myself the first chapter of an article, "The Turning-Point in My Life," which he was preparing for *Harper's Bazar*. He had begun it with one of his impossible burlesque fancies, and he felt our attitude of disappointment even before any word had been said. Suddenly he rose, and laying his hand on his breast said, "I must lie down," and started toward the stair. I supported him to his room and hurriedly poured out the hot water. He drank it and dropped back on the bed.

"Don't speak to me," he said; "don't make me talk."

Jean came in, and we sat there several moments in silence. I think we both wondered if this might not be the end; but presently he spoke of his own accord, declaring he was better, and ready for billiards.

We played for at least an hour afterward, and he seemed no worse for the attack. It is a curious malady—that angina; even the doctors are acquainted with its manifestations, rather than its cause. Clemens's general habits of body and mind were probably not such as to delay its progress; furthermore, there had befallen him that year one of those misfortunes which his confiding nature peculiarly invited—a betrayal of trust by those in whom it had been boundlessly placed—and it seems likely that the resulting humiliation aggravated his complaint. The writing of a detailed history of this episode afforded him occupation and a certain amusement, but probably did not contribute to his health. One day he sent for his attorney, Mr. Charles T. Lark, and made some final revisions in his will.[1]

[1] Mark Twain's estate, later appraised at something more than $600,000, was left in the hands of trustees for his daughters. The trustees were Edward E. Loomis, Jervis Langdon, and Zoheth S. Freeman. The direction of his literary affairs was left to his daughter Clara and the writer of this history.

AUTUMN DAYS

To see him you would never have suspected that he was ill. He was in good flesh, and his movement was as airy and his eye as bright and his face as full of bloom as at any time during the period I had known him; also, he was as light-hearted and full of ideas and plans, and he was even gentler—having grown mellow with age and retirement, like good wine.

And of course he would find amusement in his condition. He said:

"I have always pretended to be sick to escape visitors; now, for the first time, I have got a genuine excuse. It makes me feel so honest."

And once, when Jean reported a caller in the living-room, he said:

"Jean, I can't see her. Tell her I am likely to drop dead any minute and it would be most embarrassing."

But he did see her, for it was a poet—Angela Morgan —and he read her poem, "God's Man," aloud with great feeling, and later he sold it for her to *Collier's Weekly*.

He still had violent rages now and then, remembering some of the most notable of his mistakes; and once, after denouncing himself, rather inclusively, as an idiot, he said:

"I wish to God the lightning would strike me; but I've wished that fifty thousand times and never got anything out of it yet. I have missed several good chances. Mrs. Clemens was afraid of lightning, and would never let me bare my head to the storm."

The element of humor was never lacking, and the rages became less violent and less frequent.

I was at Stormfield steadily now, and there was a regular routine of afternoon sessions of billiards or reading, in which we were generally alone; for Jean, occupied with her farming and her secretary labors, seldom appeared except at meal-times. Occasionally she joined in the billiard games; but it was difficult learning and her interest was not great. She would have made a fine player, for she had a natural talent for games, as she had for languages, and she could have mastered the science of angles as she had mastered tennis and French and German and Italian. She had naturally a fine intellect, with many of her father's characteristics, and a tender heart that made every dumb creature her friend.

Katie Leary, who had been Jean's nurse, once told how, as a little child, Jean had not been particularly interested in a picture of the Lisbon earthquake, where the people were being swallowed up; but on looking at the next page, which showed a number of animals being overwhelmed, she had said:

"Poor things!"

Katie said:

"Why, you didn't say that about the people!"

But Jean answered:

"Oh, they could speak."

One night at the dinner-table her father was saying how difficult it must be for a man who had led a busy life to give up the habit of work.

"That is why the Rogerses kill themselves," he said. "They would rather kill themselves in the old tread-mill than stop and try to kill time. They have forgotten how to rest. They know nothing but to keep on till they drop."

I told of something I had read not long before. It was about an aged lion that had broken loose from his cage at Coney Island. He had not offered to hurt any one; but after wandering about a little, rather aimlessly, he had come to a picket-fence, and a moment later began pacing up and down in front of it, just the length of his cage. They had come and led him back to his prison without trouble, and he had rushed eagerly into it. I noticed that Jean was listening anxiously, and when I finished she said:

AUTUMN DAYS

"Is that a true story?"

She had forgotten altogether the point in illustration. She was concerned only with the poor old beast that had found no joy in his liberty.

Among the letters that Clemens wrote just then was one to Miss Wallace, in which he described the glory of the fall colors as seen from his windows.

The autumn splendors passed you by? What a pity! I wish you had been here. It was beyond words! It was heaven & hell & sunset & rainbows & the aurora all fused into one divine harmony, & you couldn't look at it and keep the tears back.

Such a singing together, & such a whispering together, & such a snuggling together of cozy, soft colors, & such kissing & caressing, & such pretty blushing when the sun breaks out & catches those dainty weeds at it—you remember that weed-garden of mine?—& then—then the far hills sleeping in a dim blue trance—oh, hearing about it is nothing, you should be here to see it!

In the same letter he refers to some work that he was writing for his own satisfaction—*Letters from the Earth;* said letters supposed to have been written by an immortal visitant and addressed to other immortals in some remote sphere.

I'll read passages to you. This book will never be published —in fact it couldn't be, because it would be felony . . . Paine enjoys it, but Paine is going to be damned one of these days, I suppose.

I very well remember his writing those *Letters from the Earth*. He read them to me from time to time as he wrote them, and they were fairly overflowing with humor and philosophy and satire concerning the human race. The immortal visitor pointed out, one after another, the absurdities of mankind, his ridiculous conception of heaven, and his special conceit in believing that he was the Creator's pet—the particular form of

1531

life for which all the universe was created. Clemens allowed his exuberant fancy free rein, being under no restrictions as to the possibility of print or public offense. He enjoyed them himself, too, as he read them aloud, and we laughed ourselves weak over his bold imaginings.

One admissible extract will carry something of the flavor of these chapters. It is where the celestial correspondent describes man's religion.

His heaven is like himself: strange, interesting, astonishing, grotesque. I give you my word it has not a single feature in it that he *actually values*. It consists—utterly and entirely—of diversions which he cares next to nothing about here in the earth, yet he is quite sure he will like in heaven. Isn't it curious? Isn't it interesting? You must not think I am exaggerating, for it is not so. I will give you the details.

Most men do not sing, most men cannot sing, most men will not stay where others are singing if it be continued more than two hours. Note that.

Only about two men in a hundred can play upon a musical instrument, and not four in a hundred have any wish to learn how. Set that down.

Many men pray, not many of them like to do it. A few pray long, the others make a short-cut.

More men go to church than want to.

To forty-nine men in fifty the Sabbath day is a dreary, dreary bore.

Further, all sane people detest noise.

All people, sane or insane, like to have variety in their lives. Monotony quickly wearies them.

Now then, you have the facts. You know what men don't enjoy. Well, they have invented a heaven, out of their own heads, all by themselves; guess what it is like? In fifteen hundred years you couldn't do it. They have left out the very things they care for most—their dearest pleasures—and replaced them with prayer!

In man's heaven *everybody sings*. There are no exceptions. The man who did not sing on earth sings there; the man who *could* not sing on earth sings there. This universal singing is not casual, not occasional, not relieved by intervals of quiet; it goes on all day long and every day during a stretch of twelve hours. *And everybody stays* where on earth the place would be empty in two hours. The singing is of hymns alone. Nay, it is *one* hymn alone. The words are always the same—in number they are only about a dozen—there is no rhyme—there is no poetry. "Hosanna, hosanna, hosanna unto the highest!" and a few such phrases constitute the whole service.

Meantime, every person is playing on a harp! Consider the deafening hurricane of sound. Consider, further, it is a praise service—a service of compliment, flattery, adulation. Do you ask who it is that is willing to endure this strange compliment, this insane compliment, and who not only endures it but likes it, enjoys it, requires it, commands it? Hold your breath: It is God! This race's God I mean—their own pet invention.

Most of the ideas presented in this his last commentary on human absurdities were new only as to phrasing. He had exhausted the topic long ago, in one way or another, but it was one of the themes in which he never lost interest. Many subjects became stale to him at last; but the curious invention called man remained a novelty to him to the end.

From my note-book:

October 25. I am constantly amazed at his knowledge of history—all history—religious, political, military. He seems to have read everything in the world concerning Rome, France, and England particularly.

Last night we stopped playing billiards while he reviewed, in the most vivid and picturesque phrasing, the reasons of Rome's decline. Such a presentation would have enthralled any audience—I could not help feeling a great pity that he had not devoted some of his public effort to work of that sort. No one could have equaled him at it. He concluded with some comments on the possibility of America following Rome's example, though he thought the vote of the people would always, or at least for a long period, prevent imperialism.

November 1. To-day he has been absorbed in his old interest in shorthand. "It is the only rational alphabet," he declared. "All this spelling reform is nonsense. What we need is alphabet reform, and shorthand is the thing. Take the letter M, for instance; it is made with one stroke in shorthand, while in longhand it requires at least three. The word Mephistopheles can be written in shorthand with one-sixth the number of strokes that is required in longhand. I tell you shorthand should be adopted as the alphabet."

I said: "There is this objection: the characters are so slightly different that each writer soon forms a system of his own and it is seldom that two can read each other's notes."

"You are talking of stenographic reporting," he said, rather warmly. "Nothing of the kind is true in the case of the regular alphabet. It is perfectly clear and legible."

"Would you have it in the schools, then?"

"Yes, it should be taught in the schools, not for stenographic purposes, but only for use in writing to save time."

He was very much in earnest, and said he had undertaken an article on the subject.

November 3. He said he could not sleep last night, for thinking what a fool he had been in his various investments.

"I have always been the victim of somebody," he said, "and always an idiot myself, doing things that even a child would not do. Never asking anybody's advice—never taking it when it was offered. I can't see how anybody could do the things I have done and have kept right on doing."

I could see that the thought agitated him, and I suggested that we go to his room and read, which we did, and had a riotous time over the most recent chapters of the *Letters from the Earth*, and some notes he had made for future chapters on infant damnation and other distinctive features of orthodox creeds. He told an anecdote of an old minister who declared that Presbyterianism without infant damnation would be like the dog on the train that couldn't be identified because it had lost its tag.

Somewhat on the defensive I said, "But we must admit that the so-called Christian nations are the most enlightened and progressive."

He answered, "Yes, but in spite of their religion, not because of it. The Church has opposed every innovation and discovery from the day of Galileo down to our own time, when the use of anesthetics in child-birth was regarded as a sin because it avoided the biblical curse pronounced against Eve. And every step in astronomy and geology ever taken has been opposed by bigotry and superstition. The Greeks surpassed us in artistic culture and in architecture five hundred years before the Christian religion was born.

"I have been reading Gibbon's celebrated Fifteenth Chapter," he said later, "and I don't see what Christians found against it. It is so mild—so gentle in its sarcasm." He added that he had been reading also a little book of brief biographies and had found in it the saying of Darwin's father, "Unitarianism is a feather-bed to catch falling Christians."

"I was glad to find and identify that saying," he said; "it is so good."

He finished the evening by reading a chapter from Carlyle's *French Revolution*—a fine pyrotechnic passage—the gathering at Versailles. I said that Carlyle somehow reminded me of a fervid stump-speaker who pounded his fists and went at his audience fiercely, determined to convince them.

"Yes," he said, "but he is the best one that ever lived."

November 10. This morning early he heard me stirring and called. I went in and found him propped up with a book, as usual. He said:

"I seldom read Christmas stories, but this is very beautiful. It has made me cry. I want you to read it." (It was Booth Tarkington's *Beasley's Christmas Party*.) "Tarkington has the true touch," he said; "his work always satisfies me." Another book he has been reading with great enjoyment is James Branch Cabell's *Chivalry*. He cannot say enough of the subtle poetic art with which Cabell has flung the light of romance about dark and sordid chapters of history.

CCLXXXVII

MARK TWAIN'S READING

PERHAPS here one may speak of Mark Twain's reading in general. On the table by him, and on his bed, and in the billiard-room shelves he kept the books he read most. They were not many—not more than a dozen—but they were manifestly of familiar and frequent usage. All, or nearly all, had annotations—spontaneously uttered marginal notes, title prefatories, or concluding comments. They were the books he had read again and again, and it was seldom that he had not had something to say with each fresh reading.

There were the three big volumes by Saint-Simon— the *Memoirs*—which he once told me he had read no less than twenty times. On the fly-leaf of the first volume he wrote:

This, & Casanova & Pepys, set in parallel columns, could afford a good coup d'œil of French & English high life of that epoch.

All through those finely printed volumes are his commentaries, sometimes no more than a word, sometimes a filled, closely written margin. He found little to admire in the human nature of Saint-Simon's period—little to approve in Saint-Simon himself beyond his unrestrained frankness, which he admired without stint, and in one paragraph where the details of that early period are set down with startling fidelity he wrote: "Oh, incomparable Saint-Simon!"

Saint-Simon is always frank, and Mark Twain was equally so. Where the former tells one of the unspeakable compulsions of Louis XIV., the latter has commented:

We have to grant that God made this royal hog; we may also be permitted to believe that it was a crime to do so.

And on another page:

In her memories of this period the Duchesse de St. Clair makes this striking remark: "Sometimes one could tell a gentleman, but it was only by his manner of using his fork."

His comments on the orthodox religion of Saint-Simon's period are not marked by gentleness. Of the author's reference to the Edict of Nantes, which he says depopulated half of the realm, ruined its commerce, and "authorized torments and punishments by which so many innocent people of both sexes were killed by thousands," Clemens writes:

So much blood has been shed by the Church because of an omission from the Gospel: "Ye shall be *indifferent* as to what your neighbor's religion is." Not merely tolerant of it, but indifferent to it. Divinity is claimed for many religions; but no religion is great enough or divine enough to add that new law to its code.

In the place where Saint-Simon describes the death of Monseigneur, son of the king, and the court hypocrites are wailing their extravagantly pretended sorrow, Clemens wrote:

It is all so true, all so human. God made these animals. He must have noticed this scene; I wish I knew how it struck Him.

There were not many notes in the Suetonius, nor in the Carlyle *Revolution*, though these were among the volumes he read oftenest. Perhaps they expressed for him too completely and too richly their subject-matter to require anything at his hand. Here and there are marked passages and occasional cross-references to related history and circumstance.

There was not much room for comment on the narrow margins of the old copy of Pepys, which he had read steadily since the early seventies; only here and there a few crisp words, but the underscoring and marked passages are plentiful enough to convey his devotion to that quaint record which, perhaps next to Suetonius, was the book he read and quoted most.

Francis Parkman's *Canadian Histories* he had read periodically, especially the story of the *Old Régime* and of the *Jesuits in North America*. As late as January, 1908, he wrote on the title-page of the *Old Régime:*

Very interesting. It tells how people religiously and otherwise insane came over from France and colonized Canada.

He was not always complimentary to those who undertook to Christianize the Indians; but he did not fail to write his admiration of their courage—their very willingness to endure privation and even the fiendish savage tortures for the sake of their faith. "What manner of men are these?" he wrote, apropos of the account of Bressani, who had undergone the most devilish inflictions which savage ingenuity could devise, and yet returned maimed and disfigured the following spring to "dare again the knives and fiery brand of the Iroquois." Clemens was likely to be on the side of the Indians, but hardly in their barbarism. In one place he wrote:

That men should be willing to leave their happy homes and endure what the missionaries endured in order to teach these Indians the road to hell would be rational, understandable, but why they should want to teach them a way to heaven is a thing which the mind somehow cannot grasp.

Other histories, mainly English and French, showed how he had read them—read and digested every word and line. There were two volumes of Lecky, much worn; Andrew D. White's *Science and Theology*—a chief interest for at least one summer—and among the collection a well-worn copy of *Modern English Literature—Its Blemishes and Defects*, by Henry H. Breen. On the title-page of this book Clemens had written:

HARTFORD, 1876. Use with care, for it is a scarce book. England had to be ransacked in order to get it—or the bookseller speaketh falsely.

He once wrote a paper for the Saturday Morning Club, using for his text examples of slipshod English which Breen had noted.

Clemens had a passion for biography, and especially for autobiography, diaries, letters, and such intimate human history. Greville's *Journal of the Reigns of George IV. and William IV.* he had read much and annotated freely. Greville, while he admired Byron's talents, abhorred the poet's personality, and in one place condemns him as a vicious person and a debauchee. He adds:

Then he despises pretenders and charlatans of all sorts, while he is himself a pretender, as all men are who assume a character which does not belong to them and affect to be something which they are all the time conscious they are not in reality.

Clemens wrote on the margin:

But, dear sir, you are forgetting that what a man sees in the human race is merely himself in the deep and honest privacy of his own heart. Byron despised the race because he despised himself. I feel as Byron did, and for the same reason. Do you admire the race (& consequently yourself)?

A little further along, where Greville laments that

MARK TWAIN

Byron can take no profit to himself from the sinful characters he depicts so faithfully, Clemens commented:

If Byron—if any man—draws 50 characters, they are all him-self—50 shades, 50 moods, of his own character. And when the man draws them well why do they stir my admiration? Because they are me—I recognize myself.

A volume of Plutarch was among the biographies that showed usage, and the *Life of P. T. Barnum, Written by Himself*. *Two Years Before the Mast* he loved, and never tired of. The more recent *Memoirs* of Andrew D. White and Moncure D. Conway both, I remember, gave him enjoyment, as did the *Letters of Lowell*. A volume of the *Letters of Madame de Sévigné* had some annotated margins which were not complimentary to the translator, or for that matter to Sévigné herself, whom he once designates as a "nauseating" person, many of whose letters had been uselessly translated, as well as poorly arranged for read-ing. But he would read any volume of letters or per-sonal memoirs; none were too poor that had the throb of life in them, however slight.

Of such sort were the books that Mark Twain had loved best, and such were a few of his words concerning them. Some of them belong to his earlier reading, and among these is Darwin's *Descent of Man*, a book whose influence was always present, though I believe he did not read it any more in later years. In the days I knew him he read steadily not much besides Suetonius and Pepys and Carlyle. These and his simple astronomies and geol-ogies and the *Morte Arthure* and the poems of Kipling were seldom far from his hand.

CCLXXXVIII

A BERMUDA BIRTHDAY

IT was the middle of November, 1909, when Clemens decided to take another Bermuda vacation, and it was the 19th that we sailed. I went to New York a day ahead and arranged matters, and on the evening of the 18th received the news that Richard Watson Gilder had suddenly died.

Next morning there was other news. Clemens's old friend, William M. Laffan, of the *Sun*, had died while undergoing a surgical operation. I met Clemens at the train. He had already heard about Gilder; but he had not yet learned of Laffan's death. He said:

"That's just it. Gilder and Laffan get all the good things that come along and I never get anything."

Then, suddenly remembering, he added:

"How curious it is! I have been thinking of Laffan, coming down on the train, and mentally writing a letter to him on this Stetson-Eddy affair."

I asked when he had begun thinking of Laffan.

He said: "Within the hour."

It was within the hour that I had received the news, and naturally in my mind had carried it instantly to him. Perhaps there was something telepathic in it.

He was not at all ill going down to Bermuda, which was a fortunate thing, for the water was rough and I was quite disqualified. We did not even discuss astronomy, though there was what seemed most important news—the reported discovery of a new planet.

1541

But there was plenty of talk on the subject as soon as we got settled in the Hamilton Hotel. It was windy and rainy out-of-doors, and we looked out on the drenched semi-tropical foliage with a great bamboo swaying and bending in the foreground, while he speculated on the vast distance that the new planet must lie from our sun, to which it was still a satellite. The report had said that it was probably four hundred billions of miles distant, and that on this far frontier of the solar system the sun could not appear to it larger than the blaze of a tallow candle. To us it was wholly incredible how, in that dim remoteness, it could still hold true to the central force and follow at a snail-pace, yet with unvarying exactitude, its stupendous orbit. Clemens said that heretofore Neptune, the planetary outpost of our system, had been called the tortoise of the skies, but that comparatively it was rapid in its motion, and had become a near neighbor. He was a good deal excited at first, having somehow the impression that this new planet traveled out beyond the nearest fixed star; but then he remembered that the distance to that first solar neighbor was estimated in trillions, not billions, and that our little system, even with its new additions, was a child's handbreadth on the plane of the sky. He had brought along a small book called *The Pith of Astronomy*—a fascinating little volume—and he read from it about the great tempest of fire in the sun, where the waves of flame roll up two thousand miles high, though the sun itself is such a tiny star in the deeps of the universe.

If I dwell unwarrantably on this phase of Mark Twain's character, it is because it was always so fascinating to me, and the contemplation of the drama of the skies always meant so much to him, and somehow always seemed akin to him in its proportions. He had been born under a flaming star, a wanderer of the skies. He was himself, to me, always a comet rushing through space, from mystery to mystery, regardless of suns and systems.

It is not likely to rain long in Bermuda, and when the sun comes back it brings summer, whatever the season. Within a day after our arrival we were driving about those coral roads along the beaches, and by that marvelously variegated water. We went often to the south shore, especially to Devonshire Bay, where the reefs and the sea coloring seem more beautiful than elsewhere. Usually, when we reached the bay, we got out to walk along the indurated shore, stopping here and there to look out over the jeweled water—liquid turquoise, emerald, lapis-lazuli, jade, the imperial garment of the Lord.

At first we went alone with only the colored driver, Clifford Trott, whose name Clemens could not recollect, though he was always attempting resemblances with ludicrous results. A little later Helen Allen, an early angel-fish member already mentioned, was with us and directed the drives, for she had been born on the island and knew every attractive locality, though, for that matter, it would be hard to find there a place that was not attractive.

Clemens, in fact, remained not many days regularly at the hotel. He kept a room and his wardrobe there; but he paid a visit to Bay House—the lovely and quiet home of Helen's parents—and prolonged it from day to day, and from week to week, because it was a quiet and peaceful place with affectionate attention and limitless welcome. Clifford Trott had orders to come with the carriage each afternoon, and we drove down to Bay House for Mark Twain and his playmate, and then went wandering at will among the labyrinth of blossom-bordered, perfectly kept roadways of a dainty paradise, that never, I believe, becomes quite a reality even to those who know it best.

Clemens had an occasional paroxysm during these

weeks, but they were not likely to be severe or protracted; and I have no doubt the peace of his surroundings, the remoteness from disturbing events, as well as the balmy temperature, all contributed to his improved condition.

He talked pretty continuously during these drives, and he by no means restricted his subjects to juvenile matters. He discussed history and his favorite sciences and philosophies, and I am sure that his drift was rarely beyond the understanding of his young companion, for it was Mark Twain's gift to phrase his thought so that it commanded not only the respect of age, but the comprehension and the interest of youth.

I remember that once he talked, during an afternoon's drive, on the French Revolution and the ridiculous episode of Anacharsis Cloots, "orator and advocate of the human race," collecting the vast populace of France to swear allegiance to a king even then doomed to the block. The very name of Cloots suggested humor, and nothing could have been more delightful and graphic than the whole episode as he related it.

Helen asked if he thought such a thing as that could ever happen in America.

"No," he said, "the American sense of humor would have laughed it out of court in a week; and the Frenchman dreads ridicule, too, though he never seems to realize how ridiculous he is—the most ridiculous creature in the world."

On the morning of his seventy-fourth birthday he was looking wonderfully well after a night of sound sleep, his face full of color and freshness, his eyes bright and keen and full of good-humor. I presented him with a pair of cuff-buttons silver-enameled with the Bermuda lily, and I thought he seemed pleased with them.

It was rather gloomy outside, so we remained indoors by the fire and played cards, game after game of hearts, at which he excelled, and he was usually kept happy by winning. There were no visitors, and after dinner Helen asked him to read some of her favorite episodes from *Tom Sawyer*, so he read the whitewashing scene, Peter and the Pain-killer, and such chapters until tea-time. Then there was a birthday cake, and afterward cigars and talk and a quiet fireside evening.

Once, in the course of his talk, he forgot a word and denounced his poor memory:

"I'll forget the Lord's middle name some time," he declared, "right in the midst of a storm, when I need all the help I can get."

Later he said:

"Nobody dreamed, seventy-four years ago to-day, that I would be in Bermuda now." And I thought he meant a good deal more than the words conveyed.

It was during this Bermuda visit that Mark Twain added the finishing paragraph to his article, "The Turning-Point in My Life," which, at Howells's suggestion, he had been preparing for *Harper's Bazar*. It was a characteristic touch, and, as the last summary of his philosophy of human life, may be repeated here.

Necessarily the scene of the real turning-point of my life (and of yours) was the Garden of Eden. It was there that the first link was forged of the chain that was ultimately to lead to the emptying of me into the literary guild. Adam's *temperament* was the first command the Deity ever issued to a human being on this planet. And it was the only command Adam would *never* be able to disobey. It said, "Be weak, be water, be characterless, be cheaply persuadable." The later command, to let the fruit alone, was certain to be disobeyed. Not by Adam himself, but by his *temperament*—which he did not create and had no authority over. For the *temperament* is the man; the thing tricked out with clothes and named Man is merely its Shadow, nothing more. The law of the tiger's temperament is, Thou shalt kill; the law of the sheep's temperament is, Thou shalt

not kill. To issue later commands requiring the tiger to let
the fat stranger alone, and requiring the sheep to imbrue its
hands in the blood of the lion is not worth while, for those commands *can't* be obeyed. They would invite to violations of the
law of *temperament*, which is supreme, and takes precedence of
all other authorities. I cannot help feeling disappointed in
Adam and Eve. That is, in their temperaments. Not in *them*,
poor helpless young creatures—afflicted with temperaments made
out of butter, which butter was commanded to get into contact
with fire and *be melted*. What I cannot help wishing is, that
Adam and Eve had been postponed, and Martin Luther and Joan
of Arc put in their place—that splendid pair equipped with temperaments not made of butter, but of asbestos. By neither
sugary persuasions nor by hell-fire could Satan have beguiled
them to eat the apple.

There would have been results! Indeed yes. The apple
would be intact to-day; there would be no human race; there
would be no *you;* there would be no *me*. And the old, old
creation-dawn scheme of ultimately launching me into the literary guild would have been defeated.

CCLXXXIX

THE DEATH OF JEAN

HE decided to go home for the holidays, and how fortunate it seems now that he did so! We sailed for America on the 18th of December, arriving the 20th. Jean was at the wharf to meet us, blue and shivering with the cold, for it was wretchedly bleak there, and I had the feeling that she should not have come.

She went directly, I think, to Stormfield, he following a day or two later. On the 23d I was lunching with Jean alone. She was full of interest in her Christmas preparations. She had a handsome tree set up in the loggia, and the packages were piled about it, with new ones constantly arriving. With her farm management, her housekeeping, her secretary work, and her Christmas preparations, it seemed to me that she had her hands overfull. Such a mental pressure could not be good for her. I suggested that for a time at least I might assume a part of her burden.

I was to remain at my own home that night, and I think it was as I left Stormfield that I passed Jean on the stair. She said, cheerfully, that she felt a little tired and was going up to lie down, so that she would be fresh for the evening. I did not go back, and I never saw her alive again.

I was at breakfast next morning when word was brought in that one of the men from Stormfield was outside and wished to see me immediately. When I went out he said: "Miss Jean is dead. They have just found her in her bath-room. Mr. Clemens sent me to bring you."

It was as incomprehensible as such things always are. I could not realize at all that Jean, so full of plans and industries and action less than a day before, had passed into that voiceless mystery which we call death.

Harry Iles drove me rapidly up the hill. As I entered Clemens's room he looked at me helplessly and said:

"Well, I suppose you have heard of this final disaster."

He was not violent or broken down with grief. He had come to that place where, whatever the shock or the ill-turn of fortune, he could accept it, and even in that first moment of loss he realized that, for Jean at least, the fortune was not ill. Her malady had never been cured, and it had been one of his deepest dreads that he would leave her behind him. It was believed, at first, that Jean had drowned, and Dr. Smith tried methods of resuscitation; but then he found that it was simply a case of heart cessation caused by the cold shock of her bath.

The Gabrilowitsches were by this time in Europe, and Clemens cabled them not to come. Later in the day he asked me if we would be willing to close our home for the winter and come to Stormfield. He said that he should probably go back to Bermuda before long; but that he wished to keep the house open so that it would be there for him to come to at any time that he might need it.

We came, of course, for there was no thought among any of his friends but for his comfort and peace of mind. Jervis Langdon was summoned from Elmira, for Jean would lie there with the others.

In the loggia stood the half-trimmed Christmas tree, and all about lay the packages of gifts, and in Jean's room, on the chairs and upon her desk, were piled other packages. Nobody had been forgotten. For her father she had bought a handsome globe; he had always wanted one. Once when I went into his room he said:

"I have been looking in at Jean and envying her. I

have never greatly envied any one but the dead. I always envy the dead."

He told me how the night before they had dined together alone; how he had urged her to turn over a part of her work to me; how she had clung to every duty as if now, after all the years, she was determined to make up for lost time.

While they were at dinner a telephone inquiry had come concerning his health, for the papers had reported him as returning from Bermuda in a critical condition. He had written this playful answer:

MANAGER ASSOCIATED PRESS,
    New York.

I hear the newspapers say I am dying. The charge is not true. I would not do such a thing at my time of life. I am behaving as good as I can.

Merry Christmas to everybody!   MARK TWAIN.

Jean telephoned it for him to the press. It had been the last secretary service she had ever rendered.

She had kissed his hand, he said, when they parted, for she had a severe cold and would not wish to impart it to him; then happily she had said good night, and he had not seen her again. The reciting of this was good to him, for it brought the comfort of tears.

Later, when I went in again, he was writing:

"I am setting it down," he said—"everything. It is a relief to me to write it. It furnishes me an excuse for thinking."

He continued writing most of the day, and at intervals during the next day, and the next.

It was on Christmas Day that they went with Jean on her last journey. Katie Leary, her baby nurse, had dressed her in the dainty gown which she had worn for Clara's wedding, and they had pinned on it a pretty buckle which her father had brought her from Bermuda, and which she had not seen. No Greek statue was ever more classically beautiful than she was, lying there in the great living-room, which in its brief history had seen so much of the round of life.

They were to start with Jean at about six o'clock, and a little before that time Clemens (he was unable to make the journey) asked me what had been her favorite music. I said that she seemed always to care most for the Schubert Impromptu.[1] Then he said:

"Play it when they get ready to leave with her, and add the Intermezzo for Susy and the Largo for Mrs. Clemens. When I hear the music I shall know that they are starting. Tell them to set lanterns at the door, so I can look down and see them go."

So I sat at the organ and began playing as they lifted and bore her away. A soft, heavy snow was falling, and the gloom of those shortest days was closing in. There was not the least wind or noise, the whole world was muffled. The lanterns at the door threw their light out on the thickly falling flakes. I remained at the organ; but the little group at the door saw him come to the window above—the light on his white hair as he stood mournfully gazing down, watching Jean going away from him for the last time. I played steadily on as he had instructed, the Impromptu, the Intermezzo from "Cavalleria," and Handel's Largo. When I had finished I went up and found him.

"Poor little Jean," he said: "but for her it is so good to go."

In his own story of it he wrote:

From my windows I saw the hearse and the carriages wind along the road and gradually grow vague and spectral in the falling snow, and presently disappear. Jean was gone out of my life, and would not come back any more. The cousin she

---

[1] Op. 142, No. 2.

had played with when they were babies together—he and her beloved old Katie—were conducting her to her distant childhood home, where she will lie by her mother's side once more, in the company of Susy and Langdon.

He did not come down to dinner, and when I went up afterward I found him curiously agitated. He said:

"For one who does not believe in spirits I have had a most peculiar experience. I went into the bath-room just now and closed the door. You know how warm it always is in there, and there are no draughts. All at once I felt a cold current of air about me. I thought the door must be open; but it was closed. I said, 'Jean, is this you trying to let me know you have found the others?' Then the cold air was gone."

I saw that the incident had made a very great impression upon him; but I don't remember that he ever mentioned it afterward.

Next day the storm had turned into a fearful blizzard; the whole hilltop was a raging, driving mass of white. He wrote most of the day, but stopped now and then to read some of the telegrams or letters of condolence which came flooding in. Sometimes he walked over to the window to look out on the furious tempest. Once, during the afternoon, he said:

"Jean always so loved to see a storm like this, and just now at Elmira they are burying her."

Later he read aloud some lines by Alfred Austin, which Mrs. Crane had sent him—lines which he had remembered in the sorrow for Susy:

> When last came sorrow, around barn and byre
>   Wind-carven snow, the year's white sepulchre, lay.
> "Come in," I said, "and warm you by the fire":
>   And there she sits and never goes away.

It was that evening that he came into the room where Mrs. Paine and I sat by the fire bringing his manuscript.

"I have finished my story of Jean's death," he said. "It is the end of my autobiography. I shall never write any more. I can't judge it myself at all. One of you read it aloud to the other, and let me know what you think of it. If it is worthy, perhaps some day it may be published."

It was, in fact, one of the most exquisite and tender pieces of writing in the language. He had ended his literary labors with that perfect thing which so marvelously speaks the loftiness and tenderness of his soul. It was thoroughly in keeping with his entire career that he should, with this rare dramatic touch, bring it to a close. A paragraph which he omitted may be printed now:

December 27. Did I know Jean's value? No, I only thought I did. I knew a ten-thousandth fraction of it, that was all. It is always so, with us, it has always been so. We are like the poor ignorant private soldier—dead, now, four hundred years—who picked up the great Sancy diamond on the field of the lost battle and sold it for a franc. Later he knew what he had done.

Shall I ever be cheerful again, happy again? Yes. And soon. For I know my temperament. And I know that the temperament is *master of the man*, and that he is its fettered and helpless slave and must in all things do as it commands. A man's temperament is born in him, and no circumstances can ever change it.

My temperament has never allowed my spirits to remain depressed long at a time.

That was a feature of Jean's temperament, too. She inherited it from me. I think she got the rest of it from her mother.

Jean Clemens had two natural endowments: the gift of justice and a genuine passion for all nature. In a little paper found in her desk she had written:

I know a few people who love the country as I do, but not many. Most of my acquaintances are enthusiastic over the spring and summer months, but very few care much for it the year round. A few people are interested in the spring foliage and the development of the wild flowers—nearly all enjoy the autumn colors—while comparatively few pay much attention to the coming and going of the birds, the changes in their plumage and songs, the apparent springing into life on some warm April day of the chipmunks and woodchucks, the skurrying of baby rabbits, and again in the fall the equally sudden disappearance of some of the animals and the growing shyness of others. To me it is all as fascinating as a book—more so, since I have never lost interest in it.

It is simple and frank, like Thoreau. Perhaps, had she exercised it, there was a third gift—the gift of written thought.

Clemens remained at Stormfield ten days after Jean was gone. The weather was fiercely cold, the landscape desolate, the house full of tragedy. He kept pretty closely to his room, where he had me bring the heaps of letters, a few of which he answered personally; for the others he prepared a simple card of acknowledgment. He was for the most part in gentle mood during these days, though he would break out now and then, and rage at the hardness of a fate that had laid an unearned burden of illness on Jean and shadowed her life.

They were days not wholly without humor—none of his days could be altogether without that, though it was likely to be of a melancholy sort.

Many of the letters offered orthodox comfort, saying, in effect: "God does not willingly punish us."

When he had read a number of these he said:

"Well, why does He do it then? We don't invite it. Why does He give Himself the trouble?"

I suggested that it was a sentiment that probably gave comfort to the writer of it.

"So it does," he said, "and I am glad of it—glad of anything that gives comfort to anybody."

He spoke of the larger God—the God of the great unvarying laws, and by and by dropped off to sleep, quite peacefully, and indeed peace came more and more to him each day with the thought that Jean and Susy and their mother could not be troubled any more. To Mrs. Gabrilowitsch he wrote:

REDDING, CONN., *December 29, 1909.*

O, Clara, Clara dear, I am so glad she is out of it & safe—safe! I am not melancholy; I shall never be melancholy again, I think.

You see, I was in such distress when I came to realize that you were gone far away & no one stood between her & danger but me—& I could die at any moment, & *then*—oh then what would become of her! For she was wilful, you know, & would not have been governable.

You can't imagine what a darling she was that last two or three days; & how *fine,* & good, & sweet, & noble—& *joyful,* thank Heaven!—& how intellectually brilliant. I had never been acquainted with Jean before. I recognized that.

But I mustn't try to write about her—I *can't.* I have already poured my heart out with the pen, recording that last day or two. I will send you that—& you must let no one but Ossip read it.

Good-by. I love you so! And Ossip.

FATHER.

CCXC

THE RETURN TO BERMUDA

I DON'T think he attempted any further writing for print. His mind was busy with ideas, but he was willing to talk, rather than to write, rather even than to play billiards, it seemed, although we had a few quiet games—the last we should ever play together. Evenings he asked for music, preferring the Scotch airs, such as "Bonnie Doon" and "The Campbells are Coming." I remember that once, after playing the latter for him, he told, with great feeling, how the Highlanders, led by Gen. Colin Campbell, had charged at Lucknow, inspired by that stirring air. When he had retired I usually sat with him, and he drifted into literature, or theology, or science, or history—the story of the universe and man.

One evening he spoke of those who had written but one immortal thing and stopped there. He mentioned "Ben Bolt."

"I met that man once," he said. "In my childhood I sang 'Sweet Alice, Ben Bolt,' and in my old age, fifteen years ago, I met the man who wrote it. His name was Brown.[1] He was aged, forgotten, a mere memory. I remember how it thrilled me to realize that this was the very author of 'Sweet Alice, Ben Bolt.' He was just an accident. He had a vision and echoed it. A good many persons do that—the thing they do is to put in compact

---

[1] Thomas Dunn English. Mr. Clemens apparently remembered only the name satirically conferred upon him by Edgar Allan Poe, "Thomas Dunn Brown."

form the thing which we have all vaguely felt. 'Twenty Years Ago' is just like it—'I have wandered through the village, Tom, and sat beneath the tree'—and Holmes's 'Last Leaf' is another: the memory of the hallowed past, and the gravestones of those we love. It is all so beautiful—the past is always beautiful."

He quoted, with great feeling and effect:

> The mossy marbles rest
> On the lips that we have pressed
> In their bloom,
> And the names we love to hear
> Have been carved for many a year
> On the tomb.

He continued in this strain for an hour or more. He spoke of humor, and thought it must be one of the chief attributes of God. He cited plants and animals that were distinctly humorous in form and in their characteristics. These he declared were God's jokes.

"Why," he said, "humor is mankind's greatest blessing."

"Your own case is an example," I answered. "Without it, whatever your reputation as a philosopher, you could never have had the wide-spread affection that is shown by the writers of that great heap of letters."

"Yes," he said, gently, "they have liked to be amused."

I tucked him in for the night, promising to send him to Bermuda, with Claude to take care of him, if he felt he could undertake the journey in two days more.

He was able, and he was eager to go, for he longed for that sunny island, and for the quiet peace of the Allen home. His niece, Mrs. Loomis, came up to spend the last evening in Stormfield, a happy evening full of quiet talk, and next morning, in the old closed carriage that had been his wedding-gift, he was driven to the railway station. This was on January 4, 1910.

THE RETURN TO BERMUDA

He was to sail next day, and that night, at Mr. Loomis's, Howells came in, and for an hour or two they reviewed some of the questions they had so long ago settled, or left forever unsettled, and laid away. I remember that at dinner Clemens spoke of his old Hartford butler, George, and how he had once brought George to New York and introduced him at the various publishing houses as his friend, with curious and sometimes rather embarrassing results.

The talk drifted to sociology and to the labor-unions, which Clemens defended as being the only means by which the workman could obtain recognition of his rights.

Howells in his book mentions this evening, which he says "was made memorable to me by the kind, clear, judicial sense with which he explained and justified the labor-unions as the sole present help of the weak against the strong."

They discussed dreams, and then in a little while Howells rose to go. I went also, and as we walked to his near-by apartment he spoke of Mark Twain's supremacy. He said:

"I turn to his books for cheer when I am down-hearted. There was never anybody like him; there never will be."

Clemens sailed next morning. They did not meet again.

CCXCI

STORMFIELD was solemn and empty without Mark Twain; but he wrote by every steamer, at first with his own hand, and during the last week by the hand of one of his enlisted secretaries—some member of the Allen family—usually Helen. His letters were full of brightness and pleasantry—always concerned more or less with business matters, though he was no longer disturbed by them, for Bermuda was too peaceful and too far away, and, besides, he had faith in the Mark Twain Company's ability to look after his affairs. I cannot do better, I believe, than to offer some portions of these letters here.

He reached Bermuda on the 7th of January, 1910, and on the 11th he wrote:

Again I am living the ideal life. There is nothing to mar it but the bloody-minded bandit Arthur,[1] who still fetches and carries Helen. Presently he will be found drowned. Claude comes to Bay House twice a day to see if I need any service. He is invaluable. There was a military lecture last night at the Officers' Mess Prospect; as the lecturer honored me with a special urgent invitation, and said he wanted to lecture to *me* particularly, I naturally took Helen and her mother into the private carriage and went.

As soon as we landed at the door with the crowd the Governor

---

[1] A small playmate of Helen's of whom Clemens pretended to be fiercely jealous. Once he wrote a memorandum to Helen: "Let Arthur read this book. There is a page in it that is poisoned."

came to me & was very cordial. I "met up" with that charming Colonel Chapman [we had known him on the previous visit] and other officers of the regiment & had a good time.

A few days later he wrote:

Thanks for your letter & for its contenting news of the situation in that foreign & far-off & vaguely remembered country where you & Loomis & Lark and other beloved friends are.

I had a letter from Clara this morning. She is solicitous & wants me well & watchfully taken care of. My, my, she ought to see Helen & her parents & Claude administer that trust. Also she says, "I hope to hear from you or Mr. Paine very soon."

I am writing her & I know you will respond to your part of her prayer. She is pretty desolate now after Jean's emancipation —the only kindness that God ever did that poor, unoffending child in all her hard life.

Send Clara a copy of Howells's gorgeous letter.

The "gorgeous letter" mentioned was an appreciation of his recent *Bazar* article, "The Turning-Point in My Life," and here follows:

January 18, 1910.

DEAR CLEMENS,—While your wonderful words are warm in my mind yet I want to tell you what you know already: that you never wrote anything greater, finer, than that turning-point paper of yours.

I shall feel it honor enough if they put on my tombstone "He was born in the same century and general section of Middle Western country with Dr. S. L. Clemens, Oxon., and had his degree three years before him through a mistake of the University."

I hope you are worse. You will never be riper for a purely intellectual life, and it is a pity to have you lagging along with a worn-out material body on top of your soul.

Yours ever,

W. D. HOWELLS.

On the margin of this letter Clemens had written:

I reckon this spontaneous outburst from the first critic of the day is good to keep, ain't it, Paine?

January 24th he wrote again of his contentment:

Life continues here the same as usual. There isn't a fault in it—good times, good home, tranquil contentment all day & every day without a break.

On February 5th he wrote that the climate and condition of his health might require him to stay in Bermuda pretty continuously, but that he wished Stormfield kept open so that he might come to it at any time. And he added:

Yesterday Mr. Allen took us on an excursion in Mr. Hamilton's big motor-boat. Present: Mrs. Allen, Mr. & Mrs. & Miss Sloane, Helen, Mildred Howells, Claude, & me. Several hours' swift skimming over ravishing blue seas, a brilliant sun; also a couple of hours of picnicking & lazying under the cedars in a secluded place.

The *Orotava* is arriving with 260 passengers—I shall get letters by her, no doubt.

P.S.—Please send me the *Standard Unabridged* that is on the table in my bedroom. I have no dictionary here.

There is no mention in any of these letters of his trouble; but he was having occasional spasms of pain, though in that soft climate they would seem to have come with less frequency, and there was so little to disturb him, and much that contributed to his peace. Among the callers at the Bay House to see him was Woodrow Wilson, and the two put in some pleasant hours at miniature golf, "putting" on the Allen lawn. Once when he had been beaten, Clemens said:

"Wilson, you will be the next President of the United States."

Of course a catastrophe would come along now and

then—such things could not always be guarded against. In a letter toward the end of February he wrote:

It is 2.30 in the morning & I am writing because I can't sleep. I can't sleep because a professional pianist is coming to-morrow afternoon *to play for me.* My God! I wouldn't allow Paderewski or Gabrilowitsch to do that. I would rather have a leg amputated. I knew he was coming, but I never dreamed it was to play for *me.* When I heard the horrible news 4 hours ago, be d—d if I didn't come near screaming. I meant to slip out and be absent, but now I can't. Don't pray for me. The thing is just as d—d bad as it can be already.

Clemens's love for music did not include the piano, except for very gentle melodies, and he probably did not anticipate these from a professional player. He did not report the sequel of the matter; but it is likely that his imagination had discounted its tortures. Sometimes his letters were pure nonsense. Once he sent a sheet, on one side of which was written:

BAY HOUSE,
March 5, 1910.

Received of S. L. C.
Two Dollars and Forty Cents
in return for my promise to believe everything he says hereafter.
HELEN S. ALLEN.

and on the reverse:

FOR SALE

The proprietor of the hereinbefore mentioned Promise desires to part with it on account of ill health and obliged to go away somewheres so as to let it recipricate, and will take any reasonable amount for it above 2 percent of its face because experienced parties think it will not keep but only a little while in this kind of weather & is a kind of proppity that don't give a cuss for cold storage nohow.

Clearly, however serious Mark Twain regarded his

physical condition, he did not allow it to make him gloomy. He wrote that matters were going everywhere to his satisfaction; that Clara was happy; that his household and business affairs no longer troubled him; that his personal surroundings were of the pleasantest sort. Sometimes he wrote of what he was reading, and once spoke particularly of Prof. William Lyon Phelps's *Literary Essays*, which he said he had been unable to lay down until he had finished the book.[1]

So his days seemed full of comfort. But in March I noticed that he generally dictated his letters, and once when he sent some small photographs I thought he looked thinner and older. Still he kept up his merriment. In one letter he said:

> While the matter is in my mind I will remark that if you ever send me another letter which is not paged at the top I will write you with my own hand, so that I may use with utter freedom & without embarrassment the kind of words which alone can describe such a criminal, towit, —— ——; you will have to put into words those dashes because propriety will not allow me to do it myself in my secretary's hearing. You are forgiven, but don't let it occur again.

He had still made no mention of his illness; but on the 25th of March he wrote something of his plans for coming home. He had engaged passage on the *Bermudian* for April 23d, he said; and he added:

> But don't tell anybody. I don't want it known. I may have to go sooner if the pain in my breast does not mend its ways pretty considerable. I don't want to die here, for this is an unkind place for a person in that condition. I should have to

---

[1] To Phelps himself he wrote: "I thank you ever so much for the book, which I find charming—so charming, indeed, that I read it through in a single night, & did not regret the lost night's sleep. I am glad if I deserve what you have said about me; & even if I don't I am proud & well contented, since you *think* I deserve it."

lie in the undertaker's cellar until the ship would remove me
& it is dark down there & unpleasant.

The Colliers will meet me on the pier, & I may stay with them
a week or two before going home. It all depends on the breast
pain. I don't want to die there. I am growing more and more
particular about the place.

But in the same letter he spoke of plans for the summer, suggesting that we must look into the magic-lantern
possibilities, so that library entertainments could be given
at Stormfield. I confess that this letter, in spite of its
light tone, made me uneasy, and I was tempted to sail
for Bermuda to bring him home. Three days later he
wrote again:

I have been having a most uncomfortable time for the past
four days with that breast pain, which turns out to be an affection of the heart, just as I originally suspected. The news from
New York is to the effect that non-bronchial weather has arrived there at last; therefore, if I can get my breast trouble in
traveling condition I may sail for home a week or two earlier
than has been proposed.

The same mail that brought this brought a letter from
Mr. Allen, who frankly stated that matters had become
very serious indeed. Mr. Clemens had had some dangerous attacks, and the physicians considered his condition
critical.

These letters arrived April 1st. I went to New York
at once and sailed next morning. Before sailing I consulted with Dr. Quintard, who provided me with some
opiates and instructed me in the use of the hypodermic
needle. He also joined me in a cablegram to the Gabrilowitsches, then in Italy, advising them to sail without
delay.

CCXCII

THE VOYAGE HOME

I SENT no word to Bermuda that I was coming, and when on the second morning I arrived at Hamilton, I stepped quickly ashore from the tender and hurried to Bay House. The doors were all open, as they usually are in that summer island, and no one was visible. I was familiar with the place, and, without knocking, I went through to the room occupied by Mark Twain. As I entered I saw that he was alone, sitting in a large chair, clad in the familiar dressing-gown.

Bay House stands upon the water, and the morning light, reflected in at the window, had an unusual quality. He was not yet shaven, and he seemed unnaturally pale and gray; certainly he was much thinner. I was too startled, for the moment, to say anything. When he turned and saw me he seemed a little dazed.

"Why," he said, holding out his hand, "you didn't tell us you were coming."

"No," I said, "it is rather sudden. I didn't quite like the sound of your last letters."

"But those were not serious," he protested. "You shouldn't have come on *my* account."

I said then that I had come on my own account; that I had felt the need of recreation, and had decided to run down and come home with him.

"That's—very—good," he said, in his slow, gentle fashion. "*Now* I'm glad to see you."

His breakfast came in and he ate with an appetite

When he had been shaved and freshly propped up in his pillows it seemed to me, after all, that I must have been mistaken in thinking him so changed. Certainly he was thinner, but his color was fine, his eyes were bright; he had no appearance of a man whose life was believed to be in danger. He told me then of the fierce attacks he had gone through, how the pains had torn at him, and how it had been necessary for him to have hypodermic injections, which he amusingly termed "hypnotic injunctions" and "subcutaneous applications," and he had his humor out of it, as of course he must have, even though Death should stand there in person.

From Mr. and Mrs. Allen and from the physician I learned how slender had been his chances and how uncertain were the days ahead. Mr. Allen had already engaged passage on the *Oceana* for the 12th, and the one purpose now was to get him physically in condition for the trip.

How devoted those kind friends had been to him! They had devised every imaginable thing for his comfort. Mr. Allen had rigged an electric bell which connected with his own room, so that he could be aroused instantly at any hour of the night. Clemens had refused to have a nurse, for it was only during the period of his extreme suffering that he needed any one, and he did not wish to have a nurse always around. When the pains were gone he was as bright and cheerful, and, seemingly, as well as ever.

On the afternoon of my arrival we drove out, as formerly, and he discussed some of the old subjects in quite the old way. He had been re-reading Macaulay, he said, and spoke at considerable length of the hypocrisy and intrigue of the English court under James II. He spoke, too, of the Redding Library. I had sold for him that portion of the land where Jean's farm-house had stood, and it was in his mind to use the money for some sort of a memorial to Jean. I had written, suggesting that perhaps he would like to put up a small library building, as the Adams lot faced the corner where Jean had passed every day when she rode to the station for the mail. He had been thinking this over, he said, and wished the idea carried out. He asked me to write at once to his lawyer, Mr. Lark, and have a paper prepared appointing trustees for a memorial library fund.

The pain did not trouble him that afternoon, nor during several succeeding days. He was gay and quite himself, and he often went out on the lawn; but we did not drive out again. For the most part, he sat propped up in his bed, reading or smoking, or talking in the old way; and as I looked at him he seemed so full of vigor and the joy of life that I could not convince myself that he would not outlive us all. I found that he had been really very much alive during those three months—too much for his own good, sometimes—for he had not been careful of his hours or his diet, and had suffered in consequence.

He had not been writing, though he had scribbled some playful valentines and he had amused himself one day by preparing a chapter of advice—for me it appeared— which, after reading it aloud to the Allens and receiving their approval, he declared he intended to have printed for my benefit. As it would seem to have been the last bit of continued writing he ever did, and because it is characteristic and amusing, a few paragraphs may be admitted. The "advice" is concerning deportment on reaching the Gate which St. Peter is supposed to guard:

Upon arrival do not speak to St. Peter until spoken to. It is not your place to begin.

Do not begin any remark with "Say."

When applying for a ticket avoid trying to make conversation. If you *must* talk let the weather alone. St. Peter cares not a damn for the weather. And don't ask him what time the 4.30 train goes; there aren't any trains in heaven, except through trains, and the less information you get about them the better for you.

You can ask him for his autograph—there is no harm in that—but be careful and don't remark that it is one of the penalties of greatness. He has heard *that* before.

Don't try to kodak him. Hell is full of people who have made that mistake.

Leave your dog outside. Heaven goes by favor. If it went by merit you would stay out and the dog would go in.

You will be wanting to slip down at night and smuggle water to those poor little chaps (the infant damned), but don't you try it. You would be caught, and nobody in heaven would respect you after that.

Explain to Helen why I don't come. If you can.

There were several pages of this counsel. One paragraph was written in shorthand. I meant to ask him to translate it; but there were many other things to think of, and I did not remember.

I spent most of each day with him, merely sitting by the bed and reading while he himself read or dozed. His nights were wakeful—he found it easier to sleep by day—and he liked to think that some one was there. He became interested in Hardy's *Jude*, and spoke of it with high approval, urging me to read it. He dwelt a good deal on the morals of it, or rather on the lack of them. He followed the tale to the end, finishing it the afternoon before we sailed. It was his last continuous reading.

I noticed, when he slept, that his breathing was difficult, and I could see from day to day that he did not improve; but each evening he would be gay and lively, and he liked the entire family to gather around, while he became really hilarious over the various happenings of the day.

It was only a few days before we sailed that the very severe attacks returned. The night of the 8th was a hard one. The doctors were summoned, and it was only after repeated injections of morphine that the pain had been eased. When I returned in the early morning he was sitting in his chair trying to sing, after his old morning habit. He took my hand and said:

"Well, I had a picturesque night. Every pain I had was on exhibition." He looked out the window at the sunlight on the bay and green dotted islands. "'Sparkling and bright in the liquid light,'" he quoted. "That's Hoffman. Anything left of Hoffman?"

"No," I said.

"I must watch for the *Bermudian* and see if she salutes," he said, presently. "The captain knows I am here sick, and he blows two short whistles just as they come up behind that little island. Those are for me."

He said he could breathe easier if he could lean forward, and I placed a card-table in front of him. His breakfast came in, and a little later he became quite gay. He drifted to Macaulay again, and spoke of King James's plot to assassinate William III., and how the clergy had brought themselves to see that there was no difference between killing a king in battle and by assassination. He had taken his seat by the window to watch for the *Bermudian*. She came down the bay presently, her bright-red stacks towering vividly above the green island. It was a brilliant morning, the sky and the water a marvelous blue. He watched her anxiously and without speaking. Suddenly there were two white puffs of steam, and two short, hoarse notes went up from her.

"Those are for me," he said, his face full of contentment. "Captain Fraser does not forget me."

There followed another bad night. My room was only a little distance away, and Claude came for me. I do not think any of us thought he would survive it; but he slept at last, or at least dozed. In the morning he said:

"That breast pain stands watch all night and the short

breath all day. I am losing enough sleep to supply a worn-out army. I want a jugful of that hypnotic injunction every night and every morning."

We began to fear now that he would not be able to sail on the 12th; but by great good-fortune he had wonderfully improved by the 11th, so much so that I began to believe, if once he could be in Stormfield, where the air was more vigorous, he might easily survive the summer. The humid atmosphere of the season increased the difficulty of his breathing.

That evening he was unusually merry. Mr. and Mrs. Allen and Helen and myself went in to wish him good night. He was loath to let us leave, but was reminded that he would sail in the morning, and that the doctor had insisted that he must be quiet and lie still in bed and rest. He was never one to be very obedient. A little later Mrs. Allen and I, in the sitting-room, heard some one walking softly outside on the veranda. We went out there, and he was marching up and down in his dressing-gown as unconcerned as if he were not an invalid at all. He hadn't felt sleepy, he said, and thought a little exercise would do him good. Perhaps it did, for he slept soundly that night—a great blessing.

Mr. Allen had chartered a special tug to come to Bay House landing in the morning and take him to the ship. He was carried in a little hand-chair to the tug, and all the way out he seemed light-spirited, anything but an invalid. The sailors carried him again in the chair to his state-room, and he bade those dear Bermuda friends good-by, and we sailed away.

As long as I remember anything I shall remember the forty-eight hours of that homeward voyage. It was a brief two days as time is measured; but as time is lived it has taken its place among those unmeasured periods by the side of which even years do not count.

At first he seemed quite his natural self, and asked for

a catalogue of the ship's library, and selected some me
moirs of the Countess of Cardigan for his reading. He
asked also for the second volume of Carlyle's *French
Revolution*, which he had with him. But we ran immediately into the more humid, more oppressive air of the Gulf
Stream, and his breathing became at first difficult, then
next to impossible. There were two large port-holes,
which I opened; but presently he suggested that it would
be better outside. It was only a step to the main-deck,
and no passengers were there. I had a steamer-chair
brought, and with Claude supported him to it and bundled him with rugs; but it had grown damp and chilly,
and his breathing did not improve. It seemed to me
that the end might come at any moment, and this thought
was in his own mind, for once in the effort for breath he
managed to say:

"I am going—I shall be gone in a moment."

Breath came; but I realized then that even his cabin
was better than this. I steadied him back to his berth
and shut out most of that deadly dampness. He asked
for the "hypnotic injunction" (for his humor never left
him), and though it was not yet the hour prescribed I
could not deny it. It was impossible for him to lie down,
even to recline, without great distress. The opiate made
him drowsy, and he longed for the relief of sleep; but
when it seemed about to possess him the struggle for air
would bring him upright.

During the more comfortable moments he spoke quite
in the old way, and time and again made an effort to
read, and reached for his pipe or a cigar which lay in the
little berth hammock at his side. I held the match, and
he would take a puff or two with satisfaction. Then the
peace of it would bring drowsiness, and while I supported
him there would come a few moments, perhaps, of precious sleep. Only a few moments, for the devil of suffocation was always lying in wait to bring him back for fresh

tortures. Over and over again this was repeated, varied by him being steadied on his feet or sitting on the couch opposite the berth. In spite of his suffering, two dominant characteristics remained—the sense of humor, and tender consideration for another.

Once when the ship rolled and his hat fell from the hook, and made the circuit of the cabin floor, he said:

"The ship is passing the hat."

Again he said:

"I am sorry for you, Paine, but I can't help it—I can't hurry this dying business. Can't you give me enough of the hypnotic injunction to put an end to me?"

He thought if I could arrange the pillows so he could sit straight up it would not be necessary to support him, and then I could sit on the couch and read while he tried to doze. He wanted me to read *Jude*, he said, so we could talk about it. I got all the pillows I could and built them up around him, and sat down with the book, and this seemed to give him contentment. He would doze off a little and then come up with a start, his piercing, agate eyes searching me out to see if I was still there. Over and over—twenty times in an hour—this was repeated. When I could deny him no longer I administered the opiate, but it never completely possessed him or gave him entire relief.

As I looked at him there, so reduced in his estate, I could not but remember all the labor of his years, and all the splendid honor which the world had paid to him. Something of this may have entered his mind, too, for once, when I offered him some of the milder remedies which we had brought, he said:

"After forty years of public effort I have become just a target for medicines."

The program of change from berth to the floor, from floor to the couch, from the couch back to the berth among the pillows, was repeated again and again, he always thinking of the trouble he might be making, rarely uttering any complaint; but once he said:

"I never guessed that I was not going to outlive John Bigelow." And again:

"This is such a mysterious disease. If we only had a bill of particulars we'd have something to swear at."

Time and again he picked up Carlyle or the Cardigan *Memoirs*, and read, or seemed to read, a few lines; but then the drowsiness would come and the book would fall. Time and again he attempted to smoke, or in his drowse simulated the motion of placing a cigar to his lips and puffing in the old way.

Two dreams beset him in his momentary slumber—one of a play in which the title-rôle of the general manager was always unfilled. He spoke of this now and then when it had passed, and it seemed to amuse him. The other was a discomfort: a college assembly was attempting to confer upon him some degree which he did not want. Once, half roused, he looked at me searchingly and asked:

"Isn't there something I can resign and be out of all this? They keep trying to confer that degree upon me and I don't want it." Then realizing, he said: "I am like a bird in a cage: always expecting to get out, and always beaten back by the wires." And, somewhat later: "Oh, it is such a mystery, and it takes so long."

Toward the evening of the first day, when it grew dark outside, he asked:

"How long have we been on this voyage?"

I answered that this was the end of the first day.

"How many more are there?" he asked.

"Only one, and two nights."

"We'll never make it," he said. "It's an eternity."

"But we must on Clara's account," I told him, and I estimated that Clara would be more than half-way across the ocean by now.

"It is a losing race," he said; "no ship can outsail death."

It has been written—I do not know with what proof—that certain great dissenters have recanted with the approach of death—have become weak, and afraid to ignore old traditions in the face of the great mystery. I wish to write here that Mark Twain, as he neared the end, showed never a single tremor of fear or even of reluctance. I have dwelt upon these hours when suffering was upon him, and death the imminent shadow, in order to show that at the end he was as he had always been, neither more nor less, and never less than brave.

Once, during a moment when he was comfortable and quite himself, he said, earnestly:

"When I seem to be dying I don't want to be stimulated back to life. I want to be made comfortable to go."

There was not a vestige of hesitation; there was no grasping at straws, no suggestion of dread.

Somehow those two days and nights went by. Once, when he was partially relieved by the opiate, I slept, while Claude watched; and again, in the fading end of the last night, when we had passed at length into the cold, bracing northern air, and breath had come back to him, and with it sleep.

Relatives, physicians, and news-gatherers were at the dock to welcome him. He was awake, and the northern air had brightened him, though it was the chill, I suppose, that brought on the pains in his breast, which, fortunately, he had escaped during the voyage. It was not a prolonged attack, and it was, blessedly, the last one.

An invalid-carriage had been provided, and a compartment secured on the afternoon express to Redding—the same train that had taken him there two years before. Dr. Robert H. Halsey and Dr. Edward Quintard attended him, and he made the journey really in cheerful comfort, for he could breathe now, and in the relief came back old interests. Half reclining on the couch, he looked through the afternoon papers. It happened curiously that Charles Harvey Genung, who, something more than four years earlier, had been so largely responsible for my association with Mark Twain, was on the same train, in the same coach, bound for his country-place at New Hartford.

Lounsbury was waiting with the carriage, and on that still, sweet April evening we drove him to Stormfield much as we had driven him two years before. Now and then he mentioned the apparent backwardness of the season, for only a few of the trees were beginning to show their green. As we drove into the lane that led to the Stormfield entrance, he said:

"Can we see where you have built your billiard-room?"

The gable showed above the trees, and I pointed it out to him.

"It looks quite imposing," he said.

I think it was the last outside interest he ever showed in anything.

He had been carried from the ship and from the train, but when we drew up to Stormfield, where Mrs. Paine, with Katie Leary and others of the household, was waiting to greet him, he stepped from the carriage alone with something of his old lightness, and with all his old courtliness, and offered each one his hand. Then, in the canvas chair which we had brought, Claude and I carried him up-stairs to his room and delivered him to the physicians, and to the comforts and blessed air of home. This was Thursday evening, April 14, 1910.

CCXCIII

THE RETURN TO THE INVISIBLE

THERE would be two days more before Ossip and Clara Gabrilowitsch could arrive. Clemens remained fairly bright and comfortable during this interval, though he clearly was not improving. The physicians denied him the morphine, now, as he no longer suffered acutely. But he craved it, and once, when I went in, he said, rather mournfully:

"They won't give me the subcutaneous any more."

It was Sunday morning when Clara came. He was cheerful and able to talk quite freely. He did not dwell upon his condition, I think, but spoke rather of his plans for the summer. At all events, he did not then suggest that he counted the end so near; but a day later it became evident to all that his stay was very brief. His breathing was becoming heavier, though it seemed not to give him much discomfort. His articulation also became affected. I think the last continuous talking he did was to Dr. Halsey on the evening of April 17th—the day of Clara's arrival. A mild opiate had been administered,· and he said he wished to talk himself to sleep. He recalled one of his old subjects, Dual Personality, and discussed various instances that flitted through his mind—Jekyll and Hyde phases in literature and fact. He became drowsier as he talked. He said at last:

"This is a peculiar kind of disease. It does not invite you to read; it does not invite you to be read to; it does not invite you to talk, nor to enjoy any of the usual sick-room methods of treatment. What kind of a disease is *that?* Some kinds of sicknesses have pleasant features about them. You can read and smoke and have only to lie still."

And a little later he added:

"It is singular, very singular, the laws of mentality—vacuity. I put out my hand to reach a book or newspaper which I have been reading most glibly, and it isn't there, not a suggestion of it."

He coughed violently, and afterward commented:

"If one gets to meddling with a cough it very soon gets the upper hand and is meddling with you. That is my opinion—of seventy-four years' growth."

The news of his condition, everywhere published, brought great heaps of letters, but he could not see them. A few messages were reported to him. At intervals he read a little. Suetonius and Carlyle lay on the bed beside him, and he would pick them up as the spirit moved him and read a paragraph or a page. Sometimes, when I saw him thus—the high color still in his face, and the clear light in his eyes—I said: "It is not reality. He is not going to die." On Tuesday, the 19th, he asked me to tell Clara to come and sing to him. It was a heavy requirement, but she somehow found strength to sing some of the Scotch airs which he loved, and he seemed soothed and comforted. When she came away he bade her good-by, saying that he might not see her again.

But he lingered through the next day and the next. His mind was wandering a little on Wednesday, and his speech became less and less articulate; but there were intervals when he was quite clear, quite vigorous, and he apparently suffered little. We did not know it, then, but the mysterious messenger of his birth-year, so long anticipated by him, appeared that night in the sky.[1]

[1] The perihelion of Halley's Comet for 1835 was November 16th; for 1910 it was April 20th.

On Thursday morning, the 21st, his mind was generally clear, and it was said by the nurses that he read a little from one of the volumes on his bed, from the Suetonius, or from one of the volumes of Carlyle.   Early in the forenoon he sent word by Clara that he wished to see me, and when I came in he spoke of two unfinished manuscripts which he wished me to "throw away," as he briefly expressed it, for he had not many words left now. I assured him that I would take care of them, and he pressed my hand.   It was his last word to me.

Once or twice that morning he tried to write some request which he could not put into intelligible words.

MARK TWAIN'S LAST WRITING: A REQUEST FOR HIS SPECTACLES AND A GLASS PITCHER

And once he spoke to Gabrilowitsch, who, he said, could understand him better than the others.   Most of the time he dozed.

Somewhat after midday, when Clara was by him, he roused up and took her hand, and seemed to speak with less effort.

"Good-by," he said, and Dr. Quintard, who was standing near, thought he added: "If we meet"—but the

1577

words were very faint. He looked at her for a little while, without speaking, then he sank into a doze, and from it passed into a deeper slumber, and did not heed us any more.

Through that peaceful spring afternoon the life-wave ebbed lower and lower. It was about half past six, and the sun lay just on the horizon when Dr. Quintard noticed that the breathing, which had gradually become more subdued, broke a little. There was no suggestion of any struggle. The noble head turned a little to one side, there was a fluttering sigh, and the breath that had been unceasing through seventy-four tumultuous years had stopped forever.

He had entered into the estate envied so long. In his own words—the words of one of his latest memoranda:

"He had arrived at the dignity of death—the only earthly dignity that is not artificial—the only safe one. The others are traps that can beguile to humiliation.

"Death—the only immortal who treats us all alike, whose pity and whose peace and whose refuge are for all —the soiled and the pure—the rich and the poor—the loved and the unloved."

THE LAST RITES

IT is not often that a whole world mourns. Nations have often mourned a hero—and races—but perhaps never before had the entire world really united in tender sorrow for the death of any man.

In one of his aphorisms he wrote: "Let us endeavor so to live that when we come to die even the undertaker will be sorry." And it was thus that Mark Twain himself had lived.

No man had ever so reached the heart of the world, and one may not even attempt to explain just why. Let us only say that it was because he was so limitlessly human that every other human heart, in whatever sphere or circumstance, responded to his touch. From every remote corner of the globe the cables of condolence swept in; every printed sheet in Christendom was filled with lavish tribute; pulpits forgot his heresies and paid him honor. No king ever died that received so rich a homage as his. To quote or to individualize would be to cheapen this vast offering.

We took him to New York to the Brick Church, and Dr. Henry van Dyke spoke only a few simple words, and Joseph Twichell came from Hartford and delivered brokenly a prayer from a heart wrung with double grief, for Harmony, his wife, was nearing the journey's end, and a telegram that summoned him to her death-bed came before the services ended.

Mark Twain, dressed in the white he loved so well,

lay there with the nobility of death upon him, while a multitude of those who loved him passed by and looked at his face for the last time. The flowers, of which so many had been sent, were banked around him; but on the casket itself lay a single laurel wreath which Dan Beard and his wife had woven from the laurel which grows on Stormfield hill. He was never more beautiful than as he lay there, and it was an impressive scene to see those thousands file by, regard him for a moment gravely, thoughtfully, and pass on. All sorts were there, rich and poor; some crossed themselves, some saluted, some paused a little to take a closer look; but no one offered even to pick a flower. Howells came, and in his book he says:

I looked a moment at the face I knew so well; and it was patient with the patience I had so often seen in it: something of a puzzle, a great silent dignity, an assent to what must be from the depths of a nature whose tragical seriousness broke in the laughter which the unwise took for the whole of him.

That night we went with him to Elmira, and next day—a somber day of rain—he lay in those stately parlors that had seen his wedding-day, and where Susy had lain, and Mrs. Clemens, and Jean, while Dr. Eastman spoke the words of peace which separate us from our mortal dead. Then in the quiet, steady rain of that Sunday afternoon we laid him beside those others, where he sleeps well, though some have wished that, like De Soto, he might have been laid to rest in the bed of that great river which must always be associated with his name.

CCXCV

MARK TWAIN'S RELIGION

THERE is such a finality about death; however interesting it may be as an experience, one cannot discuss it afterward with one's friends. I have thought it a great pity that Mark Twain could not discuss, with Howells say, or with Twichell, the sensations and the particulars of the change, supposing there be a recognizable change, in that transition of which we have speculated so much, with such slender returns. No one ever debated the undiscovered country more than he. In his whimsical, semi-serious fashion he had considered all the possibilities of the future state—orthodox and otherwise—and had drawn picturesquely original conclusions. He had sent Captain Stormfield in a dream to report the aspects of the early Christian heaven. He had examined the scientific aspects of the more subtle philosophies. He had considered spiritualism, transmigration, the various esoteric doctrines, and in the end he had logically made up his mind that death concludes all, while with that less logical hunger which survives in every human heart he had never ceased to expect an existence beyond the grave. His disbelief and his pessimism were identical in their structure. They were of his mind; never of his heart.

Once a woman said to him:

"Mr. Clemens, you are not a pessimist, you only think you are." And she might have added, with equal force and truth:

"You are not a disbeliever in immortality; you only think you are."

Nothing could have conveyed more truly his attitude toward life and death. His belief in God, the Creator, was absolute; but it was a God far removed from the Creator of his early teaching. Every man builds his God according to his own capacities. Mark Twain's God was of colossal proportions—so vast, indeed, that the constellated stars were but molecules in His veins—a God as big as space itself.

Mark Twain had many moods, and he did not always approve of his own God; but when he altered his conception, it was likely to be in the direction of enlargement —a further removal from the human conception, and the problem of what we call our lives.

In 1906 he wrote:[1]

Let us now consider the real God, the genuine God, the great God, the sublime and supreme God, the authentic Creator of the real universe, whose remotenesses are visited by comets only— comets unto which incredibly distant Neptune is merely an outpost, a Sandy Hook to homeward-bound specters of the deeps of space that have not glimpsed it before for generations—a universe not made with hands and suited to an astronomical nursery, but spread abroad through the illimitable reaches of space by the fiat of the real God just mentioned, by comparison with whom the gods whose myriads infest the feeble imaginations of men are as a swarm of gnats scattered and lost in the infinitudes of the empty sky.

At an earlier period—the date is not exactly fixable, but the stationery used and the handwriting suggest the early eighties—he set down a few concisely written pages of conclusions—conclusions from which he did not deviate materially in after years. The document follows:

[1] See also 1870, chap. lxxviii; 1899, chap. ccv; and various talks, 1906-07, etc.

MARK TWAIN'S RELIGION

I believe in God the Almighty.

I do not believe He has ever sent a message to man by anybody, or delivered one to him by word of mouth, or made Himself visible to mortal eyes at any time in any place.

I believe that the Old and New Testaments were imagined and written by man, and that no line in them was authorized by God, much less inspired by Him.

I think the goodness, the justice, and the mercy of God are manifested in His works: I perceive that they are manifested toward me in this life; the logical conclusion is that they will be manifested toward me in the life to come, if there should be one.

I do not believe in special providences. I believe that the universe is governed by strict and immutable laws. If one man's family is swept away by a pestilence and another man's spared it is only the law working: God is not interfering in that small matter, either against the one man or in favor of the other.

I cannot see how eternal punishment hereafter could accomplish any good end, therefore I am not able to believe in it. To chasten a man in order to perfect him might be reasonable enough; to annihilate him when he shall have proved himself incapable of reaching perfection might be reasonable enough; but to roast him forever for the mere satisfaction of seeing him roast would not be reasonable—even the atrocious God imagined by the Jews would tire of the spectacle eventually.

There may be a hereafter and there may *not* be. I am wholly indifferent about it. If I am appointed to live again I feel sure it will be for some more sane and useful purpose than to flounder about for ages in a lake of fire and brimstone for having violated a confusion of ill-defined and contradictory rules said (but not evidenced) to be of divine institution. If annihilation is to follow death I shall not be aware of the annihilation, and therefore shall not care a straw about it.

I believe that the world's moral laws are the outcome of the world's experience. It needed no God to come down out of heaven to tell men that murder and theft and the other immoralities were bad, both for the individual who commits them and for society which suffers from them.

If I break all these moral laws I cannot see how I injure God by it, for He is beyond the reach of injury from me—I could as easily injure a planet by throwing mud at it. It seems to me that my misconduct could only injure me and other men. I cannot benefit God by obeying these moral laws—I could as easily benefit the planet by withholding my mud. (Let these sentences be read in the light of the fact that I believe I have received moral laws *only* from man — none whatever from God.) Consequently I do not see why I should be either punished or rewarded hereafter for the deeds I do here.

If the tragedies of life shook his faith in the goodness and justice and the mercy of God as manifested toward himself, he at any rate never questioned that the wider scheme of the universe was attuned to the immutable law which contemplates nothing less than absolute harmony. I never knew him to refer to this particular document; but he never destroyed it and never amended it, nor is it likely that he would have done either had it been presented to him for consideration even during the last year of his life.

He was never intentionally dogmatic. In a memorandum on a fly-leaf of Moncure D. Conway's *Sacred Anthology* he wrote:

RELIGION

The easy confidence with which I know another man's religion is folly teaches me to suspect that my own is also.

MARK TWAIN, 19th Cent. A.D.

And in another note:

I would not interfere with any one's religion, either to strengthen it or to weaken it. I am not able to believe one's religion can affect his hereafter one way or the other, no matter what that religion may be. But it may easily be a great comfort to him in this life—hence it is a valuable possession to him.

Mark Twain's religion was a faith too wide for doctrines—a benevolence too limitless for creeds. From the beginning he strove against oppression, sham, and evil in every form. He despised meanness; he resented with every drop of blood in him anything that savored of persecution or a curtailment of human liberties. It was a religion identified with his daily life and his work. He lived as he wrote, and he wrote as he believed. His favorite weapon was humor—good-humor—with logic behind it. A sort of glorified truth it was—truth wearing a smile of gentleness, hence all the more quickly heeded.

"He will be remembered with the great humorists of all time," says Howells, "with Cervantes, with Swift, or with any others worthy of his company; none of them was his equal in humanity."

Mark Twain understood the needs of men because he was himself supremely human. In one of his dictations he said:

I have found that there is no ingredient of the race which I do not possess in either a small or a large way. When it is small, as compared with the same ingredient in somebody else, there is still enough of it for all the purposes of examination.

With his strength he had inherited the weaknesses of our kind. With him, as with another, a myriad of dreams and schemes and purposes daily flitted by. With him, as with another, the spirit of desire led him often to a high mountain-top, and was not rudely put aside, but lingeringly—and often invited to return. With him, as with another, a crowd of jealousies and resentments, and wishes for the ill of others, daily went seething and scorching along the highways of the soul. With him, as with another, regret, remorse, and shame stood at the bedside during long watches of the night; and in the end, with him, the better thing triumphed—forgiveness and generosity and justice—in a word, Humanity. Certain of his aphorisms and memoranda each in itself constitutes an epitome of Mark Twain's creed. His paraphrase, "When in doubt tell the truth," is one of these, and he embodied his whole attitude toward Infinity when in one of his stray pencilings he wrote:

Why, even poor little ungodlike man holds himself responsible for the welfare of his child to the extent of his ability. It is all that we require of God.

CCXCVI

POSTSCRIPT

EVERY life is a drama—a play in all its particulars; comedy, farce, tragedy—all the elements are there. To examine in detail any life, however conspicuous or obscure, is to become amazed not only at the inevitable sequence of events, but at the interlinking of details, often far removed, into a marvelously intricate pattern which no art can hope to reproduce, and can only feebly imitate.

The biographer may reconstruct an episode, present a picture, or reflect a mood by which the reader is enabled to feel something of the glow of personality and know, perhaps, a little of the substance of the past. In so far as the historian can accomplish this his work is a success. At best his labor will be pathetically incomplete, for whatever its detail and its resemblance to life, these will record mainly but an outward expression, behind which was the mighty sweep and tumult of unwritten thought, the overwhelming proportion of any life, which no other human soul can ever really know.

Mark Twain's appearance on the stage of the world was a succession of dramatic moments. He was always exactly in the setting. Whatever he did, or whatever came to him, was timed for the instant of greatest effect. At the end he was more widely observed and loved and honored than ever before, and at the right moment and in the right manner he died.

How little one may tell of such a life as his! He traveled

POSTSCRIPT

always such a broad and brilliant highway, with plumes
flying and crowds following after. Such a whirling panorama of life, and death, and change! I have written so
much, and yet I have put so much aside—and often
the best things, it seemed afterward, perhaps because
each in its way was best and the variety infinite. One
may only strive to be faithful—and I would make it
better if I could.

APPENDIX

APPENDIX A

LETTER FROM ORION CLEMENS TO MISS WOOD CONCERNING HENRY CLEMENS

(See Chapter xxvi)

KEOKUK, IOWA, *October 3, 1858.*

MISS WOOD,—My mother having sent me your kind letter, with a request that myself and wife should write to you, I hasten to do so.

In my memory I can go away back to Henry's infancy; I see his large, blue eyes intently regarding my father when he rebuked him for his credulity in giving full faith to the boyish idea of planting his marbles, expecting a crop therefrom; then comes back the recollection of the time when, standing we three alone by our father's grave, I told them always to remember that brothers should be kind to each other; afterward I see Henry returning from school with his books for the last time. He must go into my printing-office. He learned rapidly. A word of encouragement or a word of discouragement told upon his organization electrically. I could see the effects in his day's work. Sometimes I would say, "Henry!" He would stand full front with his eyes upon mine—all attention. If I commanded him to do something, without a word he was off instantly, probably in a run. If a cat was to be drowned or shot Sam (though unwilling yet firm) was selected for the work. If a stray kitten was to be fed and taken care of Henry was expected to attend to it, and he would faithfully do so. So they grew up, and many was the grave lecture commenced by ma, to the effect that Sam was misleading and spoiling Henry. But the lectures were never concluded, for Sam would reply with a witticism, or dry, unexpected humor, that would drive the lecture clean out of my mother's mind, and change it to a

1591

laugh. Those were happier days. My mother was as lively as any girl of sixteen. She is not so now. And sister Pamela I have described in describing Henry; for she was his counterpart. The blow falls crushingly on her. But the boys grew up—Sam a rugged, brave, quick-tempered, generous-hearted fellow, Henry quiet, observing, thoughtful, leaning on Sam for protection; Sam and I too leaning on him for knowledge picked up from conversation or books, for Henry seemed never to forget anything, and devoted much of his leisure hours to reading.

Henry is gone! His death was horrible! How I could have sat by him, hung over him, watched day and night every change of expression, and ministered to every want in my power that I could discover. This was denied to me, but Sam, whose organization is such as to feel the utmost extreme of every feeling, was there. Both his capacity of enjoyment and his capacity of suffering are greater than mine; and knowing how it would have affected me to see so sad a scene, I can somewhat appreciate Sam's sufferings. In this time of great trouble, when my two brothers, whose heartstrings have always been a part of my own, were suffering the utmost stretch of mortal endurance, you were there, like a good angel, to aid and console, and I bless and thank you for it with my whole heart. I thank all who helped them then; I thank them for the flowers they sent to Henry, for the tears that fell for their sufferings, and when he died, and all of them for all the kind attentions they bestowed upon the poor boys. We thank the physicians, and we shall always gratefully remember the kindness of the gentleman who at so much expense to himself enabled us to deposit Henry's remains by our father.

With many kind wishes for your future welfare, I remain your earnest friend,

Respectfully,
ORION CLEMENS.

APPENDIX B

MARK TWAIN'S BURLESQUE OF CAPTAIN ISAIAH SELLERS

(See Chapter xxvii)

The item which served as a text for the "Sergeant Fathom" communication was as follows:

VICKSBURG, *May 4, 1859.*

My opinion for the benefit of the citizens of New Orleans: The water is higher this far up than it has been since 1815. My opinion is that the water will be four feet deep in Canal Street before the first of next June. Mrs. Turner's plantation at the head of Big Black Island is all under water, and it has not been since 1815. I. SELLERS.[1]

THE BURLESQUE

INTRODUCTORY

Our friend Sergeant Fathom, one of the oldest cub pilots on the river, and now on the Railroad Line steamer *Trombone,* sends us a rather bad account concerning the state of the river. Sergeant Fathom is a "cub" of much experience, and although we are loath to coincide in his view of the matter, we give his note a place in our columns, only hoping that his prophecy will not be verified in this instance. While introducing the Sergeant, "we consider it but simple justice (we quote from a friend of his) to remark that he is distinguished for being, in pilot phrase, 'close,' as well as superhumanly 'safe.'" It is a well-known fact that he has made fourteen hundred and fifty trips in the New Orleans and St. Louis trade without causing serious

---

[1] Captain Sellers, as in this case, sometimes signed his own name to his communications.

damage to a steamboat. This astonishing success is attributed to the fact that he seldom runs his boat after early candle-light. It is related of the Sergeant that upon one occasion he actually ran the chute of Glasscock's Island, down-stream, *in the night*, and at a time, too, when the river was scarcely more than bank full. His method of accomplishing this feat proves what we have just said of his "safeness"—he sounded the chute first, and then built a fire at the head of the island to run by. As to the Sergeant's "closeness," we have heard it whispered that he once went up to the right of the "Old Hen,"[1] but this is probably a pardonable little exaggeration, prompted by the love and admiration in which he is held by various ancient dames of his acquaintance (for albeit the Sergeant *may* have already numbered the allotted years of man, still his form is erect, his step is firm, his hair retains its sable hue, and, more than all, he hath a winning way about him, an air of docility and sweetness, if you will, and a smoothness of speech, together with an exhaustless fund of funny sayings; and, lastly, an overflowing stream, without beginning, or middle, or end, of astonishing reminiscences of the ancient Mississippi, which, taken together, form a *tout ensemble* which is sufficient excuse for the tender epithet which is, by common consent, applied to him by all those ancient dames aforesaid, of "che-arming creature!"). As the Sergeant has been longer on the river, and is better acquainted with it than any other "cub" extant, his remarks are entitled to far more consideration, and are always read with the deepest interest by high and low, rich and poor, from "Kiho" to Kamschatka, for let it be known that his fame extends to the uttermost parts of the earth:

THE COMMUNICATION

> R.R. Steamer *Trombone*,
> VICKSBURG, *May 8, 1859.*

The river from New Orleans up to Natchez is higher than it has been since the niggers were executed (which was in the fall of 1813), and my opinion is that if the rise continues at this rate the water will be on the roof of the St. Charles Hotel before

---

[1] Glasscock's Island and the "Old Hen" were phenomenally safe places.

APPENDIX

the middle of January. The point at Cairo, which has not even been moistened by the river since 1813, is now entirely under water.

However, Mr. Editor, the inhabitants of the Mississippi Valley should not act precipitately and sell their plantations at a sacrifice on account of this prophecy of mine, for I shall proceed to convince them of a great fact in regard to this matter, viz.: that the tendency of the Mississippi is to rise less and less high every year (with an occasional variation of the rule), that such has been the case for many centuries, and eventually that it will cease to rise at all. Therefore, I would hint to the planters, as we say in an innocent little parlor game commonly called "draw," that if they can only "stand the rise" this time they may enjoy the comfortable assurance that the old river's banks will never hold a "full" again during their natural lives.

In the summer of 1763 I came down the river on the old first *Jubilee*. She was new then, however; a singular sort of a single-engine boat, with a Chinese captain and a Choctaw crew, forecastle on her stern, wheels in the center, and the jackstaff "nowhere," for I steered her with a window-shutter, and when we wanted to land we sent a line ashore and "rounded her to" with a yoke of oxen.

Well, sir, we wooded off the top of the big bluff above Selma—the only dry land visible—and waited there three weeks, swapping knives and playing "seven up" with the Indians, waiting for the river to fall. Finally, it fell about a hundred feet, and we went on. One day we rounded to, and I got in a horse-trough, which my partner borrowed from the Indians up there at Selma while they were at prayers, and went down to sound around No. 8, and while I was gone my partner got aground on the hills at Hickman. After three days' labor we finally succeeded in sparring her off with a capstan bar, and went on to Memphis. By the time we got there the river had subsided to such an extent that we were able to land where the Gayoso House now stands. We finished loading at Memphis, and loaded part of the stone for the present St. Louis Court House (which was then in process of erection), to be taken up on our return trip.

You can form some conception, by these memoranda, of how high the water was in 1763. In 1775 it did not rise so high by thirty feet; in 1790 it missed the original mark at least sixty-five feet; in 1797, one hundred and fifty feet; and in 1806, nearly two hundred and fifty feet. These were "high-water" years. The "high waters" since then have been so insignificant that I have scarcely taken the trouble to notice them. Thus, you will perceive that the planters need not feel uneasy. The river may make an occasional spasmodic effort at a flood, but the time is approaching when it will cease to rise altogether.

In conclusion, sir, I will condescend to hint at the foundation of these arguments: When me and De Soto discovered the Mississippi I could stand at Bolivar Landing (several miles above "Roaring Waters Bar") and pitch a biscuit to the main shore on the other side, and in low water we waded across at Donaldsonville. The gradual widening and deepening of the river is the whole secret of the matter.

Yours, etc.

SERGEANT FATHOM.

APPENDIX C

I

MARK TWAIN'S EMPIRE CITY HOAX

(See Chapter xli)

THE LATEST SENSATION

A Victim to Jeremy Diddling Trustees—He Cuts his Throat from Ear to Ear, Scalps his Wife, and Dashes Out the Brains of Six Helpless Children!

From Abram Curry, who arrived here yesterday afternoon from Carson, we learn the following particulars concerning a bloody massacre which was committed in Ormsby County night before last. It seems that during the past six months a man named P. Hopkins, or Philip Hopkins, has been residing with his family in the old log-house just at the edge of the great pine forest which lies between Empire City and Dutch Nick's. The family consisted of nine children—five girls and four boys— the oldest of the group, Mary, being nineteen years old, and the youngest, Tommy, about a year and a half. Twice in the past two months Mrs. Hopkins, while visiting Carson, expressed fears concerning the sanity of her husband, remarking that of late he had been subject to fits of violence, and that during the prevalence of one of these he had threatened to take her life. It was Mrs. Hopkins's misfortune to be given to exaggeration, however, and but little attention was given to what she said.

About 10 o'clock on Monday evening Hopkins dashed into Carson on horseback, with his throat cut from ear to ear, and bearing in his hand a reeking scalp, from which the warm, smoking blood was still dripping, and fell in a dying condition in front of the Magnolia saloon. Hopkins expired, in the course of five minutes, without speaking. The long, red hair of the scalp he bore marked it as that of Mrs. Hopkins. A number of citizens, headed by Sheriff Gasherie, mounted at once and rode down to Hopkins's house, where a ghastly scene met their eyes. The scalpless corpse of Mrs. Hopkins lay across the threshold, with her head split open and her right hand almost severed from the wrist. Near her lay the ax with which the murderous deed had been committed. In one of the bedrooms six of the children were found, one in bed and the others scattered about the floor. They were all dead. Their brains had evidently been dashed out with a club, and every mark about them seemed to have been made with a blunt instrument. The children must have struggled hard for their lives, as articles of clothing and broken furniture were strewn about the room in the utmost confusion. Julia and Emma, aged respectively fourteen and seventeen, were found in the kitchen, bruised and insensible, but it is thought their recovery is possible. The eldest girl, Mary, must have sought refuge, in her terror, in the garret, as her body was found there frightfully mutilated, and the knife with which her wounds had been inflicted still sticking in her side. The two girls Julia and Emma, who had recovered sufficiently to be able to talk yesterday morning, declare that their father knocked them down with a billet of wood and stamped on them. They think they were the first attacked. They further state that Hopkins had shown evidence of derangement all day, but had exhibited no violence. He flew into a passion and attempted to murder them because they advised him to go to bed and compose his mind.

Curry says Hopkins was about forty-two years of age, and a native of western Pennsylvania; he was always affable and polite, and until very recently no one had ever heard of his ill-treating his family. He had been a heavy owner in the best mines of Virginia and Gold Hill, but when the San Francisco papers exposed our game of cooking dividends in order to bolster up our stocks he grew afraid and sold out, and invested an immense amount in the Spring Valley Water Company, of San Francisco. He was advised to do this by a relative of his, one of the editors of the San Francisco *Bulletin*, who had suffered pecuniarily by the dividend-cooking system as applied to the Daney Mining Company recently. Hopkins had not long ceased to own in the various claims on the Comstock lead, however,

APPENDIX

when several dividends were cooked on his newly acquired property, their water totally dried up, and Spring Valley stock went down to nothing. It is presumed that this misfortune drove him mad, and resulted in his killing himself and the greater portion of his family. The newspapers of San Francisco permitted this water company to go on borrowing money and cooking dividends, under cover of which the cunning financiers crept out of the tottering concern, leaving the crash to come upon poor and unsuspecting stockholders, without offering to expose the villainy at work. We hope the fearful massacre detailed above may prove the saddest result of their silence.

II

A POEM BY DAN DE QUILLE, WRITTEN DURING MARK TWAIN'S ABSENCE IN SAN FRANCISCO

TO MARK TWAIN

Mount Davidson still soars aloof
  And grandly frowns on Cedar Hill;
The sunshine gilds the Sugar Loaf
  And glimmers on the Desert still;
The Goose Creek Mountains far beyond
  On Heaven's glowing bosom rest—
As often, in your moments fond,
  Your head has lain upon this breast.
    Mark Twain, Mark Twain,
    Ah, when again
  Shall this breast be divinely pressed!

The May returns with many a bird,
  And many a flower of loveliest hue;
The warbling donkey's notes are heard!—
  The sage-bush takes its deepest blue;
And every lovely sight and sound
  Awakens memories sweet and choice

MARK TWAIN

Of hours when I have sat spellbound,
  Charmed by your gentle eyes and voice.
    Mark Twain, Mark Twain,
    Ah, when again
  Shall your voice bid my heart rejoice!

Rude sounds of life in discord blent,
  Rise harshly from the crowded street,
Where sordid souls on trade intent,
  Perfect their groveling schemes in feet;
But brightly on the hill above
  The silver croppings rise to view—
Sweetly as in its first strong love
  My maiden heart cropped out to you.
    Mark Twain, Mark Twain,
    Ah, when again
  That heart will you locate anew!

At morn, at noon, in evening light,
  As in a dream I move around,
For Heaven has lost its loveliest sight
  And earth its sweetest sound—
Do fond emotions softly swell
  For her for whom your steps have strayed—
Or has some flaunting city belle
  Eclipsed your plighted sage-brush maid?
    Mark Twain, Mark Twain,
    Ah, haste again
  To her whose true love you betrayed!

APPENDIX D

FROM MARK TWAIN'S FIRST LECTURE, DELIVERED OCTOBER 2, 1866

(See Chapter liv)

HAWAIIAN IMPORTANCE TO AMERICA

After a full elucidation of the sugar industry of the Sandwich Islands, its profits and possibilities, he said:

I have dwelt upon this subject to show you that these islands have a genuine importance to America—an importance which is not generally appreciated by our citizens. They pay revenues into the United States Treasury now amounting to over a half a million a year.

I do not know what the sugar yield of the world is now, but ten years ago, according to the Patent Office reports, it was 800,000 hogsheads. The Sandwich Islands, properly cultivated by go-ahead Americans, are capable of providing one-third as much themselves. With the Pacific Railroad built, the great China Mail Line of steamers touching at Honolulu—we could stock the islands with Americans and supply a third of the civilized world with sugar—and with the silkiest, longest-stapled cotton this side of the Sea Islands, and the very best quality of rice. . . . The property has got to fall to some heir, and why not the United States?

NATIVE PASSION FOR FUNERALS

They are very fond of funerals. Big funerals are their main weakness. Fine grave clothes, fine funeral appointments, and a long procession are things they take a generous delight in. They are fond of their chief and their king; they reverence them with a genuine reverence and love them with a warm affection, and often look forward to the happiness they will experience in burying them. They will beg, borrow, or steal money enough, and flock from all the islands, to be present at a royal funeral on Oahu. Years ago a Kanaka and his wife were condemned to be hanged for murder. They received the sentence with manifest satisfaction because it gave an opening for a funeral, you know. All they care for is a funeral. It makes but little difference to them whose it is; they would as soon attend their own funeral as anybody else's. This couple were people of consequence, and had landed estates. They sold every foot of ground they had and laid it out in fine clothes to be hung in. And the woman appeared on the scaffold in a white satin dress and slippers and fathoms of gaudy ribbon, and the man was arrayed in a gorgeous vest, blue claw-hammer coat and brass buttons, and white kid gloves. As the noose was adjusted around his neck, he blew his nose with a grand theatrical flourish, so as to show his embroidered white handkerchief. I never, never knew of a couple who enjoyed hanging more than they did.

VIEW FROM HALEAKALA

It is a solemn pleasure to stand upon the summit of the extinct crater of Haleakala, ten thousand feet above the sea, and gaze down into its awful crater, 27 miles in circumference and 220 feet deep, and to picture to yourself the seething world of fire that once swept up out of the tremendous abyss ages ago.

The prodigious funnel is dead and silent now, and even has bushes growing far down in its bottom, where the deep-sea line could hardly have reached in the old times, when the place was filled with liquid lava. These bushes look like parlor shrubs from the summit where you stand, and the file of visitors moving through them on their mules is diminished to a detachment of mice almost; and to them you, standing so high up against the sun, ten thousand feet above their heads, look no larger than a grasshopper.

This in the morning; but at three or four in the afternoon a thousand little patches of white clouds, like handfuls of wool, come drifting noiselessly, one after another, into the crater, like a procession of shrouded phantoms, and circle round and round the vast sides, and settle gradually down and mingle together until the colossal basin is filled to the brim with snowy fog, and all its seared and desolate wonders are hidden from sight.

And then you may turn your back to the crater and look far away upon the broad valley below, with its sugar-houses glinting like white specks in the distance, and the great sugar-fields diminished to green veils amid the lighter-tinted verdure around them, and abroad upon the limitless ocean. But I should not say you look down; you look *up* at these things.

You are ten thousand feet above them, but yet you seem to stand in a basin, with the green islands here and there, and the valleys and the wide ocean, and the remote snow-peak of Mauna Loa, all raised up before and above you, and pictured out like a brightly tinted map hung at the ceiling of a room.

You look up at everything; nothing is below you. It has a singular and startling effect to see a miniature world thus seemingly hung in mid-air.

But soon the white clouds come trooping along in ghostly squadrons and mingle together in heavy masses a quarter of a mile below you and shut out everything—completely hide the sea and all the earth save the pinnacle you stand on. As far as the eye can reach, it finds nothing to rest upon but a boundless plain of clouds tumbled into all manner of fantastic shapes—a billowy ocean of wool aflame with the gold and purple and crimson splendors of the setting sun! And so firm does this grand cloud pavement look that you can hardly persuade yourself that you could not walk upon it; that if you stepped upon it you would plunge headlong and astonish your friends at dinner ten thousand feet below.

Standing on that peak, with all the world shut out by that vast plain of clouds, a feeling of loneliness comes over a man which suggests to his mind the last man at the flood, perched high upon the last rock, with nothing visible on any side but a mournful waste of waters, and the ark departing dimly through the distant mists and leaving him to storm and night and solitude and death!

NOTICE OF MARK TWAIN'S LECTURE

"THE TROUBLE IS OVER"

"The inimitable 'Mark Twain' delivered himself last night of his first lecture on the Sandwich Islands, or anything else.

MARK TWAIN

Some time before the hour appointed to open his head the Academy of Music (on Pine Street) was densely crowded with one of the most fashionable audiences it was ever my privilege to witness during my long residence in this city. The élite of the town were there, and so was the Governor of the State, occupying one of the boxes, whose rotund face was suffused with a halo of mirth during the whole entertainment. The audience promptly notified Mark by the usual sign—stamping—that the auspicious hour had arrived, and presently the lecturer came sidling and swinging out from the left of the stage. His very manner produced a generally vociferous laugh from the assemblage. He opened with an apology, by saying that he had partly succeeded in obtaining a band, but at the last moment the party engaged backed out. He explained that he had hired a man to play the trombone, but he, on learning that he was the only person engaged, came at the last moment and informed him that he could not play. This placed Mark in a bad predicament, and wishing to know his reasons for deserting him at that critical moment, he replied, 'That he wasn't going to make a fool of himself by sitting up there on the stage and blowing his horn all by himself.' After the applause subsided, he assumed a very grave countenance and commenced his remarks proper with the following well-known sentence: 'When, in the course of human events,' etc. He lectured fully an hour and a quarter, and his humorous sayings were interspersed with geographical, agricultural, and statistical remarks, sometimes branching off and reaching beyond, soaring, in the very choicest language, up to the very pinnacle of descriptive power."

COOPER INSTITUTE

The Sandwich Islands.

By Invitation of a large number of prominent Californians and
Citizens of New York,

MARK TWAIN

WILL DELIVER A

Serio-Humorous Lecture

CONCERNING

KANAKADOM

OR,

THE SANDWICH ISLANDS,

AT

COOPER INSTITUTE,

On Monday Evening, May 6, 1867.

TICKETS FIFTY CENTS.

For Sale at CHICKERING & SONS, 652 Broadway, and at the Principal
Hotels.

Doors open at 7 o'clock. The Wisdom will begin to flow at 8.

BROOKLYN ACADEMY OF MUSIC, FEB. 7th

Tickets at 244 Fulton St. and
172 Montague St.

POSTER USED BY MARK TWAIN FOR A BROOKLYN LECTURE,
ABOUT 1869. FROM THE LENOX LIBRARY COLLECTION

APPENDIX E

FROM "THE JUMPING FROG" BOOK (MARK TWAIN'S FIRST PUBLISHED VOLUME)

(See Chapters lviii and lix)

I

ADVERTISEMENT

"Mark Twain" is too well known to the public to require a formal introduction at my hands. By his story of the *Frog* he scaled the heights of popularity at a single jump and won for himself the *sobriquet* of The Wild Humorist of the Pacific Slope. He is also known to fame as The Moralist of the Main; and it is not unlikely that as such he will go down to posterity. It is in his secondary character, as humorist, however, rather than in the primal one of moralist, that I aim to present him in the present volume. And here a ready explanation will be found for the somewhat fragmentary character of many of these sketches; for it was necessary to snatch threads of humor wherever they could be found—very often detaching them from serious articles and moral essays with which they were woven and entangled. Originally written for newspaper publication, many of the articles referred to events of the day, the interest of which has now passed away, and contained local allusions, which the general reader would fail to understand; in such cases excision became imperative. Further than this, remark or comment is unnecessary. Mark Twain never resorts to tricks of spelling nor rhetorical buffoonery for the purpose of provoking a laugh; the vein of his humor runs too rich and deep to make surface gliding necessary. But there are few who can resist the quaint similes, keen satire, and hard, good sense which form the staple of his writing. J. P.

II

"MORAL STATISTICIAN"—I don't want any of your statistics. I took your whole batch and lit my pipe with it. I hate your kind of people. You are always ciphering out how much a man's health is injured, and how much his intellect is impaired, and how many pitiful dollars and cents he wastes in the course of ninety-two years' indulgence in the fatal practice of smoking; and in the equally fatal practice of drinking coffee; and in playing billiards occasionally; and in taking a glass of wine at dinner, etc., etc., etc. . . .

Of course you can save money by denying yourself all these vicious little enjoyments for fifty years; but then what can you do with it? What use can you put it to? Money can't save your infinitesimal soul. All the use that money can be put to is to purchase comfort and enjoyment in this life; therefore, as you are an enemy to comfort and enjoyment, where is the use in accumulating cash? It won't do for you to say that you can use it to better purpose in furnishing good table, and in charities, and in supporting tract societies, because you know yourself that you people who have no petty vices are never known to give away a cent, and that you stint yourselves so in the matter of food that you are always feeble and hungry. And you never dare to laugh in the daytime for fear some poor wretch, seeing you in a good-humor, will try to borrow a dollar of you; and in church you are always down on your knees, with your eyes buried in the cushion, when the contribution-box comes around; and you never give the revenue-officers a true statement of your income. Now you all know all these things yourself, don't you? Very well, then, what is the use of your stringing out your miserable lives to a clean and withered old age? What is the use of your saving money that is so utterly worthless to you? In a word, why don't you go off somewhere and die, and not be always trying to seduce people into becoming as "ornery" and unlovable as you are yourselves, by your ceaseless and villainous "moral statistics"? Now, I don't approve of dissipation, and I don't indulge in it, either; but I haven't a particle of confidence in a man who has no redeeming petty vices whatever, and so I don't want to hear from you any more. I think you are the very same man who read me a long lecture last week about the degrading vice of smoking cigars and then came back, in my absence, with your vile, reprehensible fire-proof gloves on, and carried off my beautiful parlor-stove.

III

FROM "A STRANGE DREAM"

(*Example of Mark Twain's Early Descriptive Writing*)

. . . In due time I stood, with my companion, on the wall of the vast caldron which the natives, ages ago, named *Hale mau mau*—the abyss wherein they were wont to throw the remains of their chiefs, to the end that vulgar feet might never tread above them. We stood there, at dead of night, a mile above the level of the sea, and looked down a thousand feet upon a boiling, surging, roaring ocean of fire!—shaded our eyes from the blinding glare, and gazed far away over the crimson waves with a vague notion that a supernatural fleet, manned by demons and freighted with the damned, might presently sail up out of the remote distance; started when tremendous thunder-bursts shook the earth, and followed with fascinated eyes the grand jets of molten lava that sprang high up toward the zenith and exploded in a world of fiery spray that lit up the somber heavens with an infernal splendor.

"What is your little bonfire of Vesuvius to this?"

My ejaculation roused my companion from his reverie, and we fell into a conversation appropriate to the occasion and the surroundings. We came at last to speak of the ancient custom of casting the bodies of dead chieftains into this fearful caldron; and my comrade, who is of the blood royal, mentioned that the founder of his race, old King Kamehameha the First—that invincible old pagan Alexander—had found other sepulture than the burning depths of the *Hale mau mau*. I grew interested at once; I knew that the mystery of what became of the corpse of the warrior king had never been fathomed; I was aware that there was a legend connected with this matter; and I felt as if there could be no more fitting time to listen to it than the present. The descendant of the Kamehamehas said:

The dead king was brought in royal state down the long, winding road that descends from the rim of the crater to the scorched and chasm-riven plain that lies between the *Hale mau mau* and those beetling walls yonder in the distance. The guards were set and the troops of mourners began the weird wail for the departed. In the middle of the night came a sound of innumerable voices in the air and the rush of invisible wings; the funeral torches wavered, burned blue, and went out. The mourners and watchers fell to the ground paralyzed by fright, and many minutes elapsed before any one dared to move or speak; for they believed that the phantom messengers of the dread Goddess of Fire had been in their midst. When at last a torch was lighted the bier was vacant—the dead monarch had been spirited away!

APPENDIX F

"THE INNOCENTS ABROAD"

(See Chapter lx)

I

LIST OF OFFICERS AND PASSENGERS, "QUAKER CITY" HOLY
LAND PLEASURE EXCURSION

Officers of the ship:
Captain, Charles C. Duncan
Executive officer, Ira Bursley
First officer, William Jones
Second officer, Mr. Burdick
Third officer, Mr. Hinton
First engineer, John Harris
First assistant engineer, Mr.
McDonald
Second assistant engineer, Mr.
McArthur
Purser, J. William Davis

The passengers:
Allen, A. B., New York City
Andrews, Dr. E., Albany, N. Y.
Barry, Major James G., St.
Louis, Mo.
Beach, M. S. and Miss E. B.,
Brooklyn, N. Y.
Beckwith, Thomas S., Cleveland, Mo.
Bell, Mr. and Mrs. R. A. E.,
Portsmouth, O.
Birch, Dr. G. B., Hannibal, O.
Bond, Mr. and Mrs. John W.
and Miss Ada, St. Paul,
Minn.

Bond, Miss Mary E., Plaquemine, La.
Brown, Dr. L. and Miss Kate
L., Circleville, O.
Bullard, the Rev. Henry, Wayland, Mass.
Chadeyne, Miss Carrie D.,
Jersey City
Church, William F., Cincinnati, O.
Clemens, Samuel L., San Francisco
Crane, Albert and A., New
Orleans
Crocker, Mr. and Mrs. T. D.,
Cleveland, O.
Cutter, Bloodgood H., Little
Neck, L. I.
Davis, J. W., New York City
Denny, Colonel W. R., Winchester, Va.
Dimon, Mr. and Mrs. Fred,
Norwalk, Conn.
Duncan, Mrs. C. C., George,
and H., Brooklyn, N. Y.
Fairbanks, Mrs. A. W., Cleveland, O.
Foster, Colonel J. H., Pittsburg, Pa.

Gibson, Mr. and Mrs. William, Jamestown, Pa.

Green, Mrs. J. O., Washington City, D. C.

Greenwood, John, Jr., New York City

Greer, F. H., Boston, Mass.

Griswold, Mr. and Mrs. S. M., Brooklyn, N. Y.

Haldeman, J. S., Harrisburg, Pa.

Heiss, Goddard, Philadelphia, Pa.

Hoel, Captain W. R., Waynesville, O.

Hutchinson, the Rev. E. Carter, D. D., St. Louis, Mo.

Hyde, James K., Hydeville, Vt.

Isham, John G., Cincinnati, O.

Jackson, A. R., M. D., Stroudsburg, Pa.

James, William E., Boston, Mass.

Jenkins, F. F., Boston Mass.

Kinney, Colonel Peter, Portsmouth, O.

Krauss, George W., Harrisburg, Pa.

Langdon, Charles J., Elmira, N. Y.

Larrowe, Mrs. Nina, San Francisco, Cal.

Leary, Daniel D., New York City

Lee, Mrs. S. G., Brooklyn, N. Y.

Lockwood, Mr. and Mrs. E. K., Norwalk, Conn.

McDonald, Louis, Bristol, England

Moody, Captain Lucius, Canton, N. Y.

Moulton, Julius, St. Louis, Mo.

Nelson, Arba, Alton, Ill.

Nesbit, Dr. B. B., Louisville, Ky.

Nesbit, Thomas B., Fulton, Mo.

Newell, Miss Julia, Janesville, Wis.

Parsons, Samuel B., New York City

Payne, Dr. and Mrs. J. H., Boston, Mass.

Quereau, the Rev. G. W., Aurora, Ill.

Sanford, A. N., Cleveland, O.

Serfaty, M. A., Gibraltar

Severance, Mr. and Mrs. S. L., Cleveland, O.

Sexton, Nicholas, New York City

Slote, Daniel, New York City

Van Nostrand, John A., Greenville, N. J.

II

NEW YORK "HERALD" EDITORIAL ON THE RETURN OF THE "QUAKER CITY" PILGRIMAGE, NOVEMBER 19, 1867

In yesterday's *Herald* we published a most amusing letter from the pen of that most amusing American genius, Mark Twain, giving an account of that most amusing of all modern pilgrimages—the pilgrimage of the *Quaker City*. It has been amusing all through, this *Quaker City* affair. It might have be-

APPENDIX

come more serious than amusing if the ship had been sold at
Jaffa, Alexandria, or Yalta, in the Black Sea, as it appears might
have happened. In such a case the passengers would have been
more effectually sold than the ship. The descendants of the
Puritan pilgrims have, naturally enough, some of them, an
affection for ships; but if all that is said about this religious
cruise be true they have also a singularly sharp eye to business.
It was scarcely wise on the part of the pilgrims, although it was
well for the public, that so strange a genius as Mark Twain
should have found admission into the sacred circle. We are
not aware whether Mr. Twain intends giving us a book on this
pilgrimage, but we do know that a book written from his own
peculiar standpoint, giving an account of the characters and
events on board ship and of the scenes which the pilgrims wit-
nessed, would command an almost unprecedented sale. There
are varieties of genius peculiar to America. Of one of these
varieties Mark Twain is a striking specimen. For the development of his peculiar genius he has never had a more fitting
opportunity. Besides, there are some things which he knows,
and which the world ought to know, about this last edition of
the *Mayflower*.

APPENDIX G

MARK TWAIN AT THE CORRESPONDENTS CLUB
WASHINGTON
(See Chapter lxiii)

WOMAN
A EULOGY OF THE FAIR SEX

The Washington Correspondents Club held its anniversary on Saturday night. Mr. Clemens, better known as Mark Twain, responded to the toast, "Woman, the pride of the professions and the jewel of ours." He said:

Mr. President,—I do not know why I should have been singled out to receive the greatest distinction of the evening—for so the office of replying to the toast to woman has been regarded in every age. [Applause.] I do not know why I have received this distinction, unless it be that I am a trifle less homely than the other members of the club. But, be this as it may, Mr. President, I am proud of the position, and you could not have chosen any one who would have accepted it more gladly, or labored with a heartier good - will to do the subject justice, than I. Because, sir, I love the sex. [Laughter.] I love all the women, sir, irrespective of age or color. [Laughter.]

Human intelligence cannot estimate what we owe to woman, sir. She sews on our buttons [laughter]; she mends our clothes [laughter]; she ropes us in at the church fairs; she confides in us; she tells us whatever she can find out about the private affairs of the neighbors; she gives good advice, and plenty of it; she gives us a piece of her mind sometimes—and sometimes all of it; she soothes our aching brows; she bears our children.

APPENDIX

In all relations of life, sir, it is but just and a graceful tribute to woman to say of her that she is a brick. [Great laughter.]

Wheresoever you place woman, sir—in whatsoever position or estate—she is an ornament to that place she occupies, and a treasure to the world. [Here Mr. Twain paused, looked inquiringly at his hearers, and remarked that the applause should come in at this point. It came in. Mr. Twain resumed his eulogy.] Look at the noble names of history! Look at Cleopatra! Look at Desdemona! Look at Florence Nightingale! Look at Joan of Arc! Look at Lucretia Borgia! [Disapprobation expressed. "Well," said Mr. Twain, scratching his head, doubtfully, "suppose we let Lucretia slide."] Look at Joyce Heth! Look at Mother Eve! I repeat, sir, look at the illustrious names of history! Look at the Widow Machree! Look at Lucy Stone! Look at Elizabeth Cady Stanton! Look at George Francis Train! [Great laughter.] And, sir, I say with bowed head and deepest veneration, look at the mother of Washington! She raised a boy that could not lie—could not lie. [Applause.] But he never had any chance. It might have been different with him if he had belonged to a newspaper correspondents' club. [Laughter, groans, hisses, cries of "put him out." Mark looked around placidly upon his excited audience, and resumed.]

I repeat, sir, that in whatsoever position you place a woman she is an ornament to society and a treasure to the world. As a sweetheart she has few equals and no superior [laughter]; as a cousin she is convenient; as a wealthy grandmother with an incurable distemper she is precious; as a wet nurse she has no equal among men! [Laughter.]

What, sir, would the people of this earth be without woman? They would be scarce, sir. Then let us cherish her, let us protect her, let us give her our support, our encouragement, our sympathy—ourselves, if we get a chance. [Laughter.]

But, jesting aside, Mr. President, woman is lovable, gracious, kind of heart, beautiful; worthy of all respect, of all esteem, of all deference. Not any here will refuse to drink her health right cordially, for each and every one of us has personally known, loved, and honored the very best one of them all—his own mother! [Applause.]

APPENDIX H

ANNOUNCEMENT FOR LECTURE OF JULY 2, 1868

(See Chapter lxvi)

(See Chapter lxvi)

THE PUBLIC TO MARK TWAIN—CORRESPONDENCE

SAN FRANCISCO, *June 30th.*

MR. MARK TWAIN—DEAR SIR,—Hearing that you are about to sail for New York in the P. M. S. S. Company's steamer of the 6th July, to publish a book, and learning with the deepest concern that you propose to read a chapter or two of that book in public before you go, we take this method of expressing our cordial desire that you will not. We beg and implore you do not. There is a limit to human endurance.

We are your personal friends. We have your welfare at heart. We desire to see you prosper. And it is upon these accounts, and upon these only, that we urge you to desist from the new atrocity you contemplate. Yours truly,

Wm. H. L. Barnes	Cal. Labor Exch'e
Rear-Ad'l Thatcher	Ex-Gov. Low
Samuel Williams	Brig.-Gen. Leonard
Gen. McCook	Robt. Rockwell
Geo. R. Barnes	Stephen J. Field
Noah Brooks	B. C. Horn
Maj.-Gen. Halleck	Geo. Pen Johnson
J. B. Bowman	Maj.-Gen. Ord
Leland Stanford	Bret Harte
John McComb	J. W. Tucker
Capt. Pease	R. B. Swain
A. Badlam	Ned Ellis
John Skae	Judge Lake
Abner Barker	Joseph H. Jones
Dr. Bruner	Col. Catherwood

APPENDIX

Louis Cohn
Mercantile Library
T. J. Lamb
Prop'rs Occidental
Prop'rs Russ House
Prop'rs Cosmopolitan
Prop'rs Lick House
Michael Reese
Frank Soule
Dr. Shorb
Pioche Bayerque & Co.
Asa D. Nudd
Ben. Truman
O. O. Eldridge
Board of Aldermen
The Masons

Dr. McNulty
A. J. Marsh
Sam. Platt
Wm. C. Ralston
Mayor McCoppin
E. B. Rail
R. L. Ogden
Thos. Cash
M. B. Cox
The Citizen Military
The Odd Fellows
The Orphan Asyl'm
Various Benevolent Societies, Citizens on Foot and Horseback, and 1,500 in the Steerage

(REPLY)

SAN FRANCISCO, *June 30th.*

TO THE 1,500 AND OTHERS,—It seems to me that your course is entirely unprecedented. Heretofore, when lecturers, singers, actors, and other frauds have said they were about to leave town, you have always been the very first people to come out in a card beseeching them to hold on for just one night more, and inflict just one more performance on the public, but as soon as I want to take a farewell benefit you come after me, with a card signed by the whole community and the board of aldermen, praying me not to do it. But it isn't of any use. You cannot move me from my fell purpose. I will torment the people if I want to. I have a better right to do it than these strange lecturers and orators that come here from abroad. It only costs the public a dollar apiece, and if they can't stand it what do they stay here for? Am I to go away and let them have peace and quiet for a year and a half, and then come back and only lecture them twice? What do you take me for?

No, gentlemen, ask of me anything else and I will do it cheerfully; but do not ask me not to afflict the people. I wish to tell them all I know about VENICE. I wish to tell them about the City of the Sea—that most venerable, most brilliant, and proudest Republic the world has ever seen. I wish to hint at what it achieved in twelve hundred years, and what it lost in two hundred. I wish to furnish a deal of pleasant information, somewhat highly spiced, but still palatable, digestible, and eminently fitted for the intellectual stomach. My last lecture was not as fine as I thought it was, but I have submitted this discourse to several able critics, and they have pronounced it good. Now, therefore, why should I withhold it?

Let me talk only just this once, and I will sail positively on the 6th of July, and stay away until I return from China—two years. Yours truly, MARK TWAIN.

(FURTHER REMONSTRANCE)

SAN FRANCISCO, *June 30th.*

MR. MARK TWAIN,—Learning with profound regret that you have concluded to postpone your departure until the 6th July, and learning also, with unspeakable grief, that you propose to read from your forthcoming book, or lecture again before you go, at the New Mercantile Library, we hasten to beg of you that you will not do it. Curb this spirit of lawless violence, and emigrate at once. Have the vessel's bill for your passage sent to us. We will pay it.

Your friends,
Pacific Board of Brokers
[and other important financial and social institutions].

SAN FRANCISCO, *June 30th.*

MR. MARK TWAIN—DEAR SIR,—Will you start now, without any unnecessary delay?

Yours truly,
Proprietors of the *Alta, Bulletin, Times, Call, Examiner*
[and other San Francisco publications].

SAN FRANCISCO, *June 30th.*

MR. MARK TWAIN—DEAR SIR,—Do not delay your departure. You can come back and lecture another time. In the language of the worldly—you can "cut and come again."

Your friends,
THE CLERGY.

APPENDIX

SAN FRANCISCO, *June 30th.*

MR. MARK TWAIN—DEAR SIR,—You had better go.

Yours,   THE CHIEF OF POLICE.

(REPLY)

SAN FRANCISCO, *June 30th.*

GENTLEMEN,—Restrain your emotions; you observe that they cannot avail. Read:

NEW MERCANTILE LIBRARY
Bush Street

Thursday Evening, July 2, 1868
One Night Only

FAREWELL LECTURE
of
MARK TWAIN
Subject:
The Oldest of the Republics
VENICE
PAST AND PRESENT

Box-Office open Wednesday and Thursday
No extra charge for reserved seats

ADMISSION . . . . ONE DOLLAR

Doors open at 7   Orgies to commence at 8 P. M.

The public displays and ceremonies projected to give fitting *éclat* to this occasion have been unavoidably delayed until the 4th. The lecture will be delivered certainly on the 2d, and the event will be celebrated two days afterward by a discharge of artillery on the 4th, a procession of citizens, the reading of the Declaration of Independence, and by a gorgeous display of fireworks from Russian Hill in the evening, which I have ordered at my sole expense, the cost amounting to eighty thousand dollars.

——————o——————

AT NEW MERCANTILE LIBRARY
Bush Street
Thursday Evening, July 2, 1868

APPENDIX I

MARK TWAIN'S CHAMPIONSHIP OF THOMAS K. BEECHER

(See Chapter lxxiv)

There was a religious turmoil in Elmira in 1869; a disturbance among the ministers, due to the success of Thomas K. Beecher in a series of meetings he was conducting in the Opera House. Mr. Beecher's teachings had never been very orthodox or doctrinal, but up to this time they had been seemingly unobjectionable to his brother clergymen, who fraternized with him and joined with him in the Monday meetings of the Ministerial Union of Elmira, when each Monday a sermon was read by one of the members. The situation presently changed. Mr. Beecher was preaching his doubtful theology to large and nightly increasing audiences, and it was time to check the exodus. The Ministerial Union of Elmira not only declined to recognize and abet the Opera House gatherings, but they requested him to withdraw from their Monday meetings, on the ground that his teachings were pernicious. Mr. Beecher said nothing of the matter, and it was not made public until a notice of it appeared in a religious paper. Naturally such a course did not meet with the approval of the Langdon family, and awoke the scorn of a man who so detested bigotry in any form as Mark Twain. He was a stranger in the place, and not justified to speak over his own signature, but he wrote an article and read it to members of the Langdon family and to Dr. and Mrs. Taylor, their intimate friends, who were spending an evening in the Langdon home. It was universally approved, and the next morning appeared in the Elmira *Advertiser,* over the signature of "S'cat." It created a stir, of course.

The article follows:

APPENDIX

MR. BEECHER AND THE CLERGY

" The Ministerial Union of Elmira, N. Y., at a recent meeting passed resolutions disapproving the teachings of Rev. T. K. Beecher, declining to co-operate with him in his Sunday evening services at the Opera House, and requesting him to withdraw from their Monday morning meeting. This has resulted in his withdrawal, and thus the pastors are relieved from further responsibility as to his action."—*N. Y. Evangelist.*

Poor Beecher! All this time he could do whatever he pleased that was wrong, and then be perfectly serene and comfortable over it, because the Ministerial Union of Elmira was responsible to God for it. He could lie if he wanted to, and those ministers had to answer for it; he could promote discord in the church of Christ, and those parties had to make it right with the Deity as best they could; he could teach false doctrines to empty operahouses, and those sorrowing lambs of the Ministerial Union had to get out their sackcloth and ashes and stand responsible for it. He had such a comfortable thing of it! But he went too far. In an evil hour he slaughtered the simple geese that laid the golden egg of responsibility for him, and now they will uncover their customary complacency, and lift up their customary cackle in his behalf no more. And so, at last, he finds himself in the novel position of being responsible to God for his acts, instead of to the Ministerial Union of Elmira. To say that this is appalling is to state it with a degree of mildness which amounts to insipidity.

We cannot justly estimate this calamity, without first reviewing certain facts that conspired to bring it about. Mr. Beecher was and is in the habit of preaching to a full congregation in the Independent Congregational Church, in this city. The meeting-house was not large enough to accommodate all the people who desired admittance. Mr. Beecher regularly attended the meetings of the Ministerial Union of Elmira every Monday morning, and they received him into their fellowship, and never objected to the doctrines which he taught in his church. So, in an unfortunate moment, he conceived the strange idea that they would connive at the teaching of the same doctrines in the same way in a larger house. Therefore he secured the Opera

House and proceeded to preach there every Sunday evening to assemblages comprising from a thousand to fifteen hundred persons. He felt warranted in this course by a passage of Scripture which says, "Go ye into all the world and preach the gospel unto every creature." Opera-houses were not ruled out specifically in this passage, and so he considered it proper to regard opera-houses as a part of "all the world." He looked upon the people who assembled there as coming under the head of "every creature." These ideas were as absurd as they were far-fetched, but still they were the honest ebullitions of a diseased mind. His great mistake was in supposing that when he had the Saviour's indorsement of his conduct he had all that was necessary. He overlooked the fact that there might possibly be a conflict of opinion between the Saviour and the Ministerial Union of Elmira. And there was. Wherefore, blind and foolish Mr. Beecher went to his destruction. The Ministerial Union withdrew their approbation, and left him dangling in the air, with no other support than the countenance and approval of the gospel of Christ.

Mr. Beecher invited his brother ministers to join forces with him and help him conduct the Opera House meetings. They declined with great unanimity. In this they were wrong. Since they did not approve of those meetings, it was a duty they owed to their consciences and their God to contrive their discontinuance. They knew this. They felt it. Yet they turned coldly away and refused to help at those meetings, when they well knew that their help, earnestly and persistently given, was able to kill any great religious enterprise that ever was conceived of.

The ministers refused, and the calamitous meetings at the Opera House continued; and not only continued, but grew in interest and importance, and sapped of their congregations churches where the Gospel was preached with that sweet monotonous tranquillity and that impenetrable profundity which stir up such consternation in the strongholds of sin. It is a pity to have to record here that one clergyman refused to preach at the Opera House at Mr. Beecher's request, even when that incendiary was sick and disabled; and if that man's conscience justifies him in that refusal I do not. Under the plea of charity for a sick brother he could have preached to that Opera House multitude a sermon that would have done incalculable damage to the Opera House experiment. And he need not have been particular about the sermon he chose, either. He could have relied on any he had in his barrel.

The Opera House meetings went on; other congregations were thin, and grew thinner, but the Opera House assemblages were vast. Every Sunday night, in spite of sense and reason, multitudes passed by the churches where they might have been saved, and marched deliberately to the Opera House to be damned. The community talked, talked, talked. Everybody discussed the fact that the Ministerial Union disapproved of the Opera House meetings; also the fact that they disapproved of the teachings put forth there. And everybody wondered how the Ministerial Union could tell whether to approve or disapprove of those teachings, seeing that those clergymen had never attended an Opera House meeting, and therefore didn't know what was taught there. Everybody wondered over that curious question, and they had to take it out in wondering.

Mr. Beecher asked the Ministerial Union to state their objections to the Opera House matter. They could not—at least they did not. He said to them that if they would come squarely out and tell him that they desired the discontinuance of those meetings he would discontinue them. They declined to do that. Why should they have declined? They had no right to decline, and no excuse to decline, if they honestly believed that those meetings interfered in the slightest degree with the best interests of religion. (That is a proposition which the profoundest head among them cannot get around.)

But the Opera House meetings went on. That was the mischief of it. And so, one Monday morning, when Mr. B. appeared at the usual Ministers' meeting, his brother clergymen desired him to come there no more. He asked why. They gave no reason. They simply declined to have his company longer. Mr. B. said he could not accept of this execution without a trial, and since he loved them and had nothing against them he must insist upon meeting with them in the future just the same as ever. And so, after that, they met in secret, and thus got rid of this man's importunate affection.

The Ministerial Union had ruled out Beecher—a point gained. He would get up an excitement about it in public. But that was a miscalculation. He never mentioned it. They waited and waited for the grand crash, but it never came. After all their labor-pains, their ministerial mountain had brought forth only a mouse—and a still-born one at that. Beecher had not told on them; Beecher malignantly persisted in not telling on them. The opportunity was slipping away. Alas, for the humiliation of it, they had to come out and tell it themselves! And after all, their bombshell did not hurt anybody when they did explode it. They had ceased to be responsible to God for Beecher, and yet nobody seemed paralyzed about it. Somehow, it was not even of sufficient importance, apparently, to get into the papers, though even the poor little facts that Smith has bought a trotting team and Alderman Jones's child has the measles are chronicled there with avidity. Something must be done. As the Ministerial Union had told about their desolating action, when nobody else considered it of enough importance to tell, they would also publish it, now that the reporters failed to see anything in it important enough to print. And so they startled the entire religious world no doubt by solemnly printing in the *Evangelist* the paragraph which heads this article. They have got their excommunication-bull started at last. It is going along quite lively now, and making considerable stir, let us hope. They even know it in Podunk, wherever that may be. It excited a two-line paragraph there. Happy, happy world, that knows at last that a little congress of congregationless clergymen of whom it had never neard before have crushed a famous Beecher, and reduced his audiences from fifteen hundred down to fourteen hundred and seventy-five at one fell blow! Happy, happy world, that knows at last that these obscure innocents are no longer responsible for the blemishless teachings, the power, the pathos, the logic, and the other and manifold intellectual pyrotechnics that seduce, but to damn, the Opera House assemblages every Sunday night in Elmira! And miserable, O thrice miserable Beecher! For the Ministerial Union of Elmira will never, no, never more be responsible to God for his shortcomings. (Excuse these tears.)

(For the protection of a man who is uniformly charged with all the newspaper deviltry that sees the light in Elmira journals, I take this opportunity of stating, under oath, duly subscribed before a magistrate, that Mr. Beecher did not write this article.

APPENDIX

And further still, that he did not inspire it. And further still, the Ministerial Union of Elmira did not write it. And finally, the Ministerial Union did not ask me to write it. No, I have taken up this cudgel in defense of the Ministerial Union of Elmira solely from a love of justice. Without solicitation, I have constituted myself the champion of the Ministerial Union of Elmira, and it shall be a labor of love with me to conduct their side of a quarrel in print for them whenever they desire me to do it; or if they are busy, and have not the time to ask me, I will cheerfully do it anyhow. In closing this I must remark that if any question the right of the clergymen of Elmira to turn Mr. Beecher out of the Ministerial Union, to such I answer that Mr. Beecher recreated that institution after it had been dead for many years, and invited those gentlemen to come into it, which they did, and so of course they have a right to turn him out if they want to. The difference between Beecher and the man who put an adder in his bosom is, that Beecher put in more adders than he did, and consequently had a proportionately livelier time of it when they got warmed up.)

Cheerfully,

S'CAT.

APPENDIX J

THE INDIGNITY PUT UPON THE REMAINS OF GEORGE HOLLAND BY THE REV. MR. SABINE

(See Chapter lxxvii)

What a ludicrous satire it was upon Christian charity!—even upon the vague, theoretical idea of it which doubtless this small saint mouths from his own pulpit every Sunday. Contemplate this freak of nature, and think what a Cardiff giant of self-righteousness is crowded into his pigmy skin. If we probe, and dissect, and lay open this diseased, this cancerous piety of his, we are forced to the conviction that it is the production of an impression on his part that his guild do about all the good that is done on the earth, and hence are better than common clay—hence are competent to say to such as George Holland, "You are unworthy; you are a play-actor, and consequently a sinner; I cannot take the responsibility of recommending you to the mercy of Heaven." It must have had its origin in that impression, else he would have thought, "We are all instruments for the carrying out of God's purposes; it is not for me to pass judgment upon your appointed share of the work, or to praise or to revile it; I have divine authority for it that we are all sinners, and therefore it is not for me to discriminate and say we will supplicate for this sinner, for he was a merchant prince or a banker, but we will beseech no forgiveness for this other one, for he was a play-actor."

It surely requires the furthest possible reach of self-righteousness to enable a man to lift his scornful nose in the air and turn his back upon so poor and pitiable a thing as a dead stranger come to beg the last kindness that humanity can do in its behalf. This creature has violated the letter of the Gospel, and judged George Holland—not George Holland, either, but his profession through him. Then it is, in a measure, fair that we judge this creature's guild through him. In effect he has said, "We are the salt of the earth; we do all the good work that is done; to learn how to be good and do good men must come to us; actors and such are obstacles to moral progress." Pray look at the thing reasonably a moment, laying aside all biases of education and custom. If a common public impression is fair evidence of a thing then this minister's legitimate, recognized, and acceptable business is to tell people calmly, coldly, and in stiff, written sentences, from the pulpit, to go and do right, be just, be merciful, be charitable. And his congregation forget it all between church and home. But for fifty years it was George Holland's business on the stage to make his audience go and do right, and be just, merciful, and charitable—because by his living, breathing, feeling pictures he showed them what it was to do these things, and how to do them, and how instant and ample was the reward! Is it not a singular teacher of men, this reverend gentleman who is so poorly informed himself as to put the whole stage under ban, and say, "I do not think it teaches moral lessons"? Where was ever a sermon preached that could make filial ingratitude so hateful to men as the sinful play of "King Lear"? Or where was there ever a sermon that could so convince men of the wrong and the cruelty of harboring a pampered and unanalyzed jealousy as the sinful play of "Othello"? And where are there ten preachers who can stand in the pulpit preaching heroism, unselfish devotion, and lofty patriotism, and hold their own against any one of five hundred William Tells that can be raised upon five hundred stages in the land at a day's notice? It is almost fair and just to aver (although it is profanity) that nine-tenths of all the kindness and forbearance and Christian charity and generosity in the hearts of the American people to-day got there by being filtered down from their fountain-head, the gospel of Christ, through dramas and tragedies and comedies on the stage, and through the despised novel and the Christmas story, and through the thousand and one lessons, suggestions, and narratives of generous deeds that stir the pulses, and exalt and augment the nobility of the nation day by day from the teeming columns of ten thousand newspapers, and not from the drowsy pulpit.

All that is great and good in our particular civilization came straight from the hand of Jesus Christ, and many creatures, and of divers sorts, were doubtless appointed to disseminate it; and let us believe that this seed and the result are the main thing, and not the cut of the sower's garment; and that whosoever, in his way and according to his opportunity, sows the one and produces the other, has done high service and worthy. And further, let us try with all our strength to believe that whenever old simple-hearted George Holland sowed this seed, and reared his crop of broader charities and better impulses in men's hearts, it was just as acceptable before the Throne as if the seed had been scattered in vapid platitudes from the pulpit of the ineffable Sabine himself.

Am I saying that the pulpit does not do its share toward disseminating the marrow, the meat of the gospel of Christ? (For we are not talking of ceremonies and wire-drawn creeds now, but the living heart and soul of what is pretty often only a specter.)

No, I am not saying that. The pulpit teaches assemblages of people twice a week—nearly two hours altogether—and does what it can in that time. The theater teaches large audiences seven times a week—28 or 30 hours altogether—and the novels and newspapers plead, and argue, and illustrate, stir, move, thrill, thunder, urge, persuade, and supplicate, at the feet of millions and millions of people every single day, and all day long and far into the night; and so these vast agencies till nine-tenths of the vineyard, and the pulpit tills the other tenth. Yet now and then some complacent blind idiot says, "You un-anointed are coarse clay and useless; you are not as we, the regen-erators of the world; go, bury yourselves elsewhere, for we can-not take the responsibility of recommending idlers and sinners to the yearning mercy of Heaven." How does a soul like that stay in a carcass without getting mixed with the secretions and sweated out through the pores? Think of this insect con-demning the whole theatrical service as a disseminator of bad morals because it has Black Crooks in it; forgetting that if that were sufficient ground people would condemn the pulpit because it had Crooks and Kallochs and Sabines in it!

No, I am not trying to rob the pulpit of any atom of its full share and credit in the work of disseminating the meat and mar-row of the gospel of Christ; but I am trying to get a moment's hearing for worthy agencies in the same work, that with overwrought modesty seldom or never claim a recognition of their great services. I am aware that the pulpit does its excellent one-tenth (and credits itself with it now and then, though most of the time a press of business causes it to forget it); I am aware that in its honest and well-meaning way it bores the people with uninflammable truisms about doing good; bores them with correct compositions on charity; bores them, chloroforms them, stupefies them with argumentative mercy without a flaw in the grammar or an emotion which the minister could put in in the right place if he turned his back and took his finger off the manuscript. And in doing these things the pulpit is doing its duty, and let us believe that it is likewise doing its best, and doing it in the most harmless and respectable way. And so I have said, and shall keep on saying, let us give the pulpit its full share of credit in elevating and ennobling the people; but when a pulpit takes to itself authority to pass judgment upon the work and worth of just as legitimate an instrument of God as itself, who spent a long life preaching from the stage the self-same gospel without the alteration of a single sentiment or a single axiom of right, it is fair and just that somebody who believes that actors were made for a high and good purpose, and that they accomplish the object of their creation and accomplish it well, should protest. And having protested, it is also fair and just—being driven to it, as it were—to whisper to the Sabine pattern of clergyman, under the breath, a simple, instructive truth, and say, "Ministers are not the only servants of God upon earth, nor his most efficient ones, either, by a very, very long distance!" Sensible ministers already know this, and it may do the other kind good to find it out.

But to cease teaching and go back to the beginning again, was it not pitiable—that spectacle? Honored and honorable old George Holland, whose theatrical ministry had for fifty years softened hard hearts, bred generosity in cold ones, kindled emotion in dead ones, uplifted base ones, broadened bigoted ones, and made many and many a stricken one glad and filled it brimful of gratitude, figuratively spit upon in his unoffending coffin by this crawling, slimy, sanctimonious, self-righteous reptile!

APPENDIX K

A SUBSTITUTE FOR RULOFF

HAVE WE A SIDNEY CARTON AMONG US?

(See Chapter lxxxii)

To EDITOR OF *Tribune.*

SIR,—I believe in capital punishment. I believe that when a murder has been done it should be answered for with blood. I have all my life been taught to feel this way, and the fetters of education are strong. The fact that the death-law is rendered almost inoperative by its very severity does not alter my belief in its righteousness. The fact that in England the proportion of executions to condemnations is one to sixteen, and in this country only one to twenty-two, and in France only one to thirty-eight, does not shake my steadfast confidence in the propriety of retaining the death-penalty. It is better to hang one murderer in sixteen, twenty-two, thirty-eight than not to hang any at all.

Feeling as I do, I am not sorry that Ruloff is to be hanged, but I am sincerely sorry that he himself has made it necessary that his vast capabilities for usefulness should be lost to the world. In this, mine and the public's is a common regret. For it is plain that in the person of Ruloff one of the most marvelous of intellects that any age has produced is about to be sacrificed, and that, too, while half the mystery of its strange powers is yet a secret. Here is a man who has never entered the doors of a college or a university, and yet by the sheer might of his innate gifts has made himself such a colossus in abstruse learning that the ablest of our scholars are but pigmies in his presence. By the evidence of Professor Mather, Mr. Surbridge, Mr. Richmond, and other men qualified to testify, this man is as familiar with the broad domain of philology as common men are with the

1628

APPENDIX

passing events of the day. His memory has such a limitless grasp that he is able to quote sentence after sentence, paragraph after paragraph, chapter after chapter, from a gnarled and knotty ancient literature that ordinary scholars are capable of achieving little more than a bowing acquaintance with. But his memory is the least of his great endowments. By the testimony of the gentlemen above referred to he is able to *critically analyze* the works of the old masters of literature, and while pointing out the beauties of the originals with a pure and discriminating taste is as quick to detect the defects of the accepted translations; and in the latter case, if exceptions be taken to his judgment, he straightway opens up the quarries of his exhaustless knowledge, and builds a very Chinese wall of evidence around his position. Every learned man who enters Ruloff's presence leaves it amazed and confounded by his prodigious capabilities and attainments. One scholar said he did not believe that in matters of subtle analysis, vast knowledge in his peculiar field of research, comprehensive grasp of subject, and serene kingship over its limitless and bewildering details, any land or any era of modern times had given birth to Ruloff's intellectual equal. What miracles this murderer might have wrought, and what luster he might have shed upon his country, if he had not put a forfeit upon his life so foolishly! But what if the law could be satisfied, and the gifted criminal still be saved. If a life be offered up on the gallows to atone for the murder Ruloff did, will that suffice? If so, give me the proofs, for in all earnestness and truth I aver that in such a case I will instantly bring forward a man who, in the interests of learning and science, will take *Ruloff's crime upon himself, and submit to be hanged in Ruloff's place.* I can, and will do this thing; and I propose this matter, and make this offer in good faith. You know me, and know my address.

SAMUEL LANGHORNE.

April 29, 1871.

APPENDIX L

ABOUT LONDON

ADDRESS AT A DINNER GIVEN BY THE SAVAGE CLUB, LONDON,
SEPTEMBER 28, 1872

(See Chapter lxxxvii)

Reported by Moncure D. Conway in the Cincinnati *Commercial*

It affords me sincere pleasure to meet this distinguished club,
a club which has extended its hospitalities and its cordial welcome to so many of my countrymen. I hope [and here the
speaker's voice became low and fluttering] you will excuse these
clothes. I am going to the theater; that will explain these
clothes. I have other clothes than these. Judging human
nature by what I have seen of it, I suppose that the customary
thing for a stranger to do when he stands here is to make a pun
on the name of this club, under the impression, of course, that
he is the first man that that idea has occurred to. It is a credit
to our human nature, not a blemish upon it; for it shows that
underlying all our depravity (and God knows and you know we
are depraved enough) and all our sophistication, and untarnished
by them, there is a sweet germ of innocence and simplicity still.
When a stranger says to me, with a glow of inspiration in his
eye, some gentle, innocuous little thing about "Twain and one
flesh" and all that sort of thing, I don't try to crush that man
into the earth—no. I feel like saying, "Let me take you by
the hand, sir; let me embrace you; I have not heard that pun
for weeks." We will deal in palpable puns. We will call parties
named King "your Majesty" and we will say to the Smiths that
we think we have heard that name before somewhere. Such is
human nature. We cannot alter this. It is God that made us
so for some good and wise purpose. Let us not repine. But
though I may seem strange, may seem eccentric, I mean to re-

frain from punning upon the name of this club, though I could make a very good one if I had time to think about it—a week.

I cannot express to you what entire enjoyment I find in this first visit to this prodigious metropolis of yours. Its wonders seem to me to be limitless. I go about as in a dream—as in a realm of enchantment—where many things are rare and beautiful, and all things are strange and marvelous. Hour after hour I stand—I stand spellbound, as it were—and gaze upon the statuary in Leicester Square. [Leicester Square being a horrible chaos, with the relic of an equestrian statue in the center, the king being headless and limbless, and the horse in little better condition.] I visit the mortuary effigies of noble old Henry VIII., and Judge Jeffreys, and the preserved gorilla, and try to make up my mind which of my ancestors I admire the most. I go to that matchless Hyde Park and drive all around it, and then I start to enter it at the Marble Arch—and am induced to "change my mind." [Cabs are not permitted in Hyde Park—nothing less aristocratic than a private carriage.] It is a great benefaction—is Hyde Park. There, in his hansom cab, the invalid can go—the poor, sad child of misfortune—and insert his nose between the railings, and breathe the pure, health-giving air of the country and of heaven. And if he is a swell invalid who isn't obliged to depend upon parks for his country air he can drive inside—if he owns his vehicle. I drive round and round Hyde Park and the more I see of the edges of it the more grateful I am that the margin is extensive.

And I have been to the Zoological Gardens. What a wonderful place that is! I have never seen such a curious and interesting variety of wild animals in any garden before—except Mabille. I never believed before there were so many different kinds of animals in the world as you can find there—and I don't believe it yet. I have been to the British Museum. I would advise you to drop in there some time when you have nothing to do for—five minutes—if you have never been there. It seems to me the noblest monument this nation has yet erected to her greatness. I say to her, our greatness—as a nation. True, she has built other monuments, and stately ones, as well; but these she has uplifted in honor of two or three colossal demigods who have stalked across the world's stage, destroying tyrants and delivering nations, and whose prodigies will still live in the memories of men ages after their monuments shall have crumbled to dust—I refer to the Wellington and Nelson monuments, and —the Albert memorial. [Sarcasm. The Albert memorial is the finest monument in the world, and celebrates the existence of as commonplace a person as good luck ever lifted out of obscurity.]

The Library at the British Museum I find particularly astounding. I have read there hours together, and hardly made an impression on it. I revere that library. It is the author's friend. I don't care how mean a book is, it always takes one copy. [A copy of every book printed in Great Britain must by law be sent to the British Museum, a law much complained of by publishers.] And then every day that author goes there to gaze at that book, and is encouraged to go on in the good work. And what a touching sight it is of a Saturday afternoon to see the poor, careworn clergymen gathered together in that vast reading-room cabbaging sermons for Sunday! You will pardon my referring to these things. Everything in this monster city interests me, and I cannot keep from talking, even at the risk of being instructive. People here seem always to express distances by parables. To a stranger it is just a little confusing to be so parabolic—so to speak. I collar a citizen, and I think I am going to get some valuable information out of him. I ask him how far it is to Birmingham, and he says it is twenty-one shillings and sixpence. Now we know that doesn't help a man who is trying to learn. I find myself down-town somewhere, and I want to get some sort of idea where I am—being usually lost when alone—and I stop a citizen and say, "How far is it to Charing Cross?" "Shilling fare in a cab," and off he goes. I suppose if I were to ask a Londoner how far it is from the sublime to the ridiculous he would try to express it in a coin. But I am trespassing upon your time with these geological statistics and historical reflections. I will not longer keep you from your orgies. 'Tis a real pleasure for me to be here, and I thank you for it. The name of the Savage Club is associated in my mind with the kindly interest and the friendly offices which you lavished upon an old friend of mine who came among you a stranger, and you opened your English hearts to him and gave him a welcome and a home—Artemus Ward. Asking that you will join me, I give you his Memory.

APPENDIX M

LETTER WRITTEN TO MRS. CLEMENS FROM BOSTON, NOVEMBER, 1874, PROPHESYING A MONARCHY IN SIXTY-ONE YEARS

(See Chapter xcvii)

BOSTON, *November 16, 1935.*

DEAR LIVY,—You observe I still call this beloved old place by the name it had when I was young. *Limerick!* It is enough to make a body sick.

The gentlemen-in-waiting stare to see me sit here *telegraphing* this letter to you, and no doubt they are smiling in their sleeves. But *let* them! The slow old fashions are good enough for me, thank God, and I will none other. When I see one of these modern fools sit absorbed, holding the end of a telegraph wire in his hand, and reflect that a thousand miles away there is another fool hitched to the other end of it, it makes me frantic with rage; and then I am more implacably fixed and resolved than ever to continue taking twenty minutes to telegraph you what I might communicate in ten seconds by the new way if I would so debase myself. And when I see a whole silent, solemn drawing-room full of idiots sitting with their hands on each other's foreheads "communing" I tug the white hairs from my head and curse till my asthma brings me the blessed relief of suffocation. In our old day such a gathering talked pure drivel and "rot," mostly, but better that, a thousand times, than these dreary conversational funerals that oppress our spirits in this mad generation.

It is sixty years since I was here before. I walked hither then with my precious old friend. It seems incredible now that we did it in two days, but such is my recollection. I no longer mention that we walked back in a single day, it makes me so furious to see doubt in the face of the hearer. Men were *men* in those old times. Think of one of the puerile organisms in this effeminate age attempting such a feat.

My air-ship was delayed by a collision with a fellow from China loaded with the usual cargo of jabbering, copper-colored missionaries, and so I was nearly an hour on my journey. But by the goodness of God thirteen of the missionaries were crippled and several killed, so I was content to lose the time. I love to lose time anyway because it brings soothing reminiscences of the creeping railroad days of old, now lost to us forever.

Our game was neatly played, and successfully. None expected us, of course. You should have seen the guards at the ducal palace stare when I said, "Announce his Grace the Archbishop of Dublin and the Right Honorable the Earl of Hartford." Arrived within, we were all eyes to see the Duke of Cambridge and his Duchess, wondering if we might remember their faces and they ours. In a moment they came tottering in; he, bent and withered and bald; she, blooming with wholesome old age. He peered through his glasses a moment, then screeched in a reedy voice, "Come to my arms! Away with titles—I'll know ye by no names but Twain and Twichell!" Then fell he on our necks and jammed his trumpet in his ear, the which we filled with shoutings to this effect: "God bless you, old Howells, what is left of you!"

We *talked* late that night—none of your silent idiot "communings" for us—of the olden time. We rolled a stream of ancient anecdotes over our tongues and drank till the Lord Archbishop grew so mellow in the mellow past that Dublin ceased to be Dublin to him, and resumed its sweeter, forgotten name of New York. In truth he almost got back into his ancient religion, too, good Jesuit as he has always been since O'Mulligan the First established that faith in the empire.

And we canvassed everybody. Bailey Aldrich, Marquis of Ponkapog, came in, got nobly drunk, and told us all about how poor Osgood lost his earldom and was hanged for conspiring against the second Emperor; but he didn't mention how near he himself came to being hanged, too, for engaging in the same enterprise. He was as chaffy as he was sixty years ago, too, and swore the Archbishop and I never walked to Boston; but there was never a day that Ponkapog wouldn't lie, so be it by the grace of God he got the opportunity.

The Lord High Admiral came in, a hale gentleman close upon

seventy and bronzed by the suns and storms of many climes and scarred by the wounds got in many battles, and I told him how I had seen him sit in a high-chair and eat fruit and cakes and answer to the name of Johnny. His granddaughter (the eldest) is but lately married to the youngest of the Grand Dukes, and so who knows but a day may come when the blood of the Howellses may reign in the land? I must not forget to say, while I think of it, that your new false teeth are done, my dear, and your wig. Keep your head well bundled with a shawl till the latter comes, and so cheat your persecuting neuralgias and rheumatisms. Would you believe it?—the Duchess of Cambridge is deafer than you—deafer than her husband. They call her to breakfast with a salvo of artillery; and usually when it thunders she looks up expectantly and says, "Come in." But she has become subdued and gentle with age and never destroys the furniture now, except when uncommonly vexed. God knows, my dear, it would be a happy thing if you and old Lady Harmony would imitate this spirit. But indeed the older you grow the less secure becomes the furniture. When *I* throw chairs through the window I have sufficient reason to back it. But you—you are but a creature of passion.

The monument to the author of *Gloverson and His Silent Partners* is finished.[1] It is the stateliest and the costliest ever erected to the memory of any man. This noble classic has now been translated into all the languages of the earth and is adored by all nations and known to all creatures. Yet I have conversed as familiarly with the author of it as I do with my own great-grandchildren.

I wish you could see old Cambridge and Ponkapog. I love them as dearly as ever, but privately, my dear, they are not much improvement on idiots. It is melancholy to hear them jabber over the same pointless anecdotes three and four times of an evening, forgetting that they had jabbered them over three or four times the evening before. Ponkapog still writes poetry, but the old-time fire has mostly gone out of it. Perhaps his best effort of late years is this:

> O soul, soul, soul of mine!
> Soul, soul, soul of thine!

[1] Ralph Keeler. See chap. lxxxiii.

MARK TWAIN

Thy soul, my soul, two souls entwine,
And sing thy lauds in crystal wine!

This he goes about repeating to everybody, daily and nightly insomuch that he is become a sore affliction to all that know him.

But I must desist. There are draughts here everywhere and my gout is something frightful. My left foot hath resemblance to a snuff-bladder. God be with you.   HARTFORD.

These to Lady Hartford, in the earldom of Hartford, in the upper portion of the city of Dublin.

APPENDIX N

MARK TWAIN AND COPYRIGHT

I

PETITION

Concerning Copyright (1875)

(See Chapter cii)

To the Senate and House of Representatives of the United States in Congress Assembled.

We, your petitioners, do respectfully represent as follows, *viz.:* That *justice*, plain and simple, is a thing which right-feeling men stand ready at all times to accord to brothers and strangers alike. All such men will concede that it is but plain, simple justice that American authors should be protected by copyright in Europe; also, that European authors should be protected by copyright here.

Both divisions of this proposition being true, it behooves our government to concern itself with that division of it which comes peculiarly within its province—*viz.*, the latter moiety—and to grant to foreign authors with all convenient despatch a full and effective copyright in America *without marring the grace of the act by stopping to inquire whether a similar justice will be done our own authors by foreign governments.* If it were even known that those governments would not extend this justice to us it would still not justify us in withholding this manifest right from their authors. If a thing is right *it ought to be done*—the thing called "expediency" or "policy" has no concern with such a matter. And we desire to repeat, with all respect, that it is not a grace or a privilege we ask for our foreign brethren, but a right —a right received from God, and only denied them by man. We hold no ownership in these authors, and when we take their work from them, as at present, without their consent, it is robbery. The fact that the handiwork of our own authors is seized in the same way in foreign lands neither excuses nor mitigates our sin.

With your permission we will say here, over our signatures, and earnestly and sincerely, that we very greatly desire that you shall grant a full copyright to foreign authors (the copyright fee for the entry in the office of the Congressional Librarian to be the same as we pay ourselves), and we also as greatly desire that this grant shall be made without a single hampering stipulation that American authors shall receive in turn an advantage of any kind from foreign governments.

Since no author who was applied to hesitated for a moment to append his signature to this petition we are satisfied that if time had permitted we could have procured the signature of every writer in the United States, great and small, obscure or famous. As it is, the list comprises the names of about all our writers whose works have at present a European market, and who are therefore chiefly concerned in this matter.

No objection to our proposition can come from any reputable publisher among us—or does come from such a quarter, as the appended signatures of our greatest publishing firms will attest. A European copyright here would be a manifest advantage to them. As the matter stands now the moment they have thoroughly advertised a desirable foreign book, and thus at great expense aroused public interest in it, some small-spirited speculator (who has lain still in his kennel and spent nothing) rushes the same book on the market and robs the respectable publisher of half the gains.

Then, since neither our authors nor the decent among our publishing firms will object to granting an American copyright to foreign authors and artists, who can there be to object? Surely nobody whose protest is entitled to any weight.

Trusting in the righteousness of our cause we, your petitioners, will ever pray, etc.

With great respect,   Your Ob't Serv'ts.

CIRCULAR TO AMERICAN AUTHORS AND PUBLISHERS

DEAR SIR,—We believe that you will recognize the justice and the righteousness of the thing we desire to accomplish through the accompanying petition. And we believe that you will be willing that our country shall be the first in the world to grant to all authors alike the free exercise of their manifest right to do as they please with the fruit of their own labor without inquiring what flag they live under. If the sentiments of the petition meet your views, will you do us the favor to sign it and forward it by post at your earliest convenience to our secretary?

} Committee

Address

_____

Secretary of the Committee.

II

Communications supposed to have been written by the Tsar of Russia and the Sultan of Turkey to Mark Twain on the subject of International Copyright, about 1890.

St. Petersburg, *February.*

Col. Mark Twain, Washington.

Your cablegram received. It should have been transmitted through my minister, but let that pass. I am opposed to international copyright. At present American literature is harmless here because we doctor it in such a way as to make it approve the various beneficent devices which we use to keep our people favorable to fetters as jewelry and pleased with Siberia as a summer resort. But your bill would spoil this. We should be obliged to let you say your say in your own way. Voilà! my empire would be a republic in five years and I should be sampling Siberia myself.

If you should run across Mr. Kennan[1] please ask him to come over and give some readings. I will take good care of him.

Alexander III.

144—Collect.

[1] George Kennan, who had graphically pictured the fearful conditions of Siberian exile.

MARK TWAIN

DR. MARK TWAIN, Washington.

Great Scott, no! By the beard of the Prophet, no! How can you ask such a thing of me? I am a man of family. I cannot take chances, like other people. I cannot let a literature come in here which teaches that a man's wife is as good as the man himself. Such a doctrine cannot do any particular harm, of course, where the man has only one wife, for then it is a dead-level between them, and there is no humiliating inequality, and no resulting disorder; but you take an extremely married person, like me, and go to teaching that his wife is 964 times as good as he is, and what's hell to that harem, dear friend? I never saw such a fool as you. Do not mind that expression; I already regret it, and would replace it with a softer one if I could do it without debauching the truth. I beseech you, do not pass that bill. Roberts College is quite all the American product we can stand just now. On top of that, do you want to send us a flood of freedom-shrieking literature which we can't edit the poison out of, but must let it go among our people just as it is? My friend, we should be a republic inside of ten years.

ABDUL II.

III

MARK TWAIN'S LAST SUGGESTION ON COPYRIGHT

A MEMORIAL RESPECTFULLY TENDERED TO THE MEMBERS OF THE SENATE AND THE HOUSE OF REPRESENTATIVES

(Prepared early in 1909 at the suggestion of Mr. Champ Clark but not offered. A bill adding fourteen years to the copyright period was passed about this time.)

The Policy of Congress   Nineteen or twenty years ago James Russell Lowell, George Haven Putnam, and the undersigned appeared before the Senate Committee on Patents in the interest of Copyright. Up to that time, as explained by Senator Platt, of Connecticut, the policy of Congress had been to limit the life of a copyright by a term of years, with one definite end in view, and only one—to wit, that after an author had been permitted to enjoy for a reasonable length of time the income

APPENDIX

from literary property created by his hand and brain the property should then be transferred "to the public" as a free gift. That is still the policy of Congress to-day.

The Purpose in View The purpose in view was clear: to so reduce the price of the book as to bring it within the reach of all purses, and spread it among the millions who had not been able to buy it while it was still under the protection of copyright.

The Purpose Defeated This purpose has always been defeated. That is to say, that while the death of a copyright has sometimes reduced the price of a book by a half for a while, and in some cases by even more, it has never reduced it *vastly*, nor accomplished *any* reduction that was *permanent and secure*.

The Reason The reason is simple: Congress has never made a reduction *compulsory*. Congress was convinced that the removal of the author's royalty and the book's consequent (or at least probable) dispersal among several competing publishers would make the book cheap by force of the competition. It was an error. It has not turned out so. The reason is, a publisher cannot find profit in an *exceedingly* cheap edition if he must divide the market with competitors.

Proposed Remedy The natural remedy would seem to be, an amended law *requiring* the issue of cheap editions.

Copyright Extension I think the remedy could be accomplished in the following way, without injury to author or publisher, and with *extreme advantage to the public:* by an amendment to the existing law providing as follows—to wit: that at any time between the beginning of a book's forty-first year and the ending of its forty-second the owner of the copyright may extend its life thirty years by issuing and placing on sale an edition of the book at *one-tenth* the price of the cheapest edition hitherto issued at any time during the ten immediately preceding years. This extension to lapse and become null and void if at any time during the thirty years he shall fail during the space of three consecutive months to furnish the ten per cent. book upon demand of any person or persons desiring to buy it.

The Result The result would be that no American classic enjoying the thirty-year extension would ever be out of the reach of any American purse, let its uncompulsory price be what it might. He would get a two-dollar book for 20 cents, and he could get *none but copyright-expired classics* at any such rate.

The Final Result At the end of the thirty-year extension the copyright would again die, and the price would again *advance*. This by a natural law, the excessively cheap edition no longer carrying with it an advantage to any publisher.

Reconstruction of the Present Law Not Necessary A clause of the suggested amendment could read about as follows, and would obviate the necessity of taking the present law to pieces and building it over again:

> All books and all articles enjoying forty-two years copyright-life under the present law shall be admitted to the privilege of the thirty-year extension upon complying with the condition requiring the producing and placing upon permanent sale of one grade or form of said book or article at a price of 90 per cent. below the cheapest rate at which said book or article had been placed upon the market at any time during the immediately preceding ten years.

REMARKS

If the suggested amendment shall meet with the favor of the present Congress and become law—and I hope it will—I shall have personal experience of its effects very soon. Next year, in fact, in the person of my first book, *The Innocents Abroad*. For its forty-two-year copyright-life will then cease and its thirty-year extension begin—and with the latter the permanent low-rate edition. At present the highest price of the book is eight dollars, and its lowest price three dollars per copy. Thus the permanent low rate will be thirty cents per copy. A sweeping reduction like this is what Congress from the beginning has desired to achieve, but has not been able to accomplish because no inducement was offered to publishers to run the risk.

Respectfully submitted,

S. L. CLEMENS.

(A full and interesting elucidation of Mark Twain's views on Copyright may be found in an article entitled "Concerning Copyright," published in the *North American Review* for January, 1905.)

APPENDIX O

(See Chapter cxiv)

Address of Samuel L. Clemens (Mark Twain) from a report of the dinner given by the publishers of the *Atlantic Monthly* in honor of the Seventieth Anniversary of the Birth of John Greenleaf Whittier, at the Hotel Brunswick, Boston, December 17, 1877, as published in the Boston *Evening Transcript*, December 18, 1877.

MR. CHAIRMAN,—This is an occasion peculiarly meet for the digging up of pleasant reminiscences concerning literary folk, therefore I will drop lightly into history myself. Standing here on the shore of the Atlantic, and contemplating certain of its largest literary billows, I am reminded of a thing which happened to me thirteen years ago, when I had just succeeded in stirring up a little Nevadian literary puddle myself, whose spume-flakes were beginning to blow thinly Californiaward. I started an inspection tramp through the southern mines of California. I was callow and conceited, and I resolved to try the virtue of my *nom de guerre*. I very soon had an opportunity. I knocked at a miner's lonely log cabin in the foothills of the Sierras just at nightfall. It was snowing at the time. A jaded, melancholy man of fifty, barefooted, opened the door to me. When he heard my *nom de guerre* he looked more dejected than before. He let me in—pretty reluctantly, I thought—and after the customary bacon and beans, black coffee and hot whisky, I took a pipe. This sorrowful man had not said three words up to this time. Now he spoke up and said, in the voice of one who is secretly suffering, "You're the fourth—I'm going to move." "The fourth what?" said I. "The fourth littery man that has been here in twenty-four hours—I'm going to move." "You don't tell me!" said I; "who were the others?" "Mr. Longfellow, Mr. Emerson, and Mr. Oliver Wendell Holmes—consound the lot!"

You can easily believe I was interested. I supplicated—three hot whiskies did the rest—and finally the melancholy miner began. Said he:

"They came here just at dark yesterday evening, and I let them in, of course. Said they were going to the Yosemite. They were a rough lot, but that's nothing; everybody looks rough that travels afoot. Mr. Emerson was a seedy little bit of a chap, red-headed. Mr. Holmes was as fat as a balloon; he weighed as much as three hundred, and had double chins all the way down to his stomach. Mr. Longfellow was built like a prize-fighter. His head was cropped and bristly, like as if he had a wig made of hair-brushes. His nose lay straight down in his face, like a finger with the end joint tilted up. They had been drinking, I could see that. And what queer talk they used! Mr. Holmes inspected this cabin, then he took me by the button-hole and says he:

> "'Through the deep caves of thought
> I hear a voice that sings,
> "Build thee more stately mansions,
> O my soul!"'

"Says I, 'I can't afford it, Mr. Holmes, and moreover I don't want to.' Blamed if I liked it pretty well, either, coming from a stranger that way. However, I started to get out my bacon and beans when Mr. Emerson came and looked on awhile, and then *he* takes me aside by the buttonhole and says:

> "'Give me agates for my meat;
> Give me cantharids to eat;
> From air and ocean bring me foods,
> From all zones and altitudes.'

"Says I, 'Mr. Emerson, if you'll excuse me, this ain't no hotel.' You see, it sort of riled me—I warn't used to the ways of littery swells. But I went on a-sweating over my work, and next comes Mr. Longfellow and buttonholes me and interrupts me. Says he:

> "'Honor be to Mudjekeewis!
> You shall hear how Pau-Puk-Keewis—'

"But I broke in, and says I, 'Beg your pardon, Mr. Long-fellow, if you'll be so kind as to hold your yawp for about five minutes and let me get this grub ready, you'll do me proud.' Well, sir, after they'd filled up I set out the jug. Mr. Holmes looks at it and then he fires up all of a sudden and yells:

> "'Flash out a stream of blood-red wine!
> For I would drink to other days.'

"By George, I was getting kind of worked up. I don't deny it, I was getting kind of worked up. I turns to Mr. Holmes and says I, 'Looky here, my fat friend, I'm a-running this shanty, and if the court knows herself you'll take whisky straight or you'll go dry.' Them's the very words I said to him. Now I don't want to sass such famous littery people, but you see they kind of forced me. There ain't nothing onreasonable 'bout me. I don't mind a passel of guests a-treadin' on my tail three or four times, but when it comes to *standing* on it it's different, 'and if the court knows herself,' I says, 'you'll take whisky straight or you'll go dry.' Well, between drinks they'd swell around the cabin and strike attitudes and spout; and pretty soon they got out a greasy old deck and went to playing euchre at ten cents a corner—on trust. I began to notice some pretty suspicious things. Mr. Emerson dealt, looked at his hand, shook his head, says—

> "'I am the doubter and the doubt—'

and calmly bunched the hands and went to shuffling for a new lay-out. Says he:

> "'They reckon ill who leave me out;
> They know not well the subtle ways I keep.
> I pass and deal *again!*'

Hang'd if he didn't go ahead and do it, too! Oh, he was a cool one! Well, in about a minute things were running pretty tight, but all of a sudden I see by Mr. Emerson's eye he judged he had 'em. He had already corralled two tricks and each of the others one. So now he kind of lifts a little in his chair and says,

> "'I tire of globes and aces!—
> Too long the game is played!'

and down he fetched a right bower. Mr. Longfellow smiles as sweet as pie and says,

> "'Thanks, thanks to thee, my worthy friend,
> For the lesson thou hast taught,'

and blamed if he didn't down with *another* right bower! Emerson claps his hand on his bowie, Longfellow claps his on his revolver, and I went under a bunk. There was going to be trouble; but that monstrous Holmes rose up, wobbling his double chins, and says he, 'Order, gentlemen; the first man that draws I'll lay down on him and smother him!' All quiet on the Potomac, you bet!

"They were pretty how-come-you-so by now, and they begun to blow. Emerson says, 'The noblest thing I ever wrote was "Barbara Frietchie."' Says Longfellow, 'It don't begin with my "Bigelow Papers."' Says Holmes, 'My "Thanatopsis" lays over 'em both.' They mighty near ended in a fight. Then they wished they had some more company, and Mr. Emerson pointed to me and says:

> "'Is yonder squalid peasant all
> That this proud nursery could breed?'

He was a-whetting his bowie on his boot—so I let it pass. Well, sir, next they took it into their heads that they would like some music; so they made me stand up and sing, 'When Johnny Comes Marching Home' till I dropped—at thirteen minutes past four this morning. That's what I've been through, my friend. When I woke at seven they were leaving, thank goodness, and Mr. Longfellow had my only boots on and his'n under his arm. Says I, 'Hold on there, Evangeline, what are you going to do with *them?*' He says, 'Going to make tracks with 'em, because—

> "'Lives of great men all remind us
> We can make our lives sublime;
> And, departing, leave behind us
> Footprints on the sands of time.'

As I said, Mr. Twain, you are the fourth in twenty-four hours—and I'm going to move; I ain't suited to a littery atmosphere."

SEATING PLAN OF THE WHITTIER BIRTHDAY DINNER

APPENDIX

I said to the miner, "Why, my dear sir, *these* were not the gracious singers to whom we and the world pay loving reverence and homage; these were impostors."

The miner investigated me with a calm eye for a while; then said he, "Ah! impostors, were they? Are you?"

I did not pursue the subject, and since then I have not traveled on my *nom de guerre* enough to hurt. Such was the reminiscence I was moved to contribute, Mr. Chairman. In my enthusiasm I may have exaggerated the details a little, but you will easily forgive me that fault, since I believe it is the first time I have ever deflected from perpendicular fact on an occasion like this.

APPENDIX P

THE ADAM MONUMENT PETITION

(See Chapter cxxxiv)

To the Honorable Senate and House of Representatives of the United States in Congress Assembled.

Whereas, A number of citizens of the city of Elmira in the State of New York having covenanted among themselves to erect in that city a monument in memory of Adam, the father of mankind, being moved thereto by a sentiment of love and duty, and these having appointed the undersigned to communicate with your honorable body, we beg leave to lay before you the following facts and append to the same our humble petition.

1. As far as is known no monument has ever been raised in any part of the world to commemorate the services rendered to our race by this great man, whilst many men of far less note and worship have been rendered immortal by means of stately and indestructible memorials.

2. The common father of mankind has been suffered to lie in entire neglect, although even the Father of our Country has now, and has had for many years, a monument in course of construction.

3. No right-feeling human being can desire to see this neglect continued, but all just men, even to the farthest regions of the globe, should and will rejoice to know that he to whom we owe existence is about to have reverent and fitting recognition of his works at the hands of the people of Elmira. His labors were not in behalf of one locality, but for the extension of humanity at large and the blessings which go therewith; hence all races and all colors and all religions are interested in seeing that his name and fame shall be placed beyond the reach of the blight of oblivion by a permanent and suitable monument.

APPENDIX

4. It will be to the imperishable credit of the United States if this monument shall be set up within her borders; moreover, it will be a peculiar grace to the beneficiary if this testimonial of affection and gratitude shall be the gift of the youngest of the nations that have sprung from his loins after 6,000 years of unappreciation on the part of its elders.

5. The idea of this sacred enterprise having originated in the city of Elmira, she will be always grateful if the general government shall encourage her in the good work by securing to her a certain advantage through the exercise of its great authority.

Therefore, Your petitioners beg that your honorable body will be pleased to issue a decree restricting to Elmira the right to build a monument to Adam and inflicting a heavy penalty upon any other community within the United States that shall propose or attempt to erect a monument or other memorial to the said Adam, and to this end we will ever pray.

NAMES	NAMES
F. G. Hall	M. H. Arnot
C. Preswick	C. H. Thomson
Thad. S. Up de Graff	Theron A. Wales
Thos. K. Beecher	Wm. T. Post
John Arnot, Jr.	Seymour Dexter
S. De Witt	F. H. Atkinson
W. F. Sherwin	J. R. Reid
S. T. Reynolds	Ausburn Towner
Chas. J. Langdon	J. H. Barney
Henry E. Druke	R. R. R. Dumarz
Delos L. Holden	C. L. Harding
C. W. Brown	J. Hotchkiss
E. B. Smith	M. W. Palnue
H. G. Gilbert	Peter Wright
E. K. Waver	L. A. Humphrey
Wm. H. Ferguson	G. A. Grinley
William E. Hart	H. M. Kent
J. Richardson	T. C. Cowen
J. D. Baldwin	J. J. Bush
D. Atwater	H. V. Ransom
W. A. Ward	A. S. Fitch

MARK TWAIN

APPENDIX Q

GENERAL GRANT'S GRAMMAR

(Written in 1886. Delivered at an Army and Navy
Club dinner in New York City)

Lately a great and honored author, Matthew Arnold, has been
finding fault with General Grant's English. That would be fair
enough, maybe, if the examples of imperfect English averaged
more instances to the page in General Grant's book than they
do in Arnold's criticism on the book—but they do not. It would
be fair enough, maybe, if such instances were commoner in
General Grant's book than they are in the works of the average
standard author—but they are not. In fact, General Grant's
derelictions in the matter of grammar and construction are not
more frequent than such derelictions in the works of a majority
of the professional authors of our time, and of all previous times
—authors as exclusively and painstakingly trained to the literary trade as was General Grant to the trade of war. This is
not a random statement: it is a fact, and easily demonstrable
I have a book at home called *Modern English Literature: Its
Blemishes and Defects*, by Henry H. Breen, a countryman of
Mr. Arnold. In it I find examples of bad grammar and slovenly
English from the pens of Sydney Smith, Sheridan, Hallam,
Whately, Carlyle, Disraeli, Allison, Junius, Blair, Macaulay,
Shakespeare, Milton, Gibbon, Southey, Lamb, Landor, Smollett,
Walpole, Walker (of the dictionary), Christopher North, Kirk
White, Benjamin Franklin, Sir Walter Scott, and Mr. Lindley
Murray (who made the grammar).

In Mr. Arnold's criticism on General Grant's book we find two
grammatical crimes and more than several examples of very
crude and slovenly English, enough of them to entitle him to
a *lofty* place in the illustrious list of delinquents just named.

1651

MARK TWAIN

The following passage all by itself ought to elect him:

"Meade suggested to Grant that he might wish to have immediately under him Sherman, who had been serving with Grant in the West. He begged him not to hesitate if he thought it for the good of the service. Grant assured him that he had not thought of moving him, and in his memoirs, after relating what had passed, he adds, etc." To read that passage a couple of times would make a man dizzy; to read it four times would make him drunk.

Mr. Breen makes this discriminating remark: "To suppose that because a man is a poet or a historian he must be correct in his grammar is to suppose that an architect must be a joiner, or a physician a compounder of medicine."

People may hunt out what microscopic motes they please, but, after all, the fact remains, and cannot be dislodged, that General Grant's book is a great and, in its peculiar department, a unique and unapproachable literary masterpiece. In their line there is no higher literature than those modest, simple memoirs. Their style is at least flawless and no man could improve upon it, and great books are weighed and measured by their style and matter, and not by the trimmings and shadings of their grammar.

There is that about the sun which makes us forget his spots, and when we think of General Grant our pulses quicken and his grammar vanishes; we only remember that this is the simple soldier who, all untaught of the silken phrase-makers, linked words together with an art surpassing the art of the schools and put into them a something which will still bring to American ears, as long as America shall last, the roll of his vanished drums and the tread of his marching hosts. What do we care for grammar when we think of those thunderous phrases, "Unconditional and immediate surrender," "I propose to move immediately upon your works," "I propose to fight it out on this line if it takes all summer." Mr. Arnold would doubtless claim that that last phrase is not strictly grammatical, and yet it did certainly wake up this nation as a hundred million tons of A-number-one fourth-proof, hard-boiled, hide-bound grammar from another mouth could not have done. And finally we have that gentler phrase, that one which shows you another true side of the man, shows you that in his soldier heart there was room for other than gory war mottoes and in his tongue the gift to fitly phrase them: "Let us have peace."

APPENDIX R

PARTY ALLEGIANCE

BEING A PORTION OF A PAPER ON "CONSISTENCY," READ BEFORE
THE MONDAY EVENING CLUB IN 1887
(See Chapter clxiii)

. . . I have referred to the fact that when a man retires from
his political party he is a traitor—that he is so pronounced in
plain language. That is bold; so bold as to deceive many into
the fancy that it is true. Desertion, treason—these are the
terms applied. Their military form reveals the thought in the
man's mind who uses them: to him a political party is an army.
Well, is it? Are the two things identical? Do they even re-
semble each other? Necessarily a political party is not an army
of conscripts, for they are in the ranks by compulsion. Then
it must be a regular army or an army of volunteers. Is it a
regular army? No, for these enlist for a specified and well-
understood term, and can retire without reproach when the term
is up. Is it an army of volunteers who have enlisted for the
war, and may righteously be shot if they leave before the war is
finished? No, it is not even an army in that sense. Those fine
military terms are high-sounding, empty lies, and are no more
rationally applicable to a political party than they would be
to an oyster-bed. The volunteer soldier comes to the recruiting
office and strips himself and proves that he is so many feet high,
and has sufficiently good teeth, and no fingers gone, and is
sufficiently sound in body generally; he is accepted; but not
until he has sworn a deep oath or made other solemn form of
promise to march under that flag until that war is done or
his term of enlistment completed. What is the process when
a voter joins a party? Must he prove that he is sound in
any way, mind *or* body? Must he prove that he knows anything—is capable of anything—whatever? Does he take an
oath or make a promise of any sort?—or doesn't he leave himself

1653

entirely free? If he were informed by the political boss that if he join, it must be forever; that he must be that party's chattel and wear its brass collar the rest of his days—would not that insult him? It goes without saying. He would say some rude, unprintable thing, and turn his back on that preposterous organization. But the political boss puts no conditions upon him at all; and this volunteer makes no promises, enlists for no stated term. He has in no sense become a part of an army; he is in no way restrained of his freedom. Yet he will presently find that his bosses and his newspapers have assumed just the reverse of that: that they have blandly arrogated to themselves an iron-clad military authority over him; and within twelve months, if he is an average man, he will have surrendered his liberty, and will actually be silly enough to believe that he cannot leave that party, for any cause whatever, without being a shameful traitor, a deserter, a legitimately dishonored man.

There you have the just measure of that freedom of conscience, freedom of opinion, freedom of speech and action which we hear so much inflated foolishness about as being the precious possession of the republic. Whereas, in truth, the surest way for a man to make of himself a target for almost universal scorn, obloquy, slander, and insult is to stop twaddling about these priceless independencies and attempt to exercise one of them. If he is a preacher half his congregation will clamor for his expulsion—and *will* expel him, except they find it will injure real estate in the neighborhood; if he is a doctor his own dead will turn against him.

I repeat that the new party-member who supposed himself independent will presently find that the party have somehow got a mortgage on his soul, and that within a year he will recognize the mortgage, deliver up his liberty, and actually believe he cannot retire from that party from any motive howsoever high and right in his own eyes without shame and dishonor.

Is it possible for human wickedness to invent a doctrine more infernal and poisonous than this? Is there imaginable a baser servitude than it imposes? What slave is so degraded as the slave that is proud that he is a slave? What is the essential difference between a lifelong democrat and any other kind of lifelong slave? Is it less humiliating to dance to the lash of one master than another?

APPENDIX

This infamous doctrine of allegiance to party plays directly into the hands of politicians of the baser sort—and doubtless for that it was borrowed—or stolen—from the monarchial system. It enables them to foist upon the country officials whom no self-respecting man would vote for if he could but come to understand that loyalty to himself is his first and highest duty, not loyalty to any party name.

Shall you say the best good of the country demands allegiance to party? Shall you also say that it demands that a man kick his truth and his conscience into the gutter and become a mouthing lunatic besides? Oh no, you say; it does not demand that. But what if it produce that in spite of you? There is no obligation upon a man to do things which he ought not to do when drunk, but most men will do them just the same; and so we hear no arguments about obligations in the matter—we only hear men warned to avoid the habit of drinking; get rid of the thing that can betray men into such things.

This is a funny business all around. The same men who enthusiastically preach loyal consistency to church and party are always ready and willing and anxious to persuade a Chinaman or an Indian or a Kanaka to desert his church or a fellow-American to desert his party. The man who deserts to them is all that is high and pure and beautiful—apparently; the man who deserts from them is all that is foul and despicable. This is Consistency—with a capital C.

With the daintiest and self-complacentest sarcasm the lifelong loyalist scoffs at the Independent—or as he calls him, with cutting irony, the Mugwump; makes himself too killingly funny for anything in this world about him. But—the Mugwump can stand it, for there is a great history at his back, stretching down the centuries, and he comes of a mighty ancestry. He knows that in the whole history of the race of men no single great and high and beneficent thing was ever done for the souls and bodies, the hearts and the brains of the children of this world, but a Mugwump started it and Mugwumps carried it to victory. And their names are the stateliest in history: Washington, Garrison, Galileo, Luther, Christ. Loyalty to petrified opinions never yet broke a chain or freed a human soul in this world—and never will.

APPENDIX S

ORIGINAL PREFACE FOR "A CONNECTICUT YANKEE IN KING ARTHUR'S COURT"

(See Chapter clxxii)

My object has been to group together some of the most odious laws which have had vogue in the Christian countries within the past eight or ten centuries, and illustrate them by the incidents of a story.

There was never a time when America applied the death-penalty to more than fourteen crimes. But England, within the memory of men still living, had in her list of crimes 223 which were punishable by death! And yet from the beginning of our existence down to a time within the memory of babes England has distressed herself piteously over the ungentleness of our Connecticut Blue Laws. Those Blue Laws should have been spared English criticism for two reasons:

1. They were so insipidly mild, by contrast with the bloody and atrocious laws of England of the same period, as to seem characterless and colorless when one brings them into that awful presence.

2. *The Blue Laws never had any existence.* They were the fancy-work of an English clergyman; they were never a part of any statute-book. And yet they could have been made to serve a useful and merciful purpose; if they had been injected into the English law the dilution would have given to the whole a less lurid aspect; or, to figure the effect in another way, they would have been coca mixed into vitriol.

I have drawn no laws and no illustrations from the twin civilizations of hell and Russia. To have entered into that atmosphere would have defeated my purpose, which was to show a great and genuine progress in Christendom in these few later generations toward mercifulness—a wide and general relaxing of

APPENDIX

the grip of the law.   Russia had to be left out because exile to Siberia remains, and in that single punishment is gathered together and concentrated all the bitter inventions of all the black ages for the infliction of suffering upon human beings.   Exile for life from one's hearthstone and one's idols—this is rack, thumb-screw, the water-drop, fagot and stake, tearing asunder by horses, flaying alive—all these in one; and not compact into hours, but drawn out into years, each year a century, and the whole a mortal immortality of torture and despair.   While exile to Siberia remains one will be obliged to admit that there is one country in Christendom where the punishments of all the ages are still preserved and still inflicted, that there is one country in Christendom where no advance has been made toward modifying the medieval penalties for offenses against society and the State.

APPENDIX T

A TRIBUTE TO HENRY H. ROGERS

(See Chapter cc and earlier)

April 25, 1902. I owe more to Henry Rogers than to any other man whom I have known. He was born in Fairhaven, Connecticut, in 1839, and is my junior by four years. He was graduated from the high school there in 1853, when he was fourteen years old, and from that time forward he earned his own living, beginning at first as the bottom subordinate in the village store with hard-work privileges and a low salary. When he was twenty-four he went out to the newly discovered petroleum fields in Pennsylvania and got work; then returned home, with enough money to pay passage, married a schoolmate, and took her to the oil regions. He prospered, and by and by established the Standard Oil Trust with Mr. Rockefeller and others, and is still one of its managers and directors.

In 1893 we fell together by accident one evening in the Murray Hill Hotel, and our friendship began on the spot and at once. Ever since then he has added my business affairs to his own and carried them through, and I have had no further trouble with them. Obstructions and perplexities which would have driven me mad were simplicities to his master mind and furnished him no difficulties. He released me from my entanglements with Paige and stopped that expensive outgo; when Charles L. Webster & Company failed he saved my copyrights for Mrs. Clemens when she would have sacrificed them to the creditors although they were in no way entitled to them; he offered to lend me money wherewith to save the life of that worthless firm; when I started lecturing around the world to make the money to pay off the Webster debts he spent more than a year trying to reconcile the differences between Harper & Brothers and the American Publishing Company and patch up a working-contract between them and succeeded where any other man would have failed; as fast as I earned money and sent it to him he banked it at interest and held onto it, refusing to pay any creditor until he could pay all of the 96 alike; when I had earned enough to pay dollar for dollar he swept off the indebtedness and sent me the whole batch of complimentary letters which the creditors wrote in return; when I had earned $28,500 more, $18,500 of which was in his hands, I wrote him from Vienna to put the latter into Federal Steel and *leave* it there; he obeyed to the extent of $17,500, but sold it in two months at $25,000 profit, and said it would go ten points higher, but that it was his custom to "give the other man a chance" (and that was a true word— there was never a truer one spoken). That was at the end of '99 and beginning of 1900; and from that day to this he has continued to break up my bad schemes and put better ones in their place, to my great advantage. I do things which ought to try man's patience, but they never seem to try his; he always finds a colorable excuse for what I have done. His soul was born superhumanly sweet, and I do not think anything can sour it. I have not known his equal among men for lovable qualities. But for his cool head and wise guidance I should never have come out of the Webster difficulties on top; it was his good steering that enabled me to work out my salvation and pay a hundred cents on the dollar—the most valuable service any man ever did me.

His character is full of fine graces, but the finest is this: that he can load you down with crushing obligations and then so conduct himself that you never feel their weight. If he would only require something in return—but that is not in his nature; it would not occur to him. With the Harpers and the American Company at war those copyrights were worth but little; he engineered a peace and made them valuable. He invests $100,000 for me here, and in a few months returns a profit of $31,000. I invest (in London and here) $66,000 and must wait considerably for results (in case there shall be any). I tell him about it and he finds no fault, utters not a sarcasm. He was born serene, patient, all-enduring, where a friend is concerned, and nothing can extinguish that great quality in him. Such a man is entitled to the high gift of humor: he has it at its very best. He is not only the best friend I have ever had, but is the best man I have known.   S. L. CLEMENS.

APPENDIX U

FROM MARK TWAIN'S LAST POEM

BEGUN AT RIVERDALE, NEW YORK. FINISHED AT YORK HARBOR,
MAINE, AUGUST 18, 1902

(See Chapter ccxxiii)

(A bereft and demented mother speaks)

. . . O, I can see my darling yet: the little form
In slip of flimsy stuff all creamy white,
Pink-belted waist with ample bows,
Blue shoes scarce bigger than the house-cat's ears—
Capering in delight and choked with glee.

· · · ·

It was a summer afternoon; the hill
Rose green above me and about, and in the vale below
The distant village slept, and all the world
Was steeped in dreams. Upon me lay this peace,
And I forgot my sorrow in its spell. And now
My little maid passed by, and she
Was deep in thought upon a solemn thing:
A disobedience, and my reproof. Upon my face
She must not look until the day was done;
For she was doing penance . . . *She?*
O, it was *I!* What mother knows not that?
And so she passed, I worshiping and longing . . .
It was not wrong? You do not think me wrong?
I did it for the best. Indeed I meant it so.

· · · ·

She flits before me now:
The peach-bloom of her gauzy crêpe,
The plaited tails of hair,

APPENDIX

The ribbons floating from the summer hat,
The grieving face, dropp'd head absorbed with care.
O, dainty little form!—
I see it move, receding slow along the path,
By hovering butterflies besieged; I see it reach
The breezy top clear-cut against the sky . . .
Then pass beyond and sink from sight—forever!

.   .   .

Within, was light and cheer; without,
A blustering winter's night. There was a play;
It was her own; for she had wrought it out
Unhelped, from her own head—and she
But turned sixteen! A pretty play,
All graced with cunning fantasies,
And happy songs, and peopled all with fays,
And sylvan gods and goddesses,
And shepherds, too, that piped and danced,
And wore the guileless hours away
In care-free romps and games.
    Her girlhood mates played in the piece,
And she as well: a goddess, she,—
And looked it, as it seemed to me.
    'Twas fairyland restored—so beautiful it was
And innocent. It made us cry, we elder ones,
To live our lost youth o'er again
With these its happy heirs.
    Slowly, at last, the curtain fell.
Before us, there, she stood, all wreathed and draped
In roses pearled with dew—so sweet, so glad,
So radiant!—and flung us kisses through the storm
Of praise that crowned her triumph. . . . O,
Across the mists of time I see her yet,
My Goddess of the Flowers!
    . . . The curtain hid her. . . .
Do you comprehend? Till time shall end!
Out of my life she vanished while I looked!
    . . . Ten years are flown.
O, I have watched so long,

1661

MARK TWAIN

So long. But she will come no more. . . .
No, she will come no more.

        •   •   •   •

   It seems so strange . . . so strange . . .
Struck down unwarned!
In the unbought grace of youth laid low—
In the glory of her fresh young bloom laid low—
In the morning of her life cut down!
   And I not by! Not by
When the shadows fell, the night of death closed down.
The sun that lit my life went out. Not by to answer
When the latest whisper passed the lips
That were so dear to me—my name!
Far from my post! the world's whole breadth away.
O, sinking in the waves of death she cried to me
For mother-help, and got for answer—
Silence!

        •   •   •   •

We that are old—we comprehend; even we
That are not mad: whose grown-up scions still abide,
Their tale complete:
Their *earlier selves* we glimpse at intervals
Far in the dimming past;
We see the little forms as once they were,
And whilst we ache to take them to our hearts,
The vision fades. We know them lost to us—
Forever lost; we cannot have them back;
We miss them as we miss the dead,
We mourn them as we mourn the dead.

APPENDIX V

SELECTIONS FROM AN UNFINISHED BOOK, "3,000 YEARS AMONG THE MICROBES"

THE AUTOBIOGRAPHY OF A MICROBE, WHO, IN A FORMER EXIST-
ENCE, HAD BEEN A MAN—HIS PRESENT HABITAT BEING
THE ORGANISM OF A TRAMP, BLITZOWSKI. (WRITTEN AT
DUBLIN, NEW HAMPSHIRE, 1905)

(See Chapter ccxxxv)

Our world (the tramp) is as large and grand and awe-compel-
ling to us microscopic creatures as is man's world to man. Our
tramp is mountainous, there are vast oceans in him, and lakes
that are sea-like for size, there are many rivers (veins and
arteries) which are fifteen miles across, and of a length so stupendous as to make the Mississippi and the Amazon trifling little
Rhode Island brooks by comparison. As for our minor rivers,
they are multitudinous, and the dutiable commerce of disease
which they carry is rich beyond the dreams of the American
custom-house.

Take a man like Sir Oliver Lodge, and what secret of Nature
can be hidden from him? He says: "A billion, that is a million
millions, of atoms is truly an immense number, but the resulting
aggregate is still excessively minute. A portion of substance
consisting of a billion atoms is only barely visible with the
highest power of a microscope; and a speck or granule, in order to
be visible to the naked eye, like a grain of lycopodium-dust,
must be a million times bigger still."

The human eye could see it then—that dainty little speck.
But with my microbe-eye I could see *every individual* of the whirling billions of *atoms* that *compose* the speck. *Nothing is ever at
rest*—wood, iron, water, everything is alive, everything is raging,
whirling, whizzing, day and night and night and day, nothing

is dead, *there is no such thing as death,* everything is full of bristling life, tremendous life, even the bones of the crusader that perished before Jerusalem eight centuries ago. There are no vegetables, *all things are animal;* each electron is an animal, each molecule is a collection of animals, and each has an appointed duty to perform and a soul to be saved. Heaven was not made for man alone, and oblivion and neglect reserved for the rest of His creatures. He gave them life, He gave them humble services to perform, they have performed them, and they will not be forgotten, they will have their reward. Man—always vain, windy, conceited—thinks he will be in the majority there. He will be disappointed. Let him humble himself. But for the despised microbe and the persecuted bacillus, who needed a home and nourishment, he would not have been created. He has a mission, therefore—a reason for existing: let him do the service he was made for, and keep quiet.

Three weeks ago I was a man myself, and thought and felt as men think and feel; I have lived 3,000 years since then [microbic time], and I see the foolishness of it now. We live to learn, and fortunate are we when we are wise enough to profit by it.

In matters pertaining to microscopy we necessarily have an advantage here over the scientist of the earth, because, as I have just been indicating, we see with our naked eyes minutenesses which no man-made microscope can detect, and are therefore able to register as facts many things which exist for him as theories only. Indeed, we know as facts several things which he has not yet divined even by theory. For example, he does not suspect that there is no life but *animal* life, and that all atoms are *individual animals* endowed each with a certain degree of consciousness, great or small, each with likes and dislikes, predilections and aversions—that, in a word, each has a *character,* a character of its own. Yet such is the case. Some of the molecules of a stone have an aversion for some of those of a vegetable or any other creature and will not associate with them—and would not be allowed to, if they tried. Nothing is more particular about society than a molecule. And so there are no end of castes; in this matter India is not a circumstance.

"Tell me, Franklin [a microbe of great learning], is the ocean an individual, an animal, a creature?"

APPENDIX

"Yes."

"Then water—any water—is an individual?"

"Yes."

"Suppose you remove a drop of it? Is what is left an individual?"

"Yes, and so is the drop."

"Suppose you divide the drop?"

"Then you have two individuals."

"Suppose you separate the hydrogen and the oxygen?"

"Again you have two individuals. But you haven't water any more."

"Of course. Certainly. Well, suppose you combine them again, but in a new way: make the proportions equal—one part oxygen to one of hydrogen?"

"But you know you can't. They won't combine on equal terms."

I was ashamed to have made that blunder. I was embarrassed; to cover it I started to say we used to combine them like that where I came from, but thought better of it, and stood pat.

"Now then," I said, "it amounts to this: water is an individual, an animal, and is alive; remove the hydrogen and *it* is an animal and is alive; the remaining oxygen is also an individual, an animal, and is alive. Recapitulation: the two individuals combined constitute a third individual—and yet each *continues* to be an individual."

I glanced at Franklin, but . . . upon reflection, held my peace. I could have pointed out to him that here was mute Nature explaining the sublime mystery of the Trinity so luminously that even the commonest understanding could comprehend it, whereas many a trained master of words had labored to do *it* with speech and failed. But he would not have known what I was talking about. After a moment I resumed:

"Listen—and see if I have understood you rightly, to wit: All the atoms that constitute each oxygen molecule are separate individuals, and each is a living animal; all the atoms that constitute each hydrogen molecule are separate individuals, and each one is a living animal; each drop of water consists of millions of living animals, the drop itself is an individual, a living animal, and the wide ocean is another. Is that it?"

"Yes, that is correct."

"By George, it beats the band!"

He liked the expression, and set it down in his tablets.

"Franklin, we've got it down fine. And to think—there are other animals that are still smaller than a hydrogen atom, and yet *it* is so small that it takes five thousand of them to make a molecule—a molecule so minute that it could get into a microbe's eye and he wouldn't know it was there!"

"Yes, the wee creatures that inhabit the bodies of us germs and feed upon us, and rot us with disease. Ah, what could they have been created for? They give us pain, they make our lives miserable, they murder us—and where is the use of it all, where is the wisdom? Ah, friend *Bkshp* [microbic orthography], we live in a strange and unaccountable world; our birth is a mystery, our little life is a mystery, a trouble, we pass and are seen no more; all is mystery, mystery, mystery; we know not whence we came, nor why; we know not whither we go, nor why we go. We only know we were not made in vain, we only know we were made for a wise purpose, and that all is well! We shall not be cast aside in contumely and unblest after all we have suffered. Let us be patient, let us not repine, let us trust. The humblest of us is cared for—oh, believe it!—and this fleeting stay is not the end!"

You notice that? He did not suspect that he, also, was engaged in gnawing, torturing, defiling, rotting, and murdering a fellow-creature—he and all the swarming billions of his race. None of them suspects it. That is significant. It is suggestive—irresistibly suggestive—insistently suggestive. It hints at the possibility that the procession of known and listed devourers and persecutors is not complete. It suggests the possibility, and substantially the certainty, that man is himself a microbe, and his globe a blood-corpuscle drifting with its shining brethren of the Milky Way down a vein of the Master and Maker of all things, whose body, mayhap—glimpsed part-wise from the earth by night, and receding and lost to view in the measureless remotenesses of space—is what men name the Universe.

Yes, that was all old to me, but to find that our little old familiar microbes were *themselves* loaded up with microbes that fed *them*, enriched them, and persistently and faithfully preserved them and their poor old tramp-planet from destruction—oh, that was new, and too delicious!

I wanted to see them! I was in a fever to see them! I had

lenses to two-million power, but of course the field was no bigger than a person's finger-nail, and so it wasn't possible to compass a considerable spectacle or a landscape with them; whereas what I had been craving was a thirty-foot field, which would represent a spread of several miles of country and show up things in a way to make them worth looking at. The boys and I had often tried to contrive this improvement, but had failed.

I mentioned the matter to the Duke and it made him smile. He said it was a quite simple thing—he had it at home. I was eager to bargain for the secret, but he said it was a trifle and not worth bargaining for. He said:

"Hasn't it occurred to you that all you have to do is to bend an X-ray to an angle-value of 8.4 and refract it with a parabolism, and there you are?"

Upon my word, I had never thought of that simple thing! You could have knocked me down with a feather.

· · · · · · ·

We rigged a microscope for an exhibition at once and put a drop of my blood under it, which got mashed flat when the lens got shut down upon it. The result was beyond my dreams. The field stretched miles away, green and undulating, threaded with streams and roads, and bordered all down the mellowing distances with picturesque hills. And there was a great white city of tents; and everywhere were parks of artillery and divisions of cavalry and infantry—waiting. We had hit a lucky moment, evidently there was going to be a march-past or something like that. At the front where the chief banner flew there was a large and showy tent, with showy guards on duty, and about it were some other tents of a swell kind.

The warriors—particularly the officers—were lovely to look at, they were so trim-built and so graceful and so handsomely uniformed. They were quite distinct, vividly distinct, for it was a fine day, and they were so immensely magnified that they looked to be fully a finger-nail high.[1] Everywhere you could see officers moving smartly about, and they looked gay,

---

[1] My own expression, and a quite happy one. I said to the Duke: "Your Grace, they're just about finger-nailers!"
"How do you mean, m' lord?"
"This. You notice the stately General standing there with his

but the common soldiers looked sad. Many wife-swinks ["Swinks," an atomic race] and daughter-swinks and sweet-heart-swinks were about—crying, mainly. It seemed to indicate that this was a case of war, not a summer-camp for exercise, and that the poor labor-swinks were being torn from their planet-saving industries to go and distribute civilization and other forms of suffering among the feeble benighted somewhere; else why should the swinkesses cry?

The cavalry was very fine—shiny black horses, shapely and spirited; and presently when a flash of light struck a lifted bugle (delivering a command which we couldn't hear) and a division came tearing down on a gallop it was a stirring and gallant sight, until the dust rose an inch—the Duke thought more—and swallowed it up in a rolling and tumbling long gray cloud, with bright weapons glinting and sparkling in it.

Before long the real business of the occasion began. A battalion of priests arrived carrying sacred pictures. That settled it: this was war; these far-stretching masses of troops were bound for the front. Their little monarch came out now, the sweetest little thing that ever travestied the human shape I think, and he lifted up his hands and blessed the passing armies, and they looked as grateful as they could, and made signs of humble and real reverence as they drifted by the holy pictures.

It was beautiful—the whole thing; and wonderful, too, when those serried masses swung into line and went marching down the valley under the long array of fluttering flags.

Evidently they were going somewhere to fight for their king, which was the little manny that blessed them; and to preserve him and his brethren that occupied the other swell tents; to civilize and grasp a valuable little unwatched country for them somewhere. But the little fellow and his brethren didn't fall in—that was a noticeable particular. *They* didn't fight; they stayed at home, where it was safe, and waited for the swag.

Very well, then—what ought *we* to do? Had we no moral

hand resting upon the muzzle of a cannon? Well, if you could stick your little finger down against the ground alongside of him his plumes would just reach up to where your nail joins the flesh."

The Duke said "finger-nailers was good"—good and exact; and he afterward used it several times himself.

duty to perform? Ought we to allow this war to begin? Was it not our duty to stop it, in the name of right and righteousness? Was it not our duty to administer a rebuke to this selfish and heartless Family?

The Duke was struck by that, and greatly moved. He felt as I did about it, and was ready to do whatever was right, and thought we ought to pour boiling water on the Family and extinguish it, which we did.

It extinguished the armies, too, which was not intended. We both regretted this, but the Duke said that these people were nothing to us, and deserved extinction anyway for being so poor-spirited as to serve such a Family. He was loyally doing the like himself, and so was I, but I don't think we thought of that. And it wasn't just the same, anyway, because we were sooflaskies, and they were only swinks.

Franklin realizes that no atom is destructible; that it has always existed and will exist forever; but he thinks all atoms will go out of this world some day and continue their life in a happier one. Old Tolliver thinks no atom's life will ever end, but he also thinks Blitzowski is the only world it will ever see, and that at no time in its eternity will it be either worse off or better off than it is now and always has been. Of course he thinks the planet Blitzowski is itself eternal and indestructible—at any rate he says he thinks that. It could make me sad, only I know better. D. T. will fetch Blitzy yet one of these days.

But these are alien thoughts, human thoughts, and they falsely indicate that I do not want this tramp to go on living. What would become of me if he should disintegrate? My molecules would scatter all around and take up new quarters in hundreds of plants and animals; each would carry its special feelings along with it, each would be content in its new estate, but where should *I* be? I should not have a rag of a feeling left, after my disintegration—with his—was complete. Nothing to think with, nothing to grieve or rejoice with, nothing to hope or despair with. There would be no more *me*. I should be musing and thinking and dreaming somewhere else—in some distant animal maybe—perhaps a cat—by proxy of my oxygen I should be raging and fuming in some other creatures—a rat, perhaps; I should be smiling and hoping in still another child of Nature—

heir to my hydrogen—a weed, or a cabbage, or something; my carbonic acid (ambition) would be dreaming dreams in some lowly wood-violet that was longing for a showy career; thus my details would be doing as much feeling as ever, but I should not be aware of it, it would all be going on for the benefit of those others, and I not in it at all. I should be gradually wasting away, atom by atom, molecule by molecule, as the years went on, and at last I should be all distributed, and nothing left of what had once been Me. It is curious, and not without impressiveness: I should still be alive, intensely alive, but so scattered that I would not know it. I should not be dead—no, one cannot call it that—but I should be the next thing to it. And to think what centuries and ages and æons would drift over me before the disintegration was finished, the last bone turned to gas and blown away! I wish I knew what it is going to feel like, to lie helpless such a weary, weary time, and see my faculties decay and depart, one by one, like lights which burn low, and flicker and perish, until the ever-deepening gloom and darkness which—oh, away, away with these horrors, and let me think of something wholesome!

My tramp is only 85; there is good hope that he will live ten years longer—500,000 of my microbe years. So may it be.

Oh, dear, we are all so wise! Each of us knows it all, and *knows* he knows it all—the rest, to a man, are fools and deluded. One man knows there is a hell, the next one knows there isn't; one man knows high tariff is right, the next man knows it isn't; one man knows monarchy is best, the next one knows it isn't; one age knows there are witches, the next one knows there aren't; one sect knows its religion is the only true one, there are sixty-four thousand five hundred million sects that know it isn't so. There is not a mind present among this multitude of verdict-deliverers that is the superior of the minds that persuade and represent the rest of the divisions of the multitude. Yet this sarcastic fact does not humble the arrogance nor diminish the know-it-all bulk of a single verdict-maker of the lot by so much as a shade. Mind is plainly an ass, but it will be many ages before it finds it out, no doubt. Why do we respect the opinions of any man or any microbe that ever lived? I swear I don't know. Why do I respect my own? Well—that is different.

APPENDIX W

LITTLE BESSIE WOULD ASSIST PROVIDENCE

(See Chapter cclxxxii)

[It is dull, and I need wholesome excitements and distractions; so I will go lightly excursioning along the primrose path of theology.]

Little Bessie was nearly three years old. She was a good child, and not shallow, not frivolous, but meditative and thoughtful, and much given to thinking out the reasons of things and trying to make them harmonize with results. One day she said:

"Mama, why is there so much pain and sorrow and suffering? What is it all for?"

It was an easy question, and mama had no difficulty in answering it:

"It is for our good, my child. In His wisdom and mercy the Lord sends us these afflictions to discipline us and make us better."

"Is it *He* that sends them?"

"Yes."

"Does He send *all* of them, mama?"

"Yes, dear, all of them. None of them comes by accident; He alone sends them, and always out of love for us, and to make us better."

"Isn't it strange?"

"Strange? Why, no, I have never thought of it in that way. I have not heard any one call it strange before. It has always seemed natural and right to me, and wise and most kindly and merciful."

"Who first thought of it like that, mama? Was it you?"

"Oh no, child, I was taught it."

"Who taught you so, mama?"

"Why, really, I don't know—I can't remember. My mother,

I suppose; or the preacher. But it's a thing that everybody knows."

"Well, anyway, it does seem strange. Did He give Billy Norris the typhus?"

"Yes."

"What for?"

"Why, to discipline him and make him good."

"But he died, mama, and so it *couldn't* make him good."

"Well, then, I suppose it was for some other reason. We know it was a *good* reason, whatever it was."

"What do you think it was, mama?"

"Oh, you ask so many questions! I think it was to discipline his parents."

"Well, then, it wasn't fair, mama. Why should *his* life be taken away for their sake, when he wasn't doing anything?"

"Oh, *I* don't know! I only know it was for a good and wise and merciful reason."

"What reason, mama?"

"I think—I think—well, it was a judgment; it was to punish them for some sin they had committed."

"But *he* was the one that was punished, mama. Was that right?"

"Certainly, certainly. He does nothing that isn't right and wise and merciful. You can't understand these things now, dear, but when you are grown up you will understand them, and then you will see that they are just and wise."

After a pause:

"Did He make the roof fall in on the stranger that was trying to save the crippled old woman from the fire, mama?"

"Yes, my child. *Wait!* Don't ask me why, because I don't know. I only know it was to discipline some one, or be a judgment upon somebody, or to show His power."

"That drunken man that stuck a pitchfork into Mrs. Welch's baby when—"

"Never mind about it, you needn't go into particulars; it was to discipline the child—*that* much is certain, anyway."

"Mama, Mr. Burgess said in his sermon that billions of little creatures are sent into us to give us cholera, and typhoid, and lockjaw, and more than a thousand other sicknesses and—mama, does He send them?"

APPENDIX

"Oh, certainly, child, certainly. Of course."

"What for?"

"Oh, to *dis*cipline us! Haven't I told you so, over and over again?"

"It's awful cruel, mama! And silly! and if I—"

"Hush, oh, *hush!* Do you want to bring the lightning?"

"You know the lightning *did* come last week, mama, and struck the new church, and burnt it down. Was it to discipline the church?"

(Wearily.) "Oh, I suppose so."

"But it killed a hog that wasn't doing anything. Was it to discipline the hog, mama?"

"Dear child, don't you want to run out and play a while? If you would like to—"

"Mama, only think! Mr. Hollister says there isn't a bird, or fish, or reptile, or any other animal that hasn't got an enemy that Providence has sent to bite it and chase it and pester it and kill it and suck its blood and discipline it and make it good and religious. Is that true, mother—because if it is true why did Mr. Hollister laugh at it?"

"That Hollister is a scandalous person, and I don't want you to listen to anything he says."

"Why, mama, he is very interesting, and *I* think he tries to be good. He says the wasps catch spiders and cram them down into their nests in the ground—*alive*, mama!—and there they live and suffer days and days and days, and the hungry little wasps chewing their legs and gnawing into their bellies all the time, to make them good and religious and praise God for His infinite mercies. *I* think Mr. Hollister is just lovely, and ever so kind; for when I asked him if *he* would treat a spider like that he said he hoped to be damned if he would; and then he— *Dear* mama, have you fainted! I will run and bring help! Now *this* comes of staying in town this hot weather."

APPENDIX X

A CHRONOLOGICAL LIST OF MARK TWAIN'S WORK—PUBLISHED AND OTHERWISE—FROM 1851-1910

Note 1.—This is not a detailed bibliography, but merely a general list of Mark Twain's literary undertakings, in the order of performance, showing when, and usually where, the work was done, when and where first published, etc. An excellent Mark Twain bibliography has been compiled by Mr. Merle Johnson, to whom acknowledgments are due for important items.

Note 2.—Only a few of the more important speeches are noted. Volumes that are merely collections of tales or articles are not noted.

Note 3.—Titles are shortened to those most commonly in use, as "Huck Finn" or "Huck" for "The Adventures of Huckleberry Finn."

Names of periodicals are abbreviated.

The initials U. E. stand for the "Uniform Edition" of Mark Twain's works.

The chapter numbers in the date-lines refer to the place in this work where the items are mentioned.

1851. (See Chapter xviii of this work.)
Edited the Hannibal *Journal* during the absence of the owner and editor, Orion Clemens.
Wrote local items for the Hannibal *Journal.*
Burlesque of a rival editor in the Hannibal *Journal.*
Wrote two sketches for *The Sat. Eve. Post* (Philadelphia).
To MARY IN H—L—Hannibal *Journal.*

1852-53. (See Chapter xviii.)
JIM WOLFE AND THE FIRE—Hannibal *Journal.*
Burlesque of a rival editor in the Hannibal *Journal.*

1853. (See Chapter xix.)
Wrote obituary poems—not published.
Wrote first letters home.

1855-56. (See Chapters xx and xxi.)
First after-dinner speech; delivered at a printers' banquet in Keokuk, Iowa.
Letters from Cincinnati, November 14, 1856, signed "Snodgrass"—*Saturday Post* (Keokuk).

APPENDIX

1857. (See Chapter xxi.)
Letters from Cincinnati, March 14, 1857, signed "Snodgrass"—
Saturday Post (Keokuk).

1858.
Anonymous contributions to the New Orleans *Crescent* and probably
to St. Louis papers.

1859. (See Chapter xxvii, also Appendix B.)
Burlesque of Capt. Isaiah Sellers—*True Delta* (New Orleans), May
8 or 9.

1861. (See Chapters xxxiii to xxxv.)
Letters home, published in *The Gate City* (Keokuk).

1862. (See Chapters xxxv to xxxviii.)
Letters and sketches, signed "Josh," for the *Territorial Enterprise*
(Virginia City, Nevada).
REPORT OF THE LECTURE OF PROF. PERSONAL PRONOUN—*Enterprise.*
REPORT OF A FOURTH OF JULY ORATION—*Enterprise.*
THE PETRIFIED MAN—*Enterprise.*
Local news reporter for the *Enterprise* from August.

1863. (See Chapters xli to xliii; also Appendix C.)
Reported the Nevada Legislature for the *Enterprise.*
First used the name "Mark Twain," February 2.
ADVICE TO THE UNRELIABLE—*Enterprise.*
CURING A COLD—*Enterprise.* U. E.
INFORMATION FOR THE MILLION—*Enterprise.*
ADVICE TO GOOD LITTLE GIRLS—*Enterprise.*
THE DUTCH NICK MASSACRE—*Enterprise.*
Many other *Enterprise* sketches.
THE AGED PILOT MAN (poem)—"ROUGHING IT." U. E.

1864. (See Chapters xliv to xlvii.)
Reported the Nevada Legislature for the *Enterprise.*
Speech as "Governor of the Third House."
Letters to New York *Sunday Mercury.*
Local reporter on the San Francisco *Call.*
Articles and sketches for the *Golden Era.*
Articles and sketches for the *Californian.*
Daily letters from San Francisco to the *Enterprise.*
(Several of the *Era* and *Californian* sketches appear in SKETCHES
NEW AND OLD. U. E.)

1865. (See Chapters xlix to li; also Appendix E.)
Notes for the Jumping Frog story; Angel's Camp, February.
Sketches, etc., for the *Golden Era* and *Californian.*
Daily letter to the *Enterprise.*
THE JUMPING FROG (San Francisco)—Saturday *Press.* New
York, November 18. U. E.

1866.   (See Chapters lii to lv; also Appendix D.)
Daily letter to the *Enterprise.*
Sandwich Island letters to the Sacramento *Union.*
Lecture on the Sandwich Islands, San Francisco, October 2.
FORTY-THREE DAYS IN AN OPEN BOAT—*Harper's Magazine,*
December (error in signature made it Mark Swain).

1867.   (See Chapters lvii to lxv; also Appendices E, F, and G.)
Letters to *Alta California* from New York.
JIM WOLFE AND THE CATS—N. Y. *Sunday Mercury.*
THE JUMPING FROG—book, published by Charles Henry Webb,
May 1. U. E.
Lectured at Cooper Union, May, '66.
Letters to *Alta California* and New York *Tribune* from the *Quaker
City*—Holy Land excursion.
Letter to New York *Herald* on the return from the Holy Land.
After-dinner speech on "Women" (Washington).
Began arrangement for the publication of THE INNOCENTS
ABROAD.

1868.   (See Chapters lxvi to lxix; also Appendices H and I.)
Newspaper letters, etc., from Washington, for New York *Citizen,
Tribune, Herald,* and other papers and periodicals.
Preparing *Quaker City* letters (in Washington and San Francisco)
for book publication.
CAPTAIN WAKEMAN'S (STORMFIELD'S) VISIT TO HEAVEN (San
Francisco), published *Harper's Magazine,* December, 1907–January, 1908 (also book, Harpers).
Lectured in California and Nevada on the "Holy Land," July 2.
S'CAT! Anonymous article on T. K. Beecher (Elmira), published
in local paper.
Lecture-tour, season 1868–69.

1869.   (See Chapters lxx to lxxiii.)
THE INNOCENTS ABROAD—book (Am. Pub. Co.), July 20.   U. E.
Bought one-third ownership in the Buffalo *Express.*
Contributed editorials, sketches, etc., to the *Express.*
Contributed sketches to *Packard's Monthly, Wood's Magazine,* etc.
Lecture-tour, season 1869–70.

1870.   (See Chapters lxxiv to lxxx; also Appendix J.)
Contributed various matter to Buffalo *Express.*
Contributed various matter under general head of "MEMORANDA"
to *Galaxy Magazine,* May to April, '71.
ROUGHING IT begun in September (Buffalo).
SHEM'S DIARY (Buffalo) (unfinished).
GOD, ANCIENT AND MODERN (unpublished).

APPENDIX

1871.   (See Chapters lxxxi and lxxxii; also Appendix K.)
MEMORANDA continued in *Galaxy* to April.
AUTOBIOGRAPHY AND FIRST ROMANCE [1] — booklet (Sheldon & Co.). U. E.
ROUGHING IT finished (Quarry Farm).
Ruloff letter—*Tribune.*
Wrote several sketches and lectures (Quarry Farm).
Western play (unfinished).
Lecture-tour, season 1871-72.

1872.   (See Chapters lxxxiii to lxxxvii; also Appendix L.)
ROUGHING IT—book (Am. Pub. Co.), February. U. E.
THE MARK TWAIN SCRAP-BOOK invented (Saybrook, Connecticut).
TOM SAWYER begun as a play (Saybrook, Connecticut).
A few unimportant sketches published in "Practical Jokes," etc.
Began a book on England (London).

1873.   (See Chapters lxxxviii to xcii.)
Letters on the Sandwich Islands—*Tribune,* January 3 and 6.
THE GILDED AGE (with C. D. Warner)—book (Am. Pub. Co), December. U. E.
THE LICENSE OF THE PRESS—paper for The Monday Evening Club.
Lectured in London, October 18 and season 1873-74.

1874.   (See Chapters xciii to xcviii; also Appendix M.)
TOM SAWYER continued (in the new study at Quarry Farm).
A TRUE STORY (Quarry Farm)—*Atlantic,* November. U. E.
FABLES (Quarry Farm). U. E.
COLONEL SELLERS—play (Quarry Farm) performed by John T. Raymond.
UNDERTAKER'S LOVE-STORY (Quarry Farm) (unpublished).
OLD TIMES ON THE MISSISSIPPI (Hartford)—*Atlantic,* January to July, 1875.
Monarchy letter to Mrs. Clemens, dated 1935 (Boston).

1875.   (See Chapters c to civ; also Appendix N.)
UNIVERSAL SUFFRAGE—paper for The Monday Evening Club.
SKETCHES NEW AND OLD—book (Am. Pub. Co.), July. U. E.
TOM SAWYER concluded (Hartford).
THE CURIOUS REP. OF GONDOUR—*Atlantic,* October (unsigned).
PUNCH, CONDUCTOR, PUNCH—*Atlantic,* February, 1876. U. E.
THE SECOND ADVENT (unfinished).
THE MYSTERIOUS CHAMBER (unfinished).
AUTOBIOGRAPHY OF A DAMN FOOL (unfinished).
Petition for International Copyright.

---

[1] THE FIRST ROMANCE had appeared in the *Express* in 1870. Later included in SKETCHES.

1876. (See Chapters cvi to cx.)
Performed in THE LOAN OF THE LOVER as Peter Spuyk (Hartford).
CARNIVAL OF CRIME—paper for The Monday Evening Club—*Atlantic*, June. U. E.
HUCK FINN begun (Quarry Farm).
CANVASSER'S STORY (Quarry Farm)—*Atlantic*, December. U. E.
" 1601 " (Quarry Farm), privately printed.
AH SIN (with Bret Harte)—play (Hartford).
TOM SAWYER—book (Am. Pub. Co.), December. U. E.
Speech on "The Weather," New England Society, December 22.

1877. (See Chapters cxii to cxv; also Appendix O.)
LOVES OF ALONZO FITZ-CLARENCE, ETC. (Quarry Farm)—*Atlantic*.
IDLE EXCURSION (Quarry Farm)—*Atlantic*, October, November, December. U. E.
SIMON WHEELER, DETECTIVE—play (Quarry Farm) (not produced).
PRINCE AND PAUPER begun (Quarry Farm).
Whittier birthday speech (Boston), December.

1878. (See Chapters cxvii to cxx.)
MAGNANIMOUS INCIDENT (Hartford)—*Atlantic*, May. U. E.
A TRAMP ABROAD (Heidelberg and Munich).
MENTAL TELEGRAPHY—*Harper's Magazine*, December, 1891. U. E.
GAMBETTA DUEL—*Atlantic*, February, 1879 (included in TRAMP). U. E.
REV. IN PITCAIRN—*Atlantic*, March, 1879. U. E.
STOLEN WHITE ELEPHANT—book (Osgood & Co.), 1882. U. E.
(The three items last named were all originally a part of the TRAMP ABROAD.)

1879. (See Chapters cxxi to cxxiv; also Chapter cxxxiv and Appendix P.)
A TRAMP ABROAD continued (Paris, Elmira, and Hartford).
Adam monument scheme (Elmira).
Speech on "The Babies" (Grant dinner, Chicago), November.
Speech on "Plagiarism" (Holmes breakfast, Boston), December.

1880. (See Chapters cxxv to cxxxii.)
PRINCE AND PAUPER concluded (Hartford and Elmira).
HUCK FINN continued (Quarry Farm, Elmira).
A CAT STORY (Quarry Farm) (unpublished).
A TRAMP ABROAD—book (Am. Pub. Co.), March 13. U. E.
EDWARD MILLS AND GEO. BENTON (Hartford)—*Atlantic*, August. U. E.
MRS. MCWILLIAMS AND THE LIGHTNING (Hartford) —*Atlantic*, September. U. E.

APPENDIX

1881. (See Chapters cxxxiv to cxxxvii.)
A CURIOUS EXPERIENCE—*Century*, November. U. E.
A BIOGRAPHY OF —— (unfinished).
PRINCE AND PAUPER—book (Osgood & Co.), December.
BURLESQUE ETIQUETTE (unfinished).

1882. (See Chapters cxl and cxli.)
LIFE ON THE MISSISSIPPI (Elmira and Hartford).

1883. (See Chapters cxlii to cxlviii.)
LIFE ON THE MISSISSIPPI—book (Osgood & Co.), May. U. E.
WHAT IS HAPPINESS?—paper for The Monday Evening Club.
Introduction to Portuguese conversation book (Hartford).
HUCK FINN concluded (Quarry Farm).
HISTORY GAME (Quarry Farm).
AMERICAN CLAIMANT (with W. D. Howells)—play (Hartford),
  produced by A. P. Burbank.
Dramatized TOM SAWYER and PRINCE AND PAUPER (not pro-
  duced).

1884. (See Chapters cxlix to cliii.)
Embarked in publishing with Charles L. Webster.
THE CARSON FOOTPRINTS—the *San Franciscan*.
HUCK FINN—book (Charles L. Webster & Co.), December. U. E.
Platform readings with George W. Cable, season '84–'85.

1885. (See Chapters cliv to clvii.)
Contracted for General Grant's *Memoirs*.
A CAMPAIGN THAT FAILED—*Century*, December. U. E.
THE UNIVERSAL TINKER—*Century*, December (open letter signed
  X. Y. Z.).
Letter on the government of children—*Christian Union*.
KIDITCHIN (children's poem).

1886. (See Chapters clix to clxi; also Appendix Q.)
Introduced Henry M. Stanley (Boston).
CONNECTICUT YANKEE begun (Hartford).
ENGLISH AS SHE IS TAUGHT—*Century*, April, 1887.
LUCK—*Harper's*, August, 1891.
GENERAL GRANT AND MATTHEW ARNOLD—Army and Navy
  dinner speech.

1887. (See Chapters clxii to clxiv; also Appendix R.)
MEISTERSCHAFT—play (Hartford)—*Century*, January, 1888. U. E.
KNIGHTS OF LABOR—essay (not published).
TO THE QUEEN OF ENGLAND—*Harper's Magazine*, December.
  U. E.
CONSISTENCY—paper for The Monday Evening Club.

MARK TWAIN

1888.   (See Chapters clxv to clxviii.)
Introductory for "Unsent Letters" (unpublished).
Master of Arts degree from Yale.
Yale Alumni address (unpublished).
Copyright controversy with Brander Matthews—*Princeton Review.*
Replies to Matthew Arnold's American criticisms (unpublished).
YANKEE continued (Elmira and Hartford).
Introduction of Nye and Riley (Boston).

1889.   (See Chapters clxix to clxxiii; also Appendix S.)
A MAJESTIC LITERARY FOSSIL—*Harper's Magazine*, February,
   1890. U. E.
HUCK AND TOM AMONG THE INDIANS (unfinished).
Introduction to YANKEE (not used).
LETTER TO ELSIE LESLIE—*St Nicholas*, February, 1890.
CONNECTICUT YANKEE—book (Webster & Co.), December. U. E.

1890.   (See Chapters clxxii to clxxiv.)
Letter to Andrew Lang about English Criticism.
   (No important literary matters this year. Mark Twain engaged
in promoting the Paige typesetting-machine.)

1891.   (See Chapters clxxv to clxxvii.)
AMERICAN CLAIMANT (Hartford) syndicated; also book (Web-
   ster & Co.), May, 1892. U. E.
European letters to New York *Sun.*
DOWN THE RHONE (unfinished).
KÖRNERSTRASSE (unpublished).

1892.   (See Chapters clxxx to clxxxii.)
THE GERMAN CHICAGO (Berlin)—*Sun.* U. E.
ALL KINDS OF SHIPS (at sea). U. E.
TOM SAWYER ABROAD (Nauheim)—*St. Nicholas*, November, '93, to
   April, '94. U. E.
THOSE EXTRAORDINARY TWINS (Nauheim). U. E.
PUDD'NHEAD WILSON (Nauheim and Florence)—*Century*, Decem-
   ber, '93, to June, '94. U. E.
£1,000,000 BANK-NOTE (Florence)—*Century*, January, '93. U. E.

1893.   (See Chapters clxxxiii to clxxxvii.)
JOAN OF ARC begun (at Villa Viviani, Florence) and completed up
   to the raising of the Siege of Orleans.
CALIFORNIAN'S TALE (Florence)—*Liber Scriptorum*, also *Harper's.*
ADAM'S DIARY (Florence)—*Niagara Book*, also *Harper's.*
ESQUIMAU MAIDEN'S ROMANCE—*Cosmopolitan*, November. U. E.
IS HE LIVING OR IS HE DEAD?—*Cosmopolitan*, September. U. E.
TRAVELING WITH A REFORMER—*Cosmopolitan*, December. U. E.
IN DEFENSE OF HARRIET SHELLEY (Florence)—*N. A. Rev.*, July,
   '94. U. E.

APPENDIX

Fenimore Cooper's Literary Offenses[1] (Players, New York) —*N. A. Rev.*, July, '95. U. E.

1894. (See Chapters clxxxviii to cxc.)
Joan of Arc continued (Étretat and Paris).
What Paul Bourget Thinks of Us (Étretat)—*N. A. Rev.*, January, '95. U. E.
Tom Sawyer Abroad—book (Webster & Co.), April. U. E.
Pudd'nhead Wilson—book (Am. Pub. Co.), November. U. E.
The failure of Charles L. Webster & Co., April 18.
The Derelict—poem (Paris) (unpublished).

1895. (See Chapters clxxxix and cxcii.)
Joan of Arc finished (Paris), January 28, *Harper's Magazine*, April to December.
Mental Telegraphy Again—*Harper's*, September. U. E.
A Little Note to Paul Bourget. U. E.
Poem to Mrs. Beecher (Elmira) (not published). U. E.
Lecture-tour around the world, begun at Elmira, July 14, ended July 31.

1896. (See Chapters cxci to cxciv.)
Joan of Arc—book (Harpers), May. U. E.
Tom Sawyer, Detective, and other stories — book (Harpers), November.
Following the Equator begun (23 Tedworth Square, London).

1897. (See Chapters cxcvii to cxcix.)
Following the Equator—book (Am. Pub. Co.), November.
Queen's Jubilee (London), newspaper syndicate; book privately printed.
James Hammond Trumbull—*Century*, November.
Which was Which? (London and Switzerland) (unfinished).
Tom and Huck (Switzerland) (unfinished).
Hellfire Hotchkiss (Switzerland) (unfinished).
In Memoriam—poem (Switzerland)—*Harper's Magazine*. U. E.
Concordia Club speech (Vienna).
Stirring Times in Austria (Vienna) — *Harper's Magazine*, March, 1898. U. E.

1898. (See Chapters cc to cciii; also Appendix T.)
The Austrian Edison Keeping School Again (Vienna)— *Century*, August. U. E.
At the Appetite Cure (Vienna)—*Cosmopolitan*, August. U. E.
From the London Times, 1904 (Vienna)—*Century*, November. U. E.
About Play-acting (Vienna)—*Forum*, October. U. E.

---

[1] This may not have been written until early in 1894.

CONCERNING THE JEWS (Vienna)—*Harper's Magazine*, September, '99. U. E.

CHRISTIAN SCIENCE AND MRS. EDDY (Vienna)—*Cosmopolitan*, October. U. E.

THE MAN THAT CORRUPTED HADLEYBURG (Vienna)—*Harper's Magazine*, December, '99. U. E.

Autobiographical chapters (Vienna); some of them used in the *N. A. Rev.*, 1906–07.

WHAT IS MAN? (Kaltenleutgeben) — book (privately printed), August, 1906.

ASSASSINATION OF AN EMPRESS (Kaltenleutgeben) (unpublished).

THE MYSTERIOUS STRANGER (unfinished).

Translations of German plays (unproduced).

1899. (See Chapters cciv to ccviii.)

DIPLOMATIC PAY AND CLOTHES (Vienna)—*Forum*, March. U. E.

MY LITERARY DÉBUT (Vienna)—*Century*, December. U. E.

CHRISTIAN SCIENCE (Vienna) — *N. A. Rev.*, December, 1902, January and February, 1903.

Translated German plays (Vienna) (unproduced).

Collaborated with Siegmund Schlesinger on plays (Vienna) (unfinished).

Planned a postal-check scheme (Vienna).

Articles about the Kellgren treatment (Sanna, Sweden) (unpublished).

ST. JOAN OF ARC (London)—*Harper's Magazine*, December, 1904. U. E.

MY FIRST LIE, AND HOW I GOT OUT OF IT (London)—New York *World*. U. E.

Articles on South African War (London) (unpublished).

Uniform Edition of Mark Twain's works (Am. Pub. Co.).

1900. (See Chapters ccix to ccxii.)

TWO LITTLE TALES (London)—*Century*, November, 1901. U. E.

Spoke on "Copyright" before the House of Lords.

Delivered many speeches in London and New York.

1901. (See Chapters ccxiii to ccxviii.)

TO THE PERSON SITTING IN DARKNESS (14 West Tenth Street, New York)—*N. A. Rev.*, February.

TO MY MISSIONARY CRITICS (14 West Tenth Street, New York) —*N. A. Rev.*, April.

DOUBLE-BARREL DETECTIVE STORY (Saranac Lake, "The Lair")— *Harper's Magazine*, January and February, 1902.

Lincoln Birthday Speech, February 11.

Many other speeches.

PLAN FOR CASTING VOTE PARTY (Riverdale) (unpublished).

THE STUPENDOUS PROCESSION (Riverdale) (unpublished).

ANTE-MORTEM OBITUARIES—*Harper's Weekly*.

Received degree of Doctor of Letters from Yale.

APPENDIX

1902. (See Chapters ccxix to ccxxiv; also Appendix U.)
DOES THE RACE OF MAN LOVE A LORD? (Riverdale)—*N. A. Rev.*.
April. U. E.
FIVE BOONS OF LIFE (Riverdale)—*Harper's Weekly*, July 5. U. E.
WHY NOT ABOLISH IT? (Riverdale)—*Harper's Weekly*, July 5.
DEFENSE OF GENERAL FUNSTON (Riverdale)—*N. A. Rev.*, May.
IF I COULD BE THERE (Riverdale (unpublished).
Wrote various articles, unfinished or unpublished.
Received degree of LL.D. from the University of Missouri, June.
THE BELATED PASSPORT (York Harbor)—*Harper's Weekly*, December 6. U. E.
WAS IT HEAVEN? OR HELL? (York Harbor)—*Harper's Magazine*,
December. U. E.
Poem (Riverdale and York Harbor) (unpublished).
Sixty-seventh Birthday speech (New York), November 27.

1903. (See Chapters ccxxv to ccxxx.)
MRS. EDDY IN ERROR (Riverdale)—*N. A. Rev.*, April.
INSTRUCTIONS IN ART (Riverdale)—*Metropolitan*, April and May.
EDDYPUS, and other C. S. articles (unfinished).
A DOG'S TALE (Elmira)—*Harper's Magazine*, December. U. E.
ITALIAN WITHOUT A MASTER (Florence)—*Harper's Weekly*, January
21, 1904. U. E.
ITALIAN WITH GRAMMAR (Florence)—*Harper's Magazine*, August,
1904. U. E.
THE $30,000 BEQUEST (Florence)—*Harper's Weekly*, December 10,
1904. U. E.

1904. (See Chapters ccxxx to ccxxxiv.)
AUTOBIOGRAPHY (Florence)—portions published, *N. A. Rev.* and
Harper's Weekly.
CONCERNING COPYRIGHT (Tyringham, Massachusetts)—*N. A. Rev.*,
January, 1905.
TSAR'S SOLILOQUY (21 Fifth Avenue, New York)—*N. A. Rev.*,
March, 1905.
ADAM'S DIARY—book (Harpers), April.

1905. (See Chapters ccxxxiv to ccxxxvii; also Appendix V.)
LEOPOLD'S SOLILOQUY (21 Fifth Avenue, New York)—pamphlet,
P. R. Warren Company.
THE WAR PRAYER (21 Fifth Avenue, New York) (unpublished).
EVE'S DIARY (Dublin, New Hampshire)—*Harper's Magazine*,
December.
3,000 YEARS AMONG THE MICROBES (unfinished).
INTERPRETING THE DEITY (Dublin, New Hampshire) (unpublished).
A HORSE'S TALE (Dublin, New Hampshire)—*Harper's Magazine*,
August and September, 1906.
Seventieth Birthday speech.
W. D. HOWELLS (21 Fifth Avenue, New York)—*Harper's Magazine*,
July, 1906.

1906.   (See Chapters ccxxxix to ccli.)
Autobiography dictation (21 Fifth Avenue, New York; and Dublin, New Hampshire)—selections published, *N. A. Rev.*, 1906 and 1907.
Many speeches.
Farewell lecture, Carnegie Hall, April 19.
WHAT IS MAN?—book (privately printed).
Copyright speech (Washington), December.

1907.   (See Chapters cclvi to cclxiii.)
Autobiography dictations (21 Fifth Avenue, New York; and Tuxedo).
Degree of Doctor of Literature conferred by Oxford, June 26.
Made many London speeches.
Begum of Bengal speech (Liverpool).
CHRISTIAN SCIENCE—book (Harpers), February. U. E.
CAPTAIN STORMFIELD'S VISIT TO HEAVEN—book (Harpers).

1908.   (See Chapters cclxiv to cclxx.)
Autobiography dictations (21 Fifth Avenue, New York; and Redding, Connecticut).
Lotos Club and other speeches.
Aldrich memorial speech.

1909.   (See Chapters cclxxvi to cclxxxix; also Appendices N and W.)
Is SHAKESPEARE DEAD?—book (Harpers), April.
A FABLE—*Harper's Magazine* December.
Copyright documents (unpublished).
Address to St. Timothy School.
MARJORIE FLEMING (Stormfield)—*Harper's Bazar*, December.
THE TURNING-POINT OF MY LIFE (Stormfield)—*Harper's Bazar*, February, 1910.
BESSIE DIALOGUE (unpublished).
LETTERS FROM THE EARTH (unfinished).
THE DEATH OF JEAN—*Harper's*, December, 1910.
THE INTERNATIONAL LIGHTNING TRUST (unpublished).

1910.   (See Chapter ccxcii.)
VALENTINES TO HELEN AND OTHERS (not published).
ADVICE TO PAINE (not published).

INDEX*

*The 1912 edition of *Mark Twain*, from which this reprint was made, appeared as four volumes in two. The roman numerals in this index refer to the original volume breaks and may be ignored.

INDEX

INDEX

Clagget, W. H., i. 183–187, 220, 244.
Clapp, Henry, i. 277.
Clapp, Keziah, i. 247.
Clark, Champ, iv. 1349, 1493–1494.
Clarke, Charles Hopkins, ii. 542, 707; iii. 868–870.
Clarke, William Fayal, iii. 964.
Claude, butler, iv. 1426, 1462, 1523, 1560, 1568, 1570, 1573–1574.
Clemens, Benjamin, i. 8, 15–18, 28, 44.
Clemens, Clara, birth, ii. 509; babyhood, 577–578; trip to Germany, 617–618; in Italy, 634; saved from fire, 699; childhood at Quarry Farm, 823–825; iii. 842–843, 883; at Onteora, 900; attends school in Berlin, 957; joins family at Munich, 967; returns to America, 1001; accompanies parents in trip around the world, 1002, 1009, 1010, 1017; returns to America, 1020, 1024; winter in London, 1024–1027; studies with Leschetizky in Vienna, 1048; at Saranac Lake, 1135; nurses Olivia Clemens, 1190–1193; attack of measles, 1195; writes about house in Florence, 1200; sings at concert in Florence, 1215; at mother's death-bed, 1217–1219; ill health, 1224–1225; iv. 1308, 1323; objects to certain expressions of Mark Twain, iii. 1236; Mark Twain forwards Twichell's letters to, 1241; chooses situation for house at Redding, iv. 1323; goes to country for health, 1333; returns home, 1339–1340; gives consent to father's white costumes, 1342; opinion of Mark Twain's memory, 1369–1370; hostess at Mark

Twain's "doe" luncheons, 1434; on concert tour, 1446; goes to Stormfield, 1484; tells Mark Twain of Rogers's death, 1491; prepares for concert tour, 1505; sings at Redding concert, 1521; engagement, 1522; marriage, 1523–1524; Mark Twain's letter to, on Jean's death, 1554; anxiety about Mark Twain's health, 1559; summoned to America, 1572; arrival at Stormfield, 1575–1577.
Clemens, Gregory, i. 1–2.
Clemens, Henry, birth, i. 19; boyhood, 28, 36; characteristics of, 52–53, 81; illness of, 95; works in Orion's printing-office, 104; letter to, from Mark Twain, 109; clerk on *Pennsylvania*, 133–138; injury and death, 139–143.
Clemens, James, i. 44.
Clemens, James Ross, iii. 1025, 1039.
Clemens, Jane, girlhood and marriage, i. 3–4; life in Tennessee, 7–8; in Florida, Mo., 10–12; temper and cares, 14, 17; opinion of Sam's constitution, 29–30, 32; original of "Aunt Polly" in *Tom Sawyer*, 35–36; consoles Sam, 40; views on slavery, 41–42; takes boarders, 44, 91; consoles and advises Sam at father's death, 76; parting with Sam, 93; welcomes him back, 102; lives with Pamela, 108; makes Sam renew promise in regard to cards and liquor, 112; takes trip to New Orleans with Mark Twain, 156; letters from Mark Twain to, 175, 183, 184, 192, 233, 238–239, 312, 323, 358–360, 378; ii. 470, 696, 728; pride in Mark Twain, i. 308–309; given Bible by

INDEX

Mrs. Howells, 558; birthday letter from Mark Twain, 562; disapproval of George, 573–574; restrains Mark Twain's tendency to burlesque, 610; sails for Germany, 616–618; stay in Germany, 620–624; joins Mark Twain at Lausanne, 632; enjoyment of Italian art, 633–634; winter in Munich, 635–639; stay in Paris, 641–645; stay in England, 645–648; loss of orthodoxy, 650–651; letter to, from Mark Twain, describing Grant, 653–654; goes to Elmira for her health, 663; delights in *Prince and Pauper*, 664; household anecdotes of, 672–673, 680–681; letter from Mark Twain about Grant procession, 691; Christmas customs, 698; interest in Gerhardt's talent, 703–704; calming influence of, 721; does not share Mark Twain's speculative enthusiasms, 728; longs for simpler life, 730; takes part in Cable's joke, 768; criticism of *Huckleberry Finn*, 774–775; anecdotes of, 777; adapts *Prince and Pauper* for acting, 787–788; Mark Twain's tribute to, in *Christian Union*, 819–820; interest in Meredith's novels, iii. 847; entertains Charles Dickens, Jr., 859; Mrs. Grover Cleveland's message to, 865; depressed by Theodore Crane's death, 882; summer at Onteora, 899; loss of mother, 901; criticism of Mark Twain's portrait, 902; goes to England for her health, 919–920; summer abroad, 921–928; winter in Berlin, 929–944; trip in Southern France and Italy, Switzerland and Germany, 945–946;

funds supplied to Webster & Co., 969; waiting for good news, 972, 978–979; improvement in health, 950; in Florence, 954–957, 959; gives financial aid for Paige machine, 961–962; worry over financial matters, 965–966; H. H. Rogers declares her chief creditor of Webster & Co., 984–985; brave reception of news of failure, 986–987; summer at Étretat and winter at Paris, 989–900; necessary economy, 996; accompanies Mark Twain on tour around the world, 1002–1019; improvement in health, 1004; advises retention of anonymity in *Joan of Arc*, 1006; fiftieth birthday, 1011; letters home, 1017; receives news of Susy's illness, 1020; sails for America, 1021; return to England, 1025–1027; *Joan of Arc* dedicated to, 1033; edits Mark Twain's writings, 1040; summer in Switzerland, 1044–1047; life in Vienna, 1051–1063; opposes new lecture tour, 1073; trip to Budapest, 1078; mental telepathy between her and Mark Twain, 1083; weary of wandering, 1102; enjoyment of Dollis Hill, 1109; unable to return to Hartford, 1141; wearies of hearing about "damned human race," 1153; letter from York Harbor to Mrs. Crane, 1176; illness at York Harbor and return to Riverdale, 1178–1181; critical health of, 1190–1193, 1195; voyage to Italy, 1209; condition of health in Florence, 1211–1212, 1214; death, 1217–1218; funeral, 1222–1223; author's only meeting with. iv. 1258; Mark

INDEX

INDEX

INDEX

INDEX

INDEX

INDEX

MARK TWAIN

monument to Adam, 707–709; trip with Sherman, 710–711; asks Grant's aid for Howells's father, 711–713; Canadian trips, 715, 748–749; publishes *Prince and Pauper*, 716; newspaper attacks and reprisals, 719–722; controversy with Post-office Department, 723; interest in patents, 724–728; large financial disbursements, 729; takes Mississippi trip, 735–740; fondness for Osgood, 745; invents history game, 752–754; collaborates with Howells in play *Colonel Sellers*, 755–757, 760–762; meets Matthew Arnold, 758–759; interest in dramatic writing, 763–764; entertains G. W. Cable, 765; rides bicycle, 767; April Fool letters to, 768–770; engages in publishing business, 771–773; work on *Huckleberry Finn*, 774–775; attitude in Blaine-Cleveland campaign, 778–782; reading tour with Cable, 783–792; publishes *Huckleberry Finn*, 793; publication of Grant's *Memoirs*, 799–814; reads for Longfellow memorial, 817–818; publishes tribute to Mrs. Clemens in *Christian Union*, 819–820; letter to Mrs. Clemens, 825; fiftieth birthday, 826–831; suggestions to Webster, iii. 836; work on *Connecticut Yankee*, 840–841, 873–875, 887–888, 893; interest in mind cure, 842–843; visit to mother at Keokuk, 844–845; writes *Meisterschaft*, 648; tries memorizing system, 850–851; letter to Queen of England, 852–854; financial pressure begins, 857–858; visits to President Cleveland, 864–865; member of Players Club, 866–

867; iv. 1257–1261, 1272; degree conferred by Yale, iii. 867–869; introduces Nye and Riley, 876; readings for charity, 877–879; meets Rudyard Kipling, 880–882; embroiders slipper for Elsie Leslie, 883–884; attends New York performance of *Prince and Pauper*, 885; letter to Andrew Lang, 899–900; death of mother, 901; portrait painted by Flagg, 902; interest in Paige typesetting machine, 903–914, 961–965, 967–971, 983–985, 990–996; tries phonograph, 919; goes abroad, 920; writes travel letters from Europe, 921–923; trip down the Rhone, 924–928; winter in Berlin, 929–939; dines with Emperor, 940–944; trip through France, Italy, Switzerland, Germany, 945–946; trips to America on business, 946–948, 963, 967–968; literary work at Nauheim, 949–950; meeting with Prince of Wales, 951–952; stay at Villa Viviani in Florence, 954–966; works on *Joan of Arc*, 956–960, 988, 989, 996–998; welcome in New York, 964, 971–979; meets H. H. Rogers, 970; dines with O. W. Holmes at Mrs. Fields, 980; contributes to various magazines, 981; failure, 983–985; rests in France, 987; writes *In Defense of Harriet Shelley*, 988; business letters to Rogers, 990–994, 1081–1082; returns to America, 1000–1001; lecture tour around the world, 1002–1019; visit to President Kruger, 1019; letter to Kipling, 1006; receives news of Susy's death, 1020–1023; offers of financial aid to, 1025–1026; sadness at Susy's death, 1026–1027; *Joan*

INDEX

of Arc published in book form, 1028; preference for *Joan*, 1034; interests Rogers in Helen Keller, 1035–1037; life in London, 1038–1039, 1041; writes for American papers about Queen's Jubilee, 1043; summer in Switzerland, 1044–1046; life in Vienna, 1048–1052, 1059–1063, 1072–1083; improvement in financial affairs, 1054–1055; makes final payment to creditors, 1056; interested in various commercial enterprises, 1056–1058; letter to Theodore Stanton, 1063; letter to Twichell, 1064; not given to race distinctions, 1065–1066; Christian Science articles, 1068, 1075, 1186–1188; summer at Kaltenleutgeben, 1070–1071; collaborates with Schlesinger on German play, 1075; dinner at Budapest, 1078; audience with Emperor Francis Joseph, 1078; visit to Prince of Thurn and Taxis, 1084; trip to London, 1085–1086; summer in Sweden, 1087–1088; letter to Elizabeth Robbins, 1089; return to London, 1090; anger at editing of MSS., 1091–1093; issue of complete works, 1093–1094; sympathy with Boers, 1095–1097; interest in plasmon, 1098, 1150; plan to edit new magazine falls through, 1099–1100; appears in House of Lords to explain views on copyright, 1105–1106; banquets in London, 1106; summer at Dollis Hill House, 1108–1110; return to America, 1110; takes house, 14 West 10th Street, New York, 1112; arrangements with Harper & Brothers, 1114, 1206; entertained at various New York clubs, 1116–1120; interest in Chinese Boxers, 1120–1121; speech - making, 1121 – 1124; writes *To the Person Sitting in Darkness* and other criticisms of missionaries, 1127–1134; summer at Saranac Lake, 1135–1139; cruises on Rogers's yacht, 1139–1140, 1162–1163; takes house at Riverdale, 1141; receives degree of doctor of letters from Yale, 1143; makes speech against Croker, 1145–1146; address at Players Club, 1148; writes *Salutation from 19th to 20th Century*, 1149–1150; various investments, 1150–1151; writes papers on the Philippines, 1164–1165; trip to Missouri to receive degree conferred by University of Missouri, 1166–1175; summer at York Harbor, 1176–1178; worry over Mrs. Clemens's health, 1179–1181; sixty-seventh birthday, 1184; tribute to Thomas Reed, 1185; records notes of Mrs. Clemens's illness, 1190–1193; second winter at Riverdale, 1194–1204; fondness for mathematics, 1199–1200; lack of political ambition, 1201; refuses consent to Mark Twain day at St. Louis fair, 1202–1203; summer at Quarry Farm, 1205; stay at Villa Quarto Reale, Florence, 1209–1222; last talk with Mrs. Clemens, 1217; writes to Twichell of Mrs. Clemens's death, 1218–1219; sails for America, 1222; funeral of Mrs. Clemens, 1222–1223; summer at Tyringham, Mass., 1224; takes house in New York, 21 Fifth Avenue, 1225; publishes *Eve's Diary* and *Saint Joan*, 1225–1226; taste in music, 1227–1228; plans nu-

INDEX

Library of Humor, 841; breakdown in health, 857; death, 919.
Webster & Co., iii. 967; liabilities of, 969, 973; failure of, 983–986.
Weggis, Lake Lucerne, iii. 1044–1048.
Wells, Rolla, iii. 1173–1174.
West Indies, iii. 1162–1163.
West Point, iii. 878.
What is Happiness?, iv. 1321.
What is Man?, ii. 511, 743; iii. 1071, 1080; iv. 1321.
Wheeler, Mrs. Candace, iii. 899.
Wheeler, Dora, iii. 900.
Whipping Boy's Story, The, ii. 719.
Whipple, Edwin, ii. 474.
Whistler, James McNeill, ii. 646.
White, Andrew W., iv. 1506.
White, Richard Grant, ii. 404.
White, Stanford, iii. 973.
White, William Allen, iv. 1313.
Whiteing, Richard, ii. 643.
Whitmore, F. G., friendship with Mark Twain in Hartford, ii. 614, 678, 778; acts as business agent for Mark Twain, iii. 837–838; letter from Mark Twain to, 874; disapproves of Paige contract, 906.
Whittier, John Greenleaf, ii. 552, 603–604, 658.
Wiggin, Kate Douglas, *see* Kate Douglas Wiggin Riggs.
Wilberforce, Archdeacon Basil, iii. 1085–1086; iv. 1387, 1391.

Wilbrandt, Adolf, iii. 1067, 1084.
William, Emperor of Germany, ii. 746.
Williams, Jesse Lynch, iv. 1413.
Williams, John Sharp, iv. 1349.
Williams, True, i. 366, 384; ii. 551, 665.
Willis, Julia, i. 164.
Wilson, Francis, ii. 566.
Wilson, Woodrow, iv. 1560.
Winter, William, ii. 604.
Winters, Theodore, i. 247.
Witte, M. Sergius, iv. 1243.
Wolfe, i. 86–88, 92, 96.
Woodford, Gen. Stewart L., ii. 654; iv. 1413.
Wright, William (Dan de Quille), association with Mark Twain in Virginia City, i. 205, 210, 223, 225–228, 231–236, 239, 248; writes up mock high, vay robbery, 298–300; visits Hartford, ii. 543.
Wrightson & Co., i. 114.
Wyckoff, W. C., ii. 556.
Wydenbouck-Esterhazy, Countess of, iii. 1070.

YALTA, RUSSIA, i. 332.
York Harbor, Maine, iii. 1176-1180.
Youth's Companion, iii. 981.
Yung Wing, ii. 694.

ZANGWILL, ISRAEL, iii. 1253.
Zogbaum, Rufus, iii. 977.
Zorn, Mr., iii. 977.

THE END

A true son of Twain's Middle West, ALBERT BIGELOW PAINE was superbly qualified to write the great humorist's biography. Paine first established his reputation as a writer of children's stories and humorous travel books. His subsequent work on the editorial staff of *St. Nicholas* drew America's best-known writers to that magazine. In 1904 he completed his colorful biography of Thomas Nast and shortly afterwards became Twain's authorized biographer. He spent four years talking intimately with Twain, and the result was the impressive biography reprinted here. Paine served as editor of the Mark Twain papers until his death in 1937.

JAMES COX, Professor of English at Dartmouth College, is the author of *Mark Twain: The Fate of Humor.*